The Economics of Social Policy

The Economics of Social Policy

Peter G. Rosner

*Associate Professor, Department of Economics,
University of Vienna, Austria*

Edward Elgar
Cheltenham, UK • Northampton, MA, USA

© Peter G. Rosner, 2003

All rights reserved. No part of this publication may be reproduced, stored in a retrieval system or transmitted in any form or by any means, electronic, mechanical or photocopying, recording, or otherwise without the prior permission of the publisher.

Published by
Edward Elgar Publishing Limited
Glensanda House
Montpellier Parade
Cheltenham
Glos GL50 1UA
UK

Edward Elgar Publishing, Inc.
136 West Street
Suite 202
Northampton
Massachusetts 01060
USA

A catalogue record for this book
is available from the British Library

Library of Congress Cataloguing in Publication Data

Rosner, Peter G.
  The economics of social policy/by Peter G. Rosner.
    p. cm.
    1. Social policy—Economic aspects. I. Title.
  HN28 R67   2003
  303.3'72—dc21   2002032049

ISBN 1 84064 496 6 (cased)

Printed and bound in Great Britain by MPG Books Ltd, Bodmin, Cornwall

Contents

List of Figures	vi
List of Tables	vii
List of Boxes	x
Preface	xii
1. Introduction	1
2. Equilibrium, Welfare, Uncertainty	22
3. Economic Aspects of Social Policy	42
4. Social Health Policy	79
5. The Economics of Pensions	133
6. Social Policy and the Labour Market	196
7. Families, Children and Gender	256
8. Poverty	277
Index	340

Figures

1.1	The standard case of a consumer optimum	13
1.2	How the optimum is affected by a restriction of the amount of a good to be bought and by a tax	14
2.1	Risk-aversion	35
2.2	Fair insurance for contingent events	36
3.1	Pooling and separating equilibrium	44
3.2	The allocative effect of a tax	51
3.3	A possible effect of a tax-benefit system	52
3.4	The effects of giving goods and giving money	62
3.5	An upper limit for the amount of goods subsidised	63
3.6	A freely given good in excess of what the individual would have consumed with the same level of resources	64
3.7	Self-selection by giving a good at a specific quality	68
3.8	The area ABCD gives the compensating variation necessary when a subsidy is withdrawn	70
3.9	Lorenz curve and Gini coefficent	71
3.10	Lorenz curves can cross	72
4.1	Beneficiaries and expenditures of Medicaid programmes	96
5.1	The budget constraint under complicated pension and tax rules	171
6.1	Flows in the Austrian labour market for the year 2000	199
6.2	Survivor and hazard functions for two distributions	208
6.3	How UA affects labour supply in the case of low wages and high wages	222
6.4	The comparative static effects of fringe benefits	241
8.1	The compensation criterion according to Engel and Rothbarth	292
8.2	The budget constraint of low-wage employees in the presence of the EITC in the USA	313
8.3	Measuring efficiency of an income support scheme	316
8.4	Utility as a function of income for a log-normal distribution	328
8.5	The construction of a poverty line	329

Tables

1.1	Expenditure for the welfare state as percentage of GDP	2
3.1	The benefit–cost ratio, and the net transfer's share of the pension benefits for the retired generation	60
3.2	The benefit–cost ratio, the net transfer's share of the pension and sickness benefits, and the net transfer's share of lifetime earnings for the working generation	60
4.1	Health expenditure in OECD countries as a percentage of GDP	79
4.2	Share of public expenditure for health services in total expenditure for health services (1997)	80
4.3	Distribution of medical spending in the USA (1987)	80
4.4	Type of health insurance and coverage status, USA (1997)	95
4.5	People without health insurance for the entire year according to selected characteristics (1997)	97
4.6	Annual growth rates of health expenditure per capita	116
4.7	Total employment in health services	118
4.8	Admission rates to inpatient care institutions	119
4.9	Fictitious rate of contribution to cover expenses as percentage of income and redistribution according to income and family status	122
4.10	Expected average health costs over the life-cycle, by marital status, earnings and family size	123
5.1	Public pension expenditure as share of GDP	133
5.2	Net replacement ratios for employees with a full career in 1998	138
5.3	Average retirement age, 1993 and 1998	140
5.4	Average net replacement ratios of new pensions in relation to final income	141
5.5	Labour force participation (ages 55–64)	169
5.6	Social security wealth and its accrual for a single worker	172
5.7	Expected net benefits/payments at age 65 for different household incomes for married couples (a)	176
5.8	Expected net benefits/payments at age 65 for different household incomes for married couples (b)	176

5.9	Average rate of return according to income and according to race and education	177
5.10	Increases in life expectancy	178
5.11	Development of fertility	179
5.12	Development of dependency ratios	180
5.13	Development of pension expenditures as share of GDP	181
5.14	Equilibrium contribution rate	182
5.15	Real rate of return when retiring in year t	183
5.16	Contributions and benefits for retirement	184
5.17	Population aged 75 and over	188
5.18	Spending and people in long-term care	189
6.1	Unemployment rates	201
6.2	International comparison of employment rates for 2000	203
6.3	Unemployment rates and employment/population ratios according to sex, age and education	204
6.4	Rates of inflow into and outflow from unemployment (1993)	206
6.5	Unequal burden of unemployment in Austria (1996)	209
6.6	Unemployment benefit replacement ratios by duration and family circumstances (1991)	219
6.7	Incidence of long-term unemployment	227
7.1	Benefits and contributions over whole life in the Austrian child support system	264
8.1	The relative movement of households between deciles as ranked by expenditure and by income	280
8.2	Household characteristics by decile	281
8.3	Percentage distribution of earnings capacity and current income-poor individuals and current income-poor households, by selected socio-economic characteristics, total population	288
8.4	Estimated equivalence scales	292
8.5	Scales used in international context	293
8.6	Overlapping of poor when using different equivalence scales	294
8.7	Distribution of length of poverty spells in the USA	296
8.8	Ranking of poverty according to different poverty measures	299
8.9	Poverty according to different poverty measures for households and individuals	301
8.10	Increase in life expectancy at birth for countries with high incidence of poverty	304
8.11	Poverty thresholds in 1999 by size of family and number of related children under 18	305
8.12	Poverty rates in the USA according to demographic characteristics	306

8.13	Percentage of people who are poor at different poverty thresholds	307
8.14	Poverty gap: equivalent income deficit as percentage of poverty line	308
8.15	Gross rates of entry and exit of poverty (1993–1995)	309
8.16	Pre- and post-transfer poverty rates and poverty gaps	312
8.17	Share of beneficiaries and share of expenditure on social assistance	318
8.18	Level of social assistance entitlements as percentage of median income	320
8.19	Percentage of households receiving means-tested transfers at different levels of poverty	321
8.20	Weighted means of income, official poverty thresholds, subjective income thresholds by family size for the Netherlands and the USA	329
8.21	Change of poverty according to Sen's poverty index and decomposition into components	331
8.22	Poverty in India and Brazil since the late 1970s	333
8.23	Decomposition of the change of poverty	333

Boxes

1.1	Taxed benefits	3
1.2	Tax burden and lifetime consumption	7
2.1	The formal argument for Pareto-efficiency for an exchange economy	27
3.1	An example of non-availability of insurance against job-related risk	43
3.2	An emergency fund to avoid insurance	47
3.3	Tax-benefit incidence and empirics	53
3.4	The welfare effect of rent subsidies	64
3.5	Targeting benefits by giving goods instead of money	67
4.1	Promises of a commercial health insurance and a public health system	83
4.2	Should we attach a monetary value to health and to life?	86
4.3	An example of separation of risks	100
4.4	The WHO on health and the poor	102
4.5	Conditions which can result in denying of coverage for children	103
4.6	Special methods to acquire only good risks	104
4.7	Inequality of wealth and access to goods	105
4.8	Rationing by private insurance	106
4.9	Ranking of treatments by importance according to the Oregon Health Services Commission service category definitions	110
4.10	Are co-payments and deductibles a means to reduce costs?	113
4.11	The principal–agent problem	115
5.1	An example of risk of funds – but government is not innocent	163
5.2	Why is the market for annuities so small?	165
5.3	An example of the political risk of a PAYG system	167
5.4	The 62–65 puzzle	173
5.5	The Austrian system of care	189
6.1	Unemployment insurance through the family	212
6.2	Does unemployment cause future unemployment?	214
6.3	The measurement of the wage loss	216
6.4	How does (or did) the replacement rate in Germany influence the duration of unemployment?	224

		Boxes	xi
6.5	Forced participation for the long term unemployed		232
6.6	A pure experiment: counselling and monitoring the unemployed in the Netherlands		236
6.7	What belongs to paid labour time?		239
6.8	Who pays for workers' compensation?		242
6.9	A two-level protection of labour contracts		244
7.1	Maternity leave and the gender pay gap		269
8.1	Infant mortality and the share of the rich		284
8.2	How to predict the effects of wage supplements		314
8.3	The Bremen approach to analysing social assistance		322
8.4	A European example of activation: Denmark		324

Preface

I

Social policy always was and still is an important political issue. For some it carries the hope of a better world, particularly for many who belong to the lower half of the income distribution. They point to existing social problems – poverty, unemployment, social dependencies. Others see it as a threat to economic development and a danger for precisely those whom social policy wants to protect. Usually they invoke economic arguments, namely that social policy is not only a burden for the better-off, but also creates incentives against working, against caring for the future, against a sensible use of resources. Is it again the dismal science denying the hope of a good life for all?

If one looks into current economic research on social policy matters, one can see that this is not the case. Economists have developed reasonable arguments to show that social policy programmes can enhance welfare, but that they can also reduce it. Some of the traditional arguments of the political discourse against such programmes are misguided, but some of the hopes put into such programmes are likely to be frustrated as well. This book wants to put these arguments into a systematic framework.

It gives an introduction to the economic theory of social policy – economic theory in the sense of mainstream economics. It should enable its readers to understand the economic aspects of the discussion of social policy in economic journals and in politics. Of course, economic theory is not all one needs to make educated judgements about social policy. There are many normative problems to be tackled and an understanding of the political and of the social systems in a broader context than that provided by pure economic theory is surely not a disadvantage. Nevertheless this book concentrates on economic theory aspects. I consider it preferable to concentrate on one aspect systematically, keeping in mind that many things are left out, rather than to cover everything without systematic treatment.

Institutions of social policy should be seen as answers to specific problems. To understand the working of an institution one has to understand why it has been set up. Therefore one finds some information about institutional structures of social policy in different countries. The purpose of describing different institutions is to show that different regulations for solving a particular problem do exist. Which institutions are chosen in a country depends on its history, its political system, its social structures. Economic aspects never determine the structure of social policy institutions unambiguously. Why social insurance institutions dominate in Austria and in Germany whereas the United Kingdom has a public health service cannot be analysed by merely using the instruments of economic theory. Therefore one does not find much about it in this book.

The instruments of economic theory are useful for pursuing the question of what the consequences of different institutional structures of social policy are. In what ways do they affect the allocation of resources and how do they influence the distribution of income? Which system is a 'good' one, beyond the economist's concept of Pareto-efficiency, can only be analysed in a very restricted sense, as the question of what is a 'good' social policy, requires many normative issues to be discussed. In many instances I shall try to make clear what are the normative agenda. This I consider necessary, because what often inhibits rational discussion of social policy is that normative propositions are taken for granted without making them explicit.

II

Besides leaving out nearly all political aspects, the book has more omissions. For some of them I have arguments, for others I have to ask for pardon (I am sure readers will point to a third type.) The book concentrates on social policy in rich societies. Problems of poor countries are hardly mentioned. The problems are too different between rich and poor countries to allow for a common treatment except at a very abstract level. Take health care: providing all citizens of a country with good access to up-to-date medical treatment is a challenge in rich economies. In poor economies it is impossible. Social concern when regulating health markets therefore will result in a different policy in a poor country as compared with a rich economy.

There is also a great difference in the capacity to absorb shocks. Consider a decline of GDP *per capita* of 20 per cent. That is never an easy thing to manage. However a drop in income of about one-fifth in a rich economy, would leave people in about the same position as they held 10 to 15 years ago – when their economy was already considered to be rich. There is no economic reason why a human tragedy must be the consequence of such a decline. In many poor economies other policies are needed to avoid a tragedy.

On the other hand most poor economies have social networks which help people to absorb some risks they face. Often the extended family networks provide help in situations where in rich and individualistic societies people use formal systems – market insurance, personal savings, social transfers. Moreover in many poor economies it is possible to rely on informal production and home production to an extent unknown in rich economies. This also contributes to a different capacity for coping with those problems which are covered by social policy institutions in rich economies.

Altogether, I think that the omission of the problems of the poor countries can be excused. Less excusable is another omission: the material I use is taken almost entirely from states in Europe and the USA. Canada, Australia, New Zealand and the countries of East Asia are hardly mentioned. There is one reason: I don't know much about them. However it may be problematic to apply the concepts used in this book for the analysis of social policy of East Asia, as the social structure seems to be very different from that of other countries. First, firms are providers of social security on a level unknown in other market economies. Second, in some instances the family is still an important provider of social security. For leaving out Australia and New Zealand I cannot invoke any excuse. It was simply a lack of knowledge.

A further omission concerns a specific topic: there is no chapter on the political economy of social policy, in the sense of *new political economy* or public choice. The relation between rational, self-interested voting and social policy, between formal political structures and social policy is not discussed in the book. This is also due to a lack of deeper knowledge. However I don't believe that people calculate thoroughly expected net financial gains and losses when deciding for whom to vote.

III

I am sure that in any survey about the foremost purpose of social policy fighting poverty will be mentioned most frequently. Any attempt to curtail social policy programmes will be challenged by warning of the danger of increasing poverty, whereas extensions of programmes are argued by pointing at existing poverty. Nevertheless poverty is *not* at the heart of existing social policy programmes, particularly in Europe. The biggest programmes – measured by the amount of spending – apply for large segments of the population, if not the whole population: health provisions, pension systems, family allowances. Of course, all these systems are important for reducing poverty, but the rationale for their existence cannot be reduced to that aspect, not even in the USA, in Australia or in New Zealand, where European style social security programmes are of less importance.

I choose to present the material along the lines of the demarcation of the programmes – health services, pension systems, dealing with unemployment, supporting families. Fighting poverty as a separate programme is left for the last chapter, because in most countries poverty is reduced decisively by the aforementioned programmes, although they comprise (nearly) the whole population. Programmes which are aimed specifically at relieving poverty are nearly everywhere of small scale.

IV

This book grew out of courses on social policy held at the University of Vienna and the Central European University in Budapest. There were always students with some background in economics, sociology or political science. I hope that this book can be used in courses for students in all three subjects. This limits the use of the instruments of economic theory. However to understand the text, some knowledge of economic theory is necessary, particularly of microeconomics and of public finance. The level is not high; an understanding of basic concepts and graphical arguments suffices in most cases. Hal Varian's 'Intermediate Microeconomics' and Joseph Stiglitz's 'Public Finance' provide good introductions to the theoretical concepts as they are used in the book. Theoretical aspects requiring a deeper understanding are relegated to appendices.

Many friends, students and colleagues helped with discussing certain points, reading earlier drafts and parts of the final manuscript. Particularly I want to thank: Maria Hofmarcher, Andrea Holzmann-Jenkins, Leo Kaas, Georg Kirchsteiger, Ingrid Kubin, Herbert Obinger, Aloys Prinz, Monika Riedel, Christian Traxler, Erwin Weissel, Katharina Wick and Katharina Wrohlich. The Centre for Social Policy Research at the University of Bremen and Professor Winfried Schmähl hosted me during summer 2001. There I could discuss many points and had the opportunity to bring the manuscript to a state-of-no-return. My American cousins B. and J. Loss and H. Rosenberg answered quickly whenever I had questions concerning the use of words and problems with English grammar. Finally I have to thank the editors at Edward Elgar. Due to their help the English of the book is much better than the English which I can write.

Peter G. Rosner
Vienna

1. Introduction

The first part of this chapter provides a short review of the dimension and the objectives of social policy. As an indicator of its dimension the amount of expenditures for social policy programmes is used. We will see that social expenditures reach about 30 per cent of GDP, although to get a proper understanding of the data, it is necessary to look at their construction. Social policy programmes cover large parts of the population, in many countries nearly the whole population. Therefore social policy is more than helping the poor. In the second part it is asked: what are functions of social policy programmes besides helping the poor? The third part pursues the question of whether economics has a special way of looking at social policy programmes. The fourth part provides a short sketch of political science concepts of the welfare state. The fifth and final part gives an overview of the contents of the book.

1.1 THE EXTENT OF SOCIAL POLICY

Social policy has become an important agenda in all modern economies. The term 'welfare state' is often used in this context, indicating that there is an important difference between a pure market economy and an economy where a sizeable part of goods, services and purchasing power is allocated politically with social aspects taken into consideration. The structure of social policy and, to some extent, the size of the welfare state as well vary between different economies.

A first hint of the importance of the welfare state is given in Table 1.1 where the expenditure for social services as a percentage of GDP is presented.[1] For the USA no comprehensive data exist. Within Europe, the Scandinavian countries have the highest share of social expenditure, Ireland and the Mediterranean countries the lowest. Ireland is a special case: it is the only European country with a share of social expenditure below 20 per cent of GDP. Moreover it is also the only country with a decline in social expenditure as share of GDP.

Some social expenditures are not explicitly written down in the records of public expenditure systems. They consist primarily in special treatment of private expenditures for savings and for health insurance in the tax code – so called 'tax expenditures'. Furthermore publicly mandated private social expenditures are not covered by the data of Table 1.1. In some countries (USA, Canada, the Netherlands) they are of substantial importance (Adema, 1999).

The data of social expenditure cannot be interpreted straightforwardly. The reason is that the share of social expenditure is not a real share of GDP. To a great extent social expenditure transfers general purchasing power from one group of people to another – for example, giving money to the retired or to poor families. Sometimes purchasing power is merely given back to the same individual from whom it was taken before and people have to pay taxes although they get transfers. If social benefits are taxed or otherwise used for contributions to finance social expenditure, there is no upper limit to such expenditures. The share of social expenditure can be bigger than 100 per cent. The welfare office can send everybody each morning €1 million and collect it in the evening of the same day.[2]

Table 1.1 Expenditure for the welfare state as percentage of GDP

	1970	1980	1991	1997
Austria	21.1	27.1	27.2	28.7
Denmark				31.4
France	19.2	25.4	28.7	30.8
Germany	21.5	25.4	28.7	29.9
Greece				23.6
Ireland			19.1	17.5
Italy	17.4	19.4	24.4	25.9
Netherlands	20.8	30.8	32.4	30.3
Portugal				22.5
Sweden				33.7
United Kingdom	15.9	21.5	24.7	26.8

Source: Monatsberichte des Österreichischen Institutes für Wirtschaftsforschung, 9/1999, p. 657 and 'Bericht über die soziale Lage 1999', p. 46.

That seems to imply that policies are often not sensible. After all, what is the sense of giving money back to an individual from whom it was taken? Often it is unavoidable that recipients of transfers pay taxes. For practical reasons people who receive transfers cannot be exempted from paying value added tax, sales taxes, and so on. Only the income tax a person pays can be set against the transfers she receives.

Be that as it may, Table 1.1 allows one interpretation: social payments do not decline with the wealth of nations, neither when comparing different economies at the same time, nor when looking at the development of social expenditure. All the economies listed above were richer in 1994 than in 1970. Nevertheless, all, save Ireland, had a higher share of social expenditure in 1994. Taking the welfare state as a 'good', it is definitely a luxury good: income elasticity is – perhaps was? – bigger than one.[3]

> ## BOX 1.1 TAXED BENEFITS
>
> In the United Kingdom ... the recipient of an unemployment benefit whose last earnings were those of an average production worker (APW) and who lived in a 'one earner' family with two children received the equivalent of $18,659 in 1995, on which he or she did not pay tax. By contrast, a similar person in the Netherlands received annual unemployment benefits of $24,613 but paid $7,716 in income taxes and social-security contributions Including housing and family benefits his or her net income was $19,753. (Adema, 1999, p. 20)
>
> In Austria the biggest part of family benefit payments is given outside the income tax system. Many households get a transfer for dependent children and pay income tax. If the two systems were to be merged, social expenditure and taxes would decrease without much change of household incomes after taxes and transfers.

The fact that social expenditure as share of GDP is increasing with rising per capita income points to an important aspect: the welfare state is not only for the poor or the socially weak. Nearly all economies have social programmes which also cover middle-class people and even rich people. For example, all over Europe nearly the whole population is covered by a social health system. Even in the USA everybody above a certain age has access to Medicare. The pension systems as well cover not only the poor or socially disadvantaged. Actually in most states the flow of resources going to non-poor people through social policy programmes exceeds the means reserved for the poor.

Is this a mistake? Should the welfare state be reduced to supporting the poor? This is an important political question in all modern economies. Everywhere one finds political parties and interest groups which call for such a change and others which reject it. In this book we will have a look at this question. In particular we will ask, what is the economic rationale for the existence of the welfare state beyond helping the poor?

This question is often related to the claim that there is too much or too little of social policy. Some believe that there is an efficiency-equity trade-off: more social policy may increase equity, but the efficiency of the economy is thereby reduced. Total welfare or economic growth is curtailed by too much social policy. Empirically this claim cannot be substantiated (see Atkinson, 1999, ch.2 for an overview of the empirical literature). This does not imply that the proposition is false. The problem with such empirical studies is that data from different countries are used. These countries differ not only in the amount spent for social expenditure but also in many other aspects. Any difference between countries in growth rates or other easily accessible data as proxies for efficiency should not be seen merely in relation to social policy but in a broader context for which no general theory is available. Without such a theory the question of what is the optimal amount of social policy, cannot be investigated empirically. Therefore it is not pursued in this book.

Furthermore the welfare state is not a single entity, of which a state can have too little or too much. It consists of many different programmes with different objectives. It thus can happen that in some respects there is too little social policy and in others there is too much of it. However for such statements to be meaningful, one has to make precise what is to be understood under the term 'too little' and 'too much'. To do this it is necessary to discuss the objectives of different programmes.

We further ask what are the economic effects of the programmes of the welfare state? How do they affect the behaviour of individuals? For each programme discussed in this book we ask how it affects welfare. As this is an economic textbook the instruments of economic analysis are used. Parts of the course are positive analysis – it is asked what are the effects of existing welfare state programmes. Other parts are normative – how *should* the welfare system be organised in order to increase welfare. The latter question cannot be answered unambiguously when it comes to evaluating redistribution between different individuals. There is no economic theory to answer the question of how much should be given to poor people on ethical grounds. This question belongs to the realm of theories of justice.[4]

What belongs to the field of social policy? As it covers not only support for the poor or otherwise socially weaker segments of a population, we are in need of a delineation of the field against other topics. Take the system of education. Should it be covered in a course of social policy? Basic education is provided free nearly everywhere. University education in most European states is either free or provided at a price far below true costs. In other countries provisions exist to ensure that everybody can attend university whatever their means. This clearly affects both poor and middle-class families: expenditures for education are covered by taxes which to a great extent are paid by non-poor people. Other publicly provided goods change the income distribution as well. For example, the quality of public transportation or the accessibility of recreational areas, like parks, woods and beaches can have a great impact on the standard of living for many people.

These topics are usually not pursued in the context of social policy, and they will not be covered in this book either. For practical reasons only subjects which institutionally belong to the field of social policy will be looked at. These are (i) health insurance, (ii) provisions for retirement and old age, (iii) help for the unemployed, (iv) policies related to families, and (v) poverty. This restriction is not based on any theoretical demarcation, rather on the need to have a restriction and on the existing institutional arrangements in most countries.

Due to the multiplicity of topics covered there is no unified theory of social policy, comparable to the theory of foreign trade or optimal taxation. However the text uses, perhaps in an eclectic way, many economic concepts.

There is a further restriction, namely that the activities of firms which are voluntary or of purely contractual nature are not considered as part of social policy. In that case – firms providing health insurance or contributions to a kindergarten – we speak of fringe benefits of the labour contract. They are part of labour costs and have to be analysed in the context of the institutions of labour markets. However if such activities are mandated by law, then they are part of social policy – though they do not show in the aggregate data of social policy. We not only look at state-organised social policy but we will see that there are important cases where the state restricts its activity to regulate the behaviour of firms and of individuals in the above mentioned areas without providing services itself.

1.2 THE OBJECTIVES OF SOCIAL POLICY

As social policy covers such a wide field, it has no unambiguously given objective. In order to evaluate its effects one has to be clear on the reasons for having set up the programmes. Otherwise its welfare effects cannot be evaluated. It would be impossible to say whether a programme is beneficial or not. As mentioned already, we do not speak about social policy in general. It is preferable to speak of specific programmes – for example, unemployment benefits, public health insurance, and so on.

We distinguish between the following objectives of social policy programmes:

- fighting poverty;
- protection for contingent events (insurance);
- redistribution;

- giving structure to contracts in favour of 'weaker' partners (for example, labour law, rent control).

In different programmes the weight of these objectives can be different. Fighting poverty is hardly the main purpose of a publicly provided health insurance for the whole population, though it contributes to the reduction of poverty and is very important for poor people. A basic pension for everybody can be an important instrument for fighting poverty, but hardly qualifies for protection against risks which are typical for private retirement provisions.

The task of fighting poverty itself is clear, though there may be different normative bases for that. Some people want to fight poverty because they want to better the life of the otherwise poor. Others may see it as a means to increase social coherence or to fend off political disorder.

The reason for setting up social insurance programmes is not so clear. There are many risks individuals face. For some of them commercial insurance is available – against fire, against theft of a car, and so on. There are no social policy programmes against damage from fire or against the loss due to theft of a car. But for some contingent events social policy programmes were set up in most countries. We will therefore consider, why some risks are covered, at least to some extent, by social insurance programmes, and others are not.

The most important risks for which social programmes exist are:

- unemployment;
- illness;
- disability;
- loss of wealth in relation with retirement;
- outliving one's own resources;
- need of care.

The term 'redistribution' carries usually the association of taking from the rich and giving to the poor. That is too narrow a concept of redistribution. It hardly accounts for the size of social policy programmes. We have to distinguish between four types of redistribution:

1. *Vertical*: redistribution between individuals or households due to differences in income or wealth.
2. *Horizontal*: redistribution due to specific characteristics of individuals or households within the same income group – for example, according to the number of children.
3. *During the life-cycle of a person*: taking money from an individual or household at one point of time and giving it to the same individual or

household at another point of time – for example, support of students and financing this support by a special tax for people with an academic degree.
4. *Between different cohorts*: if individuals born at a certain date have to pay more (less) for those born earlier than they get from individuals born later, there is intergenerational redistribution in favour of cohorts born earlier (later).

Whereas redistribution of types 1, 2, and 4 amounts to *interpersonal* redistribution, namely one takes away from one person and gives to another one, redistribution of type 3 is *intrapersonal* redistribution. In most welfare state programmes we find all types of redistribution.

For a complete picture of redistribution one has to look at the income of people over a lifetime. Consider the following example: all incomes increase by 2 per cent per working year. Everybody starts with the same wage at the same age, all retire at the same age. Everybody has therefore the same income over her working life, in each year incomes are unequal. Assume that in this economy an income support scheme is introduced with the purpose of supporting those who are poor in a particular year. It is financed by a tax which is paid by those with high income in that year. We would observe in each year redistribution from the rich to the poor, but over the whole life-cycle nobody's income is altered by this tax-transfer scheme. We will see that this is an important aspect of some programmes of social policy.

This also happens in some programmes for horizontal redistribution. One of the most important reasons for horizontal redistribution is favouring families with children. But having dependent children is not a characteristic of an individual or a household, rather it is a characteristic of a household for a specific period of time. We will see in Chapter 7 that this is important when one wants to calculate the amount of redistribution when supporting families.

BOX 1.2 TAX BURDEN AND LIFETIME CONSUMPTION

Any tax on consumption is usually seen as regressive – that is households with higher incomes pay a smaller percentage of their income as taxes. This is due to the fact that the percentage of income spent on consumption is declining with income. In a life-cycle context things are different, because the share spent for consumption out of current income not only depends on income but on age as well. The rate of consumption expressed as lifetime consumption over lifetime income does not vary as much as it does when annual data are used.

> A study of the distributional effects of an introduction of a VAT in the USA by Casperson and Metcalf (1994) found that taking account of lifetime income, the burden of a VAT with a tax rate of 5 per cent changes in the following way:
>
> *Taxes as a fraction of income for a VAT on total expenditures*
>
> | Decile | Annual income | Lifetime income |
> |---|---|---|
> | 1 | 7.71 | 3.93 |
> | 2 | 6.01 | 3.85 |
> | 3 | 5.36 | 4.16 |
> | 4 | 4.66 | 3.97 |
> | 5 | 4.30 | 3.83 |
> | 6 | 3.82 | 3.68 |
> | 7 | 3.64 | 3.51 |
> | 8 | 3.33 | 3.31 |
> | 9 | 3.06 | 3.46 |
> | 10 | 2.75 | 2.95 |
>
> Using annual income and annual consumption the VAT is a much stronger burden on low incomes than on high incomes, however when using lifetime concepts the difference in burden between high and low incomes is much smaller.

There is a further problem: we have to ask who really gets the benefits and who pays for them. This is generally not an easy question to answer. For example, if university is free, who benefits? The students as they have no other income? Their parents, because they usually finance the education of their children? The future employers of the students, as the graduates will be content with a lower wage? The low-income households, because it makes access to university easier? The consumers who buy the products of the goods produced by the graduates, that is, the clients of doctors, lawyers and similar professions? The rich, because well-to-do households have a higher propensity to send children to a university than other households? The professors as the demand for their service is higher? The answer to the simple question, who benefits from free access to university education is already very complicated. To answer such questions one has to use general equilibrium models.

1.3 THE ECONOMIC APPROACH TO SOCIAL POLICY

1.3.1 Economic Analysis and Political Conclusions

Do economists have a special way of looking at social policy? There is a simple answer: they use the methods of economics for the analysis of social policy.

The basic element of this analysis is that economists ask how people act when they are confronted with different options. Economics sees social reality as the outcome of choices individuals make. That is, people decide whether to work or not, what to consume, how much to save, how many children to raise, how much education to get, and so on. Of course, people have to observe constraints when making decisions, namely their wealth, income, prices, their abilities and existing regulations. In all these decisions individuals gauge benefits – either income or more general 'utility' – and costs – either monetary costs or 'disutility'. That is the basic methodological assumption of nearly all economics.

Is this a sensible assumption? Can one say that an unemployed individual has chosen to be unemployed? Similarly has a homeless individual chosen to be homeless? Isn't it cynical to speak of choice when discussing social problems?

Concerning the unemployed, we can make two propositions: an unemployed person will surely find a job if he does not ask for payment. Therefore he will also find a job if he is content with an extremely small payment. The first proposition follows from the assumption of non-satiation: people always want more. If Adam works for Beth without getting paid, Beth is better off. Therefore she will 'employ' him.[5] The second proposition follows from a continuity assumption: a very small change in a parameter, namely of Adam's wage, does not make a big difference. Therefore, if Adam refuses to work for a very low wage, he has chosen unemployment.

Can we thus conclude that unemployment is voluntary? No, because we have to keep two things apart. If Adam refuses to work for an extremely low wage, economists conclude that he has considered it better to stay unemployed. The evidence for this is the fact that he is unemployed. But that is not what we mean when we say that somebody is voluntarily unemployed. The difference is as follows: saying that Adam's unemployment is voluntary, means that his unemployment falls within his ethical responsibility. It is a normative statement. In the political context of a market society such a statement may even imply that Adam should bear the consequences of his choice – namely being without a job is not a reason to ask for support. However the statement that Adam has opted for unemployment because he only could find a job at an extremely low wage, is not a normative statement.

There is no approval or disapproval implied. No political conclusion can be drawn.

Economics give no support to the proposition that Adam is voluntarily unemployed and should not be helped because he refuses to work for an extremely low wage. The normative statement 'Adam should be prepared to work for a specific wage' can never be a conclusion from economic analysis. The normative position is always an extra. True, some economists think that most unemployed would find a job if there were no unemployment benefits or only less generous ones and if workers and employers were allowed to make any contract they want, unhindered by minimum wage laws or collective agreements. But in general they do not expect people to work for almost nothing. They are rather convinced that reducing unemployment benefits and similar measures will not have drastic consequences for wages.

Consider the homeless: in which way did they choose their situation? Isn't it just a lack of housing which makes people homeless? Of course, one cannot say that they prefer being homeless to living in a nice house. That would be pathetic, as they could not afford a nice house. But we can say that being homeless is better for them than staying in the worst, most ramshackle building. This we conclude from the fact that they do not live in a very poor building. They consider such living conditions as not worth the expenditure, even if they can afford it.[6]

The point of that approach is that seeing homelessness as an outcome of choice prompts the question, why people choose homelessness. What makes them accept homelessness as better than the next best alternative – living in very poor housing? If one sees homelessness as lack of housing, the only way to help is to build accommodation. But if one considers it as a question of prices, incomes and quality, other policy options emerge: any increase in the supply of poor housing brings down the price of such accommodation. That can be achieved by several means other than providing housing directly. If, for example, low and middle-income groups have better access to new housing, they will be eager to give up old accommodation, which would then be free for the very poor.[7] Another possibility is to give transfers to the homeless or to increase the quality of bad housing – increasing safety standards, giving more privacy, and so on. Some of the homeless will then be prepared to pay a small amount for such accommodation. It may also turn out that the insufficient supply of very poor housing is due to public regulation: in rich societies houses usually have to conform to minimum standards concerning safety and stability. Therefore flats can be far too expensive for the current homeless. In that case different policies may be more suitable – perhaps helping the poor with the rent.

A third example: in many states, unemployment among lone mothers is higher than among married women with children. On the other hand, lone mothers more often work full time than married mothers, but less often part time.[8] Is that a question of choice? If you ask a married mother caring for small children, why does she not work full time, you will probably get the answer: how could I, I have to look after my children. Does a lone mother not have to look after her children? Of course, she has to, she even has more obligations as she might be totally without a partner to share responsibilities for the children. But the extra income by working full time is, if wages and the desire to be with the children are the same for both groups of mothers (economists call this *ceteris paribus*), much more valuable for her than for the married mother whose husband works full time. In that sense the lone mother has chosen working full time, whereas the married mother has chosen to spend more time with her children.

What about the higher rate of unemployment for lone mothers? In most states it is much easier for them to get transfers in case of unemployment than for members of other groups. In many states, the income that a woman with few qualifications can earn with part-time work can be reached by means-tested transfers. Many lone mothers therefore face the choice between a full-time job or living on transfers. For them a part-time job is an inferior solution to being unemployed and to working full time. (Whether it is good or bad that lone mothers have easier access to transfers which makes them more likely to stay at home is again an ethical question – at least to some extent.)

Summing up: to regard social states as result of choice is a sensible approach and should not be confounded with ethical statements about proper acting. Of course, there are some limitations to the use of that approach. To see them it is necessary to look at the way economics considers how the choice of individuals is structured.

Economists assume that people make rational choices. That does not mean that people always act selfishly, even less that they maximise income. It means something much weaker, namely that people make choices consistently. That is, if A is chosen when the choice was between A and B, and if B is chosen when the choice was between B and C, then A will be chosen, whenever the choice is between A and C. Though it is well documented that there are situations (in connection with uncertainty) in which people do not act consistently in that sense, economics faces tremendous difficulties when giving up this assumption. The problem is that it is then possible to prove nearly everything.[9]

Be that as it may, the assumption of consistent choices is a reasonable one for most people in most situations. But social policy is in some instances concerned with situations where the danger that otherwise rational individuals act inconsistently is not negligible. Furthermore there are individuals for whom the assumption of rational choice cannot be made: for individuals with mental problems and for addicts that is not a good assumption. These are individuals who often face severe social problems.[10]

A further point: do people really always have much choice? There are situations where it is rather cynical to speak of choice – bonded labour, in certain cultures, women are married without having been asked for their consent. Sometimes social conventions limit the possibility for choice, particularly for women. If the action of an individual is constrained by custom and force, such that there is not much choice to be made, economic analysis is not of much help. For example, economics will not help you to understand why women in Afghanistan did not work when the Taliban were ruling the country – they did not have the choice.[11]

A particularly important instance of limitation for choice is the legal framework, especially in the context of social policy. In the example of the homeless we have mentioned that public regulations of housing may contribute to an insufficient supply of very bad houses. Or a minimum wage may prevent an individual getting a job she is prepared to take.

Should such regulations be given up? Note that in the case of homeless people, they might prefer to have such bad houses instead of being homeless; a woman may prefer to work for a below-minimum wage instead of being unemployed. But this does not imply that such regulations should be given up. Bad housing may have negative effects on others. For example, a neighbourhood may deteriorate due to a few very bad houses; they can create risks for the health of people passing by. Accepting a very low wage may affect the wages of other individuals.

Whether the negative effects outweigh the positive effects is also an ethical question: how do we value the improvement of the situation of the homeless by allowing very bad housing in comparison with the increased risks for others passing by? And how should we weigh the loss of welfare due to lower wages for some against the higher welfare of those who got employment? Economic analysis cannot provide an answer.

But economic analysis can be of help in refining the ethical question and in calculating the benefits and the costs of such measures. If some individuals work for below-minimum wages, does it really have such devastating effects on the wages of others? Does the acceptance of ramshackle houses for the homeless really have such obstructing consequences as many fear? These are questions for applied economic research on social policy problems.

1.3.2 A Basic Instrument for Analysis

The instruments for the analysis of social policy are taken from the set of microeconomic tools. It is assumed that households maximise utility under constraints. The constraints consist of the budget and the existing regulations

– for example, a maximum number of working hours. The formal analysis uses the appropriate mathematics, namely the technique of constrained optimisation. For a basic understanding graphic analysis is often sufficient.

In Figure 1.1 the axes represent the amounts of goods. The line x'y' represents the budget line. The curve I is the indifference curve, which contains the relevant information about preferences. An individual facing the budget line x'y' and having preferences according to the indifference curve consumes x" of good x and y" of good y.

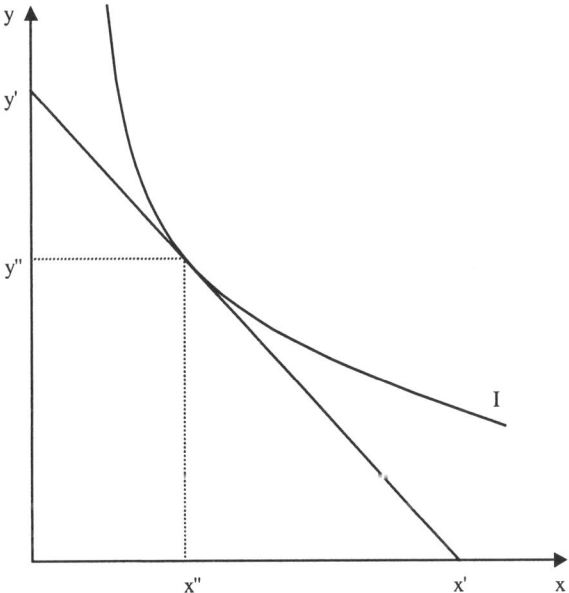

Figure 1.1 The standard case of a consumer optimum

How do regulations, taxes and transfers influence such a choice? First, through regulations (Figure 1.2, left). Let us assume that it is forbidden to buy more than x* of good x. The individual buys that amount and spends the rest of his wealth on y. Note that it reaches a lower indifference curve and therefore a lower level of utility. If he chooses in absence of regulations a point to the left of x*, the regulation has no influence.

Taxes change the budget constraint. If the same tax is levied on both goods, the new budget set is shifted parallel to the left. If only one good – in Figure 1.2, good y – is taxed then the budget line turns counter-clockwise at the point x', resulting in an optimum at a lower indifference curve (Figure 1.2, right). Whether the demand for the good y goes up or declines depends on the size of the substitution effect and the size and direction of the income effect.

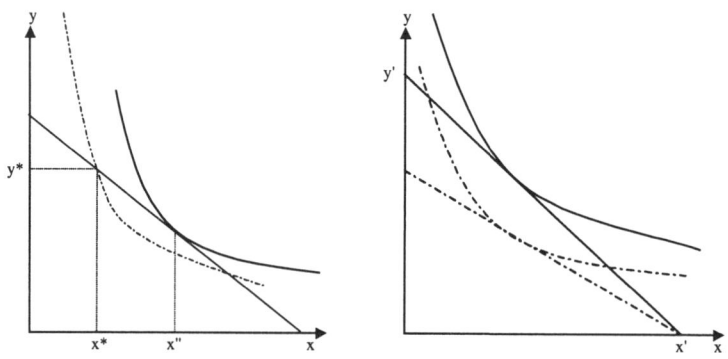

Figure 1.2 How the optimum is affected by a restriction of the amount of a good to be bought (left) and by a tax (right)

1.4 SOME POLITICAL SCIENCE ASPECTS

Though the book concentrates on the economics of social policy, it is not possible to set aside political aspects completely. There is too much political heat in all discussions on social programmes to do that. During many election campaigns, social policy issues are of major importance. However in most instances the difference between those claiming to 'defend the welfare state' and those who want to emphasise 'less state intervention and more economic efficiency' is not actually very large. Usually the real differences are concentrated around the extension or curtailment of a few specific programmes; that may be of great importance for some segments of the population, but hardly qualifies for a radical change.[12] In the 1980s, the British Prime Minister Margaret Thatcher tried to reduce the welfare state. However the National Health Service, the basic pension system, unemployment insurance and many other social services remained basically untouched, though some reforms were undertaken in conformity with the ideology of the Conservative government. Actual payments for social purposes as a percentage of GDP increased during Mrs. Thatcher's government because of the higher number of unemployed. In the 1990s, President Bill Clinton wanted to introduce a general health insurance system in the USA. That would have been a real break with the then prevailing institutions of the USA health system (see below, Chapter 4.2), but he failed completely.

On the other hand, the changes of welfare policy in the USA in 1996 (see below, Chapter 8.7.2), which had a big impact on the poor, were favoured by President Clinton, but were also in line with the changes sought by his predecessors, Ronald Reagan and George Bush (Blank and Ellwood, 2001).

For some the welfare state is a first step towards a non-capitalist economy. For those on the left this is a reason to support the welfare state; for those on the political right it is a reason to oppose the welfare state on the grounds that it restricts economic and political freedom. Now, after many decades of experience with welfare states, one can say that neither the hopes nor the fears were justified. All economies with strong social policy programmes are still capitalist market economies: the capital stock is overwhelmingly privately owned, public ownership of the capital stock has been in decline for many years; investment is made to make profits; profits and capital income is everywhere accepted as a legitimate source of income.[13] Furthermore political freedom is an important issue in all modern welfare states.

I prefer to see the welfare state as a market economy with public regulations for specific purposes – namely how the access to health services is organised, how income during retirement is safeguarded, how people are supported in case of unemployment, what are general standards for labour contracts, and so on. In that perspective the welfare state can be seen either as a means to overcome market failures and to help the poorer segments of the society – the traditional economic approach; or it can be conceived as a way to alleviate the vicissitudes of a pure market economy which otherwise would generate insecurity and poverty – the more political approach.

Be that as it may, there are different political structures for social policy. We can differentiate according to the way in which individuals are affected. Social benefits are given:

- only to the poor or primarily to the poor – social assistance programmes;
- to all those who contribute – mostly through payments related to working income;
- to all citizens.

If the first way is in the centre of social policy, poverty alleviation is its dominant purpose. This approach can be found in the English-speaking world by tradition: in the USA, in the UK, in Australia, in New Zealand. Some states in Latin America have recently opted for such a type of social policy, for example, Chile. The idea of this type of social policy can be linked to liberal ideas ('liberal' in the European sense), namely supporting the poor, but leaving everything else to the markets.[14] Many benefits are means tested.[15]

In the second case protection of the income of working people is an important objective. One finds this type of social policy in Germany, Austria, France and other European states. Most of the central European transformation countries also turn towards this type of welfare state for redesigning their social policy (Tálos, 1998). People who are poor because they are not active on the labour market are conceptually not at the centre of attention of policy makers. This type of policy is often linked to the existence of strong trade unions and/or strong Christian-social traditions.[16] A further characteristic of these states is that they provide more benefits dependent on family status than states belonging to other types of welfare state.

The third type of social policy wants to safeguard a minimum for everybody and to protect the income of working people as well. It can be found in the Scandinavian countries and the Netherlands. Social democratic ideas are considered to back such a type of policy (Esping-Andersen, 1990).

Since the 1990s the distinction between the three types of welfare states has become less clear-cut (Esping-Andersen, 1996). The economies of northern Europe have reduced some of their programmes. Other countries with a strong tradition of linking social protection to labour market attachment have begun implementing reforms to reduce income protection while increasing programmes of social assistance. When evaluating the actual working of different social policy systems, the distinction is even less clear. It was shown that the USA welfare system is less effective in fighting poverty than the German social security type welfare state (Goodin et al., 1999).

One also has to distinguish between the state as regulator of social policy and as organiser of the programmes – collecting the taxes to finance them and paying out the benefits and organising the services. A state may mandate social health insurance, collect the contributions and pay for the services, while the health services, or part of them, are provided by private actors. States may finance kindergartens, but this does not imply that the state runs kindergartens.

We can distinguish between different organisational structures of social policy:

- The state organises the activities. It supplies the services directly on central, regional or local level. An example is the National Health Service in the UK. In that case the state employs many people for delivering social services. Naturally the state has to care for financing the services, either through general taxes, contributions or earmarked taxes. Organising activities is a sensible way of provision, if equality of services is considered to be essential.
- The state sets up special institutions for social policy and provides only the basic framework for social policy. These institutions often have a

legally defined domain of organisation and a legally defined scope. In that case there is no competition between these institutions for customers or fields of activity. Such institutions are often delineated according to professional lines. For instance, health insurance for blue-collar workers, a pension system for miners. There can be different regulations for different groups. We find such institutions in many European states, particularly for those aspects of social policy which protect against income loss. The pension schemes in many countries are constructed in such a way.
- The state obliges people to care for their own welfare and perhaps subsidises the payments, but leaves the organisational structure to the market; for example, health insurance in Switzerland; income related pensions in the UK and in Australia. With such a policy the state does not have to collect contributions.

1.5 A SHORT PREVIEW

There are different ways to analyse social policy. One type of literature is primarily concerned with its historic development: why were social policy programmes introduced? Why were reforms undertaken? Such analysis relies on an underlying theory of economics and/or politics. The emergence of the welfare state may be seen as an attempt to calm the war between classes, even to fend off revolutions. Others, in a more Whiggish view of the development of modern economies, see the development of social policy as the necessary answer to the social problems created by progressing industrialism (see Talos, 1981, for Austria). Ideological developments were important for establishing social programmes (for France and the UK, see Pederson, 1993). Still others see in the welfare state a process of establishing political affiliations (for example, Skocpol, 1992, for the USA).

That type of literature is important if one wants to understand how social policy was and still is discussed by people active in the field. For example, in Germany and in Austria the introduction and extension of social programmes was one of the targets of socialist parties and of trade unions, whereas parties of the right were either hostile to such programmes or wanted to have them on a smaller scale. Some saw social policy as an attempt to pacify the working classes as they would otherwise fight for a socialist revolution. This idea underlay Bismarck's policy in Germany of introducing important social policy programmes while making the social-democratic party illegal. Some of that literature can only be understood fully if one knows what are the options the authors have in mind: a pauperisation of some parts of the population, a revolution, a break-up of political parties.

Here a different approach is used: social policy programmes are discussed as answers to problems of market societies. The only alternatives considered are pure market solutions to the underlying problem – for example, social health protection against purely market-based health insurance; or public regulation of retirement income against purely market-based provision for retirement. This approach is of course non-historical. It will not help much to understand why a country has developed this or that institution of social policy. The question is always in which way does an economy with specific institutions of social policy differ from an economy where individuals solve a particular problem by making use of market provisions. That approach is connected with a normative question: if there were no social policy programmes, should they be introduced and how should they be organised?

In the second chapter a brief summary of basic economic concepts is provided. It will be asked whether there is something like an equilibrium in all markets and if so whether that is something 'good'. It will also provide an introduction to the theory of uncertainty and of insurance. Chapter 3 gives an introduction to the economics of social policy programmes, and discusses the reasons why publicly provided programmes may be preferred to market solutions (3.1). Ways to study effects of social policy programmes will be analysed in 3.2. A further point pursued in Chapter 3 is whether it is preferable to give goods or to give money (3.3).

Chapter 4 is the first chapter to analyse a special programme. It is based on a distinction between two views on the provision of health services, namely the choice theoretic approach and the social policy view (4.1). The following part of this chapter provides some information on solutions to the problems of health provision in various countries. In 4.3 we look at the reasons why there is no country without a sizeable public health system. Problems of equity are also discussed in this section. The allocative and the distributive effects are looked at in 4.4 and in 4.5.

Pension systems, which are the biggest social policy programmes in most states, are the topic of Chapter 5. In the first part information about different pension systems is provided. In 5.2 the elements of the theory of pensions system is given by comparing unfunded and funded systems. In 5.3 we again ask what are the reasons for the widespread existence of either public pension systems or publicly regulated private schemes. In 5.4 and 5.5 the allocative and distributive effects are discussed. Finally the effects of demographic changes are analysed in 5.6.

Chapter 6 takes up the question of social policy for labour markets. That comprises unemployment (6.1 to 6.3) and regulation of labour contracts (6.4). The analysis of policies dealing with unemployment is restricted to social policy aspects. Employment policy, particularly macroeconomic policy is not covered in this book. In 6.1 we look first at indicators of labour market

Introduction 19

problems and then at the problems of the unemployed – consumption smoothing, lower wages, repeated spells of unemployment. In 6.2 some information about unemployment benefits are given and their effects on the economy are analysed. Part 6.3 covers active labour market policy, and the last part discusses why the labour market is so heavily regulated and what are the effects of these regulations. Particularly we look at regulations for terminating a labour contract.

Policies for the support of families are the topic of Chapter 7. First we will discuss reasons why families should be supported. Though it is in most states politically accepted that this should be done, it is important to be clear why this is so. Otherwise it is not possible to evaluate how the chosen policy actually supports the objectives. In 7.2 the instruments for the support of families will be described and analysed. Then there is a look at maternity rights and parental leave provisions. The chapter ends with discussion of lone parent problems.

In the last chapter we look at poverty. We are primarily interested in poverty insofar as it can be alleviated by means of social policy. Economic growth is not a topic of this chapter, though the reduction of poverty was primarily due to economic growth. First, it is necessary to define poverty. This turns out to be a tricky problem (8.1). In 8.2 problems of poverty on a household level in relation to poverty at the level of individuals are discussed, and in 8.3 we look at duration of poverty. In 8.4 we consider precisely what is meant when one says poverty has increased or decreased. In 8.5 some information about poverty and its structures are given. It is also discussed whether poverty is a structural problem of society or rather due to personal characteristics. The following part discusses wage supplements as a means to reduce poverty, the final part looks at social assistance programmes.

NOTES

1. The former planned economies also spent much for social policy purposes. However data of planned economies are not comparable with data of market economies, as prices charged for products in planned economies often reflected social concern. For example, basic food was sold at very low prices, often below cost. This allowed pensions to be kept very low without making the retired hungry. The same applies to housing and many other goods and services. It is therefore not possible to compare the data from the period before the transformation has started with current data.
2. In Austria students up to the age of 25 receive child benefits of about € 2000 per year. Recently the government introduced fees for universities of about € 800 per year. For one reason or the other the government never considered the possibility of reducing child benefits for students.
3. Note that expenditure for social programmes increased in the UK during the Conservative governments of Margaret Thatcher and John Major. These governments pursued a policy to reduce the importance of the welfare state.

4. For a philosophical theory of justice, Rawls (1971), is currently the most referred book.
5. We disregard the following: though Beth may like to have the results of Adam's labour without having paid a wage, she abhors Adam working without payment for ethical reasons.
6. In big Indian cities whole families used to sleep in the streets because the houses they could afford were too far away from the places where the jobs were. They could have lived with what they earned in the city in one of the slums in the outskirts. But they could not earn a living there. Daily transportation between the outskirts and the city was too expensive. For an analysis of the increase of homelessness in the USA along these lines, O'Flaherty, 1996.
7. It is not necessarily a sign of worsening social circumstances if some houses turn from middle-class houses into poor-family houses. It can be a sign of social improvement!
8. In the Netherlands only 13 per cent of working mothers from two-parent families worked 35 hours or more, whereas 36 per cent of working lone mothers worked such hours (Bussemaker et al.,1997). In Germany merely 14 per cent of lone mothers who participated in the labour market worked less than 21 hours, whereas 30 per cent of working married mothers did so (Laisney et al., 1999)
9. There are other assumptions necessary for deriving important results of economic theory. However in the context of social policy they are less problematic. An important assumption is that people can make choices over all pairs of states. This is a problem when too many dimensions change. You may have no problem in making a decision between being a reasonably paid analyst in London and very well paid manager in Bristol. But consider the following choice: you live as a bachelor with a middle income in the suburbs of Copenhagen with a life expectancy of 50 more years, or with a high income in the centre of Barcelona with a family of four children with a life expectancy of 40 more years. That choice may be difficult. Fortunately such choices are seldom to be made. Most choices that individuals make do not pose many problems.
10. Some methods for therapeutic treatments work with the assumption that psychological phenomena were a rational answer to some psychic problem.
11. It is possible to translate the statement that women are not allowed to work in Afghanistan into the language of economics. One has to say that for all wages the utility of working is lower than the utility of not working, because the disutility of working is increased by the fines for trespassing the law when found working. However this formulation does not give any insight beyond the original one, namely that it is forbidden to work.
12. The only case of a drastic reduction in a welfare state was that of New Zealand.
13. There is no relation between the extent of the welfare state and the taxation of capital income. Many countries with strong social policy traditions like Austria or Germany rely almost completely on payroll taxes for financing their welfare programmes.
14. In the US context 'liberal' political ideas are on the left side of the political spectrum and are usually pro-welfare state. Political philosophies which reject the welfare state are called *libertarian* in the US context. For a presentation, see Nozick, 1974.
15. This type of welfare state is often termed *Beveridge*-type welfare state after the British economist William Beveridge.
16. Often the system is called *Bismarckian*, as its roots go back to the social policy reform of the German Chancellor Bismarck in the 1880s.

REFERENCES

Adema, Willem (1999), *Net Social Expenditure*, Paris, OECD, Labour Market and Social Policy, Occasional Papers, No. 39.

Atkinson, Anthony B. (1999), *The Economic Consequences of Rolling Back the Welfare State*, Cambridge (Mass.): MIT Press.

- *Bericht über die soziale Lage 1999*, Wien: Bundesministerium für Soziale Sicherheit und Generationen, 2000.
Blank, Rebecca and David T. Ellwood (2001), *The Clinton Legacy for America's Poor*, Cambridge (Mass.), NBER Working Paper 8437.
Bussemaker Jet, Annemieke van Drenth, Trudij Knijn and Jannecke Plantenga (1997), 'Lone Mothers in the Netherlands', in: Jane Lewis (ed.), *Lone Mothers in European Welfare Regimes. Shifting Policy Logics*, London and Philadelphia: Jessica Kingsley Publishers, pp. 96–120.
Casperson, Erik and Gilbert Metcalf (1994), 'Is a Value Added Tax Regressive? Annual Versus Lifetime Incidence Measures', *National Tax Journal*, 47, pp. 731–46.
Esping-Andersen, Gosta (1990), *The Three Worlds of Welfare Capitalism*, Cambridge: Polity Press.
Esping-Andersen, Gosta (ed.) (1996), *Welfare States in Transition. National Adaptations in Global Economies*, London: Sage Publications.
Goodin, Robert E., Bruce Heady, Ruud Muffels and Henk Jan Dirven (1999), *The Real Worlds of Welfare Capitalism*, Cambridge: Cambridge University Press.
Laisney, François, Michael Lechner, Matthias Staat and Gerhard Wagenhals (1999), 'Work and welfare of single mothers in Germany', *Economie Publique*, 3, pp. 111–44.
- *Monatsberichte des Österreichischen Instituts für Wirtschaftsforschung*, Wien, 1999
Nozick, Robert (1974), *Anarchy, State and Utopia*, New York: Basic Books.
O'Flaherty, Brendan (1996), *Making Room – the Economics of Homelessness*, Cambridge (Mass.): Harvard University Press.
Pederson, Susan (1993), *Family, Dependence and the Origin of the Welfare State. Britain and France 191–1945*, Cambridge: Cambridge University Press.
Rawls, John (1971), *A Theory of Justice*, Cambridge (Mass.): Harvard University Press.
Skocpol, Theda, (1992), *Protecting Soldiers and Mothers. The Political Origin of Social Policy in the United States*, Cambridge (Mass.): Harvard University Press.
Talos, Emmerich (1981), *Staatliche Sozialpolitik in Österreich. Rekonstruktion und Analyse*, Wien: Verlag für Gesellschaftskritik.
Tálos, Emmerich (ed.) (1998), *Soziale Sicherung im Wandel*, Wien: Böhlau.

2. Equilibrium, Welfare, Uncertainty

To discuss the effects of social policy programmes it is necessary to refer to a standard for comparison. Otherwise it is impossible to state whether the introduction or extension of a programme is favourable or will reduce welfare. A suitable standard against which the effects of social policy programmes can be evaluated is the pure market economy. After all, as argued in the first chapter, the welfare state can be seen as a set of regulations and institutions supplementing a market economy.

To carry out this comparison we have to ask what would be the outcome of a pure market economy if there were no social policy programmes. This question cannot be answered empirically as all societies have some provisions for social protection. It is a theoretical question, namely economics construes a model of a pure market society and asks what difference does the introduction of social policy programmes make. The purpose of this chapter is to present an outline of the theory of such a pure market economy.

In the first section I sketch some important concepts of microeconomic theory. For those acquainted with them this section provides a short summary. In the second section an introduction to the theory of uncertainty and insurance is provided. This is important for the theory of social policy, because it deals with problems of uncertainty. This section is more comprehensive, because uncertainty is hardly dealt with in introductory economics courses.

2.1 GENERAL EQUILIBRIUM AND ITS WELFARE PROPERTIES

It was argued above that interpersonal redistribution of income is an important objective of social policy. Whether that is desirable or not is hardly an economic question. It is a political and ethical issue. The economist's job is to find how these objectives can be achieved at the lowest cost and what are the economic effects of such a policy.

But what about other programmes? Providing insurance against contingent events and safeguarding intrapersonal redistribution? Can't people care for themselves?

The traditional answer to this question was, and for some still is: NO. Workers are poor and often ignorant. They are dependent on their employers and are unable to care individually for their future. Social policy is a way to overcome collectively the social and political weakness of workers as individuals. Note that in many countries socialist parties and trade unions were important for the emergence of the welfare state.[1]

Whether this is an appropriate idea today or whether it was a good one in bygone decades will not be discussed here. It is a position only a minority holds today – which does not imply that it is wrong. Be that as it may, there are many people and political groups who are in favour of strong social policy, though they consider modern capitalism to be a reasonable economic system. They regard social policy as useful, perhaps even a necessary complement to a market economy. That is also the approach of this book.

In order to understand social policy in this context we have to ask whether it is necessary at all to interfere with the working of the market system. The first question therefore is: what is the outcome of an economy in which goods and services are allocated to individuals only via markets? This question is pursued in general equilibrium theory. There it is asked whether all markets can be in equilibrium, and if so, whether the equilibrium is something 'good'.

The basic idea of general equilibrium theory is that all markets are interrelated. That is easy to see: if people suddenly change their demand for some goods, many others experience a rise or a decline in income. This causes further shifts of demand, leading to further changes of income and so on. Any change of a price can lead to similar chain of changes. Economic theory pursues such problems by analysing how households and firms act and what is the overall result.

In order to get income for consumption, households supply labour in the labour market and capital in the capital market. With the income received households demand goods for consumption which are produced by firms. We say that households have preferences – tastes – for goods. They can be represented by a utility function. Households maximise utility. The result of the maximisation shows itself as demand for goods and as supply of labour and capital in the markets.

Firms transform inputs (labour and capital) that they have acquired in the markets into outputs which they sell to the households. Their objective is to maximise profits. The profits are handed over to households, because they are the owners of the firms.

In the simplest case it is assumed that there is perfect competition. That means that all households and firms take prices as given, though the prices are the result of the supply and demand of all households and all firms in all markets. The point is that no household and no firm considers the possibility of influencing prices by restricting or extending its demand and supply. More formally: Households are characterised by:

1. Preferences over bundles of goods and services (x, a vector). These preferences can be represented by a utility function $U(x)$. (It requires specific assumptions for a preference ordering that it can be represented by a utility function. In most applied economic literature one begins directly with the utility function.)
2. Endowments of goods, abilities, and human capital (X, a vector).
3. Shares of ownership of firms (D, a vector). These shares are normalised such that the sum taken over all households equals 1.

The income of households consists of proceeds from the sale of goods and services – first of all labour – as well as income from their shares (dividends). They maximise utility under the condition that they remain within the limit set by the income they get from the supply of their endowments and the profits of the firms.

Formally:

$$\text{maximise } U(x)$$
$$\text{subject to the condition } px \leq pX + D\pi$$
(p is the vector of all prices, π are profits)

Firms are characterised by technologies. A technology is a method of transformation of inputs into outputs, namely goods and services into other goods and services. The technologies are described by production functions.

$$y = g(z)$$

where y is a vector of outputs of a firm, and z the vector of inputs. For example, with the input of six hours of my labour, three hours of the service of my laptop and two espressos, two pages of the manuscript of this book were produced.

Firms want to maximise profits but have to consider the limits set by the technology. For example, there is no technology available for me to write two pages of this book with less than six hours of labour, even with a better laptop and a third espresso. But this is a special case. In most production one can substitute one input against another, particularly in the long run. The same amount of output can be produced with much labour and little capital or with less labour and more capital.

Formally:

$$\text{maximise } \pi(y)$$

subject to $y = g(z)$

Profits are the proceeds of the sale of goods and services minus the costs for the inputs.

The result of the interaction of supply and demand of all households and all firms is called an allocation of goods. We say that households and firms co-ordinate their plans via the market. If markets are competitive, all households and all firms make their plans under the assumptions that prices are given, even though the prices are determined in the market.

There are two questions. (i) Is there an equilibrium? (ii) If yes, is the equilibrium something 'good' – in the sense of socially desirable?

(i) An equilibrium is a vector of prices (that is, for each good and each service one price), a vector of demand for goods and services and supply of labour and capital by households and a vector of inputs and outputs, such that (a) households maximise utility, (b) firms maximise profits and (c) that for all goods demand equals supply.

This is called an equilibrium for the following reason: if neither preferences nor technologies change, the game will be played in the next period in the same way as it is played in the current period. Everything would remain the same. It is one of the important theorems of general equilibrium analysis that under certain mathematical conditions, which to a great extent can be given a meaningful economic interpretation, such an equilibrium exists. This means that people and firms can co-ordinate their plans through markets simply by taking care of their private interests. There is no need for a general co-ordinating organisation. (How does one see that markets are in equilibrium? Everybody can sell and buy at the going prices; there are no queues – neither of sellers, nor of buyers.)

(ii) Is such an equilibrium something 'good' in the sense of being socially desirable?

A simple example demonstrates that this is not necessarily the case. Assume that you take a well-paid job for a couple of months in another city. Before you start your job you look for a small flat. You realise by glancing through the ads that with your income paying for a flat is not a problem. Assume that the market is in equilibrium. Therefore you will be able to find a flat within a short time, as there will always be a few flats to let on the market. But this nice state of the market does not exclude the possibility that you will find on the way to your flat many people sleeping in the streets because they are homeless. Of course, they could also easily find a flat at the market price, but they cannot afford it. They were maximising their utility as well, but their endowments were too small to earn enough for renting a flat.

There is a further problem, particularly relevant for social policy. In some instances voluntary contracts are not socially accepted, in the sense that they will not be enforced by courts. Some are explicitly forbidden, like selling oneself into slavery or peonage. In some cases they will not be enforced by a public authority, because they are considered to be too one-sided, even though both sides have accepted the contract voluntarily. In a social policy context, labour market contracts can fall under such a clause.[2]

However under certain conditions an equilibrium is something 'good' in a specific sense. To understand this we have to introduce the concept of *Pareto-efficiency*.

Definition: *An allocation of goods and services X is called Pareto-better than another allocation Y if everybody in X is at least as well off as in Y, and at least one individual is better off in X than in Y while nobody in Y is better off than in X. An allocation is Pareto-efficient, if there is no Pareto-better allocation.*[3]

Note that 'being better', 'at least as well off' refers always to valuations of individuals.

An example of Pareto-inefficiency is the existence of involuntary unemployment. (People are involuntarily unemployed, if they are prepared to work for the current wage – and even at a slightly lower wage – and yet cannot find a job.) This is inefficient in the Pareto sense, because the unemployed would prefer working for the current wage to staying idle; their marginal product would be about the same as that of the employed workers, so it would be profitable to employ them. However they remain unemployed.[4]

A Pareto-efficient allocation is not necessarily a desirable allocation. It can be an allocation with extreme inequalities. For example, the existence of homelessness does not imply Pareto-inefficiency. If some people are too poor to afford appropriate housing, their situation can perhaps be changed by a redistribution of wealth. But any redistribution makes some people worse off. The utility a rich person loses when something is taken away from her cannot be compared to the utility a person gets from a transfer. This is a basic methodological assumption of economic theory.[5]

But one can state the reverse: a Pareto-inefficient allocation is not desirable, because in such a situation the possibility exists of making someone better off without hurting anybody else. This is the reason why so much of economic literature is concerned with Pareto-efficiency.

There is a strong theorem of general equilibrium theory concerning Pareto-efficiency. The theorem states that under certain economic conditions the market equilibrium is Pareto-efficient. It is impossible to make people better off without hurting other people (*first theorem of welfare economics*). A full proof is not presented here, however the basic argument is the following: if there are markets, people make all exchanges by which they can improve their situation. If they leave out a possibility for a market transaction they do so because they would not be better off with the market transaction. In Box 2.1 the argument is presented formally for an economy with two agents, two goods and no production. (Bringing more agents and more goods into the picture would only result in a more complicated notation, without deeper economic or mathematical insights.).

BOX 2.1 THE FORMAL ARGUMENT FOR PARETO-EFFICIENCY FOR AN EXCHANGE ECONOMY

There are two people, Adam and Eve. Each of them gets each morning an endowment, several units of two goods X and Y, namely X^A and Y^A for Adam, and X^E and Y^E for Eve. They decide to exchange some of their endowments, the price of X for Y is p, the price of Y is 1 (though there are only two people the price p must be seen as the price prevailing under competition as if there were many Adams and Eves with identical endowments and the same preferences). After having exchanged, Adam has $X^{A'}$ and $Y^{A'}$ and Eve $X^{E'}$ and $Y^{E'}$. Assume that this is not Pareto-efficient. That implies that there is a different allocation of the total amount of goods $X^{A''} + X^{E''}$, $Y^{A''} + Y^{E''}$ which is preferred by Adam and Eve and remains within the budget constraints.

$$X^{A''} + X^{E''} = X^A + X^E$$
$$Y^{A''} + Y^{E''} = Y^A + Y^E$$

and

$$(X^{A''}, Y^{A''}) \succ^A (X^{A'}, Y^{A'})$$
$$(X^{E''}, Y^{E''}) \succ^E (X^{E'}, Y^{E'})$$

($\succ^A$ is Adam's preference order, $\succ^E$ is Eve's preference order)

Adam and Eve have chosen the consumption bundles on the right-hand side and not those one on the left-hand side, though they prefer the latter. Obviously they cannot afford the preferred bundles – otherwise they would have ended up with the " allocation. Therefore:

$$p \cdot X^{A''} + Y^{A''} > p \cdot X^A + Y^A$$
$$p \cdot X^{E''} + Y^{E''} > p \cdot X^E + Y^E$$

> Adding these two inequalities yields
>
> $$p \cdot (X^{A''} + X^{E''}) + (Y^{A''} + Y^{E''}) > p \cdot (X^A + X^E) + (Y^A + Y^E)$$
>
> If one inserts the first two equations in the last inequality, there is a contradiction. Therefore $(X^{A'}, Y^{A'})$ $(X^{E'}, Y^{E'})$ is a Pareto-efficient allocation.

This theorem does not imply that everything is fine in a market economy. It merely states that if the conditions which are necessary to prove the theorem are satisfied, one cannot improve the allocation in the sense of Pareto. It is not the existence of markets per se which calls for public interference.

There are two types of reasons why one might want to change the allocation of a pure market economy: (i) One of the conditions that is important for the result of the welfare theorem is not fulfilled. In that case, a Pareto-improvement might be possible. (ii) The income distribution resulting from the exchange in the markets is considered bad. For example, the existence of an equilibrium does not imply that everybody has an apartment or a job with a living wage. In that case one may want to redistribute income or wealth. That is not a Pareto improvement – the improvement for one individual is at the expense of another.[6]

The economic condition for an equilibrium to be Pareto-efficient is basically the following: the economic activities of an individual affect only her own welfare or that of other people who consent in making a contract. The welfare of third individuals is not affected. There are many situations when this condition is not fulfilled. The technical term for such situations is *market failure*.

- Technical external effects of an activity, for example, environmental effects where the utility of third persons will be affected. In the field of social policy: individuals having a social problem tend to create some for others – they are less productive, may engage in criminal acts, become sick, and so on.
- If there is a monopoly in the market for a good, the amount of that good supplied is not efficient. In order to maximise profits, the monopolist supplies less than would be supplied in a competitive market. By forcing the monopolist to sell an increased supply, the ensuing increase in welfare for the consumers is larger than the loss of profit to the supplier. The reason is that selling an increased supply is only possible when there is a reduction of the price of the monopoly

good (at least for some consumers). This cannot be achieved by market transactions, because the monopolist would lose if she increases her supply. Though her loss will be smaller than the benefit for the consumer (this can be shown rigorously), she cannot reap the profits from selling more of the good, unless there is perfect price discrimination. A monopoly can be a due to a natural monopoly, namely if there is only one supplier in the optimum. That is the case for goods the production of which needs much research before production starts, but have low production costs when the technology is known (for example, a new medicine).
- In case of a public good. (A public good is a good whose consumption is non-rival. The marginal cost of one more consumer equals zero – for example, one more car on a non-congested road.) The usual condition of efficiency requires that marginal costs equal marginal utility. If marginal costs are zero, excluding anybody from consuming this good is a loss of welfare – one could increase welfare by allowing this person to consume the good without making him pay for it. If this applies to all consumers the good under consideration will not be supplied, as there are set-up costs for producing the good. Only marginal costs are zero!

There are other types of market failure, particularly in connection with uncertainty (see below). (For more information look at any textbook on public finance.) When there are market failures a central authority can Pareto-improve the allocation achieved by markets. This does not imply that government interference will really achieve a better outcome in the sense of Pareto: the government may be wrongly informed about preferences or production possibilities. However there is room for a Pareto-improvement. How this can be achieved depends on the type of market failure. Some possibilities in connection with social policy questions will be worked out in the book.

What about the second problem, that of redistribution? Consider the case of homeless people. What should a government do if it wants to help the homeless? They say they cannot afford a flat, because prices are too high. Should the government force prices down? In that case those with higher income will demand even more housing. Therefore a real price control which forces prices down must be supplemented by a rationing scheme – how many apartments a family is allowed to have and how big they can be. This would work, but such a policy requires a lot of bureaucratic effort and it is unlikely that such a housing regime would be politically supported even if it could be administered. Many people would be able to afford bigger apartments – some only due to keeping down rents – but they would not be allowed to acquire them. Only in special situations would such a policy be accepted, for example after a war during which a big part of the stock of houses has been destroyed or after a major earthquake.

What about public housing? The government taxes people who are better off and supplies affordable housing to those who are too poor to find a flat at market prices. This is a viable policy, however it needs a lot of activity on behalf of the government. (The housing policy of the Vienna municipality, particularly between 1923 and 1933, came close to this idea: there was a special tax on housing, the proceeds of which were used for the construction of new houses for workers.[7])

What would happen if the government simply gave something to the homeless to increase their endowments such that they can afford to buy houses? This would drive up prices further, as demand increases. But there is an important theorem of economics which shows that such a policy can work. It can be seen as a converse of the first welfare theorem – *the second welfare theorem*: it states that under slightly more restrictive conditions *each admissible Pareto-efficient allocation can be achieved by redistributing the endowments and then leaving everything else to competitive markets.* (An allocation is admissible if the amount of goods allocated does not exceed the sum of all endowments and all goods produced with the inputs available.) If it is decided that the outcome of the market allocation with the original endowments is undesirable for reasons of income distribution – perhaps some people are without a home or a wage high enough to allow a decent living – neither price fixing, nor the organisation of supply by the government is necessary. A redistribution of the endowments suffices.

The basic idea behind this theorem is that if one redistributes endowments between individuals, the ensuing demand and supply of goods and services safeguards the desired allocation. Consider the example of homeless people: if the government equips them with a sufficiently high amount of purchasing power, they will demand housing. That will drive up the price – but this is precisely the effect which safeguards an increased supply. First, some people will decide that it is optimal for them to have a smaller flat than they had before when prices were lower, and, secondly, more houses will be built.[8]

Can this theorem be used in the context of social policy? That would be a big advantage, as in that case the state could restrict its activities to redistribution. The basic content of the proposition is that a government has to tax people if it wants to favour a special group. Unfortunately things are not so easy. Taxing people and giving transfers to others has in most cases substantial allocative effects. (For an extensive treatment of this point see Myles, 1995, pp. 44–8.) Therefore redistribution without any allocative effects is not a viable option.

That does not imply that this theorem cannot be used for practical purposes. An important example is Drèze and Sen's (1989) analysis of public action in the case of hunger due to crop failures, natural catastrophes, wars, and so on. In such situations governments often relied on price controls for basic food in the hope that this allowed the victims to buy enough of it. Such a policy was often accompanied by measures such as rationing of food, political and judicial attacks against 'hoarders and speculators' and planned redistribution of basic food from surplus to deficit areas. Drèze and Sen (1989) showed in their study about famines that a different policy was very effective: give the hungry money – perhaps by introducing public work schemes. That increases demand and drives prices up. But this is warranted: firstly, as in the example of housing the homeless, some people demand less food – they are not the hungry ones – and, secondly, merchants organise the flow of food from surplus areas to deficit areas, because they can thereby make a profit. If prices were instead kept down by decree, the government would have to enforce the transfer of basic foods to the deficit areas. It would have to organise the logistics, the storage, the transport – activities which governments are often not apt to do.

2.2 ELEMENTS OF THE ANALYSIS OF UNCERTAINTY

2.2.1 The Neumann–Morgenstern Utility Function

Up to now we have not taken into account one important fact of life: there is always uncertainty. As mentioned in the introduction, social policy has a lot to do with it. Problems of health, unemployment, longevity (that is, to outlive one's own wealth), and so on are all contingent events. They are realised with a certain probability. There is no economic activity directed towards the future without uncertainty. This is true for all investment, but also when buying goods for consumption in a future period. For example, the utility I get from a new car which could last for many years will be severely reduced if I die a year after I have bought it. If I had known before, I would have acquired a wreck and would have bought with the rest of my wealth something different – perhaps a better treatment to make my life a bit longer, or some caring to make the end less painful.

Economic analysis has developed some concepts to handle problems of uncertainty. The most important one is that of the *expected utility function* (or Neumann–Morgenstern (NM) utility function, after the pioneers of this concept John von Neumann and Oskar Morgenstern). It deals with the problem of how people value uncertain events before uncertainty is resolved. Consider the following example: you get either x or y depending on a chance factor.

With probability π you receive x which gives the utility $u(x)$ and with probability $(1-\pi)$ you get y with utility $u(y)$. How will you evaluate that lottery $Z = (x, y; \pi, 1-\pi)$? How much are you prepared to pay for the purchase of such a lottery? Or how much are you prepared to pay for avoiding this lottery?

The Neumann–Morgenstern utility function states that the utility of a contingent basket is its expected utility, formally:

$$EU(Z) = u(x)\cdot\pi + u(y)\cdot(1-\pi)$$

or generally: let X be a vector with each component x_i, denoting an outcome (a good, a payment, and so on), Π is a vector of equal dimension of probabilities. The expected utility of X is defined as:

$$EU(X) = \sum u(x_i)\pi_i$$

Expected utility is the weighted sum of the utilities of all possible states; the weights are the probabilities of the states.

There are a few assumptions behind this concept, some of which are problematic:

- There is a probability distribution for all contingent events. It is clear that if this assumption is not fulfilled, one cannot calculate a sum as in the formula above. This does not mean that probabilities are 'objectively' given, rather that people have to assume probabilities for all possible events when they make decisions rationally in the face of uncertainty.
- Adding up utilities must be a sensible operation. To see the problem for economic theory: when we have a set X of goods or allocations we assume that people can order the elements of X according to their preferences. Any function $f(.)$ with $f(x) > f(y)$ whenever $x \succ y$ is called a utility function of this preference ordering. Any monotone transformation of $g(f(.))$ is also a utility function representing the same preference ordering. It does not make a difference whether one uses the utility function $f(x)$ or $f(x) + 10$, or $7f(x)$, or $\ln(f(x))$ or $\exp(f(x))$. They all refer to the same preferences. The utility function does not give any information about differences of utility. We cannot say that x is 5 times as good as y, or the difference between $f(x)$ and $f(y)$ is 10. Utility is only *ordinal*. One important consequence is that one cannot add up utilities. Therefore one cannot use such utility functions for calculating expected utility. In order to do that we need information about differences of utilities as well. Then one can add up utilities, and

multiply them with a constant. These are utility functions which are unique up to a positive affine transformation: if u is utility function then $v(u) = au + b$ represents the same preferences. To achieve that one can make the following assumption: for any two outcomes x and y with probabilities π and $1-\pi$, there is an event z such that the person is indifferent between the lottery $(x, y; \pi, 1-\pi)$ and the fixed outcome z with probability 1. This assumption is quite reasonable in many situations. The idea of demand for and supply of insurance rests on this assumption. It can be shown that this assumption is very important – though not sufficient – for the construction of NM utility functions.
- Utility of good x in situation one is independent of good y in situation two. This assumption is reasonable because events exclude each other.
- Utilities do not depend on states. The utility function remains the same in all outcomes. This is not an important problem as long as we consider utilities over different amounts of wealth, as more wealth is nearly always preferred to less wealth. It is more of a problem if the utility of goods is considered. The utility of many goods depends on the state of nature. An umbrella has a positive utility when it rains – I am prepared to pay for having one with me. But it can be a nuisance to carry one around when the weather is fine. More important for social policy is that we may have different utility functions when we are old and when we are young, different ones when we are healthy and when we are sick.[9]

The NM utility function is not the only utility concept to handle uncertainty, but it is the most important one. Nearly all economic literature uses it, particularly in applied research. The big advantage of NM functions is that they are mathematically easy to handle and that the basic results of equilibrium analysis – including the welfare theorems – hold true under appropriate modification: it is assumed that households maximise expected utility and firms expected profits.[10]

There is already an important difference compared to an economy without uncertainty which is very important for social policy. Even though the equilibrium is efficient in the Pareto sense if there are no external effects, some people may be pretty badly off after uncertainty is resolved (*ex post*) – some people may have lost their ability to work, others have become sick, or lived longer than they had expected and therefore have outlived their accumulated resources. One way to cope with such problems is insurance. That will be analysed in the remaining parts of this chapter.

2.2.2 Preferences for Risk

We need a further concept to make problems of insurance tractable for analysis. Individuals are distinguished according to their *preference for risk*. An individual who is prepared to pay for avoiding risk – that is, buying insurance – is called risk-averse; an individual who buys risk – for example, a lottery ticket – is called a risk lover. In between lies the case of risk-neutral agents.

Formally: if for an individual

$$EU(X) = \sum u(x_i)\pi_i < u(\sum x_i \pi_i) = u(E(X)),$$

where the term left of the inequality sign is the expected utility of values and the term on the right is the utility of the expected value, the agent is risk-averse: she prefers the expected outcome with probability one to the original lottery. If the sign is reversed she is a risk lover: the lottery is preferred to the safe outcome with the same size as the expected outcome. If they are considered equal then the agent is risk-neutral.

There is a close relationship between the shape of the utility function of an individual and her behaviour towards risk. Consider the case with diminishing marginal utility of income.[11] This is somehow the 'normal' case for households. If a person faces a lottery with two outcomes, x1 and x2, with x2 > x1, both with probability 0.5, she prefers the fixed payment of 0.5(x1 + x2) to the lottery, as can be seen in Figure 2.1. If she is risk-averse, she is prepared to pay something for having 0.5(x1 + x2) with probability 1 instead of the lottery (x1, x2; 0.5, 0.5). Decreasing marginal utility of income (a concave utility function) is therefore tantamount to being risk-averse. If the utility function is convex the agent is a risk-lover: the expected utility of the lottery exhibits higher utility as the utility of the expected outcome. Note that this expression is sensible only if payoffs can be added. In case of wealth or income this can be done. However when one attempts to estimate health risks, this is a meaningless operation: though one can add utilities over different health states, one cannot add up the health states without putting values on the states themselves.

What about firms? In the traditional analysis firms are considered to be profit maximisers. The utility of each outcome is simply its profit. The expected utility is therefore the expected profit. (X is the vector of outcomes, Π the vector of probabilities)

$$EU(X) = EX \cdot \Pi = \sum x_i \pi_i$$

Profit maximisers are therefore risk-neutral! To make profits they are prepared to buy risky contracts for a small premium. This is the basis for the insurance industry: risk-averse households which are prepared to pay something for reducing risk and risk-neutral firms who accept risks.[12]

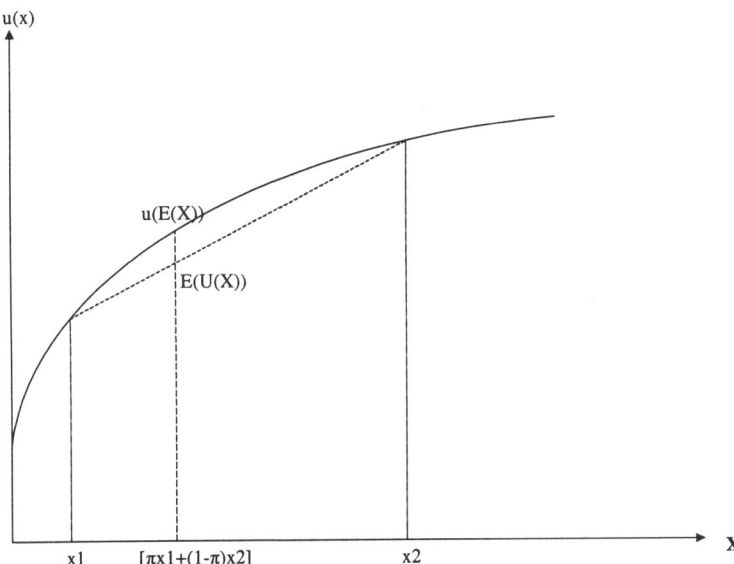

Figure 2.1 Risk-aversion

2.2.3 What Does an Insurance Do?

Assume that there are two states, wealth X in good state and Y in bad state, with $X > Y$, for example X is the value of a car, and Y is the value of the same car after an accident. There is a probability distribution over X, Y. Insurance of an amount Z means that one pays αZ ($\alpha < 1$) and when the bad state occurs one gets Z. Therefore the wealth in the good state is $(X - \alpha Z)$ and in the bad state $(Y - \alpha Z + Z)$. The probability of the bad state is π.

With probability π the insurance company has to pay Z and with $(1 - \pi)$ it has to pay nothing. In both cases the insurance collects αZ. Expected profits P are therefore:

$$P = \alpha Z - \pi Z - (1 - \pi) 0 = \alpha Z - \pi Z.$$

If expected profits are zero (perfect competition) α must equal π, the insurance premium per unit of loss is just the probability of the bad state. This is called a *fair insurance*. In reality an insurance can never be fully fair, as there are costs associated with running an insurance. The difference between a fair insurance and the real insurance is called *loading*. A loading factor of 15 per cent says that total premiums have to be 15 per cent higher than total loss payments to cover expenses.

What is the demand for insurance? How does a person value being insured? Expected utility in case of insurance is

$$E[U(Z)] = (1-\pi) \cdot u(X - \alpha Z) + \pi \cdot u(Y - \alpha Z + Z).$$

The optimal amount of insurance Z can be calculated by setting the first derivative zero:

$$\frac{[\pi * \cdot u'(Y - \alpha Z + Z)]}{[(1 - \pi) \cdot u'(X - \alpha Z)]} = \frac{\alpha}{(1 - \alpha)}$$

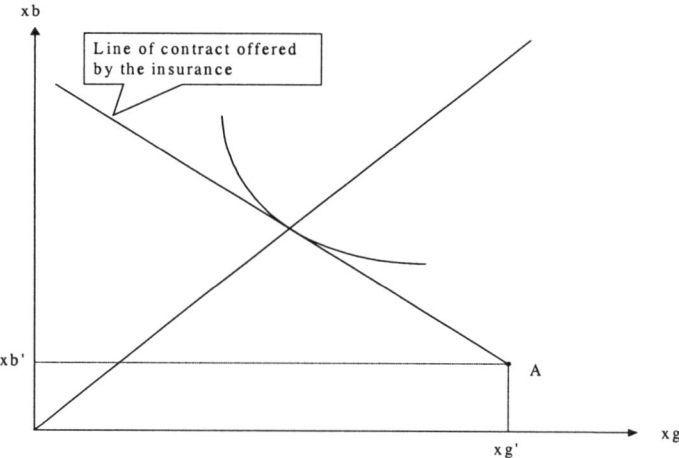

Note: Along the contract line offered by the insurance, a person can buy as many units of insurance as she wants to buy. At point A an individual has xg' units of a good in the good state and xb' units of the good in the bad state. At the 45° line income is the same in both states. If she is risk-averse, she prefers to come closer to the 45° line. If she wants to increase risk, she can move away from the 45° line. If the insurance is fair, the slope of the contract line equals $-\pi/(1-\pi)$. In that case the contract line is tangent to the indifference curve at the 45° degree line. The person has the same amount in both states of nature. She is fully insured.

Figure 2.2 Fair insurance for contingent events

The marginal rate of substitution between the two states (the expression on the left) must equal the price at which the insurance is offered (the expression on the right) (see Figure 2.2). If insurance is fair, the right hand side of the last equation equals $\pi/(1-\pi)$, because the premium must be equal to the probability of the bad outcome. This implies that marginal utility in the good state and in the bad state must be equal. This can only be achieved if consumption is independent of the state, that is, the same consumption in the good state and the bad state – full insurance. Therefore a risk-averse individual fully insures with a fair insurance. In the case that there is loading, the individual does not fully insure. She accepts some risk.

Do risky events create any problem when there are markets to cope with them? It has already been mentioned that the basic propositions of general equilibrium theory including the welfare theorems remain valid. Markets can cope with problems of uncertainty. Do we need social insurance at all? If there is a fire in a house, there is a big loss, but this is hardly a social problem, because commercial insurance against fire is available everywhere. There is no social fire insurance, and there is nobody who argues that it should be introduced. The loss through unemployment is in most cases much smaller than the loss by an incidence of fire. Most unemployed people find a job within three to four months. Their loss hardly exceeds €10 000. But unemployment is everywhere considered a problem for social policy. There is hardly an insurance company that provides unemployment insurance on a commercial basis.[13] Those that do exist are only suitable for special segments of employed people.

The fundamental question concerning social policy in relation to contingent events is:

Why are there markets to insure against some contingent events while for others such markets do not exist or are considered to be socially inadequate and must be supplemented by social policy?

Are there specific market failures in connection with uncertainty? What are the conditions for an insurance market to work efficiently – in the sense of Pareto? Amongst the conditions for an equilibrium to be efficient are the following:

(i) Independence of events. If the occurrence of a bad state for one agent increases the probability of a bad state for other people the events are correlated. This is an external effect. An insurance can hardly function with correlated events. Examples are contagious diseases; unemployment; loss of wealth due to inflation.

(ii) Absence of *asymmetric information*.[14] In the case of uncertainty there can arise a problem absent in cases of full information, namely one partner in a contract has more information than the other. This is called asymmetric information. Often the term 'private information' is used in this context. What can be known by everybody is called 'public information'. This distinction does not relate to the possibility of disguising information, but is rather to do with making information trustworthy. For example, somebody asks a bank to finance a project, the success of which depends amongst other things on her effort. The applicant cannot prove that she will undertake high effort. Whether she is prepared to work assiduously is private information. Having real estate is public or common information as long as there is a public register of real estate. It can be used as collateral.

Two problems can arise in connection with asymmetric information, resulting in a non Pareto-optimal equilibrium: (a) adverse selection and (b) moral hazard.

(a) Adverse selection – lemon's principle (*ex-ante* opportunism). Due to asymmetric information, some markets may not exist. The reason is that the quality of the good traded cannot be safeguarded. Consider the following situation: in a market for second-hand cars, there are good cars and so called 'lemons' – cars breaking down with high probability within a short period. To calculate an example: there are 1000 used cars on the market, 800 good ones and 200 lemons. The seller's reservation prices (that is the minimum price for which the sellers are prepared to sell) are 200 for a lemon and 1000 for a good car; buyers are willing to pay 300 for a lemon and 1100 for a good car.

If the buyers knew which car is a lemon – public knowledge – there would be no problem. Both types of cars could be sold. The lemons would settle for something between 200 and 300, the good cars for a price between 1000 and 1100. The allocation after exchange is Pareto-optimal, as sellers are prepared to part with their cars for less than buyers are willing to pay.

What happens though if there is only private information – only the sellers know which car is a lemon and which one is a good one? This depends on the way prospective buyers value the risk of buying a lemon, that is, on their utility function. The probability of a lemon is 0.2. Assume that they buyers are willing to pay:

$$0.2*300 + 0.8*1100 = 940$$

At the price of 940, only lemons are supplied because the reservation price for good cars is 1000. No good cars will be traded in equilibrium, a situation which is not Pareto-efficient. The underlying problem is not that there is risk, but that one party in the contract knows less than the other.

(b) Moral hazard (*ex-post* opportunism). One condition under which risky events can be insured is that the probabilities of the outcomes cannot be manipulated by partners of a contract. There are two aspects to this, first the probability of the event. My wealth is impaired in case of a hailstorm, but I cannot manipulate whether there is an hailstorm or not. In other cases manipulation is possible. For example, the probability of a fire can be manipulated. The second aspect is that of the size of the loss. Though I cannot manipulate the probability of a hailstorm, I can manipulate the size of the loss – I can leave windows open which will allow damage in my flat.

It is a problem for insurance companies if prevention is costly. If I am protected against a loss by an insurance contract, I have an incentive to avoid the costs of taking precaution against the bad outcome – that is, I avoid costs by not buying a good lock for my flat if I have insurance against burglary. Usually insurance companies prescribe which precautionary measures have to be undertaken by the insured and will control them, but this is costly and increases loading.

There are instances in which control for effort is not really viable. Consider the case of getting a loan for studying. Most successful students earn enough after graduation to be able to pay back a loan they took out to finance their studies. In a good system of higher education the probability of success for students who are prepared to make the necessary effort should be high enough that it is worthwhile for a bank to give loans to students. Some will fail and will never pay back, but as long as the probability of a failure is a given number there should be no problem in getting a loan. Unfortunately that is not the case. The amount of effort a student makes depends very much on the characteristics of a person and can be manipulated. Situations like that can lead to social problems. The problem for students and other young people is not that they are poor because of low earnings. Taking their expected income over a life time, they are not poor. However they cannot get a loan to finance current consumption. The unemployed face the same problem: most of them find a job within, at most, four months. Taken over their whole working life, unemployment often leads only to a small loss of income. But for somebody unemployed it is nevertheless very difficult to get a loan because the probability of finding another job can be affected by the unemployed individual.

NOTES

1. Some radical groups on the left were opposed to social policy as they considered it an aberration from a revolutionary path.
2. For a recent discussion of such clauses see Shiffrin (2000).
3. In older literature one often finds the expression 'Pareto-optimality' instead of Pareto-efficiency. That expression is not used anymore because by using the word 'optimality' it is implied that such an allocation is something 'good', in the sense of being desirable. But as it will become clear in the following paragraphs that is not necessarily true.
4. For decades it was asked how such a situation can be an equilibrium at all. The point is that in markets for goods and assets prices would change such that demand equals supply. Labour markets do not work in this way. See below, Chapter 6.
5. In older economic literature there is a distinction between basic needs and other desires. With this idea one can clearly compare utilities between different people: satisfying a basic need gives more utility than satisfying other desires. However this distinction, though in many situations sensible, would bring theoretical problems.
6. One can find in the literature the expression 'Pareto improving redistribution'. This concept is used in the following context. Assume that the list of arguments of the utility function of Eve contains the amount of Adam's consumption. Higher consumption by Adam increases Eve's utility ('interdependent utilities'). In that case a redistribution from Eve to Adam can increase overall utility. But one should be very careful when using such an argument. The reason is the following: by making special assumptions about the utility function, one can prove almost everything. This can be quite nice, but the theory will lose its bite – anything goes.
7. It is not clear whether the people who were put into these houses were the really poor. They were mostly skilled and semiskilled workers many of whom had a fixed job in the municipality of Vienna. Of course they were not rich, but they did not belong to the lowest quintile of the income distribution.
8. The proof of the second welfare theorem makes use of mathematical concepts which are usually not covered by introductory math-for-economics courses.
9. There are generalisations of the NM-utility function which consider state contingent utilities.
10. There is empirical evidence that in certain situations people do not behave as NM utility maximisers (Kahneman and Tversky, 1981).
11. The idea of decreasing marginal utility has no meaning in a purely ordinal utility concept.
12. There is a slight misuse of language: it is a characteristic of a person, namely of her preferences, to be risk-averse or risk lover. An insurance company has no preferences, it can spread risks and thereby reduce the variance of outcomes, while leaving the mean of the distribution invariant.
13. The occurrence of unemployment is much higher than that of fire. In Austria, in each year about 20 per cent of all employed experience a period of unemployment (see below).
14. For their analysis of the asymmetric information and its consequences for markets G. Akerlof, M. Spence and J. Stiglitz were awarded the Nobel Price for economics in 2001.

REFERENCES

Drèze, Jean and Amartya Sen (1989), *Hunger and Public Action*, Oxford: Clarendon Press.

Myles, Gareth D. (1995), *Public Economics*, Cambridge: University Press.

Shiffrin, Seana Valentine (2000), 'Paternalism, Unconscionability Doctrine, and Accommodation', *Philosophy & Public Affairs*, 29, pp. 205–50.
Tversky, Amos and Daniel Kahneman (1981), 'The Framing of Decisions and the Psychology of Choice', *Science*, 211, pp. 453–58.

3. Economic Aspects of Social Policy

In the preceding chapters it was argued that besides the wish to redistribute income market failures can be a reason why government interference into the market system may be advisable. The first part of this chapter deals with some of these problems in the context of social policy. In the second part, a framework for the analysis of the consequences of social policy programmes is discussed. The third part pursues the question as to whether goods or general purchasing power should be provided.

3.1 SOME REASONS FOR SOCIAL POLICY

3.1.1 Separation of Risks and Underprovision of Insurance

In Chapter 2 the definition of fair insurance was given, namely that the premium payments cover the expected loss of the insured person. Therefore for two individuals with different probabilities of a loss, the insurance premium must be different in a fair insurance. For example, men and women have different risks concerning health expenditure and different life expectancies. A fair health insurance therefore requires a higher premium for women; an annuity insurance must also charge higher premium payments for women or pay lower annuities. Risks will be separated if it is public knowledge to which group an individual belongs.

To see why any commercially working insurance cannot pool different risks in one type of contract assume that a 'socially minded' insurance for pensions charges the same premium for men and women. The amount of the premium must cover the expected average pension for both groups taken together. Another company can attract all men by offering a contract only for men with a lower premium. Only women remain with the first insurance which in turn must raise the premium to avoid making a loss. For two reasons a separation of risks in different insurance programmes may be socially undesirable. First, there is a normative aspect: why *should* individuals with different risks pay different premiums? Second, in case of asymmetric information the separation of risks can lead to underprovision of insurance.

The first aspect is an argument of justice; it may be considered unjust that some individuals have to pay more than others because of higher risks if they cannot control the risk. Nobody can control his or her gender. To give another example, is it acceptable that people who suffer from diabetes or high blood pressure have to pay higher premiums?

A way to avoid the separation of risks is to force a pooling of risks – a *social insurance*; an insurance that does not separate risks. Premiums are not individually fair and there is always some redistribution in the system. The redistributive aspect is often enhanced by making the contributions dependent on income and not on expected loss. A social insurance favours certain people at the cost of others.

When a social insurance is set up, it cannot compete against insurance companies which can separate risks, as the latter would take away the good risks and leave the social insurance with the bad risks. This does not imply that there can be no competition whatsoever. In the Netherlands, in Switzerland and in Germany there is competition between social health insurance systems. However in that case the separation of risks must be suppressed. That can be achieved by forcing the insurance companies to offer each contract to any applicant. Another way to overcome the difficulties due to competition between social insurance institutions consists in cross-subsidisation between these institutions: those with the goods risks have to subsidise the other ones.

BOX 3.1 AN EXAMPLE OF NON-AVAILABILITY OF INSURANCE AGAINST JOB-RELATED RISK

The Aetna Life Insurance Company imposed limits on the risks it would insure, setting death benefit maximums as low as $250 for coal miners, who faced the most dangerous working conditions in the early twentieth century. A physician, on the other hand, could insure up to $10,000 for accidental death. Further, accident insurance was noted for its high load factors. Even with the high loads, a number of companies writing accident insurance failed over the period 1917–26, whereas the surviving stock companies suffered a slight underwriting loss. The end result was that many workers were unable to purchase complete coverage, and possibly were shut out of the market altogether. (Kantor and Fishback, 1996, p. 427)

A social insurance can also 'insure' against risks which cannot be insured in a market insurance due to high probabilities of a bad outcome. For example, a child born with health defects will hardly find an insurer. Accepting it in a social insurance is a subsidy of the insured. Income is redistributed in favour of these individuals. Summing up, a social insurance is an device to insure and redistribute income in one institutional set-up.

The second aspect, that of asymmetric information, is a classical market failure argument. Consider a situation in which there are two types of risk groups – a high-risk group and a low-risk group. Both are risk-averse and therefore prefer to have full insurance. Assume that it is private information to which group an individual belongs. In Figure 3.1 there are the fair insurance lines FL^l and FL^h, with the high-risk line below the low-risk line. In between lies the fair insurance line for both groups combined (FL^c). All people prefer full insurance, as, by assumption, they are risk-averse. Therefore the indifference curves (ID^l and ID^h) are tangent to the fair odds line at the 45° line (Z^h, Z^l). No insurance company can offer such contracts, because high-risk individuals would prefer to take the low-risk contract which provides full insurance for a lower premium. The insurance company thereby makes a loss.

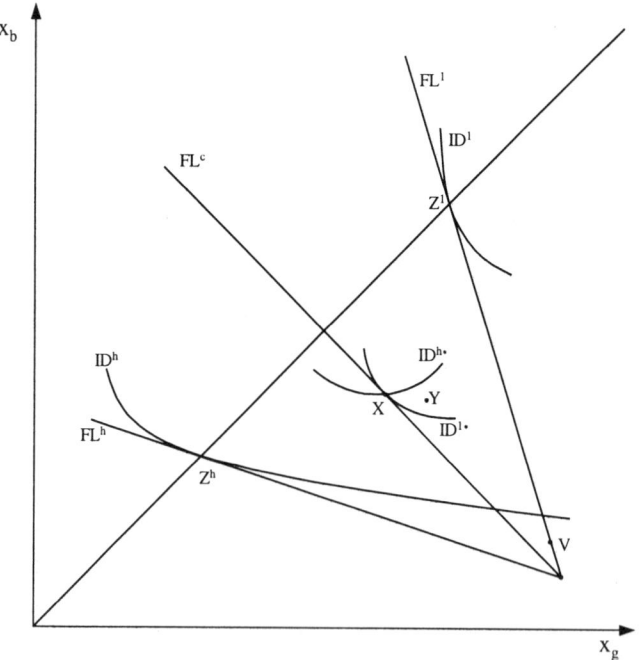

Figure 3.1 Pooling and separating equilibrium

Assume that the insurance company offers contracts along the fair odds line FL^c for the whole population, for example at point X. If there is an equilibrium, it is a *pooling equilibrium*: all have the same contract, though their risks are different. However it can happen that the indifference curves ID^{l*} and ID^{h*} through X are as in Figure 3.1. In that case X cannot be an equilibrium: if another insurance company offers a contract between the two indifference curves, for example at Y, it would attract only low-risk people and would make profits. Individuals remaining with X are high-risk individuals. Their premiums cannot cover the costs. The insurance company experiences a loss with these contracts, because the fair odds line is FL^h. Any point Y between ID^{h*} and ID^{l*} is preferred to X by people with low risks, whereas high-risk individuals prefer the contract X. This contract is not viable as only the bad risks will take it.

The contracts (V, Z^h) can be an equilibrium – a *separating equilibrium*: high-risk individuals are fully insured, low-risk individuals do not get full insurance. High-risk people do not prefer V, nor do low-risk individuals prefer Z^h. People belonging to different groups sort themselves into different contracts.

That is inefficient: low-risk people are not fully insured, though they would prefer to have full insurance. For example, they might have to pay a deductible. This is a market failure in the sense that the outcome of the market allocation is not Pareto-efficient due to asymmetric information. This may not be an important problem for social policy as it is the good risks which are not fully covered. However things are different if controlling for the group an individual belongs to creates costs. It can be shown that in that case it is the high-risk groups which are rationed in the market (Newhouse, 1996, p. 1244). That may be more of a social problem.

A digression: is adverse selection in the insurance market an important phenomenon?

Though adverse selection is a well established principle in all theoretical literature on insurance, there is not much empirical literature about it. It is not easy to find it in the data. To see why: if it is observed that different individuals buy different amounts of insurance coverage, one does not observe how expected outcome was related to the purchase of insurance – the theoretical argument. One merely observes how the actual outcome was related to the purchase of insurance. The data show the relation between different realisations of the same risk for different risk groups and the purchase of insurance. One cannot observe different probabilities facing an event, only the outcome. In order to find adverse selection as a cause for purchasing different insurance contracts, one has to model demand for high-risk and low-risk groups separately and then confront the predictions with actual data.

A further complication is that the purchase of divers insurance contracts may be influenced by other characteristics – wealth, risk aversion, and so on.

If one wants to single out the effect of different risks, one must take account of the influence of other effects. This is difficult if the other characteristics are correlated with the risk – for example, risk aversion can change with income; it may be different between men and women. However if these other characteristics, like income and gender, can be observed, one can control for them in the regression analysis.

A study by Puelz and Snow (1994) searched for adverse selection in the market for car insurance. They used the data of an insurance company offering contracts with deductibles of $100, $200 and $250. The information they used were the contracts bought, some personal characteristics influencing risk, like age, gender, type of car and whether there was an accident reported. The theory predicts that *ceteris paribus* individuals with high risks prefer to buy a contract with a low deductible. And that was precisely what Puelz and Snow found: given the fact that there was an accident, the contract showed a higher probability of having a low deductible than where there was no accident reported.

As usual in economics, other authors produced different results: for French car insurance see Chiappori and Salanié (2000); for US health insurance, Cardon and Hendel (2001). We will return to this question in Chapter 5.3 below when discussing annuities. See also Box 5.2 below.

3.1.2 Co-ordination Failures

There are certain situations in which individual self-interested action brings about Pareto-inferior results in comparison with coordinated actions. Consider the environment: if everyone protects the environment, the outcome is better for all. However given that everyone else acts accordingly it is in the private interest of each individual to avoid the costs connected with protecting the environment. The reason is that one's contribution to pollution is minimal, whereas the costs of avoidance can be substantial. Therefore the loss that an individual suffers due to not protecting the environment is, in most cases, much smaller than the costs of the protecting activity. The result is that nobody accepts the costs voluntarily, even in cases where everybody is prepared to vote in favour of a law to protect the environment which forces them to bear costs. This type of situation is called a *Prisoner's dilemma*.

For questions of social policy the following situation is discussed in the literature. Assume that there are rich people and poor people. All rich people prefer some redistribution towards the poor, some because they are altruistic, others because they consider the sight of the poor unpleasant or are afraid of a rebellion. Would this preference of the rich be enough to ensure that each of them gives voluntarily? This is a Prisoner's dilemma situation. When everybody else gives something for the poor, it is better for a rich individual not to give. She can enjoy both the social stability and her unimpaired wealth, because the individual contribution to social stability is small. The way out of this situation is a mandatory redistribution scheme in favour of the poor.

Another co-ordination failure is the so called *Samaritan's dilemma*. Assume that a society is prepared to help people who became poor by bad luck – people have altruistic preferences. In that case it would be rational not to have insurance. People rely on the altruistic preferences of others.

BOX 3.2 AN EMERGENCY FUND TO AVOID INSURANCE

In all countries farmers can insure commercially against loss caused by hailstorms. In Austria there is a public welfare fund for help in case of loss by catastrophe – floods, earthquakes, hailstorms, and so on. Farmers often do not insure against hailstorms – they save on the premiums and rely on the fund (see *Die Presse*, 27 March 1998).

3.1.3 Problems with the Rationality Assumption and Insufficient Information

Rational behaviour is an important assumption in all economic models. Its premise is that people can make choices consistently and that people use all information available. This assumption is at the heart of all economic theory. It should not be given up lightly, as nearly everything can be proved when one assumes non-rational behaviour. However social problems can arise because in one way or the other the rationality assumption is not valid. That is a special problem for decisions influencing a person's welfare for a long period.

In many instances we know that our preferences will change – for example, a person's preference for leisure is different at the age of 40 from when she is 70. Therefore most people save for retirement if there is no public pension scheme. Such problems are analysed by modelling the behaviour of individuals as having one utility function as an aggregate of utility functions for each period. Usually one takes the discounted sum of period utilities as aggregate utility. The individual is considered to maximise the aggregate utility over the whole period.

In some instances this is not adequate as a description of actual human behaviour. It implies that people make a decision just once – and that's it. This is obviously not the case for many people. Unforeseen voluntary changes in people's professional activities would not exist, nor changes in the plan of how many children to raise, and so on. Probably, most of what is important in a person's life relates in one way or the other to unforeseen events and unforeseen experiences which are connected with unforeseen changes of preferences. It is altogether questionable whether a person at the age of 50 is the same person as she was at the age of 25.[1]

This can lead to inconsistencies. A choice made from the perspective of preferences at T1, optimal at that time with consequences for a later point of time T2, may not be optimal at T2. That is important for social policy. We make many decisions which are important for our future – the amount of education a person undergoes shapes her human capital and thus future earnings; the rate of savings determines retirement income; a person's general life style has influence on her future health risks. It would be a strong assumption to say that when people make such decisions they are always considering their future preferences correctly. The future preference for the then current consumption can be different from the present preference for future consumption. Whereas it is the latter which shapes the decision to get training, to save or to get insurance, it is the former which then is decisive for welfare.

Many social policy programmes cope with such problems. Some programmes force people to take care for their future – for example, public regulation of caring for one's retirement income; helping people with labour market problems due to too little training.

A special aspect of rational behaviour concerns using available information. This does not mean that it is assumed that everybody uses all information. But in an equilibrium there are no possibilities to make profits based on publicly available information merely because only a few use part of it. People who do not act accordingly are driven out of the market. This is one important cause for the efficiency of market economies, however those who are driven out may constitute a social problem.

Indeed, with given preferences an individual needs information about prices, contingencies, odds, products and providers. In most cases we learn about them in the market. We frequently make market transactions and thereby get experience about prices, suppliers, the quality of goods, and so on. Lack of information should not be of importance in most instances, though we may lose a bit by making wrong trades – transactions we feel afterwards that we should not have made.

Under certain circumstances, a problem with information may arise: if contracts are seldom made one cannot learn about products or reliability of suppliers. If, furthermore, a large part of one's own wealth is at stake, or a contract is binding in the long term and can only be changed with high costs, one's wealth can change dramatically due to lack of information. Protection from wrong contracts and coping with the consequences of wrong contracts can be reasons for public regulations if dramatic effects for individual welfare are possible.

Examples include undergoing education or a special training; or making a long-term savings contract with a fund. Note that in such cases spreading of risks is hardly possible. A society faces a high incidence of poverty if it is not prepared to rescue people who accepted risks by not taking care. People may end up without retirement income, because they invested in a fund which promised very high returns but went bankrupt; or somebody was so convinced that he would never have a serious health problem that he had no health insurance. In most countries it is accepted that this is a problem for public policy – that poverty and lack of access to health care should be avoided. We look at the outcomes, not merely at the expected utilities. This implies that regulations are necessary to limit the autonomy of people to care for their retirement income, to decide about their education or their health insurance.

3.2 EFFECTS OF SOCIAL POLICY

3.2.1 Some Principles

Whatever the purpose of social policy programmes is, one has to consider all economic effects. This is sometimes rejected, because some people think that the purpose of social policy mandates is that economic consideration should be set aside. Such a statement would imply a misunderstanding of economics. The approach followed in this book is that it is not the business of economists to say whether a social policy programme should be implemented or not, but to analyse the likely consequences of social programmes and how social policy should be carried out to make it efficient – namely achieving its desired results at minimal costs.

There are two types of effects of social policy programmes: (i) allocative effects and (ii) distributive effects. Allocation and distribution somehow mean the same. But here we want to distinguish between two very different sets of problems: the question of allocation is how a social policy programme affects the use of resources – is aggregate saving higher or lower after introducing a pension system and how is labour supply thereby affected? How does free access to the use of health services influence their supply? It is the question of aggregate welfare, independently of how it is distributed among different people. The analysis of the consequences for distribution asks how a given sum of aggregate welfare is distributed. It pursues the question of who is favoured and who pays for it. In many instances the two problems cannot be separated neatly, however it is necessary to keep them apart.

To analyse the economic consequences one has to ask how behaviour is changed by social policy programmes. For example, how will employers react if mandatory severance payments are introduced? In which way will the labour supply of women change, if maternity leave is granted and subsidised by a public transfer? It is necessary to ask how the budget constraints change under such regulation and to see in which way households' maximisation of utility and firms' maximisation of profits are affected.

Take the example of severance payments: if employers have to pay them, they must take them into consideration not only when discharging an employee, but also when deciding to offer a job. It is clear that making workers redundant is more expensive if employers have to pay something for doing it. Therefore workers will be kept in the firms in situations in which otherwise they would been set free. It can be shown that fewer jobs are offered. Such a regulation therefore makes jobs more secure and protects the employed, but it makes it more difficult for the unemployed to find a job.

In the case of maternity leave the opportunity costs of labour market participation is high when a mother has a small child. The child needs care – that is a question of the budget constraint; some people simply want to stay with a child while it is very young – that is a question of preference. If a payment is given when staying at home, the budget constraint changes and some mothers (and perhaps some fathers as well) decide to stay at home for some time who would have worked if there were no transfer. However as the productivity of employees increases with the length of their working experience, this might in the long run cause lower productivity of mothers (or fathers) and therefore lower wages. This is currently a debated issue (see below Chapter 7.3).

For the analysis of the effects of transfers one has to look at the benefits and their financing. This is due to a very basic economic principle, namely, there is no such thing as a free lunch. In the case of social policy the principle can be phrased slightly differently:

There is no such thing as a rich uncle!

There is no rich aunt either. Somebody has to pay. To analyse allocative and distributional effects it is necessary to consider both sides – the benefits and the way they are financed.

This is particularly important – and often overlooked in politics – in the case of redistribution: one cannot redistribute in favour of everybody. It is, of course, possible to redistribute in favour of small groups – the blind, very large families, the very old. In these cases the problems of the effects of financing the scheme can be neglected. There can be a rich uncle or a rich aunt for small groups. The society can redistribute in favour of the blind. The allocative effects of a tax to favour families with at least five children (in Europe less than 1 per cent of families) can be neglected – if politics are consistent and do not develop programmes specially tailored for families with less than five children as well. But for the major programmes – general health service provision, retirement income, family programmes – one has to take into consideration the allocative and distributional consequences of the financing as well.

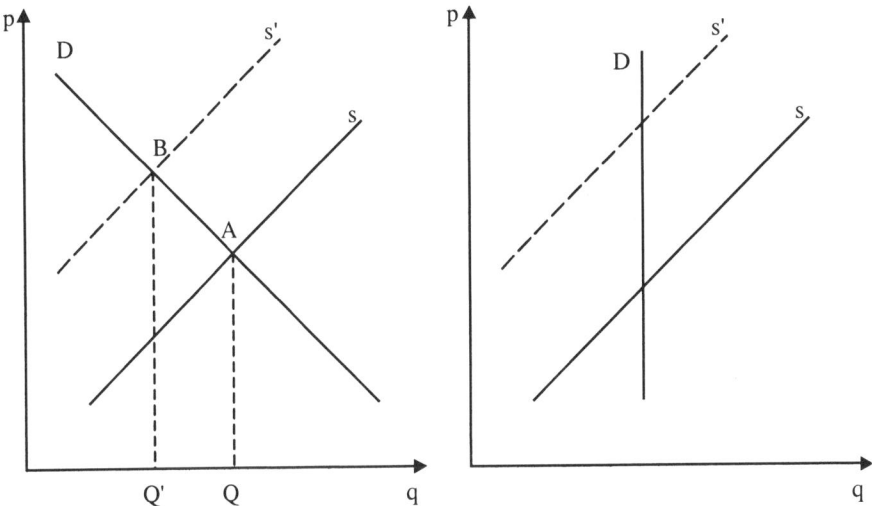

Note: The introduction of a tax, tax rate t, shifts the supply curve to the left. At the new equilibrium the amount of the good sold (and bought) is smaller by $\Delta Q = Q - Q'$.

Note: If demand is inelastic a tax does not affect the amount of the good Q.

Figure 3.2 The allocative effect of a tax

The basic ideas of the analysis of the allocative affects of taxes and transfers can be captured in Figure 3.2. The line S represents the supply of a good q without taxes, D is the demand. Point A is the equilibrium before taxes are introduced. The line S' is the supply of the good or service with the tax which has to be paid by the supplier. The point B is the new equilibrium, the reduced quantity is the allocative effect. Its size depends on the elasticity of the demand curve. In Figure 3.2 (right side) an extreme example of zero elasticity of demand is drawn. Whatever the price is, the amount of the good sold in the market does not change.

Can demand also be affected by a tax which is paid by the suppliers? No, if one only considers the tax. But that does not make sense, as it would be a tax to reduce income, and not to use its proceeds to do something useful. The proceeds of taxes are used for something – for example for a transfer to poor households. In that case the demand can change as well and the new equilibrium can be anywhere (Figure 3.3). Consider a tax on cigarettes the proceeds of which are handed over to poor households. If the poor increase their demand for cigarettes, the consumption of cigarettes may even increase.

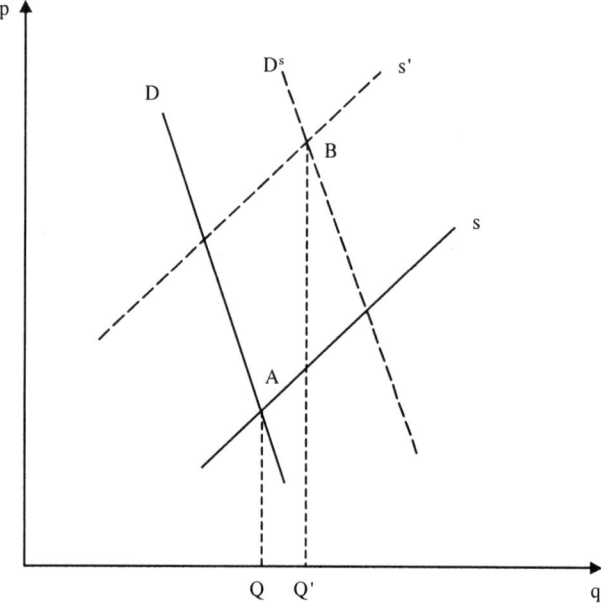

Note: If tax proceeds are given to people with high income elasticity the amount of good q may even increase.

Figure 3.3 A possible effect of a tax-benefit system

The analysis according to Figure 3.2 and Figure 3.3 is incomplete, as it neglects repercussions on other markets – a partial equilibrium approach. This is appropriate for the analysis of a tax on a good or service of minor importance – for example, a tax on shoes to finance a special support scheme for people using wheelchairs. For the big social policy programmes however such an analysis can be misleading. For a thorough analysis of the effects of big programmes it is necessary to work with general equilibrium models.

BOX 3.3 TAX-BENEFIT INCIDENCE AND EMPIRICS

There is much literature on the question of who pays for the benefits and who gets them. Unfortunately, there is no unambiguous answer. It is necessary to control for other causes which may affect wages. The contra-factual can be difficult to find: how would wages have developed if the tax or the benefit had not been introduced?

There are divers research strategies. One consists in using aggregate data and a macroeconomic framework. An example is Holmlund's study of the Swedish pay-roll taxes for financing the Swedish welfare state (Holmlund, 1983). He uses a labour demand function derived from a Cobb-Douglas production function. As a second element he uses a wage formation function from a macroeconomic model which relates wages to international prices. His results are that of each increase in payroll taxes 50 per cent are shifted back to wages, the remaining 50 per cent are shifted forward to prices.

Today, panel data for individuals are used if available. Gruber (1994) pursued the question of how the introduction of mandatory maternity benefits affected workers' wages. He used a so-called 'natural experiment'. Maternity benefits – namely that health insurance provided by firms, if any, must cover childbirth – were made mandatory in the USA in 1978. Some states however had enacted mandatory maternity benefits before 1978. By comparing the development of wages for individuals in states with and without benefits and the development before and after having made benefits mandatory Gruber's results demonstrated that the costs of mandatory benefits were shifted totally to wages. Note however that these statutes did not affect all workers equally: men and women above childbearing age were not affected. To the extent that these two groups are close substitutes for women of childbearing age this result is not surprising. The effects may be different if benefits affect all workers equally. See also Chapter 6.4 below.

3.2.2 Allocative Effects

The most important cause for allocative effects is the change of relative prices through social policy programmes. Prices are changed because certain goods or activities are made cheaper and because financing the programmes requires contributions changing relative prices of other goods or activities.

To see how a tax or a benefit affects economic activities by changing relative prices one can use the instruments of standard microeconomic analysis. In the theory of the household one distinguishes between the substitution effect and the income effect. The former asks how demand changes if prices change while keeping utility constant. The latter asks how demand changes if real income changes due to a change of the purchasing power. Whereas the direction of the substitution effect is unambiguous – namely the demand for the good whose price was increased is lower – the income effect can go either way. People may demand more of a good when their income increases or they may demand less of it (inferior goods).

According to the theory of the firm one has also to distinguish between two effects. One being the effect of the change of relative input-prices on the optimal use of inputs. This effect, similar to the substitution effect, is unambiguous – namely the factor which becomes relatively cheaper will be used more intensively. Further, when the price of a factor changes due to taxation or benefits, total costs change. This affects the optimal amount of production for firms: when costs go up, output is reduced and the demand for the factors of production declines.

There is one more effect of a change of relative input prices which is sometimes overlooked in political discussions: a change of relative prices of factors of production not only changes firms' demand for different factors, but also affects the demand of the household for the products. If labour gets more expensive, not only do firms reduce their use of labour intensive production technologies, but households reduce their demand for labour intensive products as well; for example, if wages rise, the demand for restaurants with waiter service declines, whereas that for self-service restaurants increases.

These allocative effects are currently one of the most important issues of social policy in many countries. As most social programmes are financed primarily by taxes on labour (payroll taxes and contributions), the cost of labour to firms is raised. It is often argued that the current high rates of unemployment in Europe are at least partly caused by high social security contributions. In many countries they are about 30 per cent of gross wages. It is unlikely that they have no effect on labour demand.

However one has to be careful when stating that social security contributions have the same effect as taxes. If there is a pension system (pension contributions comprise everywhere the bulk of social security contributions) which acts as fair insurance/savings system (see Chapter 5 below), the contributions cannot be considered a tax: for every euro a person pays into the system she gets the due amount after retirement. There is no redistribution.[2] Actually there is no public pension system without redistribution (but see below, about Chile and Latvia in 5.1). However there are countries with more redistribution and others with less. The smaller the redistribution, and the smaller the difference to a fair savings/insurance system, the less can contributions be considered taxes.

The most important allocative effects which are discussed in the context of social policy are:

- Demand for labour and supply of labour (pension schemes, unemployment insurance, poverty alleviation).
- Saving and consumption (pension schemes, health insurance).
- Use of goods and services supplied freely and/or at subsidised prices (health services, housing subsidies, poverty alleviation).

3.2.3 Distributive Effects

When analysing the effects on income distribution of a social programme, one has to make decisions or assumptions about some issues:

1. What is the standard for comparing distributions?
2. What is the unit we use for calculating redistribution?
3. Redistribution or insurance?
4. What is the incidence of contributions and benefits?
5. Is it better for applied research to use construed examples or real data?

1. What is the standard for comparing distributions? Should one use as standard a historically given distribution or a theoretical construed distribution? Political discussions are dominated by the first question, as by any reform some people may lose in comparison with current distribution and others win. Some incomes will be considered unjustly favoured by a reform, others to be unjustly lowered by it. Usually the losers complain and the winners press for more redistribution. But there is no reason to take the historically given distribution as the basis – why not the distribution twenty years ago? For a theoretical analysis of the distributive effects of an existing system it is preferable to use a theoretical standard. This standard should not be considered to be a normative one – a just distribution, or a very unjust one – but a distribution prevailing under specific assumptions.

Usually the distribution engendered by a special programme is compared with the situation without that programme. That is, we compare a state with a specific programme with a state in which people would have cared for themselves by using markets – a social pension programme with private provision for old age, a social health programme with a market solution to health insurance. Whether the distribution engendered by the programme is more just or less so is an altogether different question which economic theory cannot answer. Economics can analyse what changes will be brought about by a social policy programme – whether they are just is a normative question, which economists are not specially legitimised to answer.

Be that as it may, one has to assume that a market solution exists and that the two income distributions are comparable. This is a sensible procedure even in cases where market solutions may not exist due to market failures. It helps to distinguish between Pareto-improvements due to overcoming a market failure and pure redistribution. For example, profit oriented unemployment insurance is not viable due to asymmetric information. The introduction of a public unemployment programme can therefore result in a Pareto-superior situation. However some groups may get more out of it than others – some may even lose. (Pareto-improvements merely means that the losers could be compensated!) The analysis of the distributional effects asks who is better off and who loses in comparison to a situation without the market failure – as if such an insurance would exist.

2. *What is the unit we use for calculating redistribution?* In most economic literature redistribution between individuals is the issue (except redistribution over the life-cycle). We do not speak about redistribution between social groups. That is a normative position. When considering justice it is assumed that individuals should not be distinguished according to the social group they belong to, rather according to other criteria – first of all the size of income and whether they have special needs. This does not exclude that the social group a person belongs to is of relevance – being a blue-collar worker, a farmer, and so on. However these social positions are only important insofar as people belonging to a social group have specific characteristics which influence the effects of the programme – for example, life expectancy, probabilities of certain diseases.

Studies differ insofar as some of them use data for individuals, others of households or of families. That is partly a conceptual issue – whether the individuals, households or families make decisions concerning labour supply, consumption and so on. It is also a question of the availability of data. In some countries income data for households are difficult to get. Finally, it is a normative issue as well – does one consider individuals living within families as being entitled for independent access to means? (See below, section 8.2.2)

3. *Redistribution or insurance?* Whether a social policy programme provides insurance or redistributes income cannot be distinguished theoretically. It is a matter of convention. Consider the following: you want to determine the redistributive effects of a health insurance programme with contributions according to income. You calculate for a set of people what they paid into the system and what they got out of it until they died. You compound both

streams of payments for each person with the appropriate rates of interest for the time of their death. You can do this because you have the information about incomes and of uses of the resources of the health system until death. Those who got more out of the system than they had paid into it were net beneficiaries, the others were net payers. One will find that some people were net beneficiaries because they paid less due to low incomes and some were net beneficiaries because they used more resources; others were net payers due to high income or little use of the services.

There are two interpretations of these data. On the one hand, by using the actual differences between individuals the results can be interpreted as redistribution. There is no insurance. On the other hand, the same results can be interpreted as insurance: out of the data one can calculate a frequency distribution of net benefits and interpret them for the individuals as probabilities. In that case one hardly finds any redistribution. The health programme is seen not only as an insurance against high health expenditure but as an insurance against low income and the costs of living with a big family as well. Another example: a basic pension for all, financed by general taxes, can be seen as a redistribution in favour of the poor or as an insurance against poverty.

Sometimes it is a useful approach to see redistribution schemes as insurance,[3] but in general one wants to separate the different aspects of social policy. In the case of health programmes it is more sensible to ask whether high and low income people will be favoured, whether families with children are made better off, and not to treat these programmes as insurance against low incomes or against the burden of big families. Therefore when pursuing the question of vertical redistribution of a programme one takes the income stream as given; when one wants to know something about horizontal redistribution, one takes the characteristics as given — for example size of the family, probabilities of diseases, and so on (for an interesting approach, see Bird, 1995).

4. *Who gets the benefits, who pays the contributions?* The statutes of social policy laws only determine who has to pay taxes and contributions and who will receive the benefits formally. Laws cannot determine who really carries the burden of taxes and who really gets the benefits.

- Before 1834 workers in England could, in the case of high price of corn, claim some welfare payments to be financed from local taxes on land (Speenhamland system). Who were the beneficiaries? The workers because of higher real income; the capitalists because workers were prepared to work for lower wages; or the landed interest because the

increased demand for corn due to the welfare payments increased the price of corn?
- In many states social expenditures are financed by contributions which are split equally between the employees and the employers. Does this imply that employers pay 50 per cent of social benefits out of their profits?

These questions are pursued under the term *tax incidence*, namely, once more, how do relative prices change by the introduction of contributions and benefits and how does this affect supply and demand. To evaluate the question thoroughly for big social programmes one needs general equilibrium models for the economy under consideration. In most cases they hardly exist. Therefore one has to make assumptions about the incidence of taxes/contributions and benefits.

It is common to make the assumptions that benefits accrue to the recipients of the services. For example, in a public health system the recipients of the services are favoured. This can be questioned – perhaps the medical profession are the beneficiaries as the demand for their services is increased by a public health system; or the firms would have to pay higher wages if there were no public health services. However it is customary to work with the above given assumption.

If taxes and contributions to the social system are proportional to wages (payroll taxes) the employed bear the burden, whether the taxes are taken from the employed or the employers. If they are proportional to value added, the burden is on labour and capital. To work with such assumptions is not satisfactory, however it is better to be explicit about them than to equate the paying unit with the unit carrying the burden.

A special problem arises in the context of intergenerational redistribution. Consider the youth-support scheme of 'fairyland'. There is free public education up to college level. All young people attend college and get a degree.[4] Those between the age of 19 and the end of college education get a public allowance at 125 per cent of the poverty level for a single person. Suddenly the government decides that too much is given to the young. It first reduces the allowance step by step and than introduces fees for colleges and reduces other taxes accordingly. How will this affect distribution? That depends on the behaviour of the parents, namely to what extent they increase their support of their children. Note that the parents have to pay less taxes because of the reduction of transfers. Therefore their net income increases. It is possible to construe a model such that there will be no change in income distribution between cohorts due to such a change in the support of young people. We return to this question in Chapter 5.2.

5. *Using construed examples or real data?* In most research real data are preferred. But there are some problems when using them in research on social policy. These are due to analysing redistribution of income in a lifetime framework and in redistribution between cohorts. First, one would need personalised data over decades. Such data are rarely available because of a lack of systematic data processing in past decades and because the institutions which are to be analysed have not been in existence long enough. The European pension systems were introduced in the 1950s, so it has only been the case for a few years that people who were covered by one of these pension systems all their working life have been retiring. The effects of the introduction of these systems are not yet over!

Second, when using empirical data one may confound the effects of a social policy programme with structural changes. If I want to know how this or that group fared during a historic period it does not matter. However if I want to know what are the effects of a programme according to its statutes, it may be better to construe stylised facts. For example, to analyse vertical redistribution one needs data about income over the life-cycle. But incomes change in the course of time due to different circumstances. Increases of income due to per capita economic growth are immaterial for the analysis of vertical redistribution of a social policy programme for a given cohort. In other instances it may be very important – for example, when analysing redistribution between cohorts, as some cohorts have experienced high per capita economic growth and others not. In that case data about the distribution of income within a cohort is of less importance. One finds in the literature both type of data used. Some publications use both real data and construed data.

Be that as it may, there is no unique way to characterise the change of income distribution caused by social policy programmes. This is due to the fact that income distributions can only be ranked unambiguously under specific assumptions. In some research single-value indices are used to compare income distributions and change of income distributions across different economies or over a period of time (see below, Appendix 3.2). However it is more customary to pursue the question of how different groups fare in a welfare programme without summing up the results in a single-value index.

An example of such a calculation is that of the redistributive effects of the Swedish welfare state (Ståhlberg, 1989). The analysis was restricted to cash payments in connection with old age, disability and sickness benefits: (i) a flat-rate basic pension; (ii) a supplementary earnings related pension, which used the best 15 years of income as the basis for calculating the pension; (iii) a further supplement for people with low pensions, including disability pensions; (iv) sickness benefit payments. Neither were unemployment benefits, nor health services or family benefits considered.

Table 3.1   *The benefit–cost ratio, and the net transfer's share of the pension benefits for the retired generation*

	Sex and socio-economic group	Benefit–cost ratio	Net transfer's share of benefits
Men	I	3.70	0.73
	II	3.75	0.73
	III	5.01	0.80
Women	I	9.04	0.89
	II	7.20	0.86
	III	10.62	0.91

Table 3.2   *The benefit–cost ratio, the net transfer's share of the pension and sickness benefits, and the net transfer's share of lifetime earnings for the working generation*

Sex and socio-economic group	Benefit–cost ratio	Net transfer's share of the benefits	Net transfer's share of lifetime earnings
		Pensions	
Men I	0.6	−0.7	−0.08
Men II	0.6	−0.5	−0.07
Men III	0.7	−0.4	−0.05
Women I	0.8	−0.2	−0.04
Women II	0.9	−0.1	−0.02
Women III	1.0	0.0	0.00
		Pensions and sickness benefits	
Men I	0.5	−1.1	−0.15
Men II	0.6	−0.8	−0.12
Men III	0.7	−0.4	−0.07
Women I	0.7	−0.5	−0.09
Women II	0.8	−0.3	−0.06
Women III	0.9	−0.1	−0.02

Notes: Benefit-cost ratio: discounted aggregate benefits over discounted aggregate contributions.
Net transfer's share of benefits: share of benefits paid by transfers.
Net transfer's share of lifetime earnings: share of transfer in total income.

Source: Stålberg, 1989.

The study used data of 4000 people born between 1905 and 1953. For individuals born at the beginning of this period a nearly complete set of data was available, namely what they had paid and what they had received. For the younger ones the author had to work with assumptions concerning future developments. For that the author used the same method as the Swedish social insurance system for calculating disability pensions: from past earnings and the person's qualification an expected earnings profile was calculated as a basis for the disability insurance. All payroll taxes were assumed to be paid by the workers. The rate of discount was assumed to be 2 per cent.

The author compared three groups, group I being mainly white-collar workers with high incomes, group II are white-collar workers with low incomes, and group III mostly blue-collar workers.

As can be seen in Table 3.1, the already retired generation had an enormous advantage from the welfare state. Women fared better than men, blue-collar workers better than white-collar workers. These benefits were due to a shift of resources from the next generation. That the next generation fared differently can be seen in Table 3.2. Women again fared better than men, people belonging to lower socio-economic groups got more out of the system than those from groups with higher income. Overall the generation who are still working are (will be) net-payers in the schemes of the welfare state.

3.3 GIVING GOODS OR GIVING MONEY?

Let us assume that we want to change the distribution of income or wealth. How should it be done? Should we give those we want to favour goods or money? The former does not only comprise goods directly, but insurance services and the subsidy of the purchase of insurance or of goods.

It will first be shown that, in principle, it is better to give general purchasing power – that is, money – than to give goods. However there are many instances in which the free supply or the subsidy of specific goods is preferable. Before that we have to make clear what is meant under the term 'preferable': if we want an individual to achieve a level of utility she cannot achieve without the transfer, giving money is the cheapest way to do it – that is, with the lowest loss to the rest of the society. If on the other hand a certain amount of wealth is available for transfers, the biggest effect in the sense of increasing utility can be achieved by giving generalised purchasing power.

The basic idea is depicted in Figure 3.4. The original budget constraint without the transfer is C'. The consumer chooses point A. By subsidising the purchase of good x the budget constraint changes to C'', the favoured person chooses consumption at point B at a higher indifference curve.

If instead of this subsidy general purchasing power is given, relative prices between the goods are not changed. This is a parallel shift of the original budget constraint. If one wants to bring the favoured individual to the indifference curve I", this can be achieved by shifting the budget constraint to C'". Point D with the same utility as B will be chosen. This is achieved with a lower transfer.

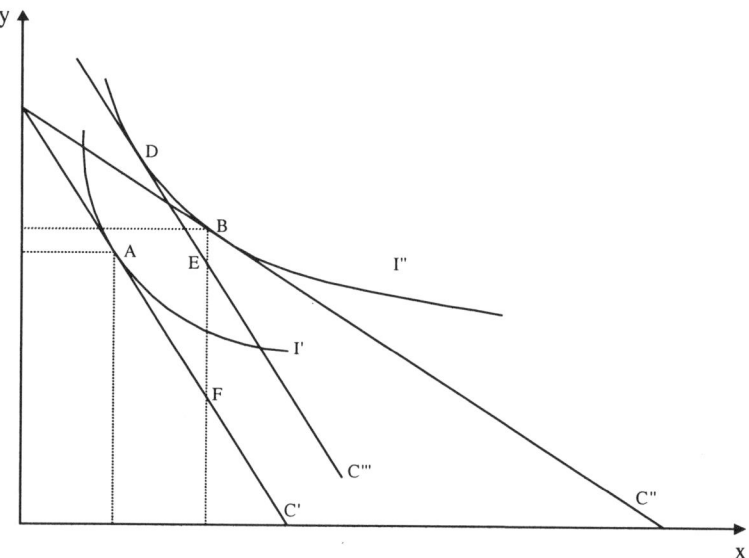

Figure 3.4 The effects of giving goods and giving money

The cost of the subsidy expressed in goods y is the amount of the distance BF. That is the difference between the original constraint and the optimal point with the subsidy. If money is given, it is sufficient to give an amount equal to the size EF. The difference BE can be saved. Therefore, one can give more and increase the welfare of the beneficiaries more and/or one can reduce the tax burden for financing the benefits.

The cause for the inefficiency of a bounded transfer is the same as that of most taxes: taxes change relative prices. There is therefore an income and a substitution effect. The welfare effect of a tax is smallest when there is no substitution effect. Transfers are nothing but negative taxes – the substitution effect reduces total welfare.

Sometimes bounded transfers or subsidised prices are only available up to a certain amount of goods acquired – for example, food stamps in the USA. This case is depicted in Figure 3.5. The maximum amount a household can buy at subsidised prices is x^{max}. If the household wants more of it, it has to pay the full market price. The budget constraint is kinked. Whether there is a loss of welfare due to the substitution effect is open. If the indifference curve is I' and point X is chosen, there is a substitution effect as argued above. If however the indifference curve is I" and Y is chosen, relative prices are not distorted by the subsidy. There is only an income effect.

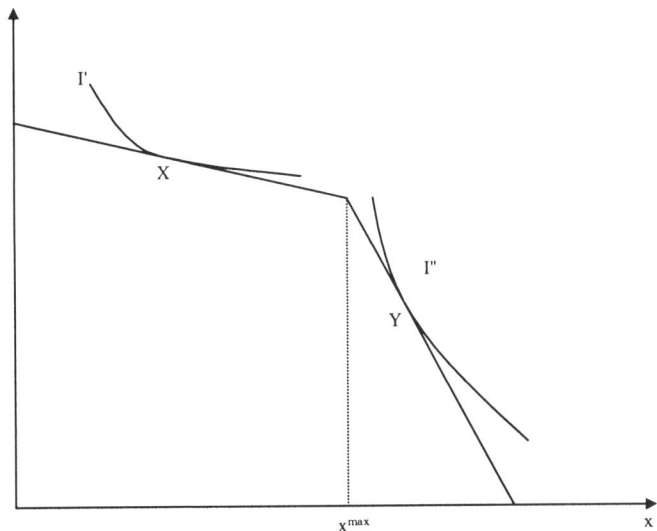

Figure 3.5 An upper limit for the amount of goods subsidised

A further case: a certain amount of the good x is given for free and households can purchase more of it at the market price. The first part of the budget constraint is horizontal. If the household purchases some extra units of x there is no substitution effect. If however the household uses all units of purchasing power for the other good, he will realise point C (Figure 3.6). In that case the indifference curve need not be tangent to any of the budget constraints. The marginal rate of substitution is not equal to the price. (Analytically, it is a corner solution to the optimisation problem of the household – not an interior solution.) The household prefers to consume less of x and more of y. This can be achieved if the household is allowed to trade some of the units of x against y. That is the idea of school vouchers: they entitle the household to a certain amount of years of schooling for each child. If this amount is in excess of minimum schooling requirements, some households will sell some of their vouchers for training to other households who perhaps want their children to attend university.

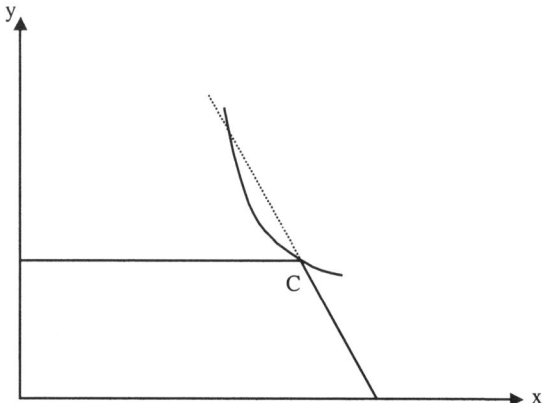

Note: The agent could reach a higher utility curve if she could exchange units of *x* against units of y along the dashed segment of the budget constraint.

Figure 3.6 A freely given good in excess of what the individual would have consumed with the same level of resources

---

BOX 3.4 THE WELFARE EFFECT OF RENT SUBSIDIES

The US had a programme to support the rent for poorer households (for a four-person family with an income not exceeding 80 per cent of area mean income). Low-income tenants were supposed to pay not more than 15 per cent of gross income or 25 per cent of net income, whichever was the greater adjusted for dependants and some expenses. The rent must not exceed a 'fair market rent'.

The amount spent on housing did not necessarily decline because households increased the size or the quality of their apartments. The increase in consumption of other goods was affected by the change of the price between housing and other consumption goods.

What were the effects on welfare of that regulation? This question was analysed (Reeder, 1985) by calculating the difference between consumption of housing with the rent subsidy and the estimated housing consumption if the households were given the same subsidy without binding it to renting an apartment. For that calculation the author used a utility function of the following form:

$$U(H,X) = [H - H^0]^\alpha [X - X^0]^{1-\alpha}$$

H is the amount of housing rented, X the amount of all other goods consumed, H^0 minimal housing, X^0 minimal consumption. H^0 and X^0 were allowed to differ between different households. The parameters of the utility functions were estimated from a set of data of recipients of this subsidy, containing information about income, family size, expenditure for housing before and after introduction of the programme and price variables. With that utility function the welfare effects could be estimated. It turned out the households spent more for accommodation with the subsidy than without it. The same effect on utility could have been achieved with a lower transfer if it were unbounded.

Mean monthly housing expenditures of Section 8 families in absence of program	$ 144
Mean monthly rent of their Section 8 unit	$ 166
Percentage increase in aggregate consumption of housing services by these families	16.3%
Mean monthly expenditure on other goods by Section 8 families in absence of program	$ 154
Mean monthly expenditure on other goods by Section 8 families under the program	$ 232
Percentage increase in aggregate consumption of other goods by these families	50.2%
Mean monthly rent paid by Section 8 families	$ 66
Mean percentage reduction in market price of housing to Section 8 families	60.1%
Mean monthly income	$ 298
Mean monthly subsidy	$ 100
Mean monthly benefit to Section 8 families**	$ 83
Mean full cost to taxpayers per Section 8 family	$ 139
Minimum external benefits	$ 56
Ratio of mean benefit to mean subsidy	0.83
Ratio of mean benefit to mean full cost to taxpayers	0.60

Notes: *This utility function is a Stone-Geary utility function. Positive utility is only ascribed to states with a consumption of all goods being arguments of the utility function in excess of a minimum. In applied research the use of this utility function is quite common, however it cannot be derived from a rational preference ordering.
**Neglects participation costs.

Source: © 1985 with permission from Elsevier Science.

Be that as it may, if bounded transfers result in welfare loss, why do we find in actual social policy so many instances of bounded transfers? This can be the consequence of a false policy although there are also economic arguments in favour of bounded transfers.

1. *Lack of rationality of the recipients of the transfers.* The above given arguments for a welfare loss assume that people act rationally. They can

optimise according to their true preferences. In many cases of poverty this is not the case – for example, in the case of addiction. Giving goods safeguards individuals against their own irrational behaviour.

2. *Lack of autonomy of the recipients of transfers.* If recipients cannot decide about the use of transfers, a bounded transfer can be a protection against exploitation by others. Many transfers are for children. Some of them must be protected against withdrawal of the transfer by adults. Bounded transfers which primarily can be consumed by children make such exploitation more difficult (Ross, 1991).

3. *Meritoric goods.* The state wants people to consume more of certain goods than they choose voluntarily to consume. The reason is that consumers do not value these goods 'appropriately' or there is positive externality when consuming them. For example, free access to controls of health can be argued that way: some do not perceive their long-term benefits correctly. However once they fall ill, they feel sorry for not having had a health check earlier. Free access to immunisation against diseases which can be transmitted from one individual to another or free access to higher education can be argued with positive external benefits.

In these cases the state not only wants to increase the utility of individuals, it also wants them to consume specific goods – paternalistic behaviour. The state tells the favoured individuals how to behave. Such arguments are not highly esteemed in economics, though in some cases there may exist good reasons for paternalistic behaviour. But even with the assumption of rationality there are instances when it is better to give goods instead of money.

4. *There is an objectively determined need with no possibility to substitute.* In that case a direct transfer does not have the welfare loss due to the substitution effect. If, for example, some surgery is necessary, it is not possible to substitute against other goods. Whether one gives the amount of money necessary to buy the service, or whether one provides the service directly does not make any difference.

5. *Samaritan's dilemma 1.* If people do not insure against contingent events because they rely on altruism, society can protect itself by forcing people to insure.

6. *Samaritan's dilemma 2.* If future productivity depends on the use of a transfer, namely for training and education, there is a Samaritan's dilemma situation as well. If the favoured person knew that in case of future poverty he will be supported, he may increase his total utility by using the transfer for immediate consumption. Binding the transfer to undergoing training can avoid this incentive.

BOX 3.5 TARGETING BENEFITS BY GIVING GOODS INSTEAD OF MONEY

If one wants to give a transfer only to the poor, one has to know who is poor. Finding them is sometimes a difficult task for a social administration which has to use resources to find them. A bounded transfer can be used for self-selection (Jacoby, 1997). The basic idea is the following: if the quality of a good freely given is fixed, poor people will take it, whereas individuals better off refrain from a take-up. Though this may lead to a stigma, it can reduce the costs of a programme. This idea is made more precise in Figure 3.7.

Assume that government provides a good freely at a certain quality $q°$. The utility function is $U(q, y)$ with q the quality of the good freely provided. The income people can use for buying goods is y. In Figure 3.7 the poor household with the lower budget constraint buys, in the absence of the transfer, a higher quality than provided freely (I). However it accepts the lower quality good and spends all its income for other goods if it reaches thereby higher utility (I'). A rich household cannot achieve higher utility by accepting the low quality good and spending all the income on other goods. There is a critical value y^* which lies on the border and makes the household indifferent between accepting the freely given good and buying the good with own income at a higher quality. This gives utility I''.

This approach was used to evaluate the Jamaican Nutrition and Milk Programme. Under this programme a free school meal at fixed quality was given. (It was paid for by a United Nations programme, therefore the authors did not consider its financing.)

Though the meal was free, only 60 per cent of the children made use of it. Quality was low insofar as there was not much variety in the food provided. From data of take-ups, income and size of households the author calculated the probabilities of a take-up dependent on income and number of children. The critical levels y^* were the following:

Number of children in the household y^*	($JMK)
1	4 838
2	6 301
> 2	6 298

Poorer households had significantly higher take-up rates than richer households. The fixed quality increased target efficiency. However one must bear in mind that what is called a low but fixed quality can lead to a stigma, which itself is a loss of welfare.

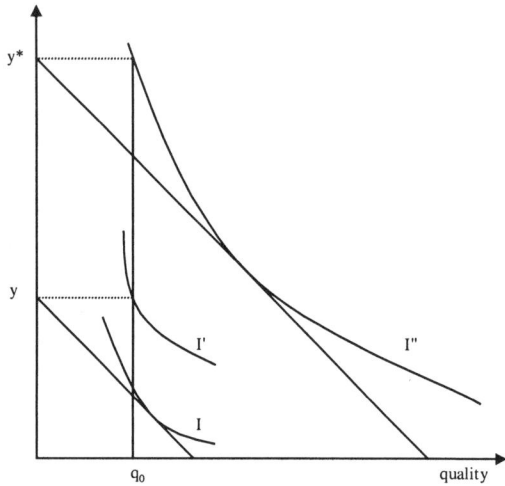

Figure 3.7 Self-selection by giving a good at a specific quality

APPENDIX 3.1

Is it Possible to Evaluate the Loss of Welfare Quantitatively?

Utility is not measurable in absolute units, because any monotone transformation of a utility function gives the same information about utility. One has to use a money metric to measure the loss of utility. The loss can be measured by answering the following question: by how much must the wealth of an individual be increased in order that she is prepared to accept a price increase (*compensating variation*)?[5]

The instrument to tackle this problem is the compensated (or Hicks') demand function. It relates the demand for goods to different prices, keeping utility constant. There is only a substitution effect, its sign is determined – a higher price of a good results in a lower demand for that good. (The Hicks' demand function cannot be observed directly. Assuming a representative consumer, it can be estimated from ordinary demand functions by using the Slutsky equations.)

The reason for using the compensated demand function for a money metric of the welfare loss is as follows: if the price vector is p^0, and with income w utility level u^0 is attainable, the minimal expenditure to reach utility u^0 at prices p^0 is w. (This sounds rather trivial, but there is an important theorem behind it: if an individual maximises her utility given prices p and the budget constraint w, she will attain a certain utility level u'. If on the other hand she minimises expenditure with the same prices p under the condition that she achieves at least utility u', she has to spend w, the original wealth.)

If prices change to p^1 – for example by withdrawing a subsidy – and wealth does not change, one reaches a different utility level u^1. The compensating variation is the difference in expenditure between the original wealth that safeguards at the new price p^1 the new utility u^1 and expenditure necessary for achieving the former utility u^0 with the new price p^1. If this difference in expenditure is given to an individual, she would be compensated for the change of prices.

Formally:

$$CV(p^0, p^1, w) = e(p^1, u^1) - e(p^1, u^0) = w - e(p^1, u^0)$$

with CV the compensating variation and e expenditure. In the present context: how much do we have to give an individual if a price subsidy is taken away in order to keep her at the same utility level as with the subsidy?

A reduction of a subsidy amounts to a price increase. Therefore when utility is kept constant the amount demanded will be lower. The relation between expenditure and the compensated demand function is as follows.

$$\partial[e(p,u)]/\partial p_m = h_m(p,u)$$

It states that the first derivative of the expenditure function with respect to the price p_m for good m is the compensated demand function for this good. The basic idea of this relation is that if the price of a good is raised by a small unit and the person was at her optimum before the rise – that is, the expenditure to achieve the utility level is at its minimum – the amount of wealth necessary to compensate her for the rise of the price is exactly the amount of the good she consumes.

With the higher price for the good the individual buys less of it. To achieve the same utility as before she has to spend more, though with the compensating transfer she does not buy the same consumption bundle as with the lower price. The amount necessary to compensate her can be calculated by using the above given relation between the compensated demand function and the expenditure function (the area ABCD in Figure 3.8).

$$CV = \int_{p^o-s}^{p^o} h(p)dp$$

The amount paid by the subsidy is the area ABCE which is bigger than ABCD. The triangle CDE is a measure of the welfare loss due to a subsidy instead of giving money.

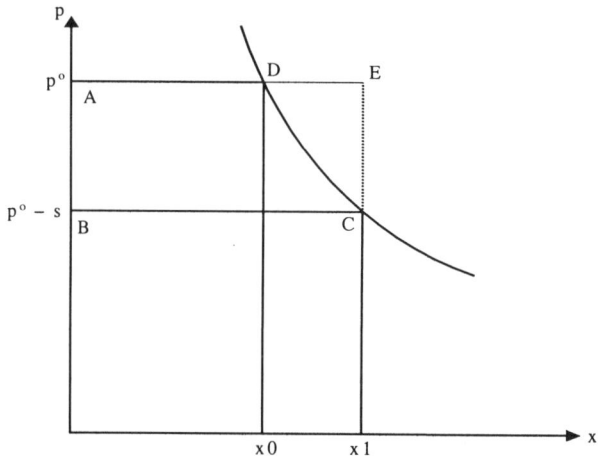

Figure 3.8 The area ABCD gives the compensating variation necessary when a subsidy is withdrawn

If there is no income effect in the ordinary demand function the latter is identical with the compensated or Hicks' demand function. It can then be used for the evaluation of the welfare loss. This is appropriate if the subsidy is given for a good of minor importance, as in that case marginal utility of income is constant.[6]

APPENDIX 3.2

Inequality and Redistribution

When analysing redistribution one asks who will be favoured by a programme and who has to pay for it. But can we say something about the change of inequality due to a programme? That is a complicated matter, as there is no unambiguous measure to characterise a distribution. Which of the following two distributions of 10 units of income is more unequal?

(i)   1; 1; 1; 7
(ii) 0.1; 3.3; 3.3; 3.3

In (i) there is equality at the bottom and a very rich unit at the top, in (ii) it is the other way round: one extremely poor unit and equality at the top.

One way to conceptualise an income distribution is the Lorenz curve. The horizontal axis represents the percentage of households ranked according to income; on the vertical axis the cumulative percentage of income up to that household is noted.

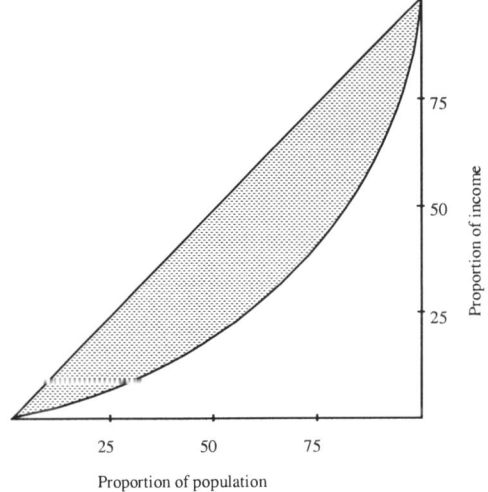

Note: The hatched area between the Lorenz curve and the diagonal represents the Gini coefficient.

Figure 3.9 Lorenz curve and Gini coefficient

If all units receive the same income the Lorenz curve is a straight line, the 45° diagonal: x per cent of households have together x per cent of total income. Any inequality moves the Lorenz curve below the 45° diagonal. The further away from the diagonal the Lorenz curve is, the more unequal is the income distribution. If one unit has all income and all other units have nothing, the Lorenz curve is a spike at the right corner.

The Lorenz curve can be characterised formally: if x is the income with density function $f(x)$, then $F(x)$, its distribution function, is the proportion of individuals with income not exceeding x. Let μ be the average income, the Lorenz curve is:

$$F_1(x) = \int x/\mu dF(x)$$

the ratio of total income of all individuals with income not exceeding x.

Another way to describe inequality, namely to summarise all information in one number, is the Gini coefficient. It is the area between the Lorenz curve and the diagonal as percentage of the total area below the diagonal. It varies between zero (total equality) and 1 (one unit gets all income). As long as different Lorenz curves do not cross, increasing values for the Gini coefficient imply increasing inequality (see Figure 3.9).

The Gini coefficient can be expressed mathematically.

$$G = 2 \int [x - F_1(x)]dx = 1 - 2 \int F_1(x)dx$$

This is precisely the hatched area in Figure 3.9.

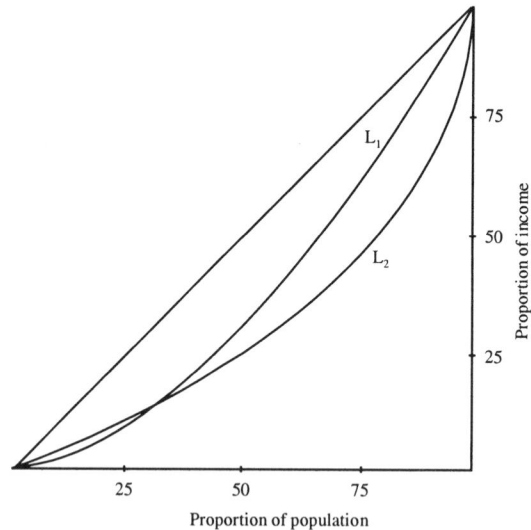

Note: The distribution represented by L_1 has more inequality at the bottom of the income distribution than L_2. An overall ranking of the two distributions is not possible.

Figure 3.10 Lorenz curves can cross

There is a problem when drawing the Lorenz curves for two income distributions in that they can cross (see Figure 3.10). That is another way of saying that income distributions cannot be ranked unambiguously according to the criterion 'more inequality'.

Income distributions after taxes need not be unambiguously more or less equal than the distribution before taxes. A tax-transfer system favouring the poor at the cost of the middle classes can decrease inequality at the lower end and increase it at the top end. However if the after-tax Lorenz curve lies above the original one, there is less inequality after taxation (and giving transfers): the tax-transfer system is progressive. If the after-tax Lorenz curve lies below the original one, the tax-transfer system increases inequality – a regressive system (for a proof see Kakwani, 1977).

The relation between the tax-transfer system and the change of income distribution is a complex issue due to the possibility of re-ranking of individuals in the income distribution. Consider a change between two distributions among four units due to taxes and transfers:

	A	B	C	D
I	1	2	3	4
II	4	3	2	1

The Lorenz curve and the Gini coefficient are the same in both distributions, however there was much redistribution. The poorest person in I became the richest in II, whereas the richest person in I finds herself at the bottom of the income distribution; B and C also changed places.

Re-ranking due to taxes or benefits looks like a violation of horizontal equity (Jenkins, 1988). There are individuals who pay more taxes than others with the same or an even higher income. However equality may not only be a question of different incomes but of other characteristics as well: family status, number of children, location of residence, health, age, and so on. Individuals with the same income are not treated equally because of specific characteristics – *unequal treatment of (income-) equals*. Furthermore the sum of all social policy programmes is usually not a coherent tax-benefit programme, but a mixture of many programmes. They often have unintended distributive consequences. Re-rankings are likely to occur. Therefore one has to distinguish between the change in inequality – comparing two distributions – and the amount of redistribution.

One measure of the change of inequality due to taxes and benefits is the difference of the Gini coefficients of the original distribution with the post-tax distribution. If there were no re-ranking, the change in inequality can be used as a measure of the extent of redistribution. A bigger difference is the result of more redistribution. With re-ranking this is no longer the case. To determine the extent of redistribution and to relate this to the change of inequality one has to delve deeper into the concepts of the Lorenz curve and the Gini coefficient.

Let $g(x)$ be a function of x, for example income after taxes as function of income before taxes. Let $F(g(x))$ be the distribution function of post-tax income when individuals are ranked according to pre-tax income. Note that this may differ from the distribution function of post-tax income, namely when individuals are ranked according to post-tax income. If γ is the average post-tax income, the concentration curve of post tax income can be defined as:

$$C(x) = F_1(g(x)) = \int g(x)/\gamma dF(x)$$

The concentration curve measures the share of post-tax income received by individuals with pre-tax income below x. The concentration curve of $g(x)$ need not be identical with the Lorenz curve of post-tax income due to the possibility of re-ranking. The recipients of the lowest 30 per cent of pre-tax income may not be identical with the recipients of the lowest 30 per cent of post-tax income.

Note also that the concentration curve can lie above the 45° line. If you draw the Lorenz curve for the distribution I, and then the concentration curve for the distribution II, you will see that the latter is nothing but a rotation of the first one around the middle point of the 45° line.

If we consider the population as consisting of different groups – single-person households, families without a child, with 1,2,3 ... children, single-parent households; people living in different regions of a state or belonging to different nationalities within a state, and so on – it is possible to derive a relation between inequality between the groups and inequality within the groups (Lambert and Aronson, 1993). This is of importance if one wants to know whether the inequality between individuals over the whole population is primarily due to differences between groups or whether it is rather the inequality within groups that determines overall inequality.

Consider the following case: the population consists of N groups, the average income of the j-th group is μ_j. If it is the case that the income of the richest individual of group j is not higher than the income of the poorest individual of group j+1 for all $j \in \{1,2...N-1\}$, the groups do not overlap. If two groups are merged, all positions remain the same. It can be shown that in this case the Gini coefficient for total population can be decomposed into the Gini coefficient of the average group incomes (G_b), the μ_j, and a weighted sum of the Gini coefficients of the different groups (G_g) – that is, there is a composition of total inequality, as measured in the Gini coefficient, in a coefficient of the between-group inequality and an expression for the within-group inequality.

$$G = G_b + \Sigma a_g G_g$$

The weights a_g are the product of population share and income share going to group g.

If there is overlapping between the groups, which will usually be the case, this neat decomposition is not valid any more. The complication arises because an individual of group j may be ranked above an individual of group j+1 if the two groups are merged into one. This is tantamount to a re-ranking. For the evaluation of redistribution one needs a residual to take account of the re-ranking.

Lambert and Aronson show that this residual can be understood in the following experiment: start with the average income of the whole population μ. If N is the size of the population, total income is $N\mu$. The given income distribution is reconstructed in three steps. (i) Give each individual the average income of her group. One gets the Lorenz curve of the group averages, $F^b_1(x)$, and the resulting Gini coefficient is precisely the Gini coefficient of the averages, G_b. (ii) Order of the whole population in the following way: rank all individuals of group 1 according to income, then all individuals of group 2 according to income, and so on without overlapping. Even if the poorest individual of group 2 has an income below some individuals of group 1, she will be ranked higher than any individual of group 1. This is done for all groups. One gets a concentration curve $C(n)$, namely the share of income going to the first n individuals. Because there may be individuals with a rank higher than n but who are actually poorer than the n-th individual, this concentration curve of the total population is different from the Lorenz curve of the total population. (iii) Introducing overlapping, that is, ordering individuals only according to income gives the Lorenz curve for the total population.

It was shown by the authors that a coefficient calculated as the Gini coefficient but using the difference between the concentration curve of step (ii) and the Lorenz curve of the averages of step (i) (expression (*)) provides the second term in the formula given above, namely the weighted sum of the Gini coefficients of within-group inequality.

$$(*) \quad 2 \int [F^b_1(x) - C(x)] dx$$

The residual can be interpreted on the basis of step (iii), namely as a coefficient derived from the difference between the concentration curve of step (ii) and the final Lorenz curve.

$$2 \int [C(x) - F_1(x)] dx$$

Using these relations we can now derive a relation between the amount of redistribution and the change of inequality as measured by the Gini coefficient (Aronson et al., 1994). Furthermore this change in the income distribution can be decomposed into a vertical component, a horizontal component and a re-ranking effect. The vertical component is due to higher taxes for higher incomes. The horizontal component is due to treating equal incomes unequally.

The change of inequality measured by the Gini coefficient can be expressed as:

$$RE = G_B - G_A$$

with G_B the pre-tax Gini coefficient and G_A the after-tax coefficient. The after-tax coefficient is as developed above:

$$G_A = G_b + \Sigma a_g G_g + R$$

with R the residual as mentioned above, G_b the Gini coefficient of post-tax incomes if only income determines taxes. The coefficients G_g are the Gini coefficients for the group of individuals with the same income. Therefore

$$RE = (G_B - G_b) - \Sigma a_g G_g - R$$

The first term is the change of income distribution if all individuals would have paid taxes only according to income. This can be seen as vertical redistribution which is inherent in the tax schedule. The second term is due to horizontal redistribution, namely making individuals with equal income pay different amounts of taxes. The third term is due to re-ranking, namely the difference between the Lorenz curve and the concentration curve based on the original ranking.

A study (van Doorslaer et al., 1999) about the redistributive effect of health care financing (private and public) in different states used these concepts to determine what affected the change in income distribution (how benefits affected the distribution was not taken into consideration):

> The results of the paper show that unequal treatment of unequals (V) [vertical redistibution P.R.] is far more important in terms of redistributive effect than

differential treatment. In general, and not surprisingly, large discrepancies between V and RE occur in the voluntary private payments, where there is little or no relationship between payment and ability to pay. Within public sources, there is, however, some variation. The discrepancy between V and RE is small in the case of taxation, despite the well known anomalies in personal income tax systems and the inevitable differences at a given level in household spending levels and patterns. By contrast, social insurance payments show a non-negligible degree of differential treatment, mainly due to varying contribution rates and exemptions on the basis of criteria other than income. (van Doorslaer et al., 1999, p. 311)

NOTES

1. According to the idea of the NM utility function, if the bad outcome is realised, people have less utility, but that's all. One considers the average outcome – sometimes one is better off, sometimes one is worse off. This makes sense as long as the average is a meaningful idea, for example, in the case of a return of assets. If an asset turns sour this year it may make up in the next year, or you have bought various assets and therefore you have some insurance against the loss a particular asset can make. The average has a real meaning. However there are situations when this is less meaningful. When you consider the option of driving fast or driving slowly, you may say, I accept the higher risks of an accident when driving fast. But after an accident which injures you for the rest of your – probably now shorter – life you cannot return to an average normal state. Your preferences will change to adapt to the different situation. The expected utility concept cannot cover such problems well.
2. There remains an allocative effect if mandatory retirement provision is in excess of what the person would have saved voluntarily (see below 5.4).
3. For a discussion of redistribution as insurance in the context of political philosophy, see Dworkin, 1981.
4. The fact that education is free until college does not make the country a fairyland. That is the case in many European states. What makes this country a fairyland is the fact that all finish college. However this assumption allows us to concentrate on question of intergenerational redistribution without considering intragenerational redistribution.
5. An alternative measure is the *equivalent variation*: taking away the subsidy makes the household worse off. How much must a household be given in order that it is indifferent between having the subsidy and not having it at the price level without subsidy.
6. The utility function can then be written in the following form $u(x, m) = \hat{u}(x) + m$, with $\hat{u}(.)$ of normal shape, $\hat{u}'(.) > 0$, $\hat{u}''(.) < 0$. That is called a quasilinear utility function.

REFERENCES

Aronson, J. Richard, Paul Johnson and Peter J. Lambert (1994), 'Redistributive Effect and Unequal Income Tax Treatment', *Economic Journal*, 104, pp. 262–70.

Bird, Edward J. (1995), 'An Explanatory Comparison of Income Risk in Germany and the United States', *Review of Income and Wealth*, 41, pp. 405–26.

Cardon, James H. and Igal Hendel (2001), 'Asymmetric information in health insurance: evidence from national medical expenditure survey', mimeo, University of Wisconsin-Madison.

Chiappori, Pierre-André and Bernard Salanié (2000), 'Testing for Asymmetric Information in Insurance Markets', *Journal of Political Economy*, 108, pp. 56–78.

Dworkin, Ronald (1981), 'What is Equality? Part 2: Equality of Resources', *Philosophy and Public Affairs*, 10, pp. 283–345, reprinted in: R. Dworkin (2000), *Sovereign Virtue*, Cambridge (Mass.): Harvard University Press, ch. 2.

Gruber, Jonathan (1994), 'The Incidence of Mandated Maternity Benefits', *American Economic Review*, 84, pp. 622–41.

Holmlund, Bertil (1983), 'Payroll Taxes and Wage Inflation', *Scandinavian Journal of Economics*, 85, pp. 1–16.

Jacoby, Hanan G. (1997), 'Self-Selection and the Redistributive Impact of in-Kind Transfers: An Econometric Analysis', *Journal of Human Resources*, 32, pp. 233–49.

Jenkins, Stephen (1988), 'Re-ranking and the Analysis of Income Redistribution', *Scottish Journal of Political Economy*, 35, pp. 65–76.

Kakwani N.C. (1977), 'Applications of Lorenz Curves in Economic Analysis', *Econometrica*, 45, pp. 719–27.

Kantor, Shawn Everett and Price V. Fishback (1996), 'Precautionary Saving, Insurance, and the Origins of Worker's Compensation', *Journal of Political Economy*, 104, pp. 419–42.

Lambert, Peter J. and J. Richard Aronson (1993), 'Inequality Decomposition Analysis and the Gini Coefficient Revisited', *Economic Journal*, 103, pp. 1221–7.

Newhouse, Joseph P. (1996), 'Reimbursing Health Plans and Health Providers: Selection Versus Efficiency in Production', *Journal of Economic Literature*, 34, pp. 1236–63.

Puelz, Robert and Arthur Snow (1994), 'Evidence on Adverse Selection: Equilibrium Signalling and Cross-Subsidization', *Journal of Political Economy*, 102, pp. 236–57.

Reeder, William J. (1985), 'The Benefits and Costs of the Section 8 Existing Housing Programme', *Journal of Public Economics*, 26, pp. 349–78.

Ross, Thomas W. (1991), 'On the Relative Efficiency of Cash Transfers and Subsidies', *Economic Inquiry*, 29, pp. 485–96.

Ståhlberg, Ann-Charlotte (1989), 'Redistribution Effects of Social Policy in a Lifetime Analytical Framework', in: B.A Gustavson et al. (eds), *The Political Economy of Social Security*, Amsterdam: North Holland, pp. 51–65.

van Doorslaer, Eddy, Adam Wagstaff, Hattem van der Burg, Terkel Christiansen, Diana De Graeve, Inge Duchesne, Ulf-G. Gerdtham, Micheal Gerfin, José Geurts, Lorna Gross, Unto Häkkinen, Jürgen John, Jan Klavus, Robert E. Leu, Brian Nolan, Owen O'Donnel, Carol Propper, Frank Puffer, Martin Schellhorn, Gun Sundberg, Olaf Winkelhake (1999), 'The redistributive effect of health care finance in twelve OECD countries', *Journal of Health Economics*, 18, pp. 291–313.

4. Social Health Policy

In discussing the problems of health care systems one has to note two things: first, health expenditure comprises a sizeable part of GDP in all societies (Table 4.1); second, a large part of health expenditure is mediated through public systems (Table 4.2).

Table 4.1   Health expenditure in OECD countries as a percentage of GDP

	1981	1990	1999	Total health spending per capita in $ 1999*
Austria	6.8	7.2	8.3	2039
Czech Republic			7.6	995
France	7.9	8.9	9.5	2130
Germany	9.4	8.3	10.5	2476
Hungary			6.8[a]	705[a]
Italy	6.9	8.6	8.4	1839
Netherlands	8.1	8.4	8.6[a]	2070
Spain	5.8	6.9	7.5	1218
Switzerland	7.3	8.4	10.4[a]	2714[a]
United Kingdom	5.9	6.0	7.0	1583
USA	9.4	12.7	13.6	4390

Notes: [a] Value for 1998. * Expressed in $ at purchasing power parity.

Source: OECD Data Base.

Expenditure is highest in the USA where nearly one in seven dollars is spent on health services. But health expenditure is not a negligible sum in other countries. Unlike most other social expenditure health expenditure is real expenditure. It is not merely a transfer of purchasing power, it is constituted of demands for goods and services. A euro spent on health services cannot be spent on other goods. Furthermore, health expenditure rises faster than income. It seems to be a luxury good.[1]

With the exception of the USA, in all rich OECD countries at least two-thirds of health expenditure is provided or financed by public systems. Nearly everybody has access to most health services without major expenditure.

Even in the USA an individual cannot be turned away from a hospital because of insufficient insurance or lack of other means in case of emergency; everybody above a certain age is covered by the public Medicare system.

Table 4.2 Share of public expenditure for health services in total expenditure for health services (1997)

Austria	72.0
France	78.4
Germany	77.4
Ireland	75.0
Italy	69.9
Netherlands	72.0
Spain	78.7
Switzerland	69.9
United Kingdom	84.5
USA	46.7

Source: OECD Data Base, Gerdtham and Jönsson (2000).

A further specificity of health expenditures is that within any year they are concentrated among a very small segment of the population. Though a high percentage of the population sees a doctor at least once a year, that does not create high costs (Table 4.3).

Table 4.3 Distribution of medical spending in the USA (1987)

Share of distribution	Cumulative share of spending (%)
Top 1 per cent	30
Top 5 per cent	58
Top 10 per cent	72
Top 50 per cent	98
Total population	100

Source: Berk and Monheit quoted in Cutler and Zeckhauser (2000); © with permission from Elsevier Science.

In the first part of this chapter, two approaches to the analysis of health services are discussed. The second part gives some information about institutional structures of public health provision in selected OECD countries. Its purpose is to show that different solutions to the underlying problem – namely organising the access to health services – exist. The third part considers the problems that prompt states to be so active in this field. It will be shown that there are market failures; more important, however, are specific normative aspects. Problems of equity are discussed in this part as well. The fourth part looks at the causes of increasing costs, which is a feature common to all health care systems worldwide. The final part discusses the way in which income distribution is affected by public health systems.

4.1 TWO APPROACHES TO HEALTH POLICY

In the literature on health services one can find two approaches:

1. The choice theoretic method.
2. The social policy approach.

Both emphasise special aspects of health care and particular options concerning health services. Each one neglects other important aspects.

The choice theoretic method considers health as a stock of capital which decreases over time and special consumption (for example, smoking) and which can be increased by health expenditure. Agents have to make choices, taking into account prices and their preferences for health and other goods (Grossman, 1972, 2000). Health has value, because health is a source of utility; and this value can be estimated empirically. The value of health services is derived from the value of health. The instruments which are used in research based on this method are those of standard microeconomic theory and this method is the basis for most health economics research. (For an overview of estimations of the value of health see Viscusi, 1993; Johnson et al., 1997).[2]

The social policy approach bases its ideas on the assumption that in the case of a health problem there is a need for specific services which have to be satisfied and which can be satisfied if only the technology is available. There are not many possibilities for substitution between health and the consumption of other goods. This approach does not look at the utility of health, but at the utility of health services, namely their medical effectiveness for restoring health. A choice between consumption of health services and of other goods is not considered. This approach is the basis for most social policy legislation concerning health. It is also the approach used in many WHO publications.

Each method is sensible only under factual and normative assumptions. The choice theoretic method assumes that people can make decisions and should make decisions concerning their consumption of health services. Individuals are the best judges when deciding how to evaluate health. It rejects the notion that a third party – the health authority – knows better (Hurley, 2000). By choosing a particular way of living an individual affects her health. A smoker prefers smoking and the associated higher risk of lung cancer to non-smoking and a lower risk of lung cancer. People can, at least to a certain degree, affect health expenditures.[3] Some draw a specific normative conclusion, namely that people are responsible for the decisions they make and should therefore contribute accordingly.

The social policy approach on the other hand rejects this position and assumes that where there is a disease there is a need for services, which should be covered as otherwise health and life are seriously endangered. One cannot substitute between health and consumption of other goods. Furthermore a person cannot choose her life style freely, or, if it can be chosen, the actual choice does not have much influence on health. The normative consequence is that people have a right to health care.

This is exemplified in the following quotation from the Beveridge plan from 1944 which was the blueprint for the British post-war welfare state:

> A comprehensive national health service will ensure that for every citizen there is available whatever medical treatment he requires, in whatever form he requires it, domiciliary or institutional, general, specialist or consultant, and will ensure also the provision of dental, ophthalmic and surgical appliances, nursing and midwifery, and rehabilitation after accidents. (Quoted in Gordon, 1988, p. 212)

A similar idea underlies the German and Austrian social security laws. They mandate that the services of the health suppliers must be suitable for healing the disease; however they should not exceed what is 'necessary'. The Swedish Health Care Act mentions as its goal 'good health and health care under equal conditions for the entire population'. The problem is the use of the concept of a need and its satisfaction, an idea which was prominent in nineteenth-century economics, but is alien to modern economics.

We can link these two approaches of providing health services to the above mentioned difference between the *ex ante* view and the *ex post* view. The economic approach takes the *ex ante* view, as it looks at expected utilities. The social policy approach on the other hand cares for actual outcomes, the *ex post* view. Each approach taken alone is unsatisfactory, because each one neglects important aspects which are covered by the other.

First, for the choice theoretic method, there is often no real possibility of substitution once the need for a treatment has arisen. If you experience pain or if your life is seriously threatened by a disease, you cannot have less treatment than necessary in order to get more of other consumption goods. Not to have pain and not to have one's life endangered is not an extra consumption good, it is rather the basis for all experience of utility. However the possibility of substitution between different goods is important for all economic analysis.

A further problem is that when an individual is sick there are, in many instances, particularly in the expensive ones, not many options available – one needs special surgery or one does not need it. If there are a few options available, some more expensive, some less expensive, the patient – the consumer – hardly has the necessary knowledge to make an informed decision between different drugs, different treatments, and so on. It is mostly the physicians who have to make the decisions.

Concerning the possibility of influencing one's own probabilities of getting a disease, it is certainly true that a person's life style can have an effect. But it is a long way from this to considering life style to be a matter of choice in the traditional sense of economics. A young person acquiring the habit of smoking or developing obesity can hardly be considered as having made a rational choice by taking into account expected utility and future risks in the same way as a portfolio manager evaluates expected returns and risks when buying specific stock. Information about risks is often not available – the dangers of HIV were not known for some time – and there were instances where information about risks were concealed for reasons of profit, for example the danger of smoking or working with asbestos.[4]

BOX 4.1 PROMISES OF A COMMERCIAL HEALTH INSURANCE AND A PUBLIC HEALTH SYSTEM

Compare the two statements from public relations material:

To provide value to our clients through superior service and coordinated access to effective managed health programmes at an acceptable choice. (RightCHOICE Managed Care, Inc. Mission Statement; Blue Cross Blue Shield Missouri)

The fundamental purpose of the NHS [in England] is to secure through the resources available the greatest possible improvement in the physical and mental health of the people of England by promoting health, preventing ill health, diagnosing and treating injury and disease and caring for those with long term illness and disability who require the service of the NHS. (Alan Langlands, NHS Chief Executive (UK), 1995)

It is also not clear to what extent health costs depend on people's actions. From the fact that one increases the probability of getting lung cancer by smoking, it cannot be inferred that one increases one's expected total health costs. The reason is that nobody simply dies because of age, but always because of a specific disease or a non-functioning of some organs. For many people that means costly treatment and hospitalisation for a prolonged period at the end of life, irrespective of the chosen life style (Barendregt et al., 1997).

Furthermore the normative consequences of the choice of a life style for health outcome are different from other risks people accept. If an individual experiences a loss of wealth because a risky asset lost value, then it is accepted that she should bear the loss – at least if there is not a special problem of poverty. It is not customary (or at least at odds with the basic ideas of a market economy) to salvage the wealth that an individual lost in a risky speculation. But it is also accepted that a person with lung cancer should get the necessary treatment whether he was a smoker or a non-smoker, though some people accept that smokers should pay more in case of cancer. When a mountain climber has to be rescued she is asked afterwards to reimburse costs, but it would not be acceptable that a person is rescued only if she can reimburse costs, even if she had acted grossly negligent. In such instances the *ex-post* aspect usually dominates. This can be called the *rule of rescue*.

The social policy approach, on the other hand, dismisses altogether the possibilities of choice. But in some instances one can have a significant effect on one's health costs. Take dental care: cleaning teeth regularly and having regular check-ups decreases the costs of dental services over a lifetime. The fact that wages differ according to different health risks (compare Viscusi, 1992, Ch. 3–6; for a summary in a textbook see Borjas, 1996, Ch. 8) also shows that such risks are somehow 'chosen'.[5] Otherwise employers would not have to pay more for the same quality of labour merely because of bigger health risks.

There is a deeper problem for the social policy approach. To consider it as a basis for a sensible policy one has to make the following assumptions:

- One can distinguish precisely between the states 'healthy' and 'sick'.
- A disease can either be cured completely, not cured at all, or can at least by specific treatment be ameliorated in a precise way. There is satiation and the law of diminishing marginal utility does not apply.
- Expenditures for health care are only a small part of GDP, in which case an increase of spending is not a big problem.

The three assumptions together would imply that it is not necessary to ration health services. There are needs for services and they can be satisfied. Unfortunately none of the three conditions is fulfilled.

According to the definition of the WHO to be healthy means 'a state of complete physical, mental and social well-being and not merely the absence of disease or infirmity'. This definition is not merely very demanding, but neglects – amongst other things – the problem of ageing. A 30-year-old woman who cannot give birth is according to this definition not fully healthy. That makes sense. But what about a 50-year-old woman? This would merely be a question for curiosity, if there were no medical technologies available allowing a 50-year-old woman to give birth. But they are available. Should public health systems pay for reproductive treatment for a 30-year-old woman? For a 50-year-old woman? An individual not able to hike ten miles carrying a rucksack does not enjoy 'complete physical well-being'. Is a 75-year-old sick if she cannot walk the ten miles with a rucksack? At what age does that become a problem for a public health system? And what about all those problems which were considered as deviant, and therefore morally objectionable, behaviour, and are now seen as health problems: alcoholism, drug problems and other addictions, learning disabilities, and so on. To what extent should a public health system take care of them?

Concerning the second assumption, there are diseases which can be cured completely by special treatment, but when left untreated can lead to catastrophic results. Marginal utility is either the full value of health or zero. The law of diminishing marginal utility does not apply. Removal of an appendix, curing tuberculosis, syphilis, inoculation against cholera or poliomyelitis are typical examples. But many diseases are of a different type. Although full health cannot be restored, extra treatments have positive effects: marginal utility and marginal costs are different from zero. In any serious surgery, risks can nearly always be decreased further by more controls. Regular check-ups have a positive effect on the health of a population, but they can be very costly.[6] Furthermore restoring health cannot be uniquely defined. If an individual loses her teeth, is it necessary to provide very expensive implants, or is it sufficient to provide dentures? When is psychic health restored? Obviously there is no satiation. With all the modern technologies available there is no upper limit for the state of 'being healthy'.[7] Therefore the question of how many services to provide has to be answered.

The third assumption is not fulfilled either, as about 10 per cent of GDP is spent on health services. It is necessary to ration health services. This fact is often overlooked in programmatic statements of the social policy approach, though all systems contain costs in one way or another. Be that as it may, the mechanism of rationing through markets, namely that services are allocated according to the willingness-to-pay, is considered unethical by the social policy approach.

To sum up, whereas the choice theoretic approach – somehow the economist's natural method – neglects the problem of needs, the social policy approach does not take into account the economic problems of providing health services. If a health system were to be organised according to the ideas of only one of these approaches the result would be very bad. A market oriented system like that of the USA or Switzerland must take care of needs which are not satisfied by the commercially organised supply of health services and insurance. On the other hand all social policy systems have to consider costs and have to look for efficiency.

BOX 4.2 SHOULD WE ATTACH A MONETARY VALUE TO HEALTH AND TO LIFE?

Some people find the idea repulsive that a monetary value is put on health and even on life, because they think that one should not forsake life or health in favour of wealth. But what is meant when valuing life and health in monetary units is something different from putting a money value on other goods. When I value an hour of my time with €30 that means I am prepared to give up an hour of my leisure time for €30. If I value a painting I own at €1000, I will be happy to sell it if somebody offers me more than that. But if I put a price on my life, I do not intend to sell my life. It means something different, namely that I am prepared to pay a price to reduce the probability of a fatal accident.

But shouldn't one do everything to avoid such an accident?

- If you have a Porsche and if there is no speeding control, will you drive at 160 mph?
- If not, do you drive just at 40 mph on an empty freeway?

If you answer the first question with no, because you consider it too dangerous to do it, and if you answer the second question with no as well, because it would be too boring for you and you consider the extra time spent on the road as time lost, you have already set a price on the reduction of the probability of a fatal accident. The time won (and the thrill experienced) by driving at 160 mph was not worth the higher probability of having an accident in comparison to driving at just 60 to 70 mph. The even lower probability of an accident by driving at just 40 mph was not worth the time lost on the road and the accompanying boredom. The point is that you cannot avoid the possibility of a fatal accident completely, because whatever you do there is a danger of an accident. You can reduce its probability, but that creates costs. These costs have to be weighted against the increased safety.

From an empirical analysis:

> For newborns, health capital increased by $95 000 between 1970 and 1990, while health capital for the elderly increased by $169 000. The greater increase in health capital for the elderly than for the young is a result of differential changes in mortality by age. The lion's share of mortality reduction between 1970 and 1990 was a result of fewer deaths from cardiovascular disease. Since cardiovascular disease is more prominent late in life, the present value of these gains is greater for the elderly than for the young. ...
> Using cross-section data on medical spending in 1970 and 1987, we estimate that expected medical costs increased by $19 000 for infants (in 1987 dollars), and by $34 000 for people aged 65. The increase in health capital is greater than the increase in medical spending. (Cutler and Richardson, 1998, p. 99)

4.2 ORGANISATIONAL STRUCTURES

Though there is no state without a sizeable part of health expenditure mediated by the public sector, the organisational structures differ between them. One can distinguish four types of structures:

1. Publicly organised health services, for example, the National Health Service (NHS) in the United Kingdom, the Health Service in Italy, the Swedish Health Service, the Norwegian Health Service.
2. Social insurance institutions, for example, the Austrian and the German *Krankenkassen*, the French *Assurance-maladie*.
3. Publicly mandated insurance with regulations of contracts for social policy purposes and subsidy of premiums, for example, Switzerland and the Netherlands.
4. Publicly financed or subsidised access to health services for certain groups, for example, Medicare and Medicaid in the USA.

In some countries (USA, Switzerland, the Netherlands) people have a choice between more and less generous plans – which services are covered, whether there are deductibles, co-payments, and so on. In states with a publicly organised health system there cannot be a choice between different programmes. In most states with a public health insurance system there is not much choice left for the insured either. There is no choice for the insured between different types of contracts, though there may be competition between different insurance organisations.[8] In all states there is competition between different suppliers of health services.

Common to most systems is that it is accepted that everybody should have access to good health services independently of income. There should not be much difference between services provided by public systems and by privately funded systems. This is also true for Canada, New Zealand and Australia. The European transformation countries restructure their health systems along similar lines. The USA is different, because a part of the population is without health insurance. That does not leave them without access to health services, but those with low income use markedly less resources. Many developing countries also have universal public health systems; but due to the poverty of their economies, they are often of very low quality. Many people with high incomes rely primarily on privately organised systems. This also applies to most of the CIS countries.

There is a further aspect of health provision in connection with employed labour: do sick people have a right to stay at home and to receive payments, and if so, for how long? It is clear that this is very important; however it is not covered in this book.

4.2.1 Public Health Services

The NHS is the organiser of all public health services in the United Kingdom. All citizens and all individuals with the right of residence in the UK have access to its services. Within the system the services are the same for everyone. To a great extent they are financed out of general taxes (approximately 80 per cent) and to a smaller extent by a special tax (approximately 15 per cent). For some services a small co-payment is necessary. Poor people can be freed from paying the co-payment. People have to enlist with a General Practitioner (GP) whose approval is necessary to turn to a specialist or to a consultant. The GP functions as *gatekeeper* to the health system. A GP can opt for *fund-holding* status. In that case she gets a capitation fee for each patient who registers with her and has in turn to buy all the relevant services of health providers in the market (Matsaganis and Glennester, 1994).[9] Some 15 per cent of the population has private insurance as well.

The NHS is a big organisation. It has complex structures of governance with central, regional and local layers of planning institutions. Since the reforms of the 1980s local and regional health councils can buy services from different providers. The reforms were introduced in order to have some competition between providers. Nearly all hospitals are public.

The NHS is by construction not merely a health insurance but a health system. It is also active in the prevention of diseases and some of its services are closely related to social work and to community based care. It works together with other parts of the administration of social services, particularly at local levels. As a health system the NHS can set specific health policy targets.

Currently the UK spends slightly less than 7 per cent of its GDP on health services. This is amongst the lowest in rich economies. Whether its services are worse than those of other countries is difficult to judge. The number of doctors and hospital beds per 1000 inhabitants is much smaller than in most other rich economies. Life expectancy is nearly the same as in the USA, which spends almost double the amount per individual as the UK. But life expectancy depends on many factors, not merely on health expenditure. Baily and Garber (1997), for example, have shown that the UK system is more productive than the US system in the treatment of diabetes because of its public health character; in other cases (for example, removal of gallstones) the US system is more productive.[10] According to another study, survival rates for cancer treatments are higher in the USA than in the UK, and it is easier to get dialysis for kidney patients in the USA than in the UK (*The Economist*, 4 July 1998). A frequent complaint against the NHS is that there are long waiting lists for treatment. This has contributed to the increasing number of individuals taking up private insurance (Besley et al., 1999).

Other countries with public health systems are slightly different. In Italy the division between the public and the private is not as sharp as in the UK. About 10 per cent of publicly financed services are provided by the private sector. Many doctors work in both sectors with often unclear rules of demarcation (Fattore, 1999). The Swedish system was never as centralised as the NHS. There are 26 county councils with, to some extent, different provision of health services. Only when cost-containment became important was the variability of services reduced for equity reasons (Anell and Svarvar, 1999).

4.2.2 A Social Insurance Health System without Competition – Austria

In the social security system of Austria people are enlisted according to their profession in different *Krankenkassen* (health insurance). These are self-governing bodies under the control of the Ministry of Social Affairs. All laws concerning health insurance, save for those who work for the *Länder* (the provinces), are federal laws. The system is financed by contributions which are, for blue-collar workers, 7.9 per cent, and for other employees 6.9 per cent of their gross wage up to a level of €3200 per month. The contribution is shared equally between the employer and the employee. Separate systems exist for the mining industry, the self-employed, the professions, the federal public system, the regional public system and for some big firms.[11]

An individual not working is insured without further payment if she is married to an insured person or if she is a dependent child of an insured person.[12] Unemployed people and retirees remain in their *Krankenkasse*. People who quit working and have no other insurance can voluntarily insure for a fixed premium. Currently 99 per cent of the population are covered by one of the *Krankenkassen*. An individual may be without insurance before entering the labour market, when losing the connection with the labour market after prolonged periods of unemployment (if not married to an insured person), or after a divorce if neither working nor retired. The *Krankenkasse* does not cover people in need of long-term care without a chance of improvement, particularly if they are hospitalised in an institution. If they need treatment in a hospital for which they have no means, expenses are covered out of the social assistance budgets of the *Länder*.

All *Krankenkassen* in Austria function as insurance. They provide means for necessary treatment in case of need. The need must be stated by a physician. Prevention and caring are provided by the *Krankenkassen* only in special cases. This may be seen an omission, but it is due to the construction of the institution as insurance. Prevention and caring remain primarily tasks for the state.

Primary care and specialist services are mostly supplied privately. The physicians have contracts with the *Krankenkassen* and are paid by them. In order to contain costs the *Krankenkassen* limit the number of doctors to whom a contract is given; however patients can see other doctors and are reimbursed for the expenses at 80 per cent of the rate of the *Krankenkasse*.

Prices of services are fixed by a contract between a *Krankenkasse* and the Chamber of Physicians. There is a small deductible and for some groups there are co-payments. Most of the hospitals are public. They are owned by the *Länder* or the communes; the teaching hospitals tied to the universities are federally owned. Some hospitals belong to a *Krankenkasse*. There is a non-profit sector of hospitals, mostly run by religious communities, and there is a small private for-profit sector.

Hospitals get paid for the treatment of each patient by the *Krankenkasse*. The former fee-for-service payment has recently been changed into a system of diagnosis related group rates. The payments by the *Krankenkasse* do not cover all expenses. There are sizeable subsidies by the *Länder* (in case of the teaching hospitals by the federal state) out of general taxes.

Each *Krankenkasse* decides which treatments it is prepared to finance, and to what extent (for example, how many units of psychotherapeutic counselling), although the law demands that all treatments which are necessary must be provided. Some treatments and some medications require prior approval of the *Krankenkasse*. There are some differences in their 'generosity'. This is due to different economic situations. The income of the *Krankenkassen* depends on their members' income, therefore *Krankenkassen* in affluent regions have bigger budgets. The expenditures depend on the age distribution and risks of their members. For example, people in the public sector have lower risks and higher incomes than other groups of the population. Their *Krankenkasse* is therefore more 'generous'. There are some transfers between *Krankenkassen* to take care of different income/expenditure structures.

There is a further social health insurance system for all employed people. It covers accidents and diseases which are related to their job (*Unfallversicherung*). It is more generous than the *Krankenkassen* as it is supposed to cover expenses for rehabilitation after accidents and pays in many instances a pension as well. It is financed by a wage-related contribution, fully paid by the employers. It is an insurance for employers against employees' claims in relation to job related accidents or a job specific disease.[13] In the year 2000 the rate of contribution was 1.4 per cent. The *Unfallversicherung* is not merely an insurance but has, according to the law, also to care for prevention. It has to control for safety measures in firms, a task for which in other states separate government bodies are responsible (in the USA, for example, this is the Occupational Safety and Health Authority – OSHA).

4.2.3 Social Insurance with Competition – Germany

The German system is similar to the Austrian one. It has *Krankenkassen* on regional and professional basis. There is also an *Unfallversicherung* working on the same principles as in Austria. The most important differences to the Austrian system is that the premium is not fixed by statutory law, but must be fixed by the *Krankenkasse*. The law requires that the premiums be set such that all expenses are covered. Currently the average rate is approximately 13 per cent, shared by the employer and the insured. A further major difference is that people with high incomes can opt out of the system altogether. As we will see below, this reduces vertical redistribution. About 90 per cent of the population is insured in one of the *Krankenkassen* or in the system for the public sector.

Unlike in Austria where the insurance carrier is mandatory, in Germany there is the right to choose a *Krankenkasse*. In 1993 this right was introduced in order to have some competition between them. It became effective in 1996. There is primarily competition via different rates of premium. Competition via different levels of health services plays a minor role. If there were no separation of risks all *Krankenkassen* would end up with the same rate in equilibrium: individuals will switch from the more expensive ones to the cheaper ones until either all differences have vanished or the cheapest supplier has become a monopolist.

In respect to the rates of different insurers this did not occur. The difference between the cheapest and the most expensive ones was 1:2 before 1996 and has increased meanwhile. In respect to the distribution of the insured, however, this did happen. An increasing number of people leave their *Krankenkasse* each year in favour of another one (Busse, 2001). There is some separation of risks, though nobody is hindered in changing from one *Krankenkasse* to another. The cheaper *Krankenkassen* attract the good risks, the high risks remain with the more expensive ones. This has been confirmed by detailed research: those who switched from one *Krankenkasse* to another have costs of 55 per cent of the average (Schulz et al., 2001). It is primarily the young who change insurance.

In order to contain the spread of contributions there is neutralisation of risks by transfers between the *Krankenkassen*. The premiums should not differ due to different risk structures. In 2000 about €12 billion were redistributed through this system. The problem is that the transfers do not compensate fully for different risks, though there are 12 groups of risks with more than 700 categories taken into account. There is a general consensus that the transfers between the *Krankenkassen* must be set on a new footing to bring the transfers more in line with differences in morbidity, however a definite plan has not yet (fall, 2001) materialised.

4.2.4 A Two-Tier Social Insurance with Competition – the Netherlands

The Netherlands has a two-tier system of public and publicly regulated health insurance. The first tier is a mandatory public insurance against exceptional medical expenses (*Algemeene Wet Bijzondere Ziektekosten*, AWBZ). It covers long-term treatment in hospitals, caring, psychiatric treatment and treatment for physically and mentally handicapped people. These contingencies could not be insured by a profit oriented insurance. The premium is income-related, and in 1996 it was 7.35 per cent of income.

The second tier consists of an insurance for regular medical care. Employees with an income below a threshold (about €27,000 per year in 1999), individuals above 65 and some other groups have to insure in a sickness fund insurance (*Zieckenfondsbesluit*, ZFW). There is competition between different ZFWs. The self-employed and those with income above the threshold can insure with a private health insurance. About 60 per cent of the population have insurance with a ZFW, the remaining 40 per cent have private insurance. People who are not insured under these schemes and who belong to low-income and/or high-risk groups can rely on a further scheme (*Wet op de Toegang tot Ziektekostenverzekeringen*, WTZ).

Individuals who are insured with a ZWF pay for their insurance in two ways. First, there is an income-related premium in a central fund, second, a direct flat-rate premium is paid by the insured and their employers. The central fund pays to the ZWF of choice a capitation payment according to the risk group to which a person belongs. The flat-rate premiums can be different between different ZFWs and between different plans of a ZFW. Insurers have to charge the same premium to all insured for the same option, but there can be different options. There is competition between different insurers and some choice for the insured.

Although the ZFWs have to accept anyone who wants a specific contract there is the danger of cream-skimming. To inhibit it, the capitation payment is adjusted for different risks. When the current system was started only gender and age were used for grading. A regional variable and one for employment status has been added. There are now 680 risk groups (Kieke and Poelert, 2001). Nevertheless there is still an incentive to attract customers who are expected to have low costs. It can be shown, for example, that people with high health expenditure during five preceding years are more likely to have high expenditure in the following years. One way to estimate expected future health costs consists in looking at health costs in the past (van de Ven et al., 1994, 1996).

4.2.5 Mandated Insurance and Redistribution – Switzerland

The Swiss system is somehow unique. It rests on private market oriented institutions with public regulation for social purposes and public support. Among the European health systems the Swiss system comes closest to the ideas of the second welfare theorem. It supports the poor and families, but rests on a market system for the supply of insurance services. Switzerland has, after the USA and Germany, the most expensive system. About 10 per cent of GDP is spent on health services. As in Austria and in Germany independent doctors are suppliers of services. Most hospitals are run by the *Kantone* (the provinces) which also contribute to covering costs. As recently as 1996 the obligation to insure was introduced in all *Kantone*, however 99 per cent of the population were insured before that date.

Private insurers can act as social insurers. For that the insurance company has to fix for each insurance contract a single contribution for everybody independently of risk. Contracts can differ according to the size of the deductible and for acceptance of managed care (see below). Cheaper rates are possible for children. Most of the insurance companies work in only one of the *Kantone*. Insurance companies are not allowed to refuse a contract on grounds of high risk. In social insurance contracts provisions of contracts for special groups are not admitted, as this would be a way to separate risks.

Payment is independent of income, but dependent on the number of individuals insured. Rates differ between different insurers, with a differential of up to 50 per cent between the cheapest and the most expensive insurance company. There are differences in what an insurance offers, but there is a statutory minimum provision which covers primary care and specialist services, hospital costs, but also some services not provided by doctors, like chiropractice and logopedics. There is public support for low income groups. This support is a necessary complement to the obligation to insure.

4.2.6 Public Support of Access to Health Services – the USA

Amongst the industrialised countries the USA has the smallest public health system. For most working people health insurance is provided by the employer as a part of their labour contract.[14] In 1996, 160 million people were covered by insurance bought by an employer or through an employer. The share of individuals having employer-provided health insurance was slowly declining in the last decade (United States General Accounting Office, 1998). Apart from the subsidy of health provision via tax, health insurance by the employers should not be seen as a social policy programme, rather as a fringe benefit of a labour contract. Of those with insurance about 19 million also had government insurance. For 9 million the employer did not contribute to the premium (Carrasquillo et al., 1999). Less than 10 per cent of the population buys insurance directly (Cutler and Zeckhauser, 2000). (See Table 4.4)

The state subsidises the provisions of health insurance as the premium of the insurance is not taxed. The price of the average health insurance contract is thereby reduced by 27 per cent (Gruber, 2000b).[15] Furthermore group insurance is cheaper than individual insurance. This system creates some problems for the functioning of labour markets (Monheit and Cooper, 1994), because people with expected higher medical costs – for example, because of many children, or because of a handicapped child – may be affected adversely (Scott et al., 1995). Furthermore as group size is important in health insurance, big firms face lower costs when providing health insurance than small firms (Diamond, 1992).[16] Some of the insurers are for-profit companies, but there exists a big non-profit sector as well.

More than 16 per cent of the population have no insurance, although they have access to emergency room treatment.[17] A medical unit cannot turn away an individual in urgent need of treatment. Most of the uninsured have low incomes. Of those below poverty level more than 30 per cent have no insurance (United States General Accounting Office, 1997). They are either unemployed or working for employers who do not offer the benefit of health insurance, in most cases small employers. Others work on a temporary basis.[18] On average they receive about half the medical care of insured people who are otherwise similar (Diamond, 1992).

For nearly two decades, insurers have tried to regulate the supply of health services in order to contain costs: a system known as *managed care*. As pure insurers they have to pay all expenses for all treatments considered necessary by the physicians (fee-for-service). In managed care the choice of doctors is restricted and doctors are restricted in what they can do for their patients.

There are two public systems:

- For the poor: Medicaid. These are state regulated systems which are federally supported.
- For the aged: Medicare – a federal programme. All above the age of 65, and younger people who are disabled or in end-stage renal disease can take part in this programme (exceptions are federal employees and aliens with less than 5 years of residence).

Table 4.4 Type of health insurance and coverage status, USA (1997)*

Status and type of coverage	Thousand of persons (%)
Total	269 094 (100.0)
Covered	225 646 (83.9)
Private	188 533 (70.1)
Employment-based	165 092 (61.4)
Government	66 685 (24.8)
Medicare	35 590 (13.2)
Medicaid	28 956 (10.8)
Military	8 527 (3.2)
Not covered	43 448 (16.1)
Poor persons	
Total	35 574 (100.0)
Covered	24 336 (68.4)
Private	8 264 (23.2)
Employment-based	5 521 (15.5)
Government	18 585 (52.2)
Medicare	4 637 (13.0)
Medicaid	15 386 (43.3)
Not covered	11 238 (31.6)

Note: Data are from the US Census Bureau. Percentages add up to more than 100 because some people had more than one type of coverage.

Source: Kuttner (1999a).

Medicaid

Medicaid is the largest health insurance system in the USA, it covers more than 41 million people. Individual states determine eligibility and which services are covered. Federal support varies between states according to per capita income. Poorer states get up to 83 per cent of their Medicaid expenditure from the federal budget, the minimum a state gets is 50 per cent. In 1997 total expenditure was $159 billion of which nearly 60 per cent was covered by the federal budget (Iglehart, 1999).

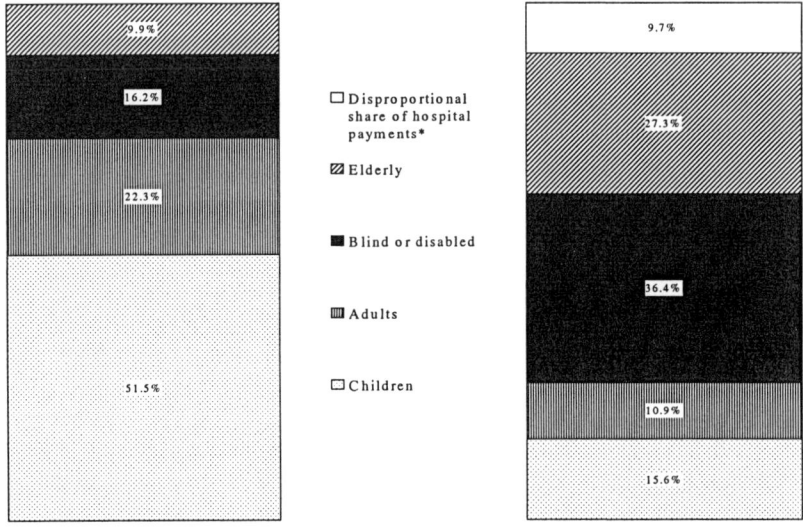

Note: *Payments to hospitals which have an above average share of low income patients.

Source: Iglehart (1999, p. 404).

Figure 4.1 Beneficiaries and expenditures of Medicaid programmes

Criteria for eligibility are defined to some extent by the federal government (advanced age, blindness, disability). The states set their criteria according to the income and assets of households. The extension or restriction of access to Medicaid is a constant issue in American politics. Up to the mid 1990s there was a close relation between receiving welfare and being eligible for Medicaid; following welfare reforms this connection has been made less strict. This seemed necessary, as changes to social assistance programmes reduced the number of individuals eligible by obliging them to accept low-paid jobs. If the affected people had lost the access to Medicaid as a result, they would have hesitated to take up such jobs (see below, Chapter 8.7.2), contrary to the intention of the reforms. Further, in 1997 it was decided that children whose parents are not eligible for Medicaid would, under certain circumstances, be covered by a special programme of Medicaid, Children's Health Insurance Programme (CHIP) or some of its sub-programmes.

Not all people who are eligible for Medicaid are enrolled in its programmes. This is a typical feature of all social programmes for the poor. Some states, for example Oregon, ask for a small premium (between $6 and $28, depending on family size) to participate in the Medicaid programme. This leads to a decrease in participation (ODAS, 1999, p. 33).[19]

Medicare

The Medicare system consists of two parts. First, a mandatory hospital insurance, which covers all hospital care with a small deductible and some home care. It is an insurance against events with high cost. It is financed by a contribution amounting to 2.9 per cent of gross income. It is therefore primarily a system of redistribution over the life-cycle – one pays all through one's working life and receives benefits in old age.

Second, there is supplementary medical insurance for the same group. It is voluntary, but subsidised. Therefore 98 per cent of those entitled take this insurance. It charges $459 per year (in 1999), and for the poor the fee is paid by Medicaid. The system pays 80 per cent of insured events.

For some years patients who have enlisted with Medicaid or Medicare have been asked to switch to managed care. Doctors are paid for Medicare patients with a capitation fee which is graded by the patient's age and sex. As in the Netherlands the grading scheme is considered as not being responsive to different expected costs for different people. Therefore insurance carriers try to attract groups with low risks (Office of Strategic Planning, 1999).

Table 4.5 People without health insurance for the entire year according to selected characteristics (1997)

Characteristic	All people (thousands)	Uninsured people (%)
Total	269 094	16.1
Sex		
Male	131 705	17.6
Female	137 390	14.8
Age (yr)		
< 18	71 682	15.0
18–24	25 201	30.1
25–34	39 354	23.3
35–44	44 462	17.3
45–64	56 313	14.1
≥ 65	32 082	1.0
Race or ethnic group		
White	221 651	15.0
Non-Hispanic white	192 179	12.0
Black	34 598	21.5
Asian or Pacific Islander	10 492	20.7
Hispanic	30 773	34.2

Source: Kuttner (1999a).

Emergency treatment

Individuals without insurance, mostly in low-wage jobs, have access to emergency treatment (see Table 4.5). No physician can turn away a person in urgent need. Actually two-thirds of private physicians provide some charity care (either free care or at a reduced rate). About 12 per cent of their working time was used for charity care (Cunningham and Tu, 1997). Charity in-patient treatment is concentrated in urban public and not-for-profit hospitals (Mann et al., 1997). There is some discussion whether not-for-profit hospitals are providing a disproportionally high share of these services.

High-risk individuals

About half the states pay for access to health insurance at a cost of 150 per cent of a standard contract for high-risk individuals who were denied a private insurance contract for previous conditions (United States General Accounting Office, 1997).

4.3 OBJECTIVES OF PUBLIC HEALTH INSURANCE AND HEALTH SUPPORT

There is no country in the world where the access to health services is not organised or subsidised by the public sector. Is this sensible? What are the reasons for it? One can distinguish between market problems and social policy questions in the narrow sense of the word.

Before discussing that, we have to look at the content of health insurance contracts. There are three different aspects, only the first of which is a traditional insurance event:
- Insurance for high-cost/low-probability events: diseases with high expenditure before being old.
- Saving for high-cost/high-probability events. Health costs are high in advanced age with high probability. One cannot enter a new health insurance contract in advanced age or when born with a serious health problem. A health insurance contract lasting until advanced age can be seen as a savings contract.
- Coverage of low cost/high probability events. Most cases of using medical services cause low expenditures. Non-poor people below a certain age without insurance would have no problem in paying directly for the visit to the doctor's office, for treatment in case of flu, after a small accident, and so on. These expenses are no bigger than other domestic expenses such as those incurred by the breakdown of a car, of a refrigerator or other costly items. Though people rarely insure against such events, most public health systems and public health insurance

institutions do take care of events with minor expenses.[20] Even in the USA, most health insurance contracts cover these events. An insurance not covering small expenditures would be cheaper, but many people prefer to have these events covered as well.[21]

There may be a reason for that: if an individual has to pay something, she would have to make choices – whether it is worth paying to see a doctor, to have a treatment, to have a special health-check. Many people prefer not to make these decisions themselves, but to leave them to the physician. Not having to take expenses into account makes that easier. Many people prefer to have a contract in which all such expenditures are covered. It is like an all-you-can-eat-buffet, or a holiday resort where you can use all facilities without extra payment. One pays for not having to make decisions as to whether the consumption of a service is worth the cost.

4.3.1 Problems of Markets

1. *Market failures in the narrow sense of the word.* Even if people make rational choices for long periods, use all information available, and estimate risks correctly, market failures arise when there are external effects of any kind. State intervention can bring about a Pareto-improvement.

One of the classic examples of external effects relating to the health system is contagious disease. If an individual with a contagious disease is cured or if somebody chooses to be inoculated against one, the probability that somebody else gets sick decreases. It is therefore a benefit for all if somebody gets treatment or is inoculated. Whether this is achieved by subsidisation or by mandating the treatment is immaterial. Be that as it may, today contagious diseases are of minor importance in rich economies, though they are still a problem in most poor economies.

A second type of market failures is due to insufficient competition. Though there are many suppliers of health services, monopoly is a problem due to medical and regional specificity of the services. In the research and marketing of new drugs decreasing average costs and natural monopolies are an important factor. In the insurance business there is a tendency towards a decreasing number of independent insurers. Whether this will result in a monopoly or whether the optimal size of insurers is small enough such that there remain sufficient insurers to maintain competition is not known.

Insufficient competition may also prevail due to the market power of the buyers of health services. Public health systems clearly dominate the market in most European states. The implications for the health industry cannot be analysed in a traditional model of monopsony, because public health systems do not maximise profits. They are part of the political system.

Adverse selection and moral hazard, both caused by asymmetric information, are a special concern in health economics. People differ in their risk for the need for health services. Insurers try to separate risks. As was argued in Chapter 3 this can lead to an inefficient under-provision of insurance (Newhouse, 1996). There has been a lot of research about the relevance of adverse selection. The overwhelming conclusion is that it is an important phenomenon (for an overview see Cutler and Zeckhauser, 2000).[22]

2. *Insurance markets work well for high-cost low-probability events (for example, fire).* However the need for health services can be high probability events: (i) there are high risk groups; (ii) for old people the probability of large medical costs is high. Such risks might be uninsurable by market insurance. Private insurance companies often increase premiums or end the contract if a client is diagnosed with a long-term disease (Cochrane, 1995). The affected people need support or publicly provided insurance.

BOX 4.3 AN EXAMPLE OF SEPARATION OF RISKS

To trim costs, Harvard in 1995 moved to a more competitive health insurance system. Under the new system, the University pegged its contribution at a fixed percentage of the lowest cost plan ...
When the new system was introduced, the cost of the PPO [Preferred-Provider-Organization P.R.] rose, and PPO enrollment fell ... about ¼ of PPO enrollees left the PPO between 1994 and 1995. These enrollees were disproportionately the younger and healthier employees in the PPO, however. As a result of biased disenrollment, the PPO lost money in 1995; in 1996, it had to raise its premium by nearly $1,000. This led to a further decline in PPO enrollment; over half the remaining PPO enrollees left the plan after 1996. Again, these employees were disproportionately younger and healthier than those that remained in the PPO. Thus the PPO premium lost money again in 1997 and would have had to increased premiums substantially in 1998. ... In fact, the required premium increase would have been too large for the insurer and Harvard to bear. The PPO was disbanded before that year. Adverse selection thus produced a death spiral, and did so very quickly. The disappearance of the PPO is a welfare loss to employees who would have chosen it at their individual-specific cost. (Cutler and Zeckhauser, 2000, p. 623)

---

3. *People do not behave rationally.* (i) An individual may underestimate risks which will lead to under-insurance in relation to her true preferences. (ii) The biggest part of health expenditure arises in the last part of one's life. Entering an insurance in old age is usually impossible. But people may abstain from paying for insurance when young or middle aged, because it

means paying for something very remote and very unpleasant to think of. This may also lead to under-insurance.

A way of overcoming this problem is to force people to take insurance, as is done in Switzerland. The payment for the Medicare hospital insurance in the USA can also be seen as an obligatory insurance for health service when old. That is a paternalistic policy. It can be defended if one assumes that the government is better informed about preferences than the people themselves.

4. *Samaritan's dilemma.* In all societies it is accepted that everybody should have access to medical treatment if urgently necessary. People may rely on it and refuse to take insurance, thereby imposing costs on others. Obliging people to take insurance can reduce this problem. The argument is different from that in the preceding paragraph, as it does not require a paternalistic policy.

5. *Contracts for health insurance are very complicated as they must contain many clauses which can only be understood with some medical training.* As contributions increase in many contracts with the age of entering the insurance there are sunk costs as well: changing insurance is costly, because an individual is older at the change than when she made the original contract. Shopping around, which is necessary for learning about the market, is hardly possible. This problem does not require a public health system, but public control of health insurance contracts.

6. *Information problems concerning future diseases and technologies.* In general one expects a health insurance to pay for all services at state-of-the-art technologies. They are not known when a contract is made. Long-term contracts create specific incentives when new problems arise (for example, AIDS) and technologies change quickly. However the development of new technologies are not given exogenously but depend on the contracts the insurance companies have with their clients and on the regulations of public health systems (see below: allocation effects).

4.3.2 Social Policy Aims – Normative Aspects

Market problems of access to health services and health insurance call for regulations and interference into the relevant markets, but can probably be solved without public health provision as they exist in most states. For policies actually pursued normative arguments are put forward, not merely pointing to some market failures.

1. *Poverty.* The income of some people is too low to buy as much insurance as is considered to be appropriate for good health services. For households in the lowest quintile of the income distribution commercial health insurance may demand more than a third of the household income. For example, the average HMO plan sponsored by an employer in the USA costs more than $150 per month for each employee and more than $450 for a family plan (Kuttner, 1999b). Poor health may even be a cause for low income. Subsidising the acquisition of health insurance is necessary, if it is accepted that the poor should have access to health services.

BOX 4.4 THE WHO ON HEALTH AND THE POOR

Since the poor are condemned to live in their bodies just as the rich are, they need protection against health risks fully as much. In contrast, where other assets such as housing are concerned, the need for such protection either does not arise, or arises only in proportion to income. (World Health Organisation, 2000, p. 4)

---

2. *Safeguarding the health of the population – public health.* Many states pursue policies to reduce the incidence of morbidity in connection with specific diseases. Fighting contagious diseases is a traditional aim of health policy, pursued over centuries. Today health authorities try to reduce the incidence of diseases which are considered to be responsible for many early deaths: the number of heart attacks, increasing early treatment of breast cancer, and so on. These are output oriented aims – the success of the policy is the increase of health. But there are also input oriented policies, namely safeguarding a good provision with health services. The numbers of doctors, of hospital beds, of nurses are widely accepted measures of quality of living standards. In the last years, input oriented policies have become less important in the industrialised countries. It has become clear that the health of the population does not always increase with an increasing number of doctors or hospital beds.

3. *Coverage for risks which cannot be insured.* Certain risks cannot be insured because it would be too expensive. This is mostly due to high probabilities and high costs of the events. For example: a long-term renal disease can lead to expulsion from private health insurance; diseases and health problems an individual is born with cannot always be insured; there are problems for HIV affected individuals. Such cases are always left for public support. In the USA individuals who are denied a private contract due to being high risk can find public insurance in about half the states (United States General Accounting Office, 1997).

> **BOX 4.5 CONDITIONS WHICH CAN RESULT IN DENYING OF COVERAGE FOR CHILDREN**
>
> Anorexia and Bulimia, Asthma, Autism, Cerebral Palsy, Cystic Fibrosis, Down's Syndrome, Epilepsy, Emotional Disorders, HIV Positive, Juvenile Diabetes, Leukemia, Muscular Dystrophy, Rheumatoid Athritis. (United States General Accounting Office, 1998, p. 10)

4. *Redistribution in favour of families.* The payment for health insurance is independent of the number of insured individuals. (The exceptions are Switzerland and the USA.) This amounts to a subsidisation of families and can be argued as any subsidy for families. (See Chapter 7 below on families.)

5. *Redistribution in favour of high-risk individuals.* Public insurance or public health services charge the same amount independently of the underlying risk. Market oriented insurance companies – whether they are non-profit or for-profit – distinguish to some extent between different risks by setting premiums, deductibles, covered events, and so on. Insurance contracts use different willingness-to-pay to equate marginal benefits and marginal costs.[23]

This is by many considered unjust. Women would have to pay higher premiums than men in private health insurance.[24] Whereas it is widely accepted that people with higher income enjoy higher utility, many consider it unacceptable that an individual with higher health risks has to pay a higher premium, particularly in the case of bad luck – for example, suffering from high blood pressure. This will become a major problem as soon as genetic screening allows better prognosis of different risks.

Even in the case of higher risks due to lifestyle, different rates are to many people objectionable.[25] Furthermore though jobs requiring the same qualification are usually better paid in the case of higher risks for health, blue-collar jobs have, on the average, more health risks than jobs which require higher qualifications. Once more, many consider it unjust that people with higher health risks due to their job and on average lower income have to pay more.

In countries with a health system combining social insurance aspects and competition between insurance companies the market is strongly regulated to inhibit the emergence of different contracts for different risks. As mentioned already Switzerland does not allow special premiums for groups, and forces the insurance companies with social health insurance to provide any contract it offers to any customer. Nobody can be excluded from a contract due to high risks. Some states in the USA also have laws to reduce cream-skimming by insurance companies (United States General Accounting Office, 1997).[26]

Transfers between different insurance companies to adjust for different risks, as in the Netherlands and in Germany, also reduce competitive pressure.

BOX 4.6 SPECIAL METHODS TO ACQUIRE ONLY GOOD RISKS

In Chapter 3 it was shown that supplying contracts with appropriate premiums and deductibles can be a way to reach out for the good risks. But sometimes insurance companies use other, less subtle methods:

... if health plans know that some omitted risk factors are relevant (e.g., AIDS, disability, prior utilization or hypochondria), but they cannot ex-ante identify the individuals with these characteristics, they may deter the high-risk consumers by selectively not contracting with physicians who have the best reputation for treating patients with such problems. Health plans also could contract with providers who have no interpreters, or whose facilities have no disabled access...

... if health plans can ex-ante identify predictably unprofitable individuals based on certain risk characteristics, they can focus their selection strategy directly on those identifiable individuals, e.g., by providing the high risk with poor quality of care or poor services (such as delayed payments of reimbursements and delayed answers to letters); by not working to coordinate the multiple visits that people with many problems may need; by selective advertising and direct mailing; by contracting with providers who practice in 'healthy districts' . (Van der Ven and Ellis, 2000, p. 774)

---

6. *Special equality.* Health services should not differ according to ability to pay (*Keine Zwei-Klassen-Medizin*; 'health services for the poor are poor health services'). Medical services should be allocated on the basis of medical needs and not only on the basis of demand, because demand is affected by the distribution of wealth. This is a widely held normative value (compare Tobin, 1970; Walzer, 1983) and is the normative basis for most European style public health systems. Giving equality in the context of health services a special place is due to considering health a basis for all human activity (Wagstaff and van Doorslaer, 2000).

There would be no problem with this if there were no constraint on resources – somehow the assumption of the social policy approach to health care. But as this is obviously not the case, there must be some rationing.

4.3.3 A Digression on Rationing, Efficiency, Rights and Equity

Allocating goods and services according to needs is uncommon in market economies. In most cases goods are allocated according to willingness-to-pay. Everybody who is prepared to spend at least the supply price for a good will get it. An individual whose willingness-to-pay is lower than the equilibrium price must do without the good, but her plans are not frustrated. She is not rationed. She does not want to buy more, given prices, her preferences and her wealth. If goods are allocated according to need, people prefer to have more of them. It is not income and prices which restrict the acquisition of a good but the plan of the allocation office. If, for example, the government provides its citizens with flats free of charge, most people would like to have a bigger and a better flat, even if the government provides each household with precisely the same flat that the household would have chosen given its wealth and given prices.

BOX 4.7 INEQUALITY OF WEALTH AND ACCESS TO GOODS

Is different access to goods due to different wealth acceptable in the following cases?
- Different access to good wine.
- Different access to housing.
- Different access to education for children.
- Different access to medical services.

Many people would accept that a society is not particularly unjust if a rich person can buy a bottle of good wine which a poorer person cannot afford. It is also widely accepted that one can buy services of a specially gifted teacher for private tuition, as long as nobody is prohibited from attending good schools because of lack of wealth. Concerning housing a minimum standard is usually seen as being within the scope of public policy – for example, families with children must always have shelter. But it is generally not accepted that the services of a specially able surgeon should be allocated to individuals only on the basis of ability to pay. It would be considered by many as 'inefficient' and unjust if the services of a very good surgeon are bought by rich people for routine operations, whereas poorer people have to turn to recently trained surgeons for complicated surgery.

Note: The word 'inefficient' was set under semiquotes as it is not to be understood in the sense of Pareto-efficiency.

Be that as it may, any administration of health services must ration consumption if they are allocated to the households according to needs. This is true not only for social policy oriented health systems but for market oriented insurance systems as well. It must be decided who will get which services and how many services should be provided altogether. The insurers in the USA ration their customers in most contracts, the NHS system in the UK does it, the Austrian and German Social Security insurance systems do it, though perhaps in a less transparent way.

The way that rationing is carried out differs between different systems. Insurers, whether private or public, limit the choice of doctors and/or the treatments the doctors can prescribe. The rules according to which the rationing is done are part of the contract the insured person accepts when signing the contract or laid down in the rules of the public health systems. In Austria the number of doctors with a contract with the *Krankenkasse* is limited and some treatments are restricted in volume. Some prescriptions need prior confirmation from the *Krankenkasse*. In Germany the prescription of drugs is restricted. In the UK patients cannot turn directly to a consultant before they have seen their general practitioner. Often they have to wait a long time for operations and sometimes it takes weeks to get appointments for an examination.

BOX 4.8 RATIONING BY PRIVATE INSURANCE

From an advertisement of Blue Cross/Blue Shield of Alabama:
Preventive Care Benefits:
Well Child Care
Inpatient newborn well baby care
Nine exams during the first two years of the baby's life*
Annual exam ages 2 through six
* Six visits the first year and three visits the second year are generally recommended guidelines
Lab/Diagnostic Screening*
Pap Smear for females – one annually age 18 and over
Mammography for females – one baseline ages 35–39; one annually age 40 and over
Prostate Specific Antigen for males – one annually age 40 and over
*One office visit per person per year associated with these services is also covered, subject to the office visit copayment.

Any rationing scheme needs principles on which it is operated, which implies that one needs a standard to decide what services to give and to whom. Two aims are usually mentioned and rank very highly: efficiency and equity. Note that allocations via competitive markets do not face these problems. A market allocation is efficient if there are no external effects. The reason is – to recapitulate the argument – that nobody will expend wealth for a service which she values less than the price. Problems of equity can be handled by a redistribution of the endowments.

Efficiency

Generally speaking, efficiency requires that the expected utility of a health service is at least as high as its expected costs. There are three different levels for discussing 'efficiency' in providing health services (Hurley, 2000): (i) efficiency in the production of health services – the technical aspect; (ii) efficiency in the use of health services – which services should be consumed in order to achieve a given level of health; (iii) efficiency in choosing the health level – weighing the utility from a marginal increase in health against the utility of a marginal increase of consumption of other goods.

In a pure market setting these distinctions do not raise any problem. If an individual buys a good, she has decided that it was worthwhile, whatever the utility was. We can further assume that she has bought the good at the cheapest supplier, that is, the supplier who has produced most efficiently in the technical sense. We do not need an absolute metric of utility, in particular there is no need to compare utilities between different people. But in the case of the allocation of health services by public authorities such a metric is necessary.

There are two options: (a) the utility of health; (b) the utility of health services. The first one is more in line with the choice theoretic approach, the second corresponds to the social policy one. No planning office can base its decision to allocate resources between different people on the utility of health, as it would necessitate comparison of the utility of a specific health status for an individual with the utility of the same health status for somebody else. In fact, the utility of health services serves as basis for planning in most instances (Torrance, 1986).

An often used metric is that of Quality-Adjusted-Life-Years (QALYs) (Broome, 1993; Dolan, 2000). This measure assumes that a person values a year of life in good health differently from a year with somehow restricted health. In order to make such judgements one has to attach a value to the health status on a cardinal scale – usually a number between 1 (full health) and 0 (death). The difference between the value of a year always in full health and the value of actual health for each year is the measure of the loss of quality through diminished health. Minimising the number of QALYs lost can be an objective for a health system.

Be that as it may, there are two questions which need to be kept separate: First, which services should be provided out of a given budget? Is it better to give Mr A the service X or Ms B with a different health problem service Y? – efficiency in the sense of (ii). Second, how big should the budget be? – efficiency in the sense of (iii). Whereas the first question cares for competing claims within a given set of resources, the second question also looks at possibilities of substitution between health services and the consumption of other goods.

If there were a pure market system of health insurers, one could rely on the market for answering the second question; insurance companies can offer contracts which are differently generous and therefore differently costly. People decide about the generosity of the health system by choosing their preferred contract. But in any system with public regulation one has to decide explicitly how much to spend for health services. It is impossible to avoid weighing the utility of more health services against the utility of more consumption of other goods.

For the second question, how to allocate services out of a given budget, one has to decide about utilities of treatments for different diseases and for different individuals. This is usually done on a medical basis: how much does a specific treatment contribute to the health of an individual? It is not asked how she values the improvement of her health. In case health can be restored completely the value of the services is the health itself, not the utility of health. If, as in many instances, the scope of a health service is the prolongation of life, the reduction of pain, the stopping of the progress of a disease, the improvement of health conditions, and so on, the value of the service is the medical effect not the utility of the medical effect – the reduced pain, and not the utility of the reduced pain.

Rights and equity

To care only for efficiency, for example, the maximisation of QALYs out of given resources, is a problematic objective for health policy. It amounts to a specific normative position, namely to judge every activity by its effect on aggregate welfare. Some of its consequences may contradict other value judgements, namely that of people's rights and that of equity (Anand and Wailoo, 2000). For example, giving an artificial hip to a 75-year-old individual provides far less QALYs than to a 50-year-old individual. The same applies when you compare the QALYs provided by an artificial hip to an HIV positive individual with the QALYs for an otherwise healthy person. Should the public health system accept age and general health as criteria when making a decision concerning the provision of an artificial hip?

Some people think that the health system should not discriminate between individuals based on future life expectancy when deciding how to ration health services. They consider it a question of a right of an individual to get treatment independently of the amounts of QALYs thereby generated. For example, everybody has the right that her life is preserved and that pain is reduced if it is technically possible.

If such rights are accepted, equity is a reasonable starting point for asking which services should be given. What does equity mean in the context of health services? Equality of outcome would mean equality of health and is not a sensible aim. If strictly applied, it would demand a reduction in the health of well individuals, if the health of sick people cannot be restored.[27] Equality of expenditure is also not a sensible rule, as healthy and sick people would get the same amount.[28] It is necessary to take needs into account. Equal utility of treatment for all is not sensible as well as the utility of a healthy person cannot be increased through health services. Equality of marginal utility of services for each individual is rather a condition of efficiency, not of equity (Culyer and Wagstaff, 1993). Furthermore, there is a danger with that concept: it would perhaps imply that a society has to spend too many of its resources for the prolongation of life, as the difference in utility between living and not living is by most people considered very big ('Rule of Rescue').

I suggest a different concept of equity: we should not compare how many resources are actually given to people with different health problems or what the effect on their health was, but whether an individual can expect any health problem to be treated equally, that is, independently of any non-health related characteristic. If within a given population the probabilities of two diseases are equally distributed, it is not a violation of equity if the health system does not care for both diseases in the same way, even if the loss of welfare is the same for both diseases. This is a case of inefficiency, not inequity. But a health system which, for example, is generous with problems of prostate cancer but less generous with problems of breast cancer does not respect equity. It discriminates against women. Or, if co-payments have the effect that, on average, poor people do not use the same amount of health services as richer people even if they suffer the same health problem, a system with co-payments would violate equity (Nolan, 1993).

The advantage of this concept of equity is that it takes account of the way people pay for health services, namely via insurance systems. People choose between different health systems on an *ex-ante* basis. We should apply the same approach when valuing different public health systems.[29]

The most ambitious programme for valuing health services designed to enable allocation of resources for Medicaid in an efficient and fair way, was undertaken in the state of Oregon (Hadorn, 1991). The idea was to rank treatments according to cost-effectiveness by considering benefits and costs. Benefits were defined by QALYs saved. The assignment of QALYs to treatments was done through consultation with doctors and citizens (see also Daniels and Sabin, 1997). The expected benefit of a treatment, a number between zero and one, was multiplied by the expected duration of the benefit; costs were then taken into account to give the treatment a ranking. The first list was criticised for not putting enough weight on they saving of life – the rule of rescue was not given the prominence it has for most people. For example, most transplants were stopped under Medicaid. In a second attempt to assign a value to different treatments, a priority list of treatments under different categories of effects was made without taking costs into account. Costs were only considered on a second level. Whereas in the first approach some high-benefit treatments were not put high on the list, because of high costs – even removal of an appendix did not rank very high – in the latter list high-benefit treatments always ranked high.[30]

BOX 4.9 RANKING OF TREATMENTS BY IMPORTANCE ACCORDING TO THE OREGON HEALTH SERVICES COMMISSION SERVICE CATEGORY DEFINITIONS

1. Treatment of acute life-threatening conditions where treatment prevents imminent death with a full recovery and return to previous health state. Exam.: Appendectomy for appendicitis, repair of deep, open wound of neck.
2. Maternity care, including disorders of newborn.
   Exam.: Obstetrical care for pregnancy, med. therapy for low birth-weight babies.
3. Treatment of acute life-threatening conditions where treatment prevents imminent death without a full recovery or return to previous health state. Exam.: Surgical treatment for head injury with prolonged loss of consciousness.
4. Prevention care for children (includes well-child care).
   Exam.: Immunizations, screening for vision or hearing problems.
5. Treatment of a fatal, chronic condition where, with treatment, one would have improvement in life span and QWB. Exam.: Medical therapy for type I diabetes mellitus, medical therapy for asthma.
6. Reproductive services (excluding maternity and infertility).
   Exam.: Contraceptive management, vasectomy, tubal ligation.
7. Comfort care.
8. Preventive dental care. Exam.: Cleaning and fluoride.
9. Preventive (A, B, C) for adults. Exam.: Mammograms, blood pressure.
10. Treatment of acute, nonfatal non-self-limited conditions with return to previous health state. Exam.: Medical therapy for acute thyroiditis, medical therapy for vaginitis.

Social Health Policy

11	One-time treatment of nonfatal, chronic conditions with improvement in QWB. Exam.: Hip replacement, laser surgery for diabetic retinopathy.
12	Treatment of acute, nonfatal conditions where treatment will improve QWB without return to prior health state. Exam.: Relocation of dislocated elbow.
13	Repetitive treatment of nonfatal, chronic (with recurrent or continuous symptoms) conditions with improvement in QWB with short-term benefit. Exam.: Medical therapy for chronic sinusitis, medical therapy for migraine headache.
14	Treatment of acute, and nonfatal, self-limited condition where treatment will expedite return to prior health state. Exam.: Medical therapy for diaper rash, medical therapy for acute conjunctivitis.
15	Infertility services. Exam.: Medical therapy for anovulation, microsurgery for tubal disease.
16	Preventive (D) for adults Exam.: Dipstick urinalysis for ematuria in adults who are younger than 60 years.
17	Treatment of fatal or nonfatal conditions with minimal or no improvement in QWB or life span. Exam.: Medical therapy for gallstones without cholecystitis.

Note: QWB refers to quality of well-being, the Commission's term for quality of life; derived from the QWB Index of Robert Kaplan and colleagues.

Source: Haddorn (1991).

An evaluation of the concept of equity in the provision of health services was undertaken by van Doorslaer et al. (2000). They compared two streams of services for different income groups. The first stream comprised the actual services consumed, the second stream referred to the services that should have been consumed if need were taken into consideration. The need for a service was defined as the average consumption of services given the health problem, independent of income. The result was that people with low incomes consume a higher percentage of all resources: however, when taking need into account, the system is equitable, because low income individuals have higher need for services.[31]

4.4 ALLOCATIVE EFFECTS

4.4.1 Health Insurance and the Efficiency Problem

A social policy oriented health system has allocative effects. It affects the use of resources in an economy. The question is whether social policy results in more efficiency or less. As in the absence of a social health system most people would insure privately against health risks, we have to separate the effects of an insurance system from that of social health provision.

The effect of health insurance is that people demand more services than they do without insurance. This is the basic idea of having insurance: wealth is shifted into the bad states. Furthermore, in many instances people would simply be unable to pay for expensive services – they do not have the means to pay for them nor can they get a loan to do it. Remember that in each year expenditure for health services is concentrated in a small segment of the population. Insurance safeguards the access to expensive services (Nyman, 1999). Third, as mentioned above, it is sort of an all-you-can-eat buffet.

The speciality of health insurance is that it does not merely protect one's current wealth, as in the case of fire insurance, rather one pays with the insurance for specified services contingent on future need. It would therefore not be sensible to claim that giving services instead of money in social health plans results in a loss of welfare, merely because people get more services with insurance than without. This is not inefficient *per se*.

Without any social provision the demand for health services is sure to be lower: poor people would be unable to buy insurance, as it is the case in the USA, and even many of the non-poor would have less insurance than under social health plans. Social health provisions increase resources used for health services compared to a situation without them. But this is not 'inefficient' if one considers that poor people have a right to treatment.[32]

In order to pursue the question of whether an insurance – be it organised in a purely profit oriented way or with social provisions – leads to an inefficient use of resources, one must ask whether the social marginal utility of a medical service is smaller than its marginal cost. This can happen because the expenses for medical services are not paid by the patient if there is insurance. Too many resources may be used. However the costs of a service are not only money expenses. Most services take time to consume them,[33] and many are painful and even can increase health risks (for example, X-ray screening). These costs are a burden to the patient. Most people take these costs into consideration when demanding a service.

A further problem is that the utility of a service often cannot be checked by its consumer – the patient. It is the physician who tells the patient which health services are necessary. In many instances he is the provider of the health service as well. This can contribute to an inefficient use of resources. Much depends on the way in which the providers of services are paid. We distinguish between the following payment systems:

- The provider is paid for each service separately: fee-for-service.

- The provider is paid a fixed amount for a patient – a capitation rate – or for the treatment of a disease: Prospective Payment Rate, Diagnosis Related Group Rate.

BOX 4.10 ARE CO-PAYMENTS AND DEDUCTIBLES A MEANS TO REDUCE COSTS?

To decrease costs most health systems ask for some out-of-pocket payments. Does this work? If payments are high enough, people are deterred from the use of some health services. That might have unacceptable consequences. One has to control for health effects.

In a famous study carried out between 1974 and 1977 – the so called Health Insurance Experiment of the Rand Study – the effects of different payment systems on the demand for health services and the medical results were studied. A random sample with more than 5000 individuals were assigned randomly to one of 14 health plans with different co-payments and stop-loss for out-of-pocket payments. (Participation was of course voluntary.)

The study shows that the demand for services declines with the price of the service – the out-of-pocket payment. Interestingly there was not much difference between rich and poor households. Outpatient care was more responsive than inpatient care, emergency room treatment was responsive as well.

The effects on health status was measured by self-report and by examination. There were no significant medical effects of the differences in the plans for adults. A sizeable negative effect for poor adults with poor health at the beginning of the experiment was statistically insignificant. Poor people suffering from diastolic blood pressure fared better in the plan without out-of-pocket payments.

The conclusion of the study was that out-of-pocket payments are a means to increase efficiency. But one has to be careful – three years may be too short a period for all effects to materialise. (See Zweifel and Manning, 2000.)

In the first case the provider has an incentive to provide more services than optimal, as this increases her income (supplier-induced-demand, SID; Labelle et al., 1994). In the second case the provider has an incentive to provide less services than optimal, because she can thereby increase her utility. Such problems are pursued in the economic literature under the heading 'principle-agent' problems (PA problems, see Box 4.11).

Public and private systems set limits by delineating which services are covered and which are not covered. They also restrict the choice of physicians to which patients might turn – managed care. A special institutional set-up of managed care are Health Maintenance Organisations (HMOs) which integrate health insurance and health service provider. The patient is registered with a physician as a gatekeeper who cares for the health of the patients. In the classic variant the physician is paid a capitation fee for each patient and has in turn to buy all services. Unlike pure insurers, HMOs encourage prevention. HMOs have became very important in the USA (Glied, 1999). More than half of Medicaid insured individuals accepted some form of managed care in the late 1990s (Gruber, 2000a). In Switzerland insurance companies offering social health insurance must also offer HMO contracts. The United Kingdom's NHS system has similar structures.

The average cost in an HMO plan is lower than in a traditional fee-for-service plan (indemnity plan), the difference is nearly $1000 per year in the USA (Altman et al., 1998). In Switzerland the price of social insurance contracts are reduced by 25 per cent if the insured person agrees to an HMO contract. It is open to what extent this is due to increased efficiency and to what extent this is due to adverse selection (Newhouse, 1996). According to Altman et al. (1998), clients who switched from indemnity plans to HMO plans are primarily low-risk individuals. To a smaller extent high-risk individuals moved from HMO systems into fee-for-service plans. The authors conclude that there is some cream-skimming by the HMOs. Cutler and Reber (1998) got similar results in a study of a reform of health insurance provided by Harvard University: people with lower expected health costs switched into managed care plans, whereas high-risks remained in the fee-for-service plans.

Today hospital services are often paid by Diagnosis Related Group Rates. For example, a hospital gets a certain amount for each removal of an appendix. If it manages to contain the costs below this fee it makes a profit, otherwise it loses. There is some research into the question of whether managed care leads to a lower quality of services, as providers have an incentive to provide less services. In a comparison of capitated and fee-for-service payments for pregnant women it was found that there was no difference in adequacy of prenatal care, of the likelihood of a caesarean or of an adverse outcome (Oleske et al., 1998; Levison and Ullman, 1998 for Medicaid patients). In another study which separated the effects of reducing the average payment for hospital treatment of a disease from the change to DRG payments the author concluded that in-hospital mortality was increased by cost reduction, but the one-year mortality was not higher. There is also a trend of higher readmission due to the switch of the payment system (Cutler, 1995). Be that as it may, it is clear that such a system needs complementary rules that control for quality in the interest of the patients – a patient's charter, an external controller.

BOX 4.11 THE PRINCIPAL–AGENT PROBLEM

There are two economic actors – the principal and the agent; the utility function or income of at least one actor depends on the action taken by the other one. There is a chance factor which affects the outcome. PA problems comprise the relationships between management and employees, between owners and managers, between the firm and its suppliers, between patients and doctors, and so on.

One actor, called the principal, has a contract with another actor, called the agent. Each one's utility function is assumed to have income or wealth and effort (whatever that is) as arguments. Each one acts independently from the other and maximises her own utility. The outcome and therefore the welfare of the principal depends on the activity of the agent and on the chance factor; for example, the profit of a firm depends on the effort of its workers and on the demand for its products. For the individual firm the demand is a stochastic variable.

Controlling the agent creates costs. It is not possible for the principal to control the activities of the agent perfectly (asymmetric information). The agent has information the principal does not have – for example, how much effort she has provided. The agent has incentives to behave opportunistically, to shirk, to use too many resources, to make too many checks and tests.

It is not possible to avoid these problems by a special payment function. This is due to the fact (i) that the outcome depends not only on the effort of the agent but on chance as well, and (ii) that the agent is risk-averse (or more risk-averse than the principal). For example, the success of a salesperson does not only depend on her effort and her ability, but also on the number of customers entering the shop. This cannot be influenced in the short run by the salesperson. If she is not prepared to accept the risks (that is perhaps the reason, why she became a salesperson and not a shop owner), the owner of the shop must take some of the risks by making the income of the employed salesperson at least partly independent from the income of the shop. In that case the salesperson has an incentive to shirk. In the context of medicine: the health of a patient not only depends on the doctor's knowledge and effort, but on a chance factor as well (and the effort of the patient). Therefore it is not possible to tie the income of the physician to the health of the patients – patients with low probability of a cure would not find a doctor to treat them.

Two types of problems are discussed in this set-up:

- *Positive questions.* How do institutional rules influence the outcome? For example, how many health services and which health services are provided if the providers are paid for each service? How will quality be affected if providers are paid a fixed fee per case.
- *Normative questions.* How should institutions be designed to achieve a good outcome? Under which circumstances is it advisable to pay simply according to attendance and minimum quality? And when is it preferable to pay according to outcome? How should doctors be paid to safeguard quality? Which system of payment should be used in order to inhibit inefficient use of resources (marginal utility smaller than marginal costs)?

For an introduction, see Sappington (1991).

4.4.2 The Increase of Costs

Health expenditures per capita increase with GDP per capita (see Table 4.6). That points to the problem of increasing costs, everywhere an important issue. What are the reasons? The arguments showing that there are incentives to use too many resources cannot explain the increase of costs.

Table 4.6 Annual growth rates of health expenditure per capita

	1960–70	1970–80	1980–90
Germany	10.6	4.5	1.5
Japan	14.0	7.1	3.7
UK	3.7	4.2	4.4
USA	6.0	4.2	4.4

Source: Poterba (1994).

These increases are due to (a) price increases, (b) political and social factors, (c) demographic changes and (d) technical progress.

a. Price increases and Baumol's disease

For quite some time the increase of costs of health services was seen as a special price increase – a specific inflation for medical services: prices of many services increased much faster than the general price level. But that does not imply that there is a higher inflation. The point is that the services change as well. If a good becomes more expensive, one has to distinguish between a rising price and rising quality (Nordhaus, 1998). When you buy a car for €20 000 and ten years later you buy a new car for €30 000 which needs only half as much petrol as the old car and all other characteristics are the same, you cannot say that the price of the car rose by 50 per cent. The new car is different. This applies to many medical treatments. They become more and more effective. In many cases the probability of surviving complicated surgery increased, in others completely new treatments were developed. Therefore rising costs are not necessarily caused by rising prices.[34] Furthermore, new health problems may have emerged. The increase in costs for all health systems due to AIDS cannot be seen as a pure price increase (Berndt et al., 2000).

There is one important factor which causes prices to increase in medical services, even if quality is kept constant. If incomes increase due to technical progress, labour-intensive production becomes more expensive than other productions. More capital-intensive technologies become profitable. If for technical reasons the possibility of substituting capital for labour is small, these goods become more expensive (Baumol's disease). For example, a string quartet needs four players. Any increase in income of the players in line with a general rise of incomes due to technical progress makes *ceteris paribus* a concert more expensive for the audience.[35]

In the production of health services the possibility of substituting capital for labour is very limited. A doctor cannot see more patients per hour in order to increase her productivity. Bringing food to patients in a hospital needs a certain amount of labour, self-service counters for patients are not viable.

There are other products which also demonstrate very narrow possibilities for substituting capital for labour. In most cases demand shifts away from goods and services produced labour intensively – for example, less demand for stately houses as they need many people to keep them running, less demand for string quartets in private homes. This possibility hardly exists in the health system, particularly in all aspects of caring. There is a need for these services. A society which substitutes CDs for string quartets in private homes, or self-service petrol stations for petrol stations with attendants does not become a bad society. But a society that forgoes some of the benefits of health services merely because increased income due to technical progress makes these services expensive is probably not considered a good society.

b. Political and social factors

In most countries more and more people get access to good health services independently of regional and social stratification. This is partly due to political and social factors, namely (i) bringing more people into the public health system, (ii) extending the services of the health systems to regions outside urban centres, and (iii) the fact that some cases of what was previously considered as deviant behaviour are now seen as health problems – learning disabilities, all kinds of addictions, and so on. Furthermore, turning to a doctor when it is advisable to do so has become more common. For instance, in rich countries there is hardly a woman who does not see a doctor at least a couple of times when pregnant. In Austria the health checks in connection with pregnancies increased in the mid-1970s when the government introduced payments for mothers which were given under the condition of undergoing some medical checks during pregnancy and of the new-borns. Currie and Gruber (1996) report that broadening eligibility for Medicaid coverage led to more early health checks of pregnant women. When the Supplemental Security Income (SSI) Programme was introduced in the USA, allowing parents to receive welfare payments where a child had special health problems, the detection and treatment of these problems increased (Kubik, 1999).

The difference in quality between the best services, available only to a few and the services for the majority, even for the poor and those living in remote areas, has decreased nearly everywhere.[36] This can be called a democratisation of the health system. It is in line with the aim of increasing equality.

Table 4.7   Total employment in health services (thousands)

	1960	1970	1980	1990
Austria		91	170	
France		438	727	1 451*
Germany	774	1 210	1 540	
Italy	173	313	850	1 000
Norway	44	69	150	188
Sweden	115	242	420	452
UK	595	764	1 200	1 331
USA	1 736	2 878	5 119	7 100

Note: * 1987.

Source: OECD (1993), vol. 1, p. 170.

The effect of that tendency can be seen in the increase of people employed in health industries (Table 4.7). As this process has come to an end in most countries, it is no longer a cause of increasing costs. The growth rate of employment in health services was very high in the 1960s and 1970s, but has decreased since. In many countries employment in health service industries declined in the 1990s (an exception was the UK).

Table 4.8 *Admission rates to inpatient care institutions (per cent of population)*

	1960	1970	1980	1990
Austria	14.1	15.5	19.5	25.2
France		7.4	19.3	23.3
Germany	13.3	15.4	18.8	20.9
Italy	9.4	15.7	18.1	15.3
Norway		13.2	15.6	16.7*
Sweden	13.4	16.6	18.3	19.5
UK	9.1	10.9	13.6	15.9*
USA	13.9	15.5	17.1	13.7

Note: * 1988.

Source: OECD (1993), vol. 1, p. 184.

That people make use of the existing facilities is shown in Table 4.8: admission rates increased in most countries. However the link between admission and health is not clear. Note the difference between the admission rates of the USA and Austria or France. Morbidity and mortality do not vary as strongly as the admission rates do.[37]

c. Demographic development

Health expenditures are not evenly distributed over an individual's lifespan. They are high for a newborn infant, then decline and finally rise again when people are old. For women they are high when giving birth. Therefore changes in demographic parameters can affect health expenditure. There are two different forces: (i) higher life expectancy, particularly at old age; (ii) changing demographic composition.

Life expectancy has increased in nearly all countries.[38] This alone does not explain increasing health expenditure, because life expectancy increased partly due to increased health. Being elderly does not imply being sick. In fact, disability among the aged is declining in many states (Jacobzone et al., 1999). A large proportion of the health expenditure a person needs arises in the last two years of life independent of age. If people die later, their health expenditures in connection with death arise later (Lubitz and Riley, 1993; Zweifel et al., 1996).[39] However it is doubtful that life expectancy has no influence on health costs – part of the increase of life expectancy is due to better treatments of diseases which would have killed people in earlier periods.

The demographic structure of most countries has changed not only because of increased life expectancy but also because of lower birth rates. There are fewer young people and more old people in a given population, more people with a high need for health services and fewer with a small need for them. This contributes to an increase of the share of health expenditure out of a given national income.

d. Technical progress

We can distinguish between two types of technical progress. Product-specific technical progress and production-specific technical progress. In the latter case a given product can be produced with less inputs, hence costs per unit must go down. In the former case a new product is developed – a new vaccination, a new treatment. Nothing can be said *a priori* about costs. A new vaccination may supplant a costly treatment and may decrease costs. A new treatment for a medical problem can be a supplement to other treatments. It may prolong life, or may result in more checks leading to an increase of costs.

Both types of technical progress can be found in medicine. Many treatments become cheaper due to production-specific technical progress (Baily and Garber, 1997). However, there is a special incentive in the health system to develop new products. Most insurance systems and public health systems cover the costs of treatments at the state-of-the-art level. Whatever is developed by new research and proves to be useful is demanded by patients (or their doctors). Research faces the uncertainty of technical success, but there is not much economic uncertainty if a new product is technically apt to contribute to better health, delayed death, less pain, and so on. There is always consent for the need for new and better treatments – against AIDS, for better control of side effects of chemotherapy. No other industry (perhaps with the exception of defence related industries) has a near guarantee that there is demand for all new products. This of course is a mighty stimulant for research into new products and contributes to the increase in costs.

Many countries have made organisational reforms to contain costs. The most important aspect was a switch from fee-for-service payments to capitation fees and similar payment systems. Such reforms can lower costs, but they cannot stop the forces which increase costs. For example, the length of stay in hospitals has decreased nearly everywhere, thereby reducing costs.[40] But there are limits to shortening inpatient treatments. In the mid-1990s, the USA was successful in containing costs, subsequently costs again started to rise.[41]

4.5 DISTRIBUTIVE EFFECTS

Social health systems have many distributive effects. There are all types of redistribution to be found in the public health systems: interpersonal redistribution – vertical, horizontal, and intergenerational – and intra-personal redistribution over the life-cycle. The basis for evaluating the interpersonal redistribution is a fair insurance. To evaluate the amount of redistribution it is necessary to make assumptions about the incidence of benefits and costs. Usually it is assumed that the benefits go to the insured and the costs are according to payments. Without a public health scheme the patients (and not, for example, their employers) would have to pay for health services directly or for private insurance. If the contributions are set according to wages then it is assumed that they are paid by the employed, whether they are deducted from the gross income of the employed or are a supplement to wages to be paid by employers. If health services are paid out of general taxes, as in the UK, one has to work with the incidence of the tax system.

We further have to assume that there is neither a deficit nor a surplus in the health system. It is sensible to base the analysis of distributional effects on the assumption that the health system is merely an insurance against the costs of health services and nothing else. It is not an insurance against low incomes or big families. Benefits are paid out according to needs. People with higher risks are favoured if they pay the same contribution.

Whether health expenditures vary systematically with social position is an open question. In general, people with low incomes have lower health status.[42] However people with poor health have lower life expectancy and may thus get less health services. Furthermore poor people may be deterred from making use of health services even if they are entitled to use them. This tendency is strengthened if poverty is regionally concentrated. In that case access to good health services may be difficult for those living in poor areas (McClellan and Skinner, 1997). The use of health services depends also on education: those with higher education tend to make more use of available resources.

4.5.1 Vertical Redistribution

All systems with contributions dependent on income redistribute in favour of low income groups – vertical redistribution. The poor pay less. The Swiss system with contributions independent of income also redistributes in favour of low-income people as there exist subsidies for the contributions that the poor have to pay which are paid out of general taxes. In the USA the Medicaid programmes are paid for by general taxes and part of the Medicare programme is financed by contributions dependent on income. Probably public health systems are the most important instrument for vertical redistribution in many countries. In Germany vertical redistribution is limited, as individuals with high income can opt out of the public system.

Table 4.9 presents the results of a study of vertical redistribution of the German health system. It used actual data to calculate a fictitious contribution rate which would have been necessary to cover expenses. By deducting the statutory contribution rate the amount of redistribution was calculated. The data are from one year only, the redistribution is between current high income and current low income. Long-term effects, namely income over the whole life, are not considered. Though the data are from 1981 there has probably not been much change since then in the relative size of health costs. Only the absolute numbers for income and expenditure have changed. The relative size of numbers to each other has remained the same. One can see that the lower the income the higher the fictitious rate as percentage of income necessary to cover actual expenditures. The data also show that for households with low incomes it would be very difficult to buy insurance in a market based system. Without redistribution low-income households would end up with far less protection in case of need.

Table 4.9 *Fictitious rate of contribution to cover expenses as percentage of income (line one) and redistribution (line two) according to income and family status*

Monthly income (DM)	Men	Women	Couples	With one child	With two children
−1250	–	20.15	–	–	–
		15.51			
−2500	9.26	11.68	16.01		
	0.89	5.80	11.06	–	–
−3750	5.92	7.72	11.15	9.62	10.51
	−2.71	1.36	4.37	0.72	1.60
−5000	–	–	8.91	6.71	8.00
			2.69	−0.45	0.42
−6250			5.70	5.39	5.86
			1.09	−0.12	0.28

Source: Becker (1985).

4.5.2 Horizontal Redistribution

In social health systems people do not pay according to individual or group specific risks. People belonging to high-risk groups are favoured. There is also redistribution in favour of families, as contributions do not rise with the size of the family; and there is redistribution in favour of single earner families, because two earner families pay more (see Table 4.10). Even in Switzerland where contributions are per insured person, there are subsidies for families.[43]

Besides the support for families, social insurance systems do not distinguish between different risks. Therefore there is substantial redistribution from people with low risks to others with high risks. As mentioned, this is in line with normative positions on which public health systems are construed.

Table 4.10 Expected average health costs over the life-cycle, by marital status, earnings and family size (DM)

Single men	96.315
Single women	121.561
Single earner households	
– without children	200.384
– with one child	213.887
– with two children	227.390
– with three children	240.893
– with four children	254.396
Double earner households	
– without children	217.876
– with one child	233.574
– with two children	250.266
– with three children	266.958
– with four children	283.239

Source: Behrens (1991).

4.5.3 Redistribution over the Life-Cycle

Contributions and the consumption of health services are not connected in time. In most cases payments are related to incomes and vary therefore over time. Young people have low incomes and therefore pay less, the incomes of many employees and in the civil service increase with age. Pensioners often have lower incomes, and their rates may be different from those of the employed.

The use of health services increases with age. A public health system therefore shifts resources towards greater age like a pension scheme. The US Medicare system makes this explicit: one pays all through one's working life into the system and becomes eligible for the services after reaching the age of 65.

4.5.4 Redistribution between Cohorts

(The following paragraphs may not be fully comprehensible until after having read the chapter on pension systems.)

All public health systems work on a pay-as-you-go basis. Demographic changes will therefore result in redistribution between cohorts. If the share of people with low health costs declines due to the ageing of the population (increased life expectancy and decreased fertility), the current young (working) population has to pay more for the health services of the old than the old had to pay when they were young for those who were then old.

To calculate intergenerational redistribution one has to consider the following: given the costs of health services, total expenditure depends on the age-distribution of the population and the number of children born. Given the rate of contribution, the amount paid into the system depends on the number of people working and on the development of their income. The number of people working depends on the share of people of working age and their rate of participation in the labour market. To calculate redistribution one has therefore to estimate the future development of the population, their participation in the labour market and their incomes.

There is a calculation for Germany (before unification) (Behrens, 1991) in which the author used data about health expenditures dependent on family status. She calculated the change in the average contribution due to changing family structures by using data from the past. With data about mortality and age specific health expenditure she could estimate the development of the expenditures. With assumptions about demographic development and participation in the labour market, she got the following results: the average rate of contribution, which was in the late 1980s about 13 per cent, must rise until the year 2030 to about 17 per cent – that is by nearly 40 per cent. Calculating the redistributive effects under the assumption that the demographic structure will be constant by the year 2150, Behrens shows that the rate of contribution will finally settle at about 16 per cent. This increase is due only to demographic shifts, the increase of health expenditure due to technical progress and other reasons were not considered in this calculation.

Naturally such a calculation should not be seen as hard prognosis, as the results depend on many parameters – assumptions about fertility, labour market participation, retirement age, mortality, and so on. But they show what will happen if the development is as assumed – which is in one way or another the assumption that society will in the coming decades develop as it has in the past.

In a recent study Cutler and Sheiner (2000) calculated the rate of return of payments into the Medicare system by cohorts born between 1910 and 1980. For those born in 1910 the rate of return was 8.4 per cent, because they had hardly paid into the system. For those born after 1960 the rate of return will be below 2 per cent, if the law remains as it is now.

NOTES

1. Actually GDP per capita seems to be the best predictor for health expenditure per capita. See Gerdtham and Jönsson (2000).
2. Cutler and Richardson (1997, 1998) estimate the increase in overall welfare in monetary units due to increased health, Murphy and Topel (1999) the increase of welfare due to medical research.
3. It is not clear that smoking increases health costs. A study (Barendregt et al., 1997) came to the following conclusion: 'If people stopped smoking, there would be a savings in health care costs, but only in the short term. Eventually, smoking cessation would lead to increased health care costs.' The reason is that giving up smoking reduces mortality and therefore increases morbidity from non-smoking related diseases.
4. On a theoretical level the problem is the following: can one really use the concept of expected utility for the analysis of demand for health services and health insurance? It is not quite clear what risk-aversion means in the context of health. One would need a cardinal utility function to add utilities at different states of health. Furthermore preferences may depend on the health status. A person may have different preferences when healthy compared to a state with a serious disease or when handicapped. These preferences may not be known to the person as long as she is healthy. The world may start to look very different to you when you realise that your life expectancy is drastically reduced or that you are severally impaired.
5. Whether differences between wages compensate fully for different risks is still an open question (Viscusi, 1993).
6. In a study of productivity of health systems, it was shown that regular screening for breast cancer of women below forty had negligible health effects but was very costly (Baily and Garber, 1997).
7. The WHO definition contains another problem. If 'well-being' means welfare in a general sense, we must see health as one determinant of well-being amongst others. To put it into different words: the WHO definition of health conflates the health and the welfare that health can provide (Hurley, 2000).
8. Interestingly, choice itself is not considered important in traditional economic theory. Preferences individuals have are defined only over allocations – that is, outcomes of choices. Two identical allocations, one being the outcome of a market system, the other one the result of a dictatorial fiat by a central authority cannot be distinguished on welfare aspects. In traditional theory choice is only regarded as something good insofar as the central authority hardly knows people's preferences.
9. A capitation fee is a fixed payment per patient to the doctor, independent of the amount of services the doctor provides.

10. Higher productivity is often confounded with reduced costs. If people prefer to have more check-ups, it is not a waste of resources to provide them. Baily and Garber are very careful in this respect.
11. The number of independent insurance organisations has declined and will be reduced further.
12. In Austria a non-working woman has to pay for health insurance if she has not given birth before.
13. It is nevertheless in the interest of the employed to have such an insurance. In case of an accident it can be very difficult to make a claim against an employer.
14. Only Hawaii mandates employers to provide health insurance (United States General Accounting Office, 1998).
15. In 1996 payments for health insurance were 7.1 per cent of total compensation for labour (Gruber, 2000b).
16. 'A recent Congressional Budget Office report cites a Hay-Huggins Company estimate relating administrative expenses to benefit costs for different size of employee groups. For group size 1 to 4, the ratio is 40%. For groups of 100 000 or more, the ratio is 5.5%' (Diamond, 1992, p. 1234).
17. This does not imply that there is a stable group – 16 per cent of the population – which is constantly without health insurance. People may switch from a job without health insurance to a job with health insurance, or they become eligible for Medicaid or Medicare. For the dynamics of non-insurance and Medicaid, see Short et al. (1998).
18. About a quarter of the uninsured are eligible for Medicaid. In case of need they would probably enlist (Cutler and Zeckhauser, 2000).
19. The report recommended to stop collecting fees.
20. Only in the Netherlands the social insurance distinguishes between the two aspects.
21. In 1991 the average deductible for a single individual was about $200 and for a family about $500 (Cutler and Zeckhauser, 2000). Recently the acceptance of high deductibles has increased (United States General Accounting Office, 1997).
22. That, of course, can only be a problem in systems where there is a choice between different contracts.
23. It is not possible to separate risks completely as this would imply huge differences in rates. 'In a competitive health plan market with unregulated premiums, the maximum premium for full health plan coverage (that is, without cost-sharing) could be expected to exceed the average premium for the same product by a factor of 10 or more, with a minimum premium of around 10 per cent of the average' (van de Ven and Ellis, 2000, p. 770). This applies to risks concerning one year. Health insurance is also an insurance against the risk of belonging to a high-risk group.
24. There is an interesting legal problem: the higher expenditure for women is partly due to giving birth. However men have a role in these events, at least up to now. Should women be compensated for that?
25. For a different view see LeGrand (1991).
26. Note that efficiency requires equating marginal costs and marginal benefits for the individual contract only if risks can be influenced. To the extent that risks are exogenous, tailoring insurance contracts to individual risks cannot bring about higher overall efficiency.
27. Culyer and Wagstaff (1993) favour equality of health, but include explicitly the clause that nobody's health should be reduced.
28. Note that the idea of school vouchers, namely giving to each young person the same amount of the right to attend a school without payment and then allowing trading of these rights implies that everybody is given the same amount out of public funds.
29. This concept has a further advantage, namely it can be applied to a discussion of whether expenditure for medical research is distributed in accordance with ideas of equity. The expected utility a health system provides depends also on the research strategy it supports. A sick person can hardly benefit from current research, as the results will only be known in future. However a healthy person may benefit from it, as the results can be of future use. When, for example, it was discovered that AIDS is a disease the occurrence of which is higher amongst homosexuals and drug abusers, it was argued that it is a question of justice

that resources should be devoted to research against AIDS. However no individual suffering from AIDS related diseases in 1995 got much help by research carried out in that year.
30. There were some complaints that this procedure discriminated against disabled persons as there was suspicion that the same therapy was valued lower for disabled individuals than for non-disabled ones (Hadorn, 1992).
31. Interestingly, poorer persons tend to make more use of the services of general practitioners but less of specialists and consultants.
32. The word 'inefficient' should not be understood in the Pareto-sense. Taking rights into consideration precludes the use of the concept of Pareto-efficiency.
33. If people can have check-ups and treatments during paid working time, the costs of time can be low.
34. If medical services are provided by public institutions measuring output directly is not possible (Berndt et al., 2000).
35. Productivity could be augmented by increasing the size of the concert halls.
36. Better infrastructure for transportation also contributed to better access to health services. Today a distance of 80 kilometres hardly needs much more than an hour. After an heart attack or a stroke this can be decisive, though very expensive for the health system.
37. Some of the differences may be due to different reporting strategies. DRG payment systems tend to produce more admissions and shorter stays: sometimes patients are discharged and readmitted with a different diagnosis.
38. Recently life expectancy decreased in some parts of Africa due to AIDS, and in Russia and other CIS countries due to the deterioration of the health system.
39. Felder et al. (2000) state that the 'cost of dying', that is, the health expenditure in a person's last months decreases with increasing age.
40. One must be careful when interpreting the data. In many countries the admission into hospitals has increased in the same period. This could be the result of admitting people with minor problems who tend to leave hospital earlier.
41. 'According to the most recent estimates by the Health Care Financing Administration, national health care expenditures have been growing at an average rate of 6.5 per cent annually from 1998 to 2001, as compared with a rate of 5 per cent from 1993 through 1996' (Blumenthal, 2001). The rate of inflation was stable during that period.
42. This is a statistical relation, it does not imply that low incomes cause poor health, nor does it imply that poor people cannot afford access to health services and are therefore more sick. There may be cases of low health causing low income as well, and there may be common causes for low income and low health – for example, little education. Furthermore inequality *per se* may effect health. See Deaton (1999).
43. In the chapter on family policy it will be discussed whether subsidisation of families cause horizontal redistribution or a redistribution over the life cycle (see below, Chapter 7.2).

REFERENCES

Altman, Daniel, David M. Cutler and Richard J. Zeckhauser (1998), 'Adverse Selection and Adverse Retention', *American Economic Review*, Papers and Proceedings, 88, pp. 122–26.

Anand, Paul and Allan Wailoo (2000), 'Utilities versus Rights to Publicly Provided Goods: Arguments and Evidence from Health Care Rationing', *Economica*, 67, pp. 543–78.

Anell, Anders and Patrick Svarvar (1999), 'Health Care Reforms and Cost Containment in Sweden', in: E. Mossalios and J. LeGrand (eds), *Health Care and Cost Containment in the European Union*, Aldershot: Ashgate, pp. 701–31.

Baily, Martin Neil and Alan M. Garber (1997), 'Health Care Productivity', *Brooking Papers on Economic Activity*, Microeconomics, pp. 143–215.

Barendregt, Jan J., Luc Bonneux and Paul J. van der Maas (1997), 'The Health Care Costs of Smoking', *New England Journal of Medicine*, 337, pp. 1052–7.

Becker, Irene (1985), 'Einkommensverteilung in der gesetzlichen Krankenversicherung', in: W. Schmähl (ed.), *Versicherungsprinzip und soziale Sicherung*, Tübingen: J.C.B.Mohr(Paul Siebeck), pp. 98–119.

Behrens, Cornelia S. (1991), *Intertemporale Verteilungswirkungen in der gesetzlichen Krankenversicherung der Bundesrepublik Deutschland*, Frankfurt am Main: Peter Lang.

Berk, M.L. and A.C. Monheit (1992), 'The concentration of health expenditures: an update', *Health Affairs*, 11, pp. 145–9.

Berndt, Ernst B., David M. Cutler, Richard G. Frank, Zvi Griliches, Joseph P. Newhouse and Jack E. Triplett (2000), 'Medical Care Prices and Output', in: A.J. Culyer and J.P. Newhouse (eds), *Handbook of Health Economics*, vol. 1, Amsterdam: Elsevier, pp. 119–76.

Besley, Timothy, John Hall and Ian Preston (1999), 'The Demand for Private Health Insurance: Do Waiting Lists Matter', *Journal of Public Economics*, 72, pp. 155–81.

Blumenthal, David (2001), 'Controlling Health Care Expenditure', *New England Journal of Medicine*, 344, pp. 766–9.

Borjas, George J. (1996), *Labor Economics*, New York: McGraw Hill.

Broome, John (1993), 'Qalys', *Journal of Public Economics*, 50, pp. 149–68.

Busse, Reinhard (2001), 'Risk structure compensation in Germany's statutory health insurance', *European Journal of Public Health*, 11, pp. 174–7.

Carrasquillo, Olveen, David U. Himmelstein, Steffie Woolhandler and David H. Bor (1999), 'A reappraisal of private employers' role in providing health insurance', *New England Journal of Medicine*, 340, pp. 109–14.

Cochrane, John H. (1995), 'Time-Consistent Health Insurance', *Journal of Political Economy*, 103, pp. 445–73.

Culyer A.J. and Adam Wagstaff (1993), 'Equity and equality in health and health care', *Journal of Health Economics*, 12, pp. 431–57.

Cunningham, Peter J. and Ha T. Tu (1997), 'A Changing Picture of Uncompensated Care', *Health Affairs*, 16(4), pp. 167–75.

Currie, Janet and Jonathan Gruber (1996), 'Saving Babies: The Efficacy and Cost of Recent Changes in the Medicaid Eligibility of Pregnant Women', *Journal of Political Economy*, 104, pp. 1263–96.

Cutler, David M. (1995), 'The Incidence of Adverse Medical Outcomes under Prospective Payments', *Econometrica*, 63, pp. 25–50.

Cutler, David M. and Sarah Reber (1998), 'Paying for Health Insurance: The Tradeoff between Competition and Adverse Selection', *Quarterly Journal of Economics*, 113, pp. 433–66.

Cutler, David M. and Elisabeth Richardson (1997), 'Measuring the Health of the U.S. Population', *Brooking Papers on Economic Activity*, Microeconomics, pp. 273–375.

Cutler, David M. and Elisabeth Richardson (1998), 'The Value of Health: 1970 – 1990', *American Economic Review*, Papers and Proceedings, 88, pp. 97–100.

Cutler, David M. and Louise Sheiner (2000), 'Generational Aspects of Medicare' *American Economic Review*, Papers and Proceedings, 90, pp. 303–7.

Cutler, David M. and Richard J. Zeckhauser (2000), 'The Anatomy of Health Insurance', in: David M. Cutler and Richard J. Zeckhauser (eds), *Handbook of Health Economics*, vol. 1, Amsterdam: Elsevier, pp. 563–642.

Daniels, Norman and James Sabin (1997), 'Limits to Health Care: Fair Procedures, Democratic Deliberation, and the Legitimacy Problem for Insurers', *Philosophy and Public Affairs*, 26, pp. 303–50.
Deaton, Angus (1999), 'Inequalities in income and inequalities in health', Princeton University, mimeo.
Diamond, Peter (1992), 'Organizing the Health Insurance Market', *Econometrica*, 60, pp. 1233–54.
Dolan, Paul (2000), 'The Measurement of Health-Related Quality of Life for Use in Resource Allocation Decision in Health Care', in: A.J. Culyer and J.P. Newhouse (eds), *Handbook of Health Economics*, vol. 2, Amsterdam: Elsevier, pp. 1723–60.
Fattore, Giovanni (1999), 'Cost Containment and Reforms in the Italian National Health Service', in: E. Mossalios, and J. LeGrand (eds), *Health Care and Cost Containment in the European Union*, Aldershot: Ashgate, pp. 513–46.
Felder Stefan, Markus Meier and Horst Schmitt (2000), 'Health care expenditure in the last months of life', *Journal of Health Economics*, 19, pp. 679–95.
Glied, Sherry (1999), *Managed Care*, Cambridge (Mass.), NBER Working Paper 7205.
Gerdtham, Ulf-G. and Bengt Jönsson (2000), 'International Comparisons of Health Expenditure: Theory Data and Econometric Analysis', in: A.J. Culyer and J.P. Newhouse (eds), *Handbook of Health Economics*, vol. 1, Amsterdam: Elsevier, pp. 11–53.
Gordon, M. (1988), *Social Security Policies in Industrial Countries*, Cambridge: Cambridge University Press.
Grossman, Michael (1972), 'On the Concept of Health Capital and the Demand for Health', *Journal of Political Economy*, 80, pp. 761–82.
Grossman, Michael (2000), 'The Human Capital Model', in: A.J. Culyer and J.P. Newhouse (eds), *Handbook of Health Economics*, vol. 1, Amsterdam: Elsevier, pp. 347–407.
Gruber, Jonathan (2000a), *MEDICAID*, Cambridge (Mass.), NBER Working Paper, 7829.
Gruber, Jonathan (2000b), 'Health Insurance and the Labor Market' in: A.J. Culyer and J.P. Newhouse (eds), *Handbook of Health Economics*, vol. 1, Amsterdam: Elsevier, pp. 645–702.
Hadorn, David C. (1991), 'Setting Health Care Priorities in Oregon. Cost-effectiveness Meets the Rule of Rescue', *Journal of the American Medical Association*, 265, pp. 2218–25.
Hadorn, David C. (1992), 'The Problem of Discrimination in Health Care Priority Setting', *Journal of the American Medical Association*, 269, pp. 1454–9.
Hurley, Jeremiah (2000), 'An Overview of the Normative Economics of the Health Sector' in: A.J. Culyer and J.P. Newhouse (eds), *Handbook of Health Economics*, vol. 1, Amsterdam: Elsevier, pp. 54–112.
Iglehart, John K. (1999), 'The American Health Care System – Medicaid', *New England Journal of Medicine*, 340, pp. 403–8.
Jacobzone S., E. Camboirs, E. Chaplain and J.M. Robine (1999), *The Health of Older Persons in OECD Countries: Is it improving fast enough to compensate for population ageing?*, Paris, OECD Labour Market and Social Policy Occasional Papers No. 37.
Johnson, Reed F., Erin E. Fries and Spencer H. Banzhaf (1997), 'Valuing morbidity: An integration of the willingness-to-pay and health-status index literatures', *Journal of Health Economics*, 16, pp. 641–65.

Kieke, G.H. Okma and Jan D. Poelert (2001), 'Implementing prospective budgeting for Dutch sickness funds', *European Journal of Public Health*, 11, pp. 178–81.

Kubik; Jeffrey D. (1999), 'Incentives for the identification and treatment of children with disabilities: the supplemental security programme', *Journal of Public Finance*, 73, pp. 187–215.

Kuttner, Robert (1999a), 'The American Health Care System – Health Insurance Coverage', *New England Journal of Medicine*, 340, pp. 163–8.

Kuttner, Robert (1999b), 'The American Health Care System – Employer-Sponsored Health Coverage', *New England Journal of Medicine*, 340, pp. 248–52.

Labelle, Roberta, Greg Stoddard and Thomas Rice (1994), 'A re-examination of the meaning and importance of supplier-induced demand', *Journal of Health Economics*, 13, pp. 347–68.

LeGrand, Julian (1991), *Equity and Choice*, London: HarperCollins.

Levison, Arik and Frank Ullman (1998), 'Medicaid managed care and infant health', *Journal of Health Economics*, 17, pp. 351–68.

Lubitz, James D. and Gerald F. Riley (1993), 'Trends in Medicare Payments in the Last Year of Life', *New England Journal of Medicine*, 328, pp. 1092–96.

McClellan, Mark and Jonathan Skinner (1997), *The Incidence of Medicare*, Cambridge (Mass.), NBER Working Paper, 6013.

Mann, Joyce M., Glenn A. Melnick, Anil Bamezai and Jack Zwanziger (1997), 'A Profile of Uncompensated Hospital Care, 1983–1995', *Health Affairs*, 16 (4), pp. 223–32.

Matsaganis, Manos and Howard Glennester (1994), 'The threat of 'cream skimming' in the post-reform NHS', *Journal of Health Economics*, 13, pp. 31–60.

Monheit, Alan C. and Philip F. Cooper (1994), 'Health Insurance and Job Mobility: Theory and Evidence', *Industrial and Labor Relations Review*, 48, pp. 68–85.

Murphy, Kevin M. and Robert H. Topel (1999), 'The Economic Value of Medical Research', University of Chicago, mimeo.

Newhouse, Joseph P. (1996), 'Reimbursing Health Plans and Health Providers: Efficiency in Production vs. Selection', *Journal of Economic Literature*, 34, pp. 1236–63.

Nolan, Brian (1993), 'Economic incentives, health status and health services utilisation', *Journal of Health Economics*, 12, pp. 151–69.

Nordhaus, William (1998), 'Quality Change in Price Indexes', *Journal of Economic Perspectives*, 12, pp. 59–68.

Nyman, John A. (1999), 'The value of health insurance: the access motive', *Journal of Health Economics*, 18, pp. 141–52.

OECD (1993), *Health Systems. Facts and Trends, 1960–1991*, Health Policy Studies 3, Paris.

Oleske, Denise M., Marta L. Branca, Julie B. Schmidt, Richard Ferguson and Edward S. Linn (1998), 'A Comparison of Capitated and Fee-for-Service Medicaid Reimbursement Methods on Pregnancy Outcomes', *Health Services Research*, 33, pp. 57–73.

Oregon Department of Administrative Services (ODAS) (1999), *Assessment of the Oregon Health Plan Medicaid Demonstration*, www.ohppr.state.or.us.

Poterba, James M. (1994), 'A Sceptic's View of Global Budget Caps', *Journal of Economic Perspectives*, 8, pp. 67–73.

Office of Strategic Planning (1999), *Proposed Method of Incorporating Health Status Risk Adjusters into Medicare + Choice Payments*, Report to the Congress, Health Care Financing Administration.

Sappington, David E.M. (1991), 'Incentives in Principal-Agent Relationships', *Journal of Economic Perspectives*, 5(2) pp. 45–66.
Schulz, Erika, Mathias Kifmann and Friedrich Breyer (2001), *Risikostrukturausgleich am Scheideweg – Senkung der Wirtschaftlichkeitsanreize für die Krankenkassen sollte vermieden werden*, DIW-Wochenbericht 14/01.
Scott, Frank A., Mark C. Berger and John E. Garen (1995), 'Do Health Insurance and Pension Costs Reduce the Job Opportunities of Older Workers?', *Industrial and Labor Relations Review*, 48, pp. 774–91.
Short, Pamela, Farley Freedman and A. Vicki (1998), 'Single Women and the Dynamics of Medicaid', *Health Service Research*, 33, pp. 1309–36.
Tobin, James (1970), 'On limiting the domain of inequality', *Journal of Law and Economics*, 13, pp. 263–77.
Torrance, George W. (1986), 'Measurement of the Health State Utilities for Economic Appraisals', *Journal of Health Economics*, 5, pp. 1–30.
United States General Accounting Office (1997), *Private Health Insurance. Millions Relying on Individual Market Face Cost and Coverage Trade-Off*, Washington D.C., HEHS-97-8.
United States General Accounting Office (1998), *Health Insurance for Children*, Washington D.C., HEHS-98-201
van de Ven, Wynarnd P.M.M., René C.J.A. van Vliet, Eric M. van Barneveld and Leida M. Lamers (1994), 'Risk-Adjusted Capitation: Recent Experiences in the Netherlands', *Health Affairs*, 13, pp. 120–36.
van de Ven, Wynarnd P.M.M., René C.J.A. van Vliet, Eric M. van Barneveld and Leida M. Lamers (1996), 'Risikoausgleich in einem wettbewerblich strukturierten Krankenversicherungsmarkt: Reichen Alter und Geschlecht aus?', in: Peter Oberender (ed.), *Alter und Gesundheit*, Baden-Baden: Nomos, pp. 175–95.
van de Ven, Wynand P.M.M. and Randall P. Ellis (2000), 'Risk Adjustment in Competitive Health Plans', in: A.J. Culyer and J.P. Newhouse (eds), *Handbook of Health Economics*, vol. 2, Amsterdam: Elsevier, pp. 756–835.
van Doorslaer, Eddy, Adam Wagstaff, Hattem van der Burg, Terkel Christiansen, Guido Citoni, Rita di Base, Ulf-G. Gerdtham, Mike Gerfin, Lorna Gross, Unto Häkkinen, Jürgen John, Paul Johnson, Jan Klavus, Claire Lachaud, Jørgen Lauritsen, Robert E. Leu, Brian Nolan, Joãa Pereira, Carol Propper, Frank Puffer, Lise Rochaix Martin Schellhorn, Gun Sundberg, Olaf Winkelhake (1999), 'The redistributive effect of health care finance in twelve OECD countries', *Journal of Health Economics*, 18, pp. 291–313.
van Doorslaer Eddy, Adam Wagstaff, Hattem van der Burg, Terkel Christiansen, Diana De Graeve, Inge Duchesne, Ulf-G. Gerdtham, Micheal Gerfin, José Geurts, Lorna Gross, Unto Häkkinen, Jürgen John, Jan Klavus, Robert E. Leu, Brian Nolan, Owen O'Donnel, Carol Propper, Frank Puffer, Martin Schellhorn, Gun Sundberg, Olaf Winkelhake (2000), 'Equity in the delivery of health care in Europe and the US.' *Journal of Health Economics*, 19, pp. 553–83.
Viscusi, Kip (1992), *Fatal Tradeoffs. Public and Private Responsibilities for Risk*, Oxford: Oxford University Press.
Viscusi, Kip (1993), 'The Value of Risks to Life and Health', *Journal of Economic Literature*, 31, pp. 1912–46.
Wagstaff, Adam, Eddy van Doorslaer, Hattem van der Burg, Samuel Calonge, Terkel Christiansen, Guido Citoni, Ulf-G. Gerdtham, Micheal Gerfin, Lorna Gross, Unto Häkkinen, Paul Johnson, Jürgen John, Jan Klavus, Claire Lachaud, Jørgen Lauritsen, Rober Leu, Brian Nolan, Encarna Perán, Joãa Pereira, Carol Propper,

Frank Puffer, Lise Rochaix, Marisol Rodrigéz, Martin Schellhorn, Gun Sundberg, Olaf Winkelhake (1999), 'Equity in the finance of health care: some further international comparisons', *Journal of Health Economics*, 18, pp. 263–90.

Wagstaff, Adam and Eddy van Doorslaer (2000), 'Equity in Health Care Finance and Delivery', in: A.J. Culyer and J.P. Newhouse (eds), *Handbook of Health Economics*, vol. 2, Amsterdam: Elsevier, pp. 1803–59.

Walzer, Michael (1983), *Spheres of Justice*, New York: Basic Books.

World Health Organisation (2000), *The World Health Report*, Geneva: WHO.

Zweifel, Peter, Stefan Felder and Markus Meier (1996), 'Demographische Alterung und Gesundheitskosten: Eine Fehlinterpretation', in: P. Oberender (ed.), *Alter und Gesundheit*, Baden Baden: Nomos, pp. 29–46.

Zweifel, Peter and Willard G. Manning (2000), 'Moral Hazard and Consumer Incentives in Health Care', in: A.J. Culyer and J.P. Newhouse (eds), *Handbook of Health Economics*, vol. 1, Amsterdam: Elsevier, pp. 409–59.

5. The Economics of Pensions

The foremost purpose of all pension systems is to provide income during retirement and this will be the aspect we are looking at in this chapter. Many pension systems are also used for other social policy purposes – disability insurance, problems of unemployment at higher age, survivor's pensions. Some pension systems take care of problems which can arise in case of a divorce. These other aspects will not be covered here systematically. We look at pension systems as means to shift wealth into later periods of life with only one further aspect taken into consideration, namely that of fighting poverty.

The organisational structures of pension systems differ widely between different countries. Whereas in most countries the access to health services is more or less the same for all, independent of the institutional structures of the health system, that is not the case concerning pensions. As the organisational structures are very different the volume of public pensions as a share of GDP varies considerably between different countries (see Table 5.1).

Table 5.1 Public pension expenditure as share of GDP (%)

Australia	4.6	Italy	15.0
Austria	14.9	Latvia	10.2
Belgium	12.0	Netherlands	11.5
Canada	5.4	New Zealand	6.5
Czech Republic	9.0	Poland	14.4
France	13.3	Sweden	11.4
Germany	12.0	Switzerland	12.6
Hungary	9.7	United Kingdom	10.2
Ireland	5.1	United States	7.2

Note: Data for 1995.

Source: OECD Database.

These data alone do not say very much, particularly they do not allow for any conclusion as to how generously a state supports its elderly population. It is also impossible to make any inference from them about the burden of pensions for the economy or about the living standard of the retirees. A public pension system which is supposed to safeguard high replacement rates leads to a higher share of pension expenditure in GDP than a pension system which is primarily an insurance against poverty in old age and leaves everything else for privately managed funds, as is the case in Australia, New Zealand and the UK. Whereas in the former case the pension systems can finance nearly all the consumption of the elderly, this is different in the latter case. Basic pensions must be supplemented by other schemes to safeguard consumption during retirement. They are also affected by regulations and subsidies which do not show in the data.

Moreover there may be other social policy programmes which shift resources to the retired. Low pensions may be supplanted by social assistance if there is no minimum pension. In some European states the pension system contributes to financing the health system because the access to health services for the elderly is connected with the pension system. In other states – for example in the USA – the pension system does not contribute directly to financing the health system.

The first part of this chapter gives an overview of different pension systems. Before that some definitions are given. The second part discusses the basic differences between funded and unfunded systems and asks what are the merits of each. The third part looks at the reasons for public provisions and the fourth part analysis the effects on labour supply. The fifth part has a look at distributional effects. The last part discusses the way in which demographic changes affect pension systems and intergenerational redistribution.

5.1 SYSTEMS OF PUBLIC RETIREMENT SCHEMES

In the first chapter different aims of social policy – fighting poverty, insurance, and redistribution – were related to different political principles. These relationships are particularly relevant within the organisation of public pension schemes. Pension systems include:

- A basic public pension independent of former income plus an income related public pension.
- A basic public pension related to former income plus a mandated supplement in relation to former income.
- Only an income related public pension plus a means tested benefit if the pension is below a certain threshold.
- A mandated, regulated and controlled savings system.

If people get pensions from different systems we say that there are different tiers, different pillars or different columns.

Basic pensions independent of former income are an important instrument for fighting poverty. In some economies basic pensions are given to the whole population above a certain age independently of former labour market participation. If income related pensions dominate, insurance of former income is also important. In that case there are often different schemes for different groups. In some countries only employed people are covered by such schemes, whereas the self-employed have to care for themselves. Some states with basic pensions as the most important public pensions system mandate supplementary pensions to be provided by employers.[1]

States regulate provision for retirement not only by establishing pension systems but in other ways as well. Many countries subsidise saving for retirement by special clauses in the tax code and subject pension funds to special regulations. These aspects are not covered in this chapter as that would make it necessary to give a description of different tax systems and public regulation of financial markets. In a detailed evaluation of pension systems and pension regulations one cannot leave them out of the picture.

Before describing and discussing different systems, it is necessary to give some definitions. There are two fundamentally different types of schemes: (i) non-funded or pay-as-you-go systems (PAYG) and (ii) funded systems. Some systems are partially funded.

(i) In a pay-as-you-go scheme the current working population supports with its contributions the currently retired population through taxes and contributions. It is a direct transfer from one part of the population to another.
(ii) In a funded system the contributions of the working population are used to buy assets. The pensions are financed by the capital income on these assets and by repayment of the principal.

It is not always clear whether a system is funded or works on a PAYG basis. A pension fund which only acquires public debt out of which the government finances public consumption should not be considered a funded pension system if due to the existence of the pensions fund public debt is increased.[2] The pensions which have to be paid are financed out of taxes and not by a return on capital in the traditional sense. Therefore there is no difference to a PAYG system.

Publicly organised schemes for the whole population or substantial parts of it are usually organised on a PAYG basis, particularly in the case of basic pensions. Publicly mandated private schemes have to be funded schemes. The reason for these structures is that a PAYG scheme can only work when there is no competition for contributors and there is mandatory membership – all employed people, all citizens, and so on. Otherwise the pension scheme cannot guarantee future payments.[3] On the other hand, a centrally managed funded public pension scheme is, for political reasons, very problematic: pension funds are extremely important actors in the capital market, as they are the biggest investors. A central pension fund run by the state or controlled by the state dominates all investment decisions. One does not have to be a dogmatic adherent to a free-market economy to find this objectionable. Actually there is no country with only a centrally managed fund for all retirement income (Iglesias and Palacios, 2001).

There is a further distinction to be made: (i) defined contribution systems; (ii) defined benefit systems.

(i) A defined contribution system regulates how much is paid into the system, usually as a percentage of current income.
(ii) A defined benefit system regulates how much a retired person receives as pension, usually as a percentage of former income.

In some states with PAYG systems the statutes fix contributions and benefits – people pay a statutorily fixed percentage of their earnings and receive statutorily fixed pensions. In a steady state this can work – the contributions determine the pensions unambiguously and vice versa. However no economy is in a steady state – there are demographic shocks, changing employment patterns and other economic changes which influence the pension system. Pension systems in which contributions and pension are fixed statutorily can easily get out of equilibrium.

Some PAYG defined contribution systems keep individual accounts for each contributor. They mimic a funded system, insofar as there is a clear relation between contributions and pension for each person on an individual basis. These accounts do not represent a property right in a private law framework, as there are no assets to back the claims. They are called *notional defined contributions* systems (Fox and Palmer, 2001).

All existing pension systems have had one very important effect: poverty among the old has been radically reduced everywhere. Though there are still many poor amongst the retired, their poverty is in most instances not deep (see Chapter 8). This is markedly different from earlier periods.

5.1.1 A Two-Tier Pay-As-You-Go System with a Minimum Pension:
France (www.observatoire-retraite.org; Blanchet and Pelé, 1999)

France has a two-tier system and a means-tested minimum pension. There is a general basic pension which is supplemented by a compulsory scheme. Both schemes are pay-as-you-go.

The general pension is state organised. The pension depends on earnings, on years of working and on the age of retirement. The amount is up to 50 per cent of average earnings over a specified period (currently it is calculated over the best 10 years; this will be increased to 25 years by the year 2008). There is an upper limit for the income that forms the basis for calculating the pension, approximately mean labour income (twice the minimum). Therefore the maximum state pension is approximately equal to the minimum wage. The pensions from the state system pay about 60 per cent of all pension incomes.

The second tier consists of pensions from pension plans which are organised along socio-professional lines. They supplement the basic pension so that retirement income for people with income above minimum wage is in line with former income. These are defined contribution systems: the contributions are turned into pension points by dividing the contribution by the price of a pension point. The price of a pension point is determined by the sum of all contributions to the plan. The points are accumulated and are turned into a stream of money by multiplying the number of points with the value of a point in the year of the pension. In that way benefits are kept in line with contributions. For periods of sickness and unemployment individuals earn pension points as well. Pensions are increased with the rate of inflation, but do not keep pace with real wages.

There are about 150 funds (not real funds) organised in two systems. The *Associations pour le regime de retraite complementaire des salaries* (ARRCO) comprises pension funds primarily for blue-collar workers, up to three times the ceiling of the first tier, the *Association génerale des institutions de retraite* des cadres (AGIRC) primarily for white-collar workers, up to eight times the ceiling. The social partners, that is the organisations of employers and employees, decide which fund to choose. The funds are run by these organisations. The state has no important role to play. There is risk pooling between the funds – otherwise they could not function on a PAYG basis – and pension points can be transferred from one fund to another, which is important for labour market mobility.

The general pension is financed by contributions of 6.5 per cent of all wage income below the social security ceiling. The other pensions are also financed by contributions, the rate is 7.5 per cent. The employed pay 40 per cent, the rest is paid by the employer. There is a further 2.4 per cent general social security tax to finance different non-contributory transfers which are partly used for pension purposes as well.

There are special schemes for farmers and the self-employed. In case a person does not get any pension and has no other means there is a guaranteed minimum pension for all over 65 (60 in case of disability). Individuals with a pension below a certain threshold get state financed supplements. Currently about one million people receive such a minimum pension.

Table 5.2 Net replacement ratios for employees with a full career in 1998

Final monthly net earnings	First tier	Second tier ARRCO	AGIRC	Others	Total
Less than €757	76	26	0	0	102
€757 – €909	69	24	0	0	94
€909 – €1212	60	26	1	0	88
€1212 – €1515	50	27	3	0	80
€1515 – €1818	42	28	10	0	80
€1818 – €2424	34	23	17	1	75
€2424 and over	20	13	32	1	66

Note: FF converted into € by the author.

Source: SESI, Ministry of Social Affairs.

5.1.2 A Pure Pay-As-You-Go System with Unclear Redistribution: Austria

Austria has a very elaborate system of PAYG pension schemes. Not only are all employed people covered by a pension scheme, but so are most self-employed individuals and all farmers. There is only one tier, save a small segment of pensions provided by firms (Rosner et al., 1997). Public pensions are related to earned income. As in the case of the *Krankenkassen* different groups – employed workers, self-employed, farmers, railway workers, people working in the mining industry, for the federal civil service, municipal workers – have different systems.

All systems are pay-as-you-go. They are defined benefit as well as defined contribution plans: the law fixes the size of the contributions as a percentage of current income and the size of the pensions as a percentage of former income. An imbalance – mostly a deficit – is therefore likely to arise.

The contributions are paid from all earned income. Employed labour pays 22.75 per cent of gross income, of which the employees pay less than half.[4] The self-employed currently pay 15 per cent and farmers 14.5 per cent. All contributions are limited (*Höchstbeitragsgrundlage*), currently this is about €3200 for employed people and €3750 for the self-employed and farmers (gross monthly income).[5] Nearly all blue-collar workers are below this limit and most other employees as well. Only the self-employed and employees in career jobs – mostly academics, mostly men – reach an income above this limit. This *Höchstbeitragsgrundlage* sets an upper limit to the pensions as well.

The pension increases with years of contribution and the amount of contributions. For each year of insurance a person gets 2 per cent of the basis. The maximum pension is 90 per cent of the basis. The replacement rate also depends on the age of retirement. The basis for calculating the pension is the average of the best 15 years' income. This will be extended to the best 18 years. The system has a deficit which is covered by the federal budget. Currently its size is more than 20 per cent of all pension payments.

There is no minimum pension, but there is a means-tested supplement (*Ausgleichszulage*) if the pension falls below a threshold (*Richtsatz*). Currently this threshold is about €620 for a one-person household and €840 per month for a two-person household, paid fourteen times a year. This is approximately 50 per cent of mean income. Households living only on such a pension are slightly below the poverty threshold currently used by the statistical office in Luxembourg. The *Ausgleichszulagen* are financed from general taxes.

Due to the stipulation that only the 15 (18) years with highest income are considered for calculating the pension and due to the means-tested supplement the relation between working income and retirement income is not strict. There is much redistribution, however there is no calculation of its extent.

Statutory retirement age for men is 65, for women 60. That was ruled to contradict the constitutional mandated equality principle. By making a constitutional law this regulation is upheld until the year 2018. Earlier retirement due to long insurance (age 61.5 for men and age 56.5 for women) is possible if contributions were paid for at least 37.5 years. Still earlier retirement is possible under special circumstances – prolonged unemployment at a later age and in case of disability. Effective retirement age is well below the 65 and 60 rule for normal old age pensions (Table 5.3). Note that even for men the effective retirement age is below 60, the then required minimum age for long insurance pension, but above 55, the equivalent limit for women. The difference in effective retirement age between men and women is far lower than 5 years.

Up to four years per child is accepted as a break in payment of contributions to allow for child rearing. This clause is mostly used by women. Periods of unemployment are also partly considered as contribution-free insurance periods.

Pensions are high in relation to former income where an individual has had a continuous working life. Gross replacement rates of well over two-thirds can easily be reached, the net replacement rates are even higher, because pensioners do not pay contributions to the pension system (10.25 per cent) nor do they pay for unemployment insurance (3 per cent).

Nearly every year all pensions are increased with the purpose that the retirees should not lose real income due to inflation, and that they should profit from real economic growth. The value of former contributions are also increased which can be seen as interest payments on the contributions. The calculation of these increases were changed a few times. Currently they are related to the growth of net wage incomes. This comes close to the 'rate of interest' of a PAYG system (see below). There is some discretionary power for the government when deciding about the increases. It usually takes budget problems (and the date of next elections) into consideration.

Table 5.3 Average retirement age, 1993 and 1998

	1993	1998
Blue-collar workers		
men	56.2	57.5
women	56.3	57.0
Employees		
men	58.7	58.8
women	56.2	56.0
Total	56.7	57.2
Self-employed		
men	63.7	59.8
women	62.9	57.7
Total	63.3	58.9
Farmers		
men	58.1	58.4
women	58.0	58.0
Total	58.0	58.2

Source: Wirtschafts- und Sozialstatistisches Taschenbuch AK (1998 and 2000).

The *Richtsatz* – the threshold for the means-tested supplement – was often increased more than the pensions. Therefore in the last decade the minimum income of pensioner households increased more than the income of households with higher pensions. During the period 1991–2000 pensions were increased by 29 per cent, the minimum by 48 per cent. Prices rose by approximately 27 per cent and real economic growth was 24 per cent during this decade. Whereas pensions above the minimum kept pace with inflation but hardly profited from real growth, the minimum rose in line with nominal GDP.[6]

The size of the deficit as a percentage of pensions paid out varies between different systems. This is partly due to different regulations concerning retirement age – railway workers and miners can retire earlier – but primarily the variation of the deficits is due to structural changes and different contribution rates between employed, self-employed and farmers. Some of the pension systems lose paying members – farmers, miners, blue-collar workers, self-employed, and others gain, primarily private sector employees.

All pensioners are covered by health insurance. They pay 3.75 per cent of the gross pension and the pension scheme pays another 7 per cent.[7]

Table 5.4 Average net replacement ratios of new pensions in relation to final income

		1994	1996	1998
Blue-collar workers	men	77.8	79.2	80.5
	women	71.0	72.7	73.5
	total	74.7	76.5	77.6
Employees	men	81.5	82.4	83.9
	women	72.1	73.3	75.3
	total	75.9	76.9	78.7

Source: Wirtschafts- und sozialstatistisches Taschenbuch der AK (2000).

5.1.3 A Strict Pay-As-You-Go System: Germany (Lampert, 1998, p. 255f)

The German retirement systems are pure PAYG. However a second pillar, namely pensions paid by employers have a greater role than in Austria. Recently the replacement rates have been slightly reduced. To make good this shortfall the state supports saving for retirement to some extent. A funded system as second pillar for all was started.

In one aspect the German system is much stricter than the Austrian one: the relation between the pension and the contributions are much closer in Germany than in Austria. First, the contribution of all years are used for calculating the pension. Second, there is no minimum – poor pensioners are required to turn to the general social assistance system.

The contributions that people pay are proportionally rated in comparison to the contribution of the average income of the same year (1999: approximately €27 000), up to a level of 183 per cent of average income. The rate of contributions is currently 19.3 per cent, half of which is paid by the employee.

The size of the pension depends on the of the contributions and the number of years for which contributions have been paid, on the age when starting to claim the pension and on the overall development of net wages. Retirement age is 65. Each month of earlier retirement reduces the pension by 0.3 per cent, for each month retirement begins later the pension rises by 0.5 per cent.

A person who has worked for 45 years and has always paid according to the average income receives less than 50 per cent of former gross income. As there are no social security contributions and no income tax on pensions she will receive about two-thirds of former net income. All pensions are adjusted to changing prices. Recently a demographic factor for calculating pensions was introduced.

Average retirement age is, as in many other countries, far below the statutory retirement age, because many employees apply for a disability pension or other early retirement schemes. For men the average retirement age is slightly below 60, for women it is slightly higher. The reason is that men are more likely than women to retreat from working by getting a disability pension. As in Austria all pensioners remain in their *Krankenkasse* and are thus covered for health expenditure.

5.1.4 A Basic Pension Related to the Minimum Wage Plus Savings: The Netherlands (Kapetyn and de Vos, 1999)

All people above the age of 65 are entitled for the general old age pension (Alegemene Ouderdomswet, AOW). It is financed by a payroll tax of 15.4 per cent (in 1996). The pension is 50 per cent of the minimum wage. This pension is given independently of any retreat from the labour market. Earlier retirement is possible in case of disability and unemployment. The path out of labour market participation via disability insurance was very popular in the 1980s which lead in the 1990s to a tightening of the conditions for claiming disability benefits.

There are many schemes of private pensions. Often they are provided by employers. They are mostly defined benefit type pensions.

5.1.5 A Combined System with a Minimum Pension: Sweden (Lißner and Wöss, 1999)

Sweden changed its pension system in 1998. The old system provided a basic pension of about $10 000 per year if living alone, otherwise the pension is 10 per cent lower. An individual who has lived in Sweden for 40 years or has worked for 30 years is entitled to this pension. There is a earnings related second tier which provides a pension of up to 60 per cent of the income of the best 15 years of up to a limit of about $3000 per month. Retirement age is 65.

For each year of earlier retirement the earnings related pension is reduced by 6 per cent. The fist system is pure PAYG, financed by contributions and out of the federal budget. For the second tier the proceeds of a small fund are used as well. When the system was started this fund was accumulated from the then existing surplus of the pension system. All contributions are split between employers and the employed. There is no upper limit for employers' contributions. This two-tier system is the system for all people born not later than 1953 and will be the dominant system for decades to come.

In the new system the basic pension and the earnings related pension are integrated. Those without a pension or on a very low pension are entitled to a guaranteed minimum which is approximately the same as the former basic pension. The new pension is financed by contributions and by the proceeds of a fund. The state provides means out of general taxes only for the guaranteed minimum. The rate of contribution is 18.5 per cent, 16 per cent is used for the PAYG system, 2.5 per cent is used to accumulate capital stock.

Whereas the old system is a defined benefit system, the new system will be a defined contribution system. The contributions are credited on an individual account. Upon retirement the accumulated value of the contributions will be used to calculate an actuarial fair pension taking account of life expectancy at the age of retirement. Pension credits can be split between spouses. Individuals can start to receive a pension at the age of 61. The effective retirement age has no influence on the system, because early retirement reduces the pension accordingly. The value of the accumulated funds (compound with profits) will be transformed into a pension as if they were private savings.

Actual retirement age is much higher than in most other OECD countries, although a number of those working above the age of 61 are on partial retirement. The net replacement rates in the old system are between 53 per cent for those with high income and more than 70 per cent for people with medium incomes. For individuals with very low incomes, the net replacement rate can exceed 100 per cent (Lißner and Wöss, 1999). In the new system the replacement rates will be lower.

5.1.6 A Flat-Rate Pension Plus a Mandated Income Insurance: The United Kingdom (Disney et al., 2001)

The United Kingdom has the smallest public pension system among the EU countries besides Ireland. For most people the public system covers only a basic pension. There are two tiers organised by the state. The basic pension depends only on years having worked but is independent of former income. It is paid to men over 65 and to women over 60. For the full pension men qualify after having worked for 44 years, women having worked for 39 years.[8] At the age of 80 everybody who has lived in the United Kingdom for at least 10 years qualifies for 60 per cent of the full pension even if no contributions were paid. This pension increases with the price level, but as a percentage of current wage income the replacement rate declines. The average retirement age is about 63 (Miles, 1999). In 2001 the full pension was £75 per week. This is about 20 per cent of average income (Miles and Timmermann, 1999). If somebody has only the flat rate pension, she can receive some means-tested benefits as well.

The second tier is a mandated income related pension. There is a public scheme only for employees, not for the self-employed (*State Earnings Related Pension Scheme*, SERPS). It is a PAYG scheme as well. An employer can decide to opt out, in which case she contracts with a private insurance company and provides pensions for her employees. Either a defined benefit or a defined contribution plan can be chosen. The employees themselves can also decide whether to accept the pension system provided by the employer, if any, or have a SERPS pension. In the case of opting out, the employer pays lower National Insurance contributions. Contributions to the SERP system are easily transferable between employers and are fully indexed. The non-state system, is more flexible and can provide higher pensions. After retirement people can withdraw some of their funds, but when they reach 75 they have to turn their remaining wealth into an annuity. SERPS pensions are no higher than 20 per cent of average income. Together with the basic pension this amounts to a maximum pension of about 40 per cent of average income. For people with high incomes it is better not to be in a SERP scheme.

By now the majority has opted out of the system, which is why the United Kingdom has the smallest public share of pension payments in Europe. But one has to be aware that the publicly financed pension safeguards only a part of the consumption of the retirees. The low share of the public pension system in GDP does not show the extent of public support for retirement, as provision for private pensions reduce tax proceeds.

In 2001 a new scheme was introduced for individuals with incomes up to £22 000 per year. It will provide better pensions than that of SERPS for individuals with low incomes and/or interrupted careers.

The public pensions are financed by contributions on a PAYG basis. The rate is 8.4 per cent for all weekly earnings between £87 and £575. For weekly earnings between £72 and £87 there are no payments, though they are treated as having contributed 10 per cent for all earnings above the lower threshold. Neither earnings below £72 nor earnings above £575 are considered for contributions. Those who did not opt out of the second state pension or SERPS have to pay another 1.6 per cent.

5.1.7 An Incomes Related Pension with Redistribution towards Low-Income Groups: USA (Murphy and Welch, 1998; Diamond and Gruber, 2000; Liebman, 2001)

The USA has a progressive public pension system which redistributes income in favour of low-income groups. Contributions are 10.7 per cent of earned income up to $80 400 per annum. Benefits are calculated by indexing all income prior to age 60 until that year and taking the ratio of the economy-wide average income when the person is 60 to the economy-wide average income of that year. The 35 years with highest (indexed) earnings are taken for calculating the pension.

The structure of the system reflects the structure of the benefits: for the first $561 monthly income an individual gets 90 per cent, for earnings between $561 and $3381 she gets 32 per cent, and for the rest, up to the maximum insured income, merely 15 per cent. The replacement ratio therefore is 90 per cent for incomes up to $6700 and then starts to decline. At an income of $30 000 the replacement rate is a bit more than 40 per cent, at an income of $70 000 it is about 25 per cent. All pensions are indexed with the change of the price level.

Individuals with high incomes have to save for retirement if they want a reasonable replacement rate. Many employers provide pension plans. The federal state supports saving for retirement by providing tax relief (for example, the so called 401(k) plans). Normal retirement age is 65, but will increase to 67. Earlier retirement is possible, but for each month of earlier retirement the pension is reduced by five-ninths of one per cent. People retiring at the earliest date get only 80 per cent of the full pension. Until the age of 70, pensions are reduced if the pensioner has earnings. Up to the age of 65 pensions are not reduced if earnings do not exceed $8280, each dollar above that level reduces the pension by $0.5. At 65 the limit rises to $12 500 and the reduction falls to $0.33 for each $ earned above that level.

The system is a PAYG system. There is currently a surplus which allows a fund to accrue. This fund was set up because the increase in birth rate in the 1950s and 1960s (the 'Baby-boom') will lead to a special burden when these cohorts retire after 2010. At the moment the fund is only allowed to buy government debt. Its future returns are therefore paid by taxes as well.[9]

5.1.8 An Integrated Two-Tier System Plus a State Supported Third Tier: Switzerland (Bundesamt für Sozialversicherung, 1995; Obinger, 1998)

The Swiss system rests on different principles than those of other countries. Usually a social welfare aspect is applied for basic pensions, whereas the standard of living for the better-off is safeguarded by an income insurance system. Switzerland has written the social welfare aspect for all public pension provision in its constitution. This principle is not only interpreted as providing a minimum for all, but to safeguard the standard of living when retiring. A further specificity is that all pension rights of couples are treated as a whole.

As in the French system there is a basic pension for all inhabitants and a second pension to safeguard the standard of living after withdrawal from the labour market. The second tier is obligatory for the employed and voluntary for the self-employed. Unlike the French system only the first tier works on a PAYG basis, the second tier is a funded system. The most important difference to other systems is the construction of the pension: the pension rights for a couple are calculated together, namely the contributions of both spouses are put together for the calculation of the pension. A couple's pension is 150 per cent of the pension of a single person. For couples with an income below sfr70 000 (per year) no deductions are made. Up to 1995 the pension was a family pension which was allotted to the husband.[10] Since then all contributions during the time of the marriage are evenly split between husband and wife and two separate pensions are calculated. In case of divorce both have their own pension.

The basic pension lies between approximately sfr1000 and sfr2000 – the upper limit is about 40 per cent of mean income. It depends on the number of years of contribution and of income. The maximum basic pension can be reached after 45 years of contributions, for each year less of contribution one forty-fourth is deducted.

The relation between pension and former income is non-linear. If the income was always below the minimum pension the replacement rate is above 100 per cent, for those with income as high as the maximum basic pension, the replacement rate is 33 per cent. This pension is financed by contributions of 8.4 per cent (plus 1.4 per cent for invalidity insurance) of wage incomes (evenly split between employers and employed) without an upper limit. The self-employed pay 7.8 per cent. Those who do not work have to contribute according to their financial position. The federal state provides 17.5 per cent of all expenditures, primarily out of taxes on cigarettes and alcohol, the *Kantone* (the provinces) a further 3 per cent out of income taxes. The share of contributions out of taxes for invalidity insurance is higher.

Both tiers together should safeguard a pension of about 60 per cent of last income. The two systems are integrated. All incomes of the employed between the upper limit of the basic pension up to about sfr70 000 per year are insured. The contributions grow with age. The youngest pay at least 7 per cent of all income between the lower limit of about sfr24 000 and the upper limit of about sfr70 000, those above 55 at most 18 per cent, again equally shared between employer and employed. There are more than 10 000 funds which have some freedom to set contributions. There is a guaranteed rate of interest of at least 4 per cent. The pension is 7.2 per cent of all accumulated and compounded contributions per year. Earlier retirement reduces the pension by 6.8 per cent for each year, postponement of retirement increases the pension by less than 6 per cent for each year.

For those without a pension from the second tier some means-tested supplementary benefits are provided. The basic pension is increased with an average of the rate of inflation and the rate of wage growth. No such increase is possible for the pension from the second tier, as the rate of return of funds is not directly related to the increase of nominal income. Contributions from both tiers are used for calculations of invalidity benefits and descendants benefits. Retirement age is 65 for men and currently 63 for women. The latter will be increased to 64 in 2005.

A third tier of pensions is voluntary; these are supported by the state through tax deductions.

5.1.9 Mandatory Savings Plans Plus a Means-Tested Basic Pension: Chile[11] (Edwards, 1996)

The current Chilean system was introduced during the military regime in 1981. Unlike in most other states, the new system is not the result of reform of an existing system but made a radical break with it. It was strongly influenced by academically trained economists who favoured a funded scheme. Such a change is hardly possible in a democratic regime.[12] Be that as it may, the Chilean system is widely discussed amongst pension economists.

The old PAYG scheme was abolished. Today there are mandatory savings plans which force employed people to save 10 per cent of their gross income. It covers disability insurance and survivor's pensions. Self-employed people can voluntarily enter the system, however only very few of them do so. The funds are publicly regulated and provide indexed annuities. A cover charge of 3.5 per cent is accepted. For people who have worked for at least 20 years there is a tax financed, means-tested minimum. (In Argentina which has a similar system the minimum is given independently of need.) People who are unemployed or work in the shadow economy do not pay contributions and are not insured. Currently only about 50 per cent of all insured pay regularly.

Upon retirement an individual has different options. The accumulated wealth can either be transformed into a guaranteed pension or it can be withdrawn stepwise. In the latter case the monthly rent is calculated anew each year by taking account of the size of the capital stock, the expected real rate of interest and the anticipated life expectancy of the retiree. If the person dies earlier, the rest of the remaining capital is paid out to the heirs. When a retired person gets older the pension decreases because the remaining life expectancy does not decrease as quickly as the capital stock. The decision to withdraw the capital can always be revoked in favour of a fixed pension.

If a fixed pension is chosen, it is calculated on an actuarial fair basis, taking into account individual life expectancy and life expectancy of any survivor with pensions rights, the size of the accumulated capital stock and the expected rate of return over the whole assumed duration of the pension. The fixed pension therefore provides an insurance against longevity. A transfer of capital to heirs is excluded. Currently about 60 per cent opt for the fixed pension, about 40 per cent for the withdrawal solution.[13]

All funds are strictly regulated and controlled by the state. The funds have to provide a minimum rate of return, either the higher of 50 per cent of the average rate of all funds or 2 percentage points below the average. There is also a maximum rate of return, namely 50 per cent or 2 percentage points above the average. Excess profits have to be put into reserves. There are some transfers from funds with very high yields to funds with yields much below the average. These regulations tend to weaken competition between the funds.

Due to the high growth rates of the economy the rates of return were very high for more than a decade. That contributed to the acceptance of the system. Meanwhile they have been reduced. The administrative costs were very high when the system was started. They have now declined.

5.1.10 A Notional Contribution Scheme on a PAYG Basis Plus a Funded Scheme: Latvia (Fox, 1997)

As in Chile, the new Latvian pension system is the result of a construction planned by economists. A complete break with the earlier system was a precondition for its enactment. But whereas in Chile a pure funded system was introduced, probably on an ideological bias, Latvia introduced a mixed system. There is a PAYG first tier, whose pension payments are strictly linked to individual contributions – save a minimum to protect the long-term poor. For contribution-free years – military service, unemployment, child-care – a payment has to be made by a corporate institution; for example, years of military service are a burden on the current defence budget. Redistribution through the pension system is made explicit. Thus the system makes it difficult to appear to the insured as being more generous than it is in reality (see 5.3.3 below).

The pension depends on the contribution and on the pensioner's average life expectancy. It is not necessary to withdraw from the labour market in order to start getting a pension. The later the pension payment starts the higher it is. The accrual of the pension due to later beginning of payments is made on an actuarially fair value.

There is a second tier which is partly funded and which allows the insured to choose among different funds. Altogether pensions will be lower in the future than in the old system. However the new system will be sustainable.

5.2   A THEORY OF PENSION SYSTEMS

In this part of the chapter, we want to discuss the merits of an unfunded system in comparison with a funded system. As the first part of the chapter shows, in most countries at least part of retirement income is financed by a PAYG system. However widespread consideration has been given to a switch towards a partially funded system. Sweden changed to a partially funded system in 1998. In 2001 Germany lowered the maximum pension of its PAYG system and now supplements retirement income by a funded scheme. In the race between George Bush and Al Gore for the presidency in the USA the idea of a switch of the USA pension system was one of the issues. Whereas Al Gore defended the existing PAYG system, George Bush favoured a funded system. Each of the contestants got support for his position by eminent pension economists. As usual, the differences were not due to one side being right and the other wrong, but each side emphasised different aspects. They will be discussed here only in relation to retirement income, although other questions are closely linked: aggregate savings in a closed economy determine the capital stock and thereby influence aggregate output. Furthermore the functioning of capital markets is intertwined with the working of a funded system, whereas a PAYG system can be a hindrance to the emergence of a capital market.

5.2.1   Basic Ideas

To understand the working of a pension system we have to start with a situation without public pensions in which everyone has to care for their own consumption during retirement. Setting aside transfers from children to parents, that can only be achieved by saving during the period an individual works. Naturally we assume that people maximise utility, that is, we ask what is the optimal amount of saving. To make things easy it is customary to make a few assumptions and to put the analysis of pension systems and savings into a special framework – the *overlapping generation* model.

We assume that people live for two periods. In each period there are two generations alive. A person works in the first period, in the second period she does not work and has to finance consumption from savings if there is no public retirement system. To be more specific: labour supply in the first period is inelastic, that is, the wage does not influence the amount of labour supplied. We assume that the person only cares for her own consumption and has no intention to leave bequests. We further assume that there is no uncertainty concerning the time of death. That implies that there are no involuntary bequests as each person will use up all her resources in her own lifetime. Formally:

$$\max U(c_1, c_2)$$

with c_1 consumption in the first period, c_2 consumption in the second period. When there is no public pension, the person has to consider the following constraints:

$$c_1 = w - s$$
$$c_2 = s(1 + r)$$

with s savings and r the rate of interest. The result is an optimal amount of saving s^*. In a closed economy accumulated savings determine the capital stock.

In order to discuss the effects of the introduction of public pension we have to distinguish between funded and unfunded systems. When a funded system is started, the constraints do not change at all if the rate of contribution is not bigger than the rate of savings people wanted to choose voluntarily (b: rate of contribution to the pension system).

$$c_1 = w(1-b) - s$$
$$c_2 = s(1+r) + bw(1+r)$$

Instead of saving voluntarily, people are forced to save. Mandatory saving crowds out voluntary saving. The optimal amount of saving s^* ($= s + bw$), of which a part is mandatory, does not change. In case mandatory contributions (bw) are higher than optimal savings, s^*, aggregate saving is increased by the introduction of a mandatory funded pension system. People are forced to shift more of their first period income into the second period than they would have done voluntarily.

If an unfunded pension scheme is introduced with a contribution rate ß and a pension p the agent faces different constraints. Assuming that the system has neither a deficit nor a surplus ß determines p and vice versa:

$$c_1 = w(1-ß) - s$$
$$c_2 = p + (1+r)s$$

One can show that $\partial s/\partial p < 0$, if consumption in both periods is a normal good.[14] The introduction of a fair unfunded pension scheme reduces private saving. This is not difficult to understand: when you are given an income during retirement you will decrease your private provision for retirement.

What are the aggregate effects? Let us compare two economies with identical and constant populations, identical technologies and the same preferences, one having a funded system the other one a PAYG system. How do the two economies differ in steady state? Note that net savings will be zero in both economies. In the PAYG country people do not have to save for old age consumption. In the other country the young save, but the old dissave. Indeed, they have to sell the capital stock to the young in order to finance consumption, whereas the young have to acquire the capital stock in order to save for their old age. If demography does not change savings and spending cancel exactly. When demography, preferences, technologies and population are constant, the capital stock must not change in steady state.

The economy with the PAYG system has a smaller capital stock. When the system was started one generation did not save in that economy, whereas in the other one there were immediate net savings. Due to the smaller capital stock the rate of interest is higher in the PAYG country and the marginal product of labour – and therefore the wage – is smaller. These are consequences of introducing an unfunded system: the consumption of the first generation is increased and all later generations have a smaller capital stock.

What does this imply for welfare? What should a state do if a pension system is going to be started? Should it be construed as an unfunded or a funded system? Under which system will aggregate welfare be higher? If an unfunded system is started, the first generation will benefit, all other generations have a smaller capital stock. With a funded system the first generation has no public pension. We therefore have to compare the gains and losses for different generations. For that analysis we assume that all people are alike, they differ only insofar as they belong to different generations. For each generation we analyse the welfare of a *representative individual*. This is tantamount to aggregation of welfare over all people of the same generation, however there is no aggregation of welfare over different generations.[15] To compare different pension systems or a system without public pension in respect to welfare one has to make the comparison for each generation.

To do so, we adopt the Pareto criterion. We compare different allocations of consumption streams for both periods across different generations. The consumption vector of an economy without a pension system with that of an economy with a funded pension system and an economy with an unfunded system.

An allocation C^A $\{(c_1^t, c_2^t), t = 1,2,...\}$ is Pareto-better against a different allocation C^B if for all t, $U^A(c_1^t, c_2^t) \geq U^B(c_1^t, c_2^t)$ and there is at least one t with $U^A(c_1^t, c_2^t) > U^B(c_1^t, c_2^t)$. An allocation is Pareto-efficient if there is no Pareto-better allocation. Loosely speaking, an allocation is efficient in the infinite intertemporal context if there is no other allocation with one generation strictly better off and no other generation worse off.

Can't we use the welfare theorems as they were mentioned in the second chapter above? No, because of the temporal structure. The proof of the welfare theorem used the idea that actors make an exchange whenever they can thereby better their situation. But this may be impossible across generations. Consider the following unrealistically simple economy: each generation lives two periods. At the beginning of the first period it is endowed with one unit of a good which it can use for all consumption purposes. (A more sensible interpretation: each generation is endowed with a unit of labour to be used for the production of consumption goods.) A part of the good has to be stored for the second period. Assume that each generation decides to consume one half of the consumption good in the first period, the other half in the second period. The allocation is:

$$(0.5, 0.5)$$
$$(0.5, 0.5)$$
$$(0.5, 0.5)$$
....

When old, generation 1 wants to get something from generation 2. This cannot be achieved by exchange, as generation 1 is no longer alive when generation 2 is old. But the introduction of a forced redistribution across generations – a pay-as-you-go pension – can result in a Pareto-improvement. If each generation t ($t > 1$) gives half of its endowment to generation $t - 1$, the resulting allocation is:

$$(0.5, 1)$$
$$(0.5, 0.5)$$
$$(0.5, 0.5)$$
....

The first generation is better off, all other generations are indifferent – a Pareto-improvement.

With a slight modification of the assumptions all generations can be made better off. Assume that each generation is bigger than the generation before by a factor N – the factor of population growth – and the endowments change accordingly. Generation t can give $0.5N^{(t-1)}$ to generation $t - 1$ and will receive in return $0.5N^t$ from generation $t + 1$. Due to the growth of population, all generations are made better off by starting a PAYG system.

Another assumption ensuring more utility for all generations by introducing an unfunded pension system is when endowments grow from one generation to the next by a factor W – this is tantamount to an increase of productivity of labour. In that case generation t can support its elders with $0.5W^{(t-1)}$ and will get in return from its descendants, $0.5W^t$.

In the first case the number of people supporting their parents is bigger than the number of the parents, in the second case the productivity of those contributing to the pension system is growing from one generation to the next. In both cases the introduction of an unfunded pension system provides higher utility for all generations. The decisive point is that generation t while young accepts handing over part of its endowment to generation $t-1$, because it knows that, when old, it will in turn get part of the endowments of generation $t+1$. There is no private contract to achieve that.[16] Note that in such a simple economy a funded system cannot come into existence: the endowment consists only of consumption goods which can be stored just for one period. There is no capital.

Things are different with a modification of the assumptions: assume that the endowment of generation t cannot only be used for consumption, but also for production by generation $t+1$ (or can be transformed into a good useful for production). In that case generation t may want to purchase goods from generation $t-1$, use them – together with its own endowment – for the production of consumption goods for itself and for generation $t-1$, but also for production goods to sell to generation $t+1$. Capital is introduced into the model. Different generations can be linked by exchange. The above given argument about the Pareto-efficiency of a PAYG system is not valid any longer. We not only have to compare a PAYG system with a no-pension system situation as in the paragraphs above but with a funded system as well.

How do the two pensions compare? It was already stated that the introduction of a funded pension scheme does not make any difference if the rate of contribution does not exceed the optimal rate of savings. The rate of return is r, the rate of interest. Does a PAYG system have a 'rate of return'? Yes, the argument was already given – assume that the population grows at rate n ($N = 1 + n$), and the productivity of labour at rate w ($W = 1 + w$). If the rate of contribution is b, constant for all generations, everybody will get for each € contribution $(1+n)(1+w)$ € pension, which is approximately $(1 + w + n)$ (as long as w and n is sufficiently small). That is easy to understand: if you pay for each € you earn b cents for the support of your parents, and you have $1 + n$ children, each earning $(1 + w)$ € for each € you have earned, they will pay you together $(1 + w + n)$ € for each € you have given to your parents if the rate of contribution remains fixed.

Therefore, to compare the two systems, we have to compare the two rates of return. If

$$(1 + w + n) > 1 + r$$

or if

$$(w + n) > r$$

a PAYG system has higher return than a funded system and is therefore better. If the rate of rate of interest is smaller than the sum of population growth and productivity growth, the introduction of a PAYG system safeguards a Pareto-improvement.

Whether that condition is fulfilled looks like an empirical question. There were decades during which the rate of interest was below the sum of the rates of growth of labour productivity and of population growth, and there were decades during which the rate of interest was higher. However it is a standard result of macroeconomics that such a situation cannot be a stable equilibrium (see for example Blanchard and Fischer, 1989). For the long run we have to assume that the rate of interest is not smaller than the sum of the rate of population growth and productivity growth.[17] That is why an unfunded system is in general not Pareto-improving.

Is a funded system Pareto-better compared with a PAYG system? No, it can be shown that with the above given assumptions – fixed labour supply, no bequests, no uncertainty concerning death – a funded system is not Pareto-better compared with a PAYG system (Breyer, 1989). The reason is that by starting a PAYG system you give the first generation a share of the resources of the second generation. It is consumed by the first generation – no-bequest assumption. The capital stock is therefore smaller and all future generations are worse off compared with a funded system. If, instead, a funded system had been introduced (or people relied on private savings) the first generation would have forgone the benefit of the redistribution in its favour and would therefore be worse off. There is no way to compensate the first generation for not having the advantages of the introduction of a PAYG system which does not decrease the welfare of future generations. (The proof given by Breyer (1989) uses the following idea: assume that a funded system is introduced and that the government wants to compensate the first generation for not having a PAYG system. It has to incur a debt to support the first generation. The question is, whether the debt can be repaid out of future contributions within a finite period of time without hurting a future generation – no it cannot. The reason is that you cannot do away with the fact that the consumption of the first generation was increased.[18])

To sum up: the conversion of a PAYG system into a funded system does not, in general, result in a Pareto-improvement. Or in the words typical of the current political discussion: at least one generation has to suffer. Either the pensions of the currently old are reduced, or the currently young – and future generations as well – have to pay for the consumption of the currently old and have to provide for their own retirement by saving as well.

5.2.2 Changing Assumptions

We have now to look at what results if some of the assumptions of the preceding analysis are changed. Each of the following assumptions will be dropped: (i) no-bequests; (ii) labour supply is fixed; (iii) length of life is certain.

(i) In general people do not consume all their wealth, otherwise bequests would not be so important (Miles, 1999). Does that make a difference? To see the point: we assumed that individuals have utility over two periods only, because they live only for two periods. To take account of bequests, the consumption of future generations must be part of a person's utility:

$$U = U(c_1, c_2, c_f)$$

where c_f signifies consumption of future generations. Consider the following possibility: parents want to leave a fixed percentage of their endowments or a fixed amount of goods to their children – a house, or an education at an expensive university. This does not change the main idea. Everybody gets something from her ancestors and gives something for the next generation. It is nothing but a reversed unfunded pension system. The introduction of an unfunded scheme has the same effects as in the situation without bequests, namely, it reduces the capital stock. However the magnitude of the effect of the introduction of the unfunded system is smaller: if everyone saves for retirement and for leaving something for the next generation the introduction of an unfunded system can only crowd out the savings for retirement consumption, but not that for the estates.[19]

Things are different if we write the utility function in a slightly different way:

$$U = U(c_1, c_2, U^{f*})$$

with U^{f*} signifying the optimal amount of utility for the next generation (from the point of view of the current generation). Because the utility of the next generation depends in the same way on the optimal utility of the following generation and so forth, the first generation has to take account of all future generations when it maximises its utility. This is tantamount to maximisation of utility over infinitely many periods. That results in a completely different model. It is no longer an overlapping generation model with each generation deciding for itself, but a model where the first generation makes all decisions for all future generations (Ramsey-model after the British economist John Ramsey).

In that case the introduction of a PAYG pension system does not have any influence on total savings and on the capital stock. Indeed, if the government decides to introduce a PAYG system, the first generation is favoured and the capital stock is decreased. As the favoured generation maximises utility for all future generations, it increases its savings to give more to the next generation! The plan of the government is frustrated by the reaction of the public, namely by increasing their savings euro for euro. They anticipate the decrease in the capital stock due to the introduction of a PAYG pension scheme and make good the shortfall with increased saving (Ricardo-equivalence, Barro theorem[20]).

There is a tremendous amount of literature on whether the Ricardo-equivalence is empirically valid, or whether a PAYG system displaces private savings. On a superficial level aggregate savings are not related to the generosity of the pension system. Austria has a very elaborated PAYG system. It was started in 1956 and benefits were often extended, and only cut a few times. The introduction of a PAYG system of public provision for care in 1993 was also a shift of resources towards the then current old population. Nevertheless, the savings rate is very high in Austria. Retired people save and leave bequests to their children and grandchildren. In the USA, with a much lower replacement rate for incomes in the middle and upper ranges, aggregate savings are much lower. That is not a proof (or a falsification) of the validity of the Ricardo-equivalence. But even methodologically refined research is inconclusive on this question. (Kohl and O'Brian (1998) gives a good overview of the literature.)

(ii) What happens if the labour supply is not fixed? If this assumption is relaxed, the change from a PAYG system to a funded system can be Pareto-improving. To see why, if the pension system redistributes income between individuals of the same generation – for example, from the rich to the poor – such that labour supply is negatively affected (see Chapter 3), a shift towards a funded system does away with this distortion of labour supply (Breyer and Straub, 1993). In that case a Pareto-improvement would be possible. Unfortunately the payments which are necessary to compensate the first generation for the loss of the PAYG system make it necessary to introduce another tax which will also distort the decision of the households (Brunner, 1996). Furthermore if the poor are subsidised by another system – social assistance – that must also be financed by a tax. It is not the pension system which distorts prices, but any support for the poor has this effect if not financed by a lump-sum tax.

(iii) How does the assumption of no uncertainty concerning the time of death affect the results? If a person gets very old she might outlive her savings. One has therefore to take care of that case – to insure against outliving one's own resources. That can be done by buying annuities: a fixed stream of income until death. If a person dies early, the insurance makes a profit. If she lives long, there is a loss for the insurance. In a fair insurance system the profits from people living shorter lives than the average cover the losses incurred by those living longer than the average. If an insurance can provide fair annuities the uncertainty of the time of death does not influence the optimal amount of saving. But if there is no insurance for that, people have to save extra – the technical term is 'precautionary saving' – to take care of the possibility of a very long life.[21] The introduction of any pension system, whether PAYG or funded, reduces saving if it provides annuities (Kotlikoff and Spivak, 1981).[22]

5.2.3 How the Two Systems Fare in Case of Shocks

We now want to compare how the two systems fare under different types of shocks, namely demographic shocks and productivity shocks.[23] For this we distinguish people according to generation (Homburg, 1988).

N_t^w : working population at t
N_t^r : retired population at t

$$n_t = \frac{N_t^w - N_{t-1}^w}{N_{t-1}^w} : \text{rate of growth of the working population}$$

$$w_t = \frac{W_t - W_{t-1}}{W_{t-1}} : \text{rate of wage growth}$$

Contribution to the pension system at t: $N_t^w \cdot W_t \cdot b_t$
Rate of contribution at t: b_t
Expenditure of the pension system at t: $N_t^r \cdot P_t$
Pensions paid at t: P_t

Each of the two schemes can be described by an equation in which the contributions are set equal to the pension payments. For a pay-as-you-go scheme the equation is:

$$N_t^w \cdot W_t \cdot b_t = N_t^r \cdot P_t$$

This year's contributions equal this year's pensions. Assuming that all working people reach retirement, that is,

gives
$$N_t^r = N_{t-1}^w$$

$$P_t = (1 + n_t) \cdot W_t \cdot b_t$$

As mentioned above, one can define a rate of return i_t, although there is no interest payment in the formal sense:

$$1 + i_t = \frac{P_{t+1}}{W_t \cdot b_t}$$

$$= \frac{(1 + n_{t+1}) \cdot W_{t+1} \cdot b_{t+1}}{W_t \cdot b_t}$$

$$= (1 + n_{t+1}) \cdot (1 + w_{t+1}) \cdot \frac{b_{t+1}}{b_t}$$

The rate of return of an unfunded system increases with the rate of growth of population, the rate of growth of wages and any increase of contributions.

A funded scheme is described by

$$N_t^r \cdot P_t = (1 + r_{t-1}) \cdot N_{t-1}^w \cdot W_{t-1} \cdot b_{t-1}$$

with r_t being the rate of interest. Last year's contributions compounded with interest equal this year's pensions, or

$$P_t = (1 + r_{t-1}) \cdot W_{t-1} \cdot b_{t-1}$$

A funded pension does not depend on this year's contribution.

How do the two systems fare under the following two policies?

(i) Keeping the rate of contribution b_t constant.
(ii) Keeping q_t, the level of pensions in relation to current income (P_t/W_t), constant.

For quite some time most countries tried to follow the second policy, namely keeping pensions in line with the income of the working generation. As this policy creates problems, we observe in some countries a switch to the first option.

(i) $b_t = b$ for all t

In a PAYG scheme the rate of return reduces to

$$(1 + i_t) = (1 + n_t)(1 + w_t)$$

All contributions are compounded with 'interest' equal to the product of wage growth and population growth. The level of pensions q_t is independent of wages and depends only on population growth. If the rate of population growth n declines, the rate of return declines as well. The same is true if wage growth declines.

In a funded scheme the rate of return is not affected by keeping b_t constant, but the level of pension q_t is affected.

$$q_t = \frac{1+r_{t-1}}{1+w_t} \cdot b$$

Any wage increase reduces the level of pensions when contributions are constant. This is due to the fact that current pensions are not related to current wages.

(ii) $q_t = q$ for all t

In a PAYG scheme the rate of contribution must be set as

$$b_t = \frac{q}{1+n_t}$$

If policy wants to keep the pensions in line with current income, the rate of contribution must increase when the working population declines. With a long-run decline in the working population, this is not a sustainable policy: the rate of contribution would have to grow forever.

In a funded system contributions have to be set in accordance with future wages.

$$b_t = \frac{1+w_{t+1}}{1+r_t} \cdot q$$

The higher the expected wage growth, the higher must be the rate of contribution.

How is the relation of the two rates of return? If the two rates are kept equal:

$$(1 + i_t) = (1 + r_t)$$

the contributions of a PAYG system must have the following path.

$$b_t = \frac{1 + r_{t-1}}{(1 + n_t) \cdot (1 + w_t)} \cdot b_{t-1}$$

If $(1 + r) > (1 + n)(1 + w)$ which, as mentioned already, is a reasonable assumption in the long run, the system will collapse, because contributions have to increase for ever.

5.3 MUST POLICY CARE FOR RETIREMENT?

5.3.1 Redistribution of Wealth over the Life-Cycle

As with any other social policy programme, we must as, what is the rationale for having publicly regulated pensions. If there were no public retirement provision, should one be introduced? This question should not be confused with the historic question as to why public pension provisions were introduced in this or in that country. The historic causes are not the same in different countries. In Austria and in Germany the idea of general public pensions was to extend the privileges of the state bureaucracy and private bureaucracies to other groups. The political context was that the working class was organised by a social-democratic party and by trade unions and fought for an organised system of retirement income as they would otherwise be poor. In the USA pensions were first introduced for veterans (of the civil war) and for mothers. The political context was that of party politics. In order to win elections each party wanted to favour groups who belonged to their traditional constituency (Skocpol, 1992).

But can one find reasons for public retirement regulations in economic theory? Let us consider a situation without such regulations. People would have to care for themselves. They would have to save or rely on the mercy of other people. The latter way is the traditional way in agricultural societies: old people lived on their descendants. If there were none, one had to beg or turn to some public relief systems – for example, poor houses, hospitals.[24] (The Austrian pension system for farmers still has regulations which take into account the fact that there are transfers from the working farmers to their parents.) In modern, rich societies most people are able to save enough to have a retirement income in line with former earned income. Only the poor are unable to save enough. Something must be given to them. This is the idea of most basic pension schemes, as in Australia, New Zealand, the UK, Chile, Argentina. The basic pension should fend off poverty.

How much wealth is necessary for retirement in order to keep consumption at approximately the same level after retirement than before retirement? For the calculation we have to make some assumptions. (i) A household starts saving at the age of 35 (before that people have to pay back any loan they took for getting started). (ii) They save for 30 years and retire at 65. Life expectancy at age 65 is 15 years. What savings rate is necessary to finance a given replacement ratio?

Wealth at age 65 is, given the rate of interest r:

$$W_{65} = (sY/r)(e^{30r} - 1)$$

with Y income per year, s rate of savings, e basic of natural logarithm. The annuity for 15 years which can be financed out of a given wealth at 65 is:

$$A = rW_{65}\, e^{15r}/(e^{15r} - 1)$$

The replacement rate φ, assuming that pensions and income are taxed at the same rate:[25]

$$\varphi = A/(1-s)\cdot Y = (s/(1-s))\cdot e^{15r}\cdot (e^{30r} - 1)/(e^{15r} - 1)$$

To achieve a replacement rate of 0.7 one would need the following savings rate depending on the rate of interest:

interest rate	0	0.01	0.02	0.03	0.04
savings rate	0.25	0.22	0.18	0.15	0.12

A rate of savings around 15 per cent of net income is nothing outstanding. (Chile demands a savings rate of 10 per cent, but people have to save all through their working life!) If we take account of income growth, the savings rates to achieve them are a bit higher. Be that as it may, the savings necessary for achieving sufficient wealth for retirement do not comprise the essential problem. Most people can earn enough to support themselves for their whole lives during their working lives – otherwise they would need a rich uncle to support them! Empirically, however, people's wealth at retirement does not only depend on income. The savings rates differ very much between individuals in the same income group (Venti and Wise, 1998).

5.3.2 Can People Care for Themselves?

It was shown that saving can solve the problem of consumption during retirement. Can't people be left alone in their provisions for old age? Is it really necessary to have public retirement regulations and retirement programmes? Probably most people would take care. But there are some problems which will be discussed in this part of the chapter. These problems are:

1. Not having saved enough.
2. Having acquired the wrong assets.
3. Too early disability to work.
4. Outliving one's wealth.
5. Having underestimated inflation.
6. Converting wealth into an annuity.

Insufficient savings
Though a savings rate of approximately 15 per cent is not very high, some people may not save enough. This behaviour is called myopic. Agents strongly preferring current consumption, but will resent their savings decisions later. Furthermore for low-income people there is a reason not to save for retirement if there is support when being poor: individuals with low income can hardly save enough for a retirement income above the poverty threshold. If they can rely on a public scheme against poverty they lose if they have some wealth; it is rational not to save. This is a Samaritan's-dilemma situation. The obvious solution to this problem is to force people to save as is done in Chile and Argentina. The mandatory private pension regulations in the UK or in Switzerland have a similar rationale. The same logic underlies the rule of the British pension law, according to which people have to buy an annuity when they are 75.

Which assets to buy?
To take care of one's own old age needs not only the decision of how much to save, but also decisions on which assets to acquire. That is a very complicated matter. It can be made easier by relying on funds which, usually carry less risk than either stocks or assets whose return depends on merely one economic activity. The decision of which fund to invest in is also no easy matter.[26] That is probably one of the reasons why in many countries employers provide pensions. It is their business to make these decisions on behalf of their employees – this saves transaction costs and firms can buy the services of specialists for making the necessary decisions.

Nevertheless private provision for old age needs control of all funds or people would be in danger of losing the assets dedicated to finance their consumption in old age. Though it is accepted that in market economies people may lose wealth due to the acquisition of the wrong assets, it is not accepted that this should result in poverty. However, if a country does not accept that people may become poor because they have acquired the wrong assets, there is an incentive for acquiring risky assets with a high expected return. This is another example of Samaritan's dilemma: if I can rely on society in case of poverty, I am more prepared to accept high risks.[27]

To see the difference it can make: a dollar invested in a fund mirroring the Dow-Jones index in the 1930s would have brought a return much higher than a dollar invested in bonds with fixed interest rates. But some of the assets forming the Dow-Jones had much lower returns. Any fund using only a subset of Dow-Jones listed stock could have had a lower return.

There is a further risk inherent in all funded systems: the volatility of financial assets is high. Even funds whose value moves with a general index of the stock exchange have higher volatility than the real economy. An extreme example is the movement of the Nikkei-index (Tokyo): in August 1978 it stood at less than 5600, it increased more or less steadily to 38 915 in December 1989. Within nine months it fell to below 21 000. It regained value and moved between 22 000 and 26 000 for two years. In October 2001 it stood at below 11 000. Though the Japanese economy did not grow much in the 1990s, it did not recede by 60 per cent. This does not imply that pensions based on funds mirror these risks completely. It is possible to hedge against them, for example, by shifting into bonds when nearing retirement age. However bonds risk losing value due to inflation. Substantial risks remain.

BOX 5.1 AN EXAMPLE OF RISK OF FUNDS – BUT GOVERNMENT IS NOT INNOCENT

For almost a decade Japan's life insurance have been losing money. Five have collapsed in the past year. Nobody expects the rest to announce anything other than awful annual results on 4 June.

The problem is years of low interest, which have led to falling annual returns. This means that life insurers are unable to match their high payout rates they have guaranteed on existing policies by investing the premiums that are paid in. In the year to 31 March, the ten biggest insurers are expected to have lost ¥1.4 trillion ($12.7 billion) from this mismatch alone. Then there were dud investments in equities and property, and also bad loans to other sickly companies.

To be fair, the fault is not wholly the life insurer's. One reason, they set unrealistically high pay-out rates in the 1980s was that the government's own life- insurance business, run by the post office, could compete in the

> knowledge that its losses would be plugged with public money. (*The Economist*, 26 May 2001)
>
> In the UK, Equitable Life, the oldest life insurer in Great Britain, also faced big problems due to falling interest rates. In the 1970 they guaranteed rates of return which then were easy to earn due to high inflation. Now inflation is much lower and nominal interest rates as well.
>
> From 1994 Equitable sought to nullify the value and the potential cost of these guarantees. That became the subject of a court case that went up to the House of Lords. Last July five law lords unanimously ruled that Equitable's earlier pledges must be honoured in full. Equitable met the estimated £1.5 billion ($2.25 billion) by freezing the value of all policies in the with-profits fund for seven months – in effect, taking from those policy-holders without guarantees to pay for those that had them. (*The Economist*, 20 January 2001)

Early disability to work

In order to make a sensible savings decision an individual has to make assumptions about his or her retirement date. Later there may be reasons to change this decision – loss of job when near retirement, too early disability to work, and so on. All countries therefore have a disability insurance. In some countries it is integrated with old-age pension schemes, in others this risk is covered by a separate insurance. In the case of private saving for retirement these risks also have to be covered in a separate insurance.

What to do with savings upon retirement?

The three other problems listed above can be discussed together, as they are closely related. If an individual has saved for retirement, she has to make a decision what to do with the accumulated savings when retiring. Using up the savings can result in outliving one's resources and poverty in very old age. One solution is to buy an annuity – that is an income stream without a definite date of end. Financial intermediaries can accept the risks. Some people die early and the funds win, others live longer and the funds lose.

Annuities carry a risk: inflation. When you buy a fixed-amount annuity its value goes down with the increase in the consumer price index (CPI). This can have dramatic effects, even with moderate rates of inflation, as they were for the last twenty years. Losing value by 2 per cent a year, reduces the value of an annuity to 82 per cent of the original value in 10 years, and to 67 per cent after 20 years.[28] With a rate of inflation of 3 per cent the values are 74 per cent and 55 per cent. People who started with a very comfortable pension may end up in poverty after 20 years!

Financial markets can cope with a steady moderate inflation. There are escalating annuities available rising each year by a rate contracted in advance. However the risk of unexpected inflation remains. Between 1970 and 1980 prices rose by 65 per cent in Germany, by 150 per cent in the USA and by 260 per cent in the UK. Three years of inflation at 10 per cent reduces a fixed-level annuity by about 25 per cent. Though the current consensus amongst economists makes it unlikely that inflation will rise again to such levels, nobody can give guarantees for decades.

Currently nominal wealth cannot be protected fully against inflation in financial markets (Brown et al., 2000). Only in Canada, the UK and the USA are there some government bonds available which promise a fixed real interest rate. This market segment is small. As mentioned, Chile has managed to provide real annuities.

BOX 5.2 WHY IS THE MARKET FOR ANNUITIES SO SMALL?

Although the purchase of an annuity is a comfortable way to hedge against the risk of outliving one's own resources, the market for annuities remains astonishingly small. There may be many reasons for that – people want to leave a bequest without committing to the size of the bequest; they may keep wealth for care when very old.

But there may be also an adverse selection problem (Brown et al., 2000; Finkelstein and Poterba 2000; Doyle et al., 2001). For individuals expecting to live long an annuity is much more interesting than for an individual with a shorter life expectancy.

In order to test whether there is adverse selection, one has in one way or another to take account of what people expected when they decided whether to buy an annuity. There is no direct way to find what individuals expected when they made the decision to buy an annuity or not to buy one. But one can compare the difference between the value of an annuity when using population-wide mortality rates, in comparison with the mortality rates of annuitants. Because the mortality of the annuitants is lower than that of the population average – individuals who buy an annuity live, on average, longer than others – an annuity is, on average, of higher value for the annuitants than for the rest of the population. Note that individuals with high life expectancy face a high risk of outliving their own resources. As the theory predicts, they find full coverage for the risk, whereas the good risk – those who tend to die early do not buy annuities.

Return for $1 when buying annuities in Australia and Singapore		
Australia	Annuitants	Population
m 60	88.89	80.97
m 65	90.40	83.73
f 60	90.26	86.65
f 65	89.38	87.04
Singapore		
m	93.92	93.44
f	95.44	96.27

Notes:
m: men, f: women, 60 (65): at the age of 60 (65).
Annuitants: using mortality rates of annuitants.
Population: using mortality rates of the whole population.

Source: Doyle et al. (2001).

5.3.3 Are Public Pensions Risk-Free?

A public non-funded pension does not face the risks of a pure savings system. Total wage income increases approximately with inflation. The development of total wage income is much steadier than that of capital income. Speculative bubbles which may drive the value of stock far above or far below the value of discounted future profits have no implications for a public PAYG system. Furthermore making the wrong decision where to invest is also not possible.

But this does not imply that there are no risks in public PAYG systems. Public pensions rest on statutory law – that can be changed. They carry the political risk that a future government wants to reduce pensions. That risk can be substantial. Whereas funded systems are obliged to show future obligations in their balances, public PAYG systems have no balance where wealth and obligations are confronted. This allows public systems to promise payments without thorough calculations of future debts. Furthermore, in the political process some groups can get favours by special clauses in the pension code – early retirement, granting contribution-free rises in pensions, and so on. That would not create a problem if financing the extra benefits were fixed at the time the benefits are mandated – for example the defence budget has to pay contributions if service is counted as a period of contribution. Unfortunately this hardly happens.

Moreover a change in any parameter of a pension system need not result in a quick change to the contribution/payment structure, as future obligations of public systems are not put on a balance sheet. For example, in a funded system an increase of life expectancy must lead to a revaluation of its obligations – if the managers acted in the appropriate way. In public PAYG systems such rules do not exist.

BOX 5.3 AN EXAMPLE OF THE POLITICAL RISK OF A PAYG SYSTEM

In 1984 the pension benefit formula was changed in Austria. To bring contributions and pensions more in line with each other, the minimum replacement rate was abolished. This affected only new pensions, beginning in 1985. The new benefit formula decreased the pensions of women drastically as they were the main beneficiaries of the former minimum replacement rate.

Average new pensions in Austria (Schilling per month)

Year	Old age pension Men	Women	Pension of women as percentage of pension of men
1983	10316	6061	58.8
1984	10787	6364	59.0
1985	11320	6385	56.4
1986	11621	6012	51.7
1987	12128	6027	49.7
1988	12256	6057	49.4
1989	12040	5908	49.1
1990	12040	6044	50.2

Source: Soziale Sicherheit 1/1993.

Whereas the pensions of new male retirees increased in line with income growth, the pension of new female retirees decreased. This was the effect of a politically engendered change of the calculation for pension benefits which was considered necessary to decrease the deficit of the pension system.

In many countries government and parliament made ample use of such opportunities, as it was a way to grant benefits without stating who should pay for them. In some countries it was accepted that effective retirement age was reduced for minimising open unemployment. The result is that many systems are currently not sustainable without either a reduction of benefits and/or increase of contributions. This is less of a problem in systems with defined benefit plans or defined contribution plans, like the Swedish or the French systems. It is a special problem for systems with statutorily fixed benefits and contributions, as in Austria, Germany and Italy. Though the law fixes precisely the pension of the insured people, the retirement income is not fixed – the law might change.[29]

5.4 ALLOCATIVE EFFECTS: LABOUR SUPPLY

Pension systems have two important allocative effects. They influence labour supply and saving. How saving and capital supply is influenced by a pension system was discussed in 5.2. In this part of the chapter we are concerned with effects on the labour supply. In order to do so, we disregard for the moment all problems of income distribution and assume that the pension system affects all people equally. That is necessary in order to separate the effects of the existence of pension systems on the labour supply from those of the changes of distribution thereby engendered.

In most countries effective retirement age has fallen (see Table 5.5). Is this due to effects of the retirement provisions? For the analysis of this question it is necessary to assume that the pension system does not change the wealth of a person – it is a fair pension. Particularly, wealth does not change if a person retires earlier or later. There is no pension system for which this condition is fulfilled, but to study the effects of an empirically given pension system on labour supply we have to separate the effects which are due the existence of a pension system from that of specific regulations.

What are the incentives to retire at a specific age if there is a fair pension scheme? (Minimum age requirements are not considered.)[30] Assume that a person's utility function is separable in consumption and leisure.

$$U(c_t) + V(l_t)$$

with c_t: consumption, l_t: leisure. A person is either working or retired, there is no partial retirement. She works from $t = 0$ to N; savings are s; pension contributions b.

$$c + b + s = 1 \quad \text{(a normalisation)}$$

For simplicity $r = 0$, therefore savings are a pure shift of wealth over time and do not influence total wealth; they can be left out of the intertemporal budget constraint. It is further assumed that there are no borrowing constraints, lifetime is certain and consumption is equalised over all periods. Utility of a year working equals $U(c)$ and of a year of retirement $(U(c) + v)$.

Table 5.5 Labour force participation (ages 55–64)

Country	Men 1990	Men 1999	Women 1990	Women 1999
France	45.8	42.6	31.1	32.5
Germany	57.7	55.1	26.4	34.3
Italy	51.7	42.8	15.0	15.9
Netherlands	45.8	49.8	16.9	22.8
Sweden	75.3	72.3	65.8	64.9
Switzerland	86.4	80.9	53.4	64.0
United Kingdom	68.1	63.5	38.7	41.1
United States	67.8	67.9	45.2	51.5

Source: OECD, Employment Outlook (2000), p. 266ff.

Lifetime utility is (T: maximal life span, c: consumption during one year):

$$U(c)N + [(U(c) + v)(T-N)] = U(c)T + (T-N)v$$

People maximise utility:

$$\text{Max: } TU(c) + (T-N)v$$
$$N, c$$

$$\text{s. t. } Tc \leq N(1-b) + (T-N)P \qquad P: \text{pension.}$$

The pension system is fair, therefore:

$$P = bN/(T-N)$$

The budget constraint reduces to

$$Tc \leq N$$

When there are no bequests people consume all they have earned during the period of working. Therefore the equality sign applies. The pension P (and the contribution b) does not influence the time of retirement N.

Things are different if there are borrowing constraints. If while working an individual wants to consume more than her income after paying the contributions for the pension, her savings during the working period are negative. She takes out a loan to be repaid during retirement. That is not unrealistic: some pension systems have high pensions – quite common in the public services of many countries.[31] Second, all pension systems demand contributions to be paid from the moment an individual starts to work. However many people take a loan when young to start their own household. In both cases, if an individual has problems in getting a loan – or, more realistically, the rate of interest for a loan is significantly higher than that for savings – the pension system can influence the retirement decision.

To see why, let c^* be the optimal amount of consumption during the period of working. If $c^* > 1 - b$, an individual cannot finance her optimal consumption if she is rationed in the market for loans. Her consumption is therefore precisely $1 - b$ during the period of working. The optimisation problem changes to (c': consumption during retirement):

$$\max_{c', N} NU(1 - b) + (T - N)[(U(c') + v]$$

$$\text{s.t. } N(1 - b) + (T - N)c' \leq N$$

In that case it can be shown that

$$\frac{\partial N}{\partial b} < 0$$

Any increase of the pension contribution, tantamount to an increase of the pension, reduces the retirement age. An individual has acquired an amount of wealth she considers sufficient for retirement earlier than in the optimal plan.

Be that as it may, hardly any pension system is really a fair system. Usually a minimum age for retirement is required, or a minimum of years of contributions. Different tax rules may apply to earned income and to retirement income. There may be special regulations for earlier retirement, special provisions in case of disability or unemployment in advanced age. For people with low income and therefore a low pension supplementary social assistance benefits can also affect the retirement decision. In some systems the pension is paid only if a person withdraws from the labour market, or the pension is reduced if she continues to work. Furthermore a person may influence her social security wealth (discounted benefits minus discounted contributions) by starting to take the pension at a specific date. Namely, if the increase of the pension due to one more year of contributing is above a certain threshold it pays to work longer; if that increase falls below this value, the social security wealth of the pensioner is reduced by contributing longer.

If it is not to affect the social security wealth of a pensioner the pension has to be reduced by approximately 6 per cent for each year of earlier retirement. This is the case in Sweden, Finland, Germany and the USA. In other countries pensions are reduced less. By withdrawing earlier from the labour market a person can increase her social security wealth. In that situation one either has to accept a decrease of the effective retirement age, or to enforce the statutory retirement strictly.

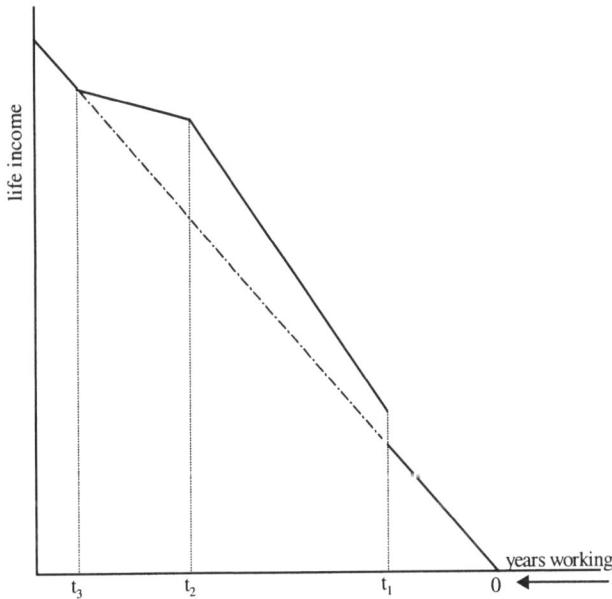

Figure 5.1 The budget constraint under complicated pension and tax rules

To show the effects of a retirement scheme, one can use a figure of the budget constraint (Figure 5.1), where the years of working are shown from right to left on the abscissa and on the ordinate is the pension wealth – that is, the discounted value of the stream of pension payments.

In Figure 5.1 it is assumed that a person has to work t_1 years to get any pension at all. Therefore the budget constraint makes a jump at t_1. Furthermore, nobody can retire before reaching age t_2. The slope of the budget constraint between t_1 and t_2 is determined by the rules of the pension system. If it is fair it must be parallel to the line of earnings, but in reality it can be steeper or flatter. If a person retires, she can have a pension and work, but (i) participation in the labour market and drawing a pension does not increase the future pension and (ii) a fixed percentage of the pension is retained. Therefore there is a kink at t_2. If an individual works beyond t_3, she can earn as much as she wants without reducing the pension. Many actual pension systems are even more complicated.

A study under the guidance of the National Bureau of Economic Research (USA) pursued the question of how does social security wealth develop for a person over the years in different systems. The data were taken from the statutes of the different systems.

Table 5.6 Social security wealth and its accrual for a single worker

Last year of work	France 1000€			UK 1000£		
	SSW	Accrual	Tax/Subsidy	SSW	Accrual	Tax/Subsidy
54	102.6			34.0		
55	113.9	11.3	−0.71	32.9	−1.1	0.10
56	125.8	11.9	−0.75	31.9	−0.9	0.09
57	131.1	5.3	−0.33	30.8	−1.2	0.10
58	129.4	−1.7	0.10	29.6	−1.2	0.10
59	127.7	−1.7	0.11	28.5	−1.2	0.10
60	116.4	−11.3	0.71	27.3	−1.1	0.10
61	105.9	−10.5	0.66	26.3	−1.0	0.09
62	95.7	−10.3	0.64	25.3	−1.0	0.09
63	86.1	−9.6	0.60	24.3	−1.0	0.09
64	76.8	−9.3	0.58	23.4	−1.0	0.09
65	67.9	−8.9	0.56	22.5	−0.9	0.09
66	59.8	−8.1	0.51	20.5	−2.0	0.20

Notes: SSW: Social security wealth; Accrual: Change of SSW in currency units.
Tax/Subsidy rate: relation of accrual to last years income. In case the rate is negative, it is a subsidy.

Sources: Blanchet and Pelé (1999); Blundell and Johnson (1999).

Calculations were made for different cases – single, married, high income, low income, and so on. Table 5.6 shows the base case for a single worker for France and the UK. In all states social security wealth decreases with increasing age. One more year of contributions has a negative rate of interest. This clearly is an incentive to stop working early.[32]

> ## BOX 5.4 THE 62–65 PUZZLE
>
> Is retirement age determined by individual optimisation, as economists look at it, or is it a kind of social convention, primarily determined by the law? In the USA there are two spikes of retirement age for people of moderate and low incomes: at 62, the age of early retirement and at 65, the age of normal retirement.
>
> When one assumes that the preferences of individuals are parametrically distributed the existence of spikes is a puzzle. One would expect that leaving the labour force is a much more gradual process. That people do not retire before the age of 62 may be due to imperfections in the capital market: it is not possible to borrow against future Social Security benefits. As households of low and medium income do not have much liquid wealth they have to finance consumption from current income. Therefore they cannot retire before they qualify for Social Security.
>
> But what about the other spike at 65? A study by John Rust and Christopher Phelan (1997) looked at the interaction of two social policy programmes: Social Security and Medicare. The former provides benefits starting at age 62, for the benefits of the latter has to wait until 65. Individuals who started to claim Social Security benefits at 62 had lower health status than the rest. However those with low health status who had no access to health services via an insurance had a much higher probability of working until 65. The authors concluded that the imperfection of the health insurance market, namely the possibility of very high health payments, was for many the reason for postponing retirement until 65.

5.5 DISTRIBUTIVE EFFECTS

(Intergenerational distributive effects will be discussed in 5.6.)
There is no general theory of distributional effects of pension systems. It all depends on how a system is construed. If pensions are closely tied to contributions there is not much redistribution. Many pension systems deliberately redistribute income, usually low income groups are favoured, but there are also unplanned redistributive effects. They are due to the interplay of income and life expectancy. People with high incomes often have higher life expectancy than people with low incomes. Therefore the planned redistribution in favour of low income groups is often attenuated due to differences in life

expectancy. Moreover to compare the redistributive effects of different pension systems it is necessary to take account of other social policy programmes which also shift resources to the elderly (Social Assistance, access to health services).[33]

Basic pension schemes financed through general taxes and/or social security contributions depending on income (UK, Switzerland, the Netherlands) redistribute income in favour of low income groups. In insurance based systems with pensions depending on previous income there is less redistribution. But there is no public insurance system with pensions calculated strictly according to contributions. The PAYG systems in particular have a large redistributional element. Some countries only consider years with high income (Austria), others exclude years with particularly low income (USA). Most countries provide some minimum in order to fight poverty.

As in the case of health care systems, redistribution must be evaluated against a fair insurance system – we compare an individual's lifetime contributions with her expected benefits, that is, the value of the pension when retiring.

Important aspects influencing the amount of redistribution are: (i) gender; (ii) income; (iii) and marital status.

(i) The life expectancy of women is higher than that of men. Any market based insurance must therefore have higher contribution rates or lower pensions for women than for men. Systems which treat men and women equally, as in all public systems, redistribute income in favour of women.

In some countries women can still retire earlier than men which also contributes to a redistribution in their favour, though the effect is small in most states. This does not exclude the fact that women have much lower pensions than men, due to their lower income and/or shorter labour market participation.

(ii) A fair pension system with insurance of former income does not redistribute income between high and low incomes. But there are usually clauses in the system making the relation between income and pension less strict. First of all, if the basis for calculating the pension does not comprise the income of all years but only a part of these years, there is redistribution in favour of high earners, because most of them will not have earned high incomes through all their working life. However, even years with low contributions are counted for the calculation of the pension as years with high income

Life expectancy varies between different income groups – there is evidence that people with high incomes have higher life expectancy at retirement. A public pension system redistributes income in favour of high income groups.

(iii) Most systems pay a survivor's pension. The majority of the recipients are women, because women's life expectancy is higher than men's, and husbands are often a bit older than their spouses. Is this a redistribution in favour of women? If there were no survivor's pension, a couple would have to safeguard the income of the surviving spouse. Because most women survive their husbands and because their pensions are much lower than that of their husbands (due to lower income and lower labour market participation) any private protection of the surviving person reduces the current consumption possibilities of the husband as well (assuming that the husband is prepared to share with his wife). The institution of survivor's pensions is therefore primarily a redistribution in favour of families. If survivors' pensions are means-tested, as for example in Austria, they provide redistribution in favour of single earner households.

5.5.1 Two Examples for Calculations of Redistributive Effects of a Pension System

The Netherlands (Nelissen, 1987)
The Netherlands had a basic pension scheme plus a supplementary pension. These were financed by contributions of 11 per cent of gross income up to a limit. The author calculated the discounted and compounded expected values of contributions and pensions at the time of retirement at 65. The rate of interest was the average of the rate for new mortgages. Incomes were assumed to grow like that of male workers in the metal industry. Pensions and contributions were considered to have developed as in the law. Imputations had to be made for the period before 1957, the year the law was enacted.

The following facts were considered: (i) demographic changes; (ii) differences between singles and couples; (iii) different life expectancies between men and women. Further assumptions were made about: (iv) development of incomes in the future; (v) development of rates for mortgages in the future; (vi) basic pension will be increased with the same rate as growth of real income; (vii) rates of mortality will not change; (viii) no marriage or remarriage after 65; (ix) people started to pay contributions at the age of 15 when the system was enacted, later this age was increased to 20; (x) age related income growth was not taken into consideration.

With these assumptions the author calculated the net return for all cohorts between 1905 and 1965 for different income groups starting with Dfl.10 000 up to Dfl.62 850 (the limit for contributions). In Table 5.7 the higher the income the lower the net benefits of the pension system. This is valid for all cohorts born between 1905 and 1965. However if one takes account of different length of working life and different life expectancy the results change (Table 5.8). It is reasonable to assume that people with low incomes have more years of contribution, because they start working life earlier. It was further assumed that people with low incomes have lower life expectancy.

Table 5.7 *Expected net benefits/payments at age 65 for different household incomes for married couples (in 1000 Dfl) (a)*

Basic variant: without differentiation of mortality.

Birth year	Income 10	20	30	40	50	60	62.85
1905	414	407	399	392	384	381	381
1915	375	355	336	316	297	290	290
1935	339	294	248	203	157	126	120
1955	320	254	189	124	59	1	−17
1965	311	236	162	88	14	−55	−82

Source: © with permission from Elsevier Science.

For the earlier cohorts, the results were actually reversed: individuals with low incomes got less than those with high incomes. For later cohorts the results of the base variant were not reversed, but there was less redistribution when taking account of different life expectancy and different length of labour market participation. It can also be seen that the first generations profited from the pension system. This, of course, is due to the fact that the pension system was introduced in 1957. The first generation won.

Table 5.8 *Expected net benefits/payments at age 65 for different household incomes for married couples (in 1000 Dfl) (b)*

Differentiation due to number of years a person worked more or less than in the base variant (a), and deviation from mean life expectancy (b_1 for men, and b_2 for women).

a	2	2	1	−1	−3	−5	−5
b_1	−4	−4	−2	0	2	4	4
b_2	−2	−2	−1	0	1	2	2
1905	363	356	374	392	409	431	431
1915	323	304	310	316	322	341	341
1935	288	242	223	203	183	177	171
1955	266	198	160	129	104	85	70
1965	257	180	133	93	58	28	9

Note: Only the result for married couples are presented and merely one of the variants.

Source: © with permission from Elsevier Science.

USA (Liebman, 2001)

As mentioned in the presentation of various pension systems in section 1 above, the USA has a progressive pension formula: the replacement rate starts with 90 per cent for very low incomes and declines to a mere 25 per cent at the upper limit of insured income. How much redistribution is there really if one takes account of different life expectancies?

The study by Liebman calculated various measures of redistribution of the Social Security system for the cohort born between 1925 to 1929. In order to concentrate on intragenerational redistribution he calculated contributions and benefits by using people's actual incomes, however he assumed that the current law always had been in force. Thus he neglected the windfall gains due to the introduction of the system.[34] The measures were (i) the internal rate of return; (ii) the average net transfer (dollars); (iii) the lifetime net tax rate. (Only the first is presented here.)

Table 5.9   Average rate of return according to income and according to race and education

Lowest quintile	2.70	
Second quintile	1.71	
Third quintile	1.32	
Fourth quintile	1.16	
Highest quintile	0.85	
	Using mortality tables that vary by age, sex, race and education	Using mortality tables that vary only by age and sex
White	1.52	1.59
Black	1.64	2.19
Hispanic	2.46	2.70
Less than high school	1.63	1.88
High school	1.46	1.52
More than high school	1.46	1.35

As can be seen in Table 5.9 the rate of return declines strongly against rising income. When estimating rates of return for groups according to race or education with group specific mortality rates, there is not much difference between rates of returns.[35] That raises the suspicion that redistribution is smaller when taking the differences in life expectancy into consideration. This suspicion is substantiated when comparing the rates of return for the groups with the rates they would have if all had the same mortality rate: big differences appear again. Obviously differences in mortality, that is, that poorer people tend to live shorter, strongly reduces the intended redistribution.

5.6 DEMOGRAPHIC CHANGES AND REDISTRIBUTION BETWEEN COHORTS

5.6.1 Demographic Developments

How do demographic developments affect a pension system? Is it justified to speak of a coming catastrophe? In the case of a PAYG system it is clear from the concept of the rate of return that demographic shocks influence returns.

$$1 + i = (1 + n)(1+ w)$$

If n, the rate of population growth, declines the rate of return goes down, unless w, the rate of growth of productivity, increases. In a funded system the rate of return, which equals the rate of interest, is also affected: as the rate of interest decreases when the capital/labour ratio increases, a decline of the size of the working population decreases the rate of interest – the value of the marginal product of capital. The value of the capital stock goes down if there are fewer people to use it. One cannot fully insure against a demographic shock by establishing a funded pension system.[36]

Table 5.10   Increases in life expectancy

	Male (60)		Female (60)		Male (70)		Female (70)	
	1977	1998	1977	1998	1977	1998	1977	1998
Austria	15.7	19.0	19.7	23.3	9.5	12.2	12.0	15.0
France	16.4	19.7	21.3	25.0	10.3	12.9	13.5	16.5
Germany	16.1	18.3	19.3	22.7	10.1	11.6	11.9	14.6
Greece	17.0	20.1	18.8	23.1	10.4	12.8	11.9	14.6
Hungary	15.4	15.0	18.6	19.7	9.3	9.7	11.3	12.4
Ireland	15.6	17.0	18.6	21.1	9.6	10.4	11.5	13.5
Italy	16.6	19.2	20.1	23.7	10.3	12.2	12.4	15.3
Norway	17.5	19.4	21.5	23.6	11.0	12.1	13.5	15.4
Spain	16.9	19.8	20.1	24.4	10.5	12.7	12.4	15.9
Sweden	17.6	20.0	21.3	24.0	10.8	12.6	13.4	15.7
Switzerland	16.7	20.2	20.3	24.6	10.3	12.8	12.6	16.2
United States	16.8	19.3	21.8	22.9	10.9	12.6	14.4	15.3

Source: UN Demographic Yearbook.

Two things have to be kept separate when looking at demography. First, the increase in life expectancy (see Table 5.10). Given retirement age, pensions as a percentage of GDP increase *ceteris paribus* if life expectancy increases. The relevant life expectancy is that of people reaching retirement age. If life expectancy increases due to a decrease in infant mortality there are more people working. Also, if the mortality of young people decreases, the ensuing increase in life expectancy makes things easier for pension systems.

Second, a decrease in the average number of children per woman decreases the number of the working population before the smaller number of people will retire. As long as fertility does not decrease below the threshold which keeps population constant that does not create a problem in the long run, although the pension system faces a serious problem for many decades. However, many industrialised states have fertility rates far below the rate necessary to keep population constant (see Table 5.11).

Table 5.11 Development of fertility (number of births/1000 women between 15 and 49)

	1962	1970	1980	Latest value
Austria	79.9	66.2	50.6	46.2 (1994)
Italy	73.3	69.0	46.3	38.7 (1991)
Japan	63.0	65.0	53.8 (1979)	39.3 (1993)
Sweden	60.2	59.5	51.0	54.7 (1994)
USA	97.3	76.3	61.5 (1979)	59.5 (1993)

Source: UN Demographic Yearbook.

Birth rates fell in all countries, although there is a big spread of birth rates between different countries, not only between rich industrialised countries and the rest, but also within the group of the rich industrialised economies. Some countries can sustain their population (birth rate per woman slightly above two), but many cannot. Whatever are the causes of this decline, it is an open question as to whether the gap in birth rates between countries will narrow, and if so at which level – at about two or at the German, Austrian, Italian and Spanish value of below 1.4.

The consequence of these two tendencies is a drastic change of the ratio of people at working age – usually defined as people between 15 and 65 – to people below working age and/or above working age. These ratios are called dependency ratios. We observe in all countries an increase in the dependency ratios (see Table 5.12), though the increase in the elderly dependency ratios overstates the problem. If birth rates decline, the number of dependent children declines as well (for the economic consequences see Holzmann, 1988a).

Table 5.12 Development of dependency ratios

	Population aged 65 and over (elderly share)				Population aged 0–14 and 65 and over			
	1990	2000	2010	2030	1990	2000	2010	2030
Austria	15.1	15.6	18.3	25.7	32.5	33.0	33.9	38.5
France	13.8	15.5	16.3	23.3	33.8	34.6	33.9	40.4
Germany	14.9	16.2	20.2	28.1	31.2	31.8	33.3	42.9
Italy	14.8	17.9	20.6	27.9	31.3	32.3	34.0	42.1
Japan	11.9	16.5	21.1	26.1	30.3	32.1	36.2	41.4
Netherlands	13.2	14.1	16.4	26.0	30.8	32.3	32.2	42.3
Sweden	17.8	17.0	18.4	23.1	35.6	36.7	36.9	41.3
UK	15.7	15.9	17.0	23.0	34.6	35.1	34.4	40.5
USA	12.6	12.5	13.6	21.9	34.1	34.2	33.5	40.5

Source: OECD (1996), p. 102.

The data for future decades are results of calculations and rest on specific assumptions about developments in life expectancy and fertility. Most studies make various calculations based on different assumptions. By that procedure one can estimate how a change in one of the assumptions influences the dependency ratios.

An increase of the dependency ratio to about 40 per cent is a problem for any pension system. This does not imply that people will become poor. The growth of productivity allows the pension system to be sustainable without making anybody poorer if only pensions are kept constant. Net income of the working population increases less than productivity, but nobody will lose in absolute terms (Bütler and Kirchsteiger, 1999). In fact, most PAYG systems increase pensions only in line with the rate of inflation.

5.6.2 Effects on Pension Systems

There are different ways to characterise the effects of demographic changes on pension systems:

1. Development of the pension burden in absolute numbers or as a percentage of GDP.
2. The development of the contribution rate to keep the system in equilibrium.
3. The development of the internal rate of return.
4. The redistribution between cohorts due to the demographic change.

These different methods should show the same tendency. But each one emphasises a different aspect. The first method considers the retired a burden for the economy as a whole: how much of GDP has to be given to the retired. The second method shows the burden on the disposable income of the working population: how does net income of the working generation change due to demographic development. The third considers contributions to the pension system as investment and asks what is the rate of return. The last way to describe the effects of a demographic change calculates the size of redistribution between cohorts.

All these calculations cover many decades, reaching far into the future. They should not be confounded with a real prognosis. They only show how the system will develop if the institutional regulations remain as they are and if the developments are as assumed. Demographics may change again in the future, as fertility may change. We also do not know how far the increase of life expectancy will continue in coming decades. Moreover how people and the political system will react to further changes is also open – perhaps increasing life expectancy will increase the labour supply of people up to the age of 70 and even beyond. Nevertheless these calculations are useful, as they show what problems might arise.

1. The development of the pension burden

If a growing percentage of the population is above the age at which people are supposed to work, a growing percentage of GDP must be set aside for their income. This is independent of the way the pension system is organised, private or public, PAYG or funded. However the data only show the expenditure of the public pension system.

The numbers in Table 5.13 are the result of calculating the effects of demographic shifts when leaving the pension system as it was in 1994. As mentioned, this is not prognosis, rather a calculation of what would happen if nothing changes. Italy, Germany, Sweden and Austria have already implemented some reforms since then.[37]

Table 5.13   Development of pension expenditures as share of GDP

	1995	2000	2010	2020	2030	2050
Austria	8.8	8.6	10.2	12.1	14.4	14.9
Germany	11.1	11.5	11.8	12.3	16.4	17.5
Italy	13.3	12.6	13.2	15.3	20.3	20.3
Japan	6.6	7.5	9.6	12.4	12.4	16.5
USA	4.1	4.2	4.5	5.2	6.6	7.0
Sweden	10.0	9.8	10.0	11.3	14.1	19.1

Source: OECD (1996), p. 36, base line scenario.

2. The growth of the contribution rate

The question is, by how much must contributions change due to demographic variations if the pension system remains the same – namely eligibility, retirement age and pensions – in order to keep the system in equilibrium? The OECD, the IMF and the EU have made such calculations for many countries.

We see in Table 5.14 that the rate of contribution has to increase everywhere. The size of the necessary increase is independent of current contributions. A strong increase from a low level as in the USA or in the UK may find less political resistance than the same increase from an already high level as in Germany or in Austria. On the other hand, the Austrian and the German systems cover nearly all retirement income. This is not the case for the UK or the USA system. There, only basic pensions are covered. People with moderate to high incomes have to pay extra for income insurance.

Table 5.14 Equilibrium contribution rate (per cent)

Country	1984	2000	2010	2020	2030	2040	2050
Austria	16.5	17.6	20.7	23.7	29.6	31.7	28.2
Belgium	14.0	13.8	14.8	17.0	21.0	22.7	21.5
Finland	8.5	9.7	11.4	16.0	18.2	17.8	17.6
France	14.3	16.5	17.3	21.6	25.3	27.0	26.6
Germany*	13.7	16.4	19.7	21.6	28.1	31.1	26.8
Italy	14.7	17.1	19.5	22.3	26.8	31.1	28.7
Netherlands	12.1	13.4	15.0	19.6	25.7	28.5	25.5
Sweden	12.9	12.1	12.8	15.9	17.0	18.0	17.0
UK	7.7	7.5	7.6	8.6	10.6	11.2	10.2
USA	8.1	8.2	8.5	11.3	14.4	14.6	14.2
Japan	6.0	9.4	12.3	14.0	13.2	15.7	15.4

Note: *West Germany.

Source: European Commission (1996).

3. The development of the internal rate of return

This method takes the view of the insured/retired person. It considers the contributions as savings and asks how does the internal rate of return of contributions change due to demographic factors. Table 5.15, taken from a study about Austria shows a drastic decline in rate of return on contributions paid. (Prices were assumed to rise by 2 per cent.)

Once more, this is not a prognosis in the strict sense, it rather states what would have happened under specific assumptions – all are made explicit in the study – and if Austria's pension systems had remained as they were in the mid-1980s, when the study was made.

Table 5.15 Real rate of return when retiring in year t

Year of retirement	r = 1.5%	r = 3%
1961	5.16	5.17
1971	4.66	4.68
1981	3.72	3.93
1991	2.46	3.09
2001	1.37	2.39
2011	0.66	1.97
2021	0.19	1.68
2031	−0.47	1.11
2041	−1.13	0.44

Source: Holzmann (1988b).

The decline is partly due to demographic changes, but the very high rates of return at the onset of the system is due to the intergenerational redistribution. When the system was started benefits were given to people who did not pay into the system.[38] That is a feature of all PAYG systems: the rate of return for those who had started the system was very high – far beyond any return of a funded system. As discussed in 5.2, such a state cannot last.

4. Redistribution between cohorts due to demographic change

The methods discussed above used real data as far as possible. To understand the effects of a pure demographic shift one has to keep everything constant save the demographic variables. In that case one has to work with fictitious data – taking the pension system under scrutiny as it is and some facts about the current economy – and calculate the long-run effects of a demographic change by assuming that the economy and the social system has always been the same. An example is given by Schulenburg (1990).

Assume that the German pension system and social health insurance system as it existed in the late 1980s, had been on the statutes since 1900, covering all individuals born after 1820. This system can be characterised by a few parameters (see Table 5.14). It was assumed that people below 20 and above 60 do not pay any contribution to the pension system, neither do people below 20 pay into health insurance. People above 60 pay only half of the contribution to the health insurance of working people – that was the law. The average pension in 1980 was DM9607 (per year). As the calculation merely concerned intergenerational redistribution, it was possible to work with data of average income.

Two calculations were made. First, the contributions (b) necessary to balance the system for each generation up to the year 2160. Keeping life expectancy and costs of the health system constant and disregarding all changes due to economic development, an annual contribution to the pension system of more than DM1500 would have been sufficient in the beginning. By the year 2000 the contribution would have had to be increased to DM3400. The maximum would be reached between 2040 and 2059 with contributions of nearly DM5900. As soon as demography returned to a steady state the necessary contribution would be above DM3600. Contributions for health insurance would have started with DM2670 at 1900, rising to a constant value of DM3200 in 2110. A maximum of DM3800 would have been reached between 2040 and 2059.

Second, it was calculated which generations were (are, will be) net payers and which ones were (are, will be) net beneficiaries. Generations born up to the 1970 are net winners in the pension system as well as in the health system. Later cohorts are net losers in both systems as they have to pay more to earlier generations than they will get from later-born generations. This net transfer will be highest for people born about 2020, and will decline until 2060 (see Table 5.16).

Table 5.16 Contributions and benefits for retirement

Age	Pensions		Health system		
	Contribution	Benefits	Contribution	Benefits	
				man	women
	$b(t,\tau)$	$l(t,\tau)$	$b(t,\tau)$	$l(t,\tau)$	$l(t,\tau)$
0–9	0	0	0	837	657
10–19	0	0	0	519	604
20–29	b(.)	0	b(.)	648	1736
30–39	b(.)	0	b(.)	802	1754
40–49	b(.)	0	b(.)	1179	1811
50–59	b(.)	0	b(.)	1816	2188
60–69	0	9607	0,5 b(.)	2653	2754
70–79	0	9607	0,5 b(.)	4174	4433
80–	0	9607	0,5 b(.)	7275	8376

Notes: $b(t, \tau,)$: contribution for people born in year t at the age of τ.
$l(t, \tau)$: benefits for people born in year t at the age of τ.

Source: Schulenburg (1990).

APPENDIX 5.1

Intergenerational Accounting

In the analysis it was shown that the basic structure of the pension system affects savings and labour supply. Savings and the labour supply affect aggregate wealth and thereby everybody's income, which in turn influences aggregate saving and labour supply. Can all things be put together, such that they can be used for estimating changes of policy in an empirically sensible way? That is the scope of *intergenerational accounting* (IA). This method was developed by Alan Auerbach and Laurence Kotlikoff (1987) from the University of Boston and is now used in many countries. The primary scope of IA was to analyse the long-run effects of public sector deficits. Their problems are similar to those of unfunded pension systems, namely that interest payments and liquidating the debt will be a burden for future generations. They also affect current economic activities and therefore future wealth.

To be empirically meaningful it is not sufficient to work with a two-periods overlapping generation model. The models need to have as many periods as an individual expects to live. In the Auerbach/Kotlikoff model that is 55 years – the life of an individual starts when entering the labour force. Children and people in education before starting to work are seen as members of their parents' household. This results in an overlapping generations model in which in each period 55 generations are alive.

Households have a utility function extending over all periods of their life. In each year they experience utility from the consumption of goods and leisure time. To keep things analytically simple lifetime utility is a weighted sum of utilities over all years.[39] The weights are discount factors, depending on time preference.

$$u_t = u(c_t, l_t) \qquad t = 1, 2, \ldots 55$$

$$U = \Sigma (1 + \delta)^{-(t-1)} f(u_t) \qquad \text{(Summation over } t = 1, \ldots 55\text{)}$$

The parameter δ is the (subjective) rate of discount. Households maximise utility over all periods. This results in specific labour supply and specific savings (capital supply). Firms are characterised by a production function. Using the assumption of competitive markets the labour demand function and the capital demand function can be derived.

The tax rates and contributions for social policy programmes have to be included in all relevant budget constraints. They are contained in all equations describing the optimum for households and firms. The state does not have to balance its budget each year as it can incur a debt or accumulate assets. However, when summing up, the discounted balances of all future years must be zero if the rate of interest cannot fall below the rate of growth in the long run: all government outlays must finally be covered by taxes and contributions.

These models cannot be solved analytically as they contain equations of order up to the number of generations concurrently alive. With simulation techniques it is possible to derive numerical solutions. The results describe for each year the state of the economy: the amount of labour and its wage, the amount of capital and the rate of interest, the income and the public sector account.

It is possible to use such models to simulate divers changes of taxes and of social policy programmes, such as introducing, extending or curtailing a pension system. The big advantage of these models is that they take account of people's reaction to changes in taxes and welfare programmes as analysed by economic theory. The model can also be used to trace the effects of demographic shocks over a long period. Of course, the numerical values of the solutions cannot be taken as an unambiguous prognosis. But they show in which way a given system of taxes and government outlays will drive an economy.

Such a model was used to evaluate the intragenerational redistributive effects of the USA public pension system (Cubeddu, 1998). The author compared the welfare of the existing unfunded system with a fully funded system in steady state. As there were by assumption no aggregate risks and no imperfections of capital markets, nor demographic risks, the funded system provided higher welfare. But taking account of variations in life expectancy and lifetime income according to gender, race (whites and non-whites) and education (with and without college) the difference between the existing PAYG system and a fully funded system was not the same for all groups. Those with a small difference are comparatively better off in the current system than those whose welfare difference is big.

The model allowed calculations of the differences in capital accumulation (labour supply was kept constant, as utility was only a function of consumption and not of leisure as well) thereby affecting old age income:

> The results confirm that males, nonwhites, and college graduates experience a greater welfare gain from eliminating social security than females, whites, and non-college graduates, respectively. These gains are on average: 39.8 percent greater for males than females, 3.8 percent greater for nonwhites than whites, and 9.1 percent greater for college graduates than noncollege graduates. Differences in life expectancy and labor productivity translate into differences in capital accumulation and labour supply distortions, that are in turn responsible for differences in welfare across types of individuals. From these findings, we can infer that the current

system is lifetime progressive across gender and education, yet lifetime regressive across race. (Cubeddu, 1998, p. 18)

APPENDIX 5.2

Care

When people are old or sick they often need not only medical health services, but other types of care as well. That comprises help in all aspects of day-to-day life: cooking, getting dressed, moving around, keeping oneself clean, and so on. These services are rarely covered by pension systems, as they require greater resources than even a generous pension programme can provide. They also do not belong to the classical field of health services with its emphasis on regaining health, prolonging life or reducing pain.

Traditionally these services were provided within the family, mostly by women. Those who could not rely on the family had to turn to local support – hospitals,[40] alms houses, and so on. Rich people were able to buy the relevant services. Note that due to the very high labour intensity of their production the ability to buy these services depends to a great extent on income differences rather than on the level of income. In a poor society many people with moderate incomes are able to pay for these services, because there are individuals who are prepared to work for some food and shelter.

In the last decades care has become a major problem in most countries. There are various reasons for that:

- More and more people can live for quite some time despite being frail and despite the malfunctioning of some important organs. This is partly due to technical progress in medical treatment, and partly due to increased wealth: care is a cause of extending life expectancy (see Table 5.17).
- People have fewer children for providing care. Furthermore regional mobility has increased and children often live far away from their parents.
- Women have increased their labour market participation and are thus less prepared to provide these services within the family.
- It is less accepted now than it was in the past to keep individuals in institutions merely to keep the costs of their support small. It has become more accepted that people should live autonomously even if they need help in day-to-day affairs.

Most countries have developed schemes to cope with the problems of care.

In some they are connected with the public health system, as for example in the UK. Such a structure is difficult to implement in public insurance systems, as in Austria or in Germany. There people in need of care are publicly supported by special transfers to enable the recipients to buy the services that they need in the market.

Table 5.17   Population aged 75 and over (% of total population)

	1990	2000	2010	2020	2030
USA	5.3	5.8	6.2	7.1	10.0
Japan	4.7	6.3	9.4	12.1	14.7
Germany	7.2	6.9	8.4	10.9	12.4
France	6.5	6.7	8.1	8.5	11.4
Italy	6.5	7.7	9.9	11.4	13.4
UK	6.8	7.3	7.9	8.8	10.6
Austria	7.1	7.2	8.3	10.1	11.6
Netherlands	5.6	6.3	7.2	8.8	12.1
Sweden	7.9	8.7	8.6	9.9	12.1

Source: OECD (1996), p. 101.

In most states the local or regional social administration provides services. This is a left-over from the time when care was a part of the administration of the poor. These services consisted to a great extent in the supply of nursing homes and in financing the stay for those who could not pay. In more recent years attempts are more usually made to keep people outside nursing homes. To care for people in institutions on an acceptable level has become very costly. That is due both to labour becoming expensive (Baumol's disease) and to a change of the acceptable level of minimum quality. Keeping frail people in huge halls with up to 20 or more beds is considered inhumane today.

Some states have enacted a legal framework on a national basis to regulate which transfers are given and what kind of services are provided and how they are to be financed.[41] In other states the rules are still decided on a regional or local level. As care is going to become more costly, local budgets will become increasingly unable to cope. States without nationwide systems are discussing their introduction.

Some traditional social assistance care programmes are means-tested at state level, whereas national systems tend to disregard means-testing. There is a special problem for means-testing in case of old-age care in that the recipients can make themselves poor by handing over any wealth to children.

All systems of care are becoming more costly, as more people remain alive well above 80. This demographic development is mitigated by the increase of health of the very old, although that does not fully compensate for their increased share (Jacobzone et al., 1998; see Table 5.18).

Table 5.18 Spending and people in long-term care

Country	(a) % GDP	(b) % GDP	(c) % of total	(d) % of total	(e) % of total
Australia	0.90	0.73	6.8	11.7	73
Denmark	n/a	2.24	7.0	20.3	80
France	n/a	0.50	6.5	6.1	59
Germany	n/a	0.82	6.8	9.6	48
Netherlands	2.70	1.80	8.8	12.0	76
Norway	2.80	2.80	6.6	17.0	63
Sweden	2.70	2.70	8.7	11.2	n/a
UK	1.30	1.00	5.1	5.5	70
USA	1.32	0.70	5.7	16.0	67
Ireland	0.86	n/a	5.0	3.5	n/a
Italy	0.58	n/a	3.9	3.0	n/a
Spain	0.56	n/a	2.8	2.0	n/a

Notes:
(a): Estimated total spending on long-term care 1992–1995.
(b): Estimated public spending on long-term care 1992–1995.
(c): Share of population aged 65 and over in institutions.
(d): Share of population aged 65 and over receiving formal help at home.
(e): Share of spending towards institutions in total public spending on long-term care.
The variation in the share of people getting help at home between states is much bigger than the variation in the share of people living in institutions. European states supporting people at home have higher shares of public spending than the other. In Italy and in Spain care provided by the family still seems to be of greater importance than in other countries.

Source: Jacobzone et al. (1998).

BOX 5.5 THE AUSTRIAN SYSTEM OF CARE

The current Austrian system was introduced in 1993. It makes up and partly supplants the older system of social assistance, given by the *Länder*. People whose need is certified by a doctor get a transfer which is not means-tested from the federal state (*Pflegegeld*). There are seven different amounts according to the hours of care needed, between approximately €150 (50 hours per month) and over €1500 (in case of total immobility and more than 180 hours per month). More than 250 000 persons receive this transfer (out of 8 millions), about half of them at level two (€270) (Badelt and Österle, 1998, vol.2). Currently about €2 billion are used for these transfers, which are financed by taxes.

The *Länder* also give some means-tested transfers, however their primary field of activity is the supply of services – nursing homes and services for people remaining in their own homes. Individuals in nursing homes who cannot fully meet the payment are also supported by the *Länder*. However people may be asked to sell their assets, including their apartment before getting supplementary help. The *Länder* can have recourse to people's estates and can even ask descendants and any other heirs for reimbursement of costs.

NOTES

1. In most countries there are separate schemes for the public sector. They will not be discussed here.
2. If the budget deficit is exogenous, the contributions to a fund financing the budget deficit increase saving. If an increase of a pension fund increases the budget deficit, saving is not increased.
3. If a group with a specialised PAYG system shrinks, its pension system faces difficulties. For example, some countries have a special pension system for miners. When the numbers of miners started to decline due to structural changes in the economy, their systems became a burden for the state budget.
4. To be precise: the law states that the employed pay 10.25 per cent and the employer 12.55 per cent of gross wages. If one considers employers' contributions to be part of wages, this amounts to 20.25 per cent of gross income including employers' contributions.
5. In Austria most employed people are paid 2 monthly incomes per year extra. Calculated on a yearly basis the *Höchstbeitragsgrundlage* is the same for the employed and the self-employed.
6. The rise of pensions were small due to a shift of income distribution in favour of capital income. As total wage income rose less than GDP the formula for the increase of pensions (and of former contributions) resulted in a slower growth of pensions.
7. Actually all pensions are 7 per cent higher than they appear to be, however the contribution for health insurance is about 10 per cent.
8. The retirement age of women will be increased to 65 by 2020.
9. That was one of the issues in the election campaign in 2000. While Al Gore favoured the status quo, George W. Bush said that he wants to allow the fund to invest in stock.
10. (The men of) Switzerland did not grant women the right to vote before the 1970s!
11. Australia has a similar system: there are means-tested benefits and mandatory savings (Jones, 1996).
12. The army which then governed the country was not brought into the new system. They were allowed to keep their old system (Edwards, 1996).
13. In certain situations the capital can be withdrawn completely at retirement.
14. A difficulty arises in the proof, as r, the rate of interest, depends in a closed economy on s (Breyer, 1989).
15. Working with the assumption of a representative individual implies that distributional questions within a generation are not considered.
16. The first article in which these ideas were laid out was Samuelson (1958).

17. To see why, assume that the rate of interest is lower than the sum of the other two rates. It would be worthwhile to take out a loan and start a new line of production. As long as the rate of interest is lower than the sum of the other rates there is no limit to that. Capital would not be scarce. Unfortunately that is not the case.
18. In the proof two cases are distinguished. One for a small open economy – the rate of interest is exogenous. In a closed economy, however the rate of interest is endogenous as savings determine capital supply.
19. If a country introduces free university education the amount that people save for the education of their children decreases.
20. See Barro, 1974. The importance of this theorem stems from its application to monetary and fiscal policy. It can be shown – and that was what Ricardo in 1817 and Barro in 1974 wanted to do – that monetary policy has no influence on aggregate demand if agents optimise over infinitely long periods.
21. Note that there will be bequests though nobody wants to leave something to children. As long as there is a positive probability of being alive tomorrow you cannot consume all your wealth today. Therefore there will always be something left over after death.
22. See the case of Chile above. People can take out their wealth and run it down. However the state guaranteed minimum can be seen as an annuity. For those with very low pensions it is worth consuming all wealth in order to qualify for the state minimum. (For means-tested retirement systems and savings, see Hubbard et al., 1995)
23. For those not familiar with the language of economics: the word 'shock' means nothing but a change of a parameter.
24. That is why fertility is not merely a question of knowledge of birth-control or religious sentiments: before the introduction of pension systems a couple without children was in danger of being unsupported in old age.
25. This can be a tricky problem. If savings for retirement are not tax deductible only a part of the annuities should be taxed, because annuities comprise interest income and paying back the principal. The latter part is not income. If savings for retirement are tax deductible things are different.
26. There are more funds than stocks.
27. One can observe quite often that people put their money into financial institutions which promise very high rates of return – but which later go bust. When that is related to poverty it does not help to say that these individuals should have thought twice about whom to trust.
28. The European Central Bank has, among its objectives, that of keeping the rate of inflation below a 2 per cent threshold. The Fed has no explicit inflation target.
29. In many countries there are incentives for interest groups to encourage such policies: if a system has a deficit covered by general taxes, they form a common resource for all. A group which manages to get more out of the pension system by special regulations redistributes wealth from other groups.
30. See Crawford and Lilien (1981).
31. The statutory contributions of people working for the public services may be low as well. But this is a fictitious calculation. To calculate the real contribution one must estimate the rate of contribution which would make the system sustainable. That part of the contribution which is not in the account is an imputed part of the wages of the public services.
32. For empirical studies one has to bear in mind that retirement income often includes pensions paid by the firm – in the US for more than 50 per cent of the labour force. In that case provisions of the private pension schemes may have a stronger influence on the retirement decision. Often firms want people to retire early, particularly where wages increase with age. For an analysis, see Stock and Wise (1990).
33. If the consumption of health services financed by Medicare is considered to be part of income, this amounts to an increase of income up to 35 per cent for an average retiree in the USA (Fuchs, 2001).
34. For intergenerational redistribution in the USA, see Burckhauser and Warlick (1981).
35. He further shows that when using a different concept of income the gradient of the rates of return according to income is even stronger. Furthermore women have a much higher rate of return than men. Unlike the approach in this chapter, Liebman considers survivors' pensions a redistribution in favour of women.

36. Sometimes one finds the idea mentioned that a population can insure a funded system by investing in another economy. That does not work, as nearly all economies face the same problem. Furthermore most economies with currently high birth rates are politically unstable and are therefore unlikely candidates for large-scale investment of pension funds. If they grow for a long time they will probably experience a decline in birth rates as well.
37. This development is not merely the result of demographic changes and changes of labour market participation, but also due to 'maturation' of the system. When a pension system is started, it takes many decades until all people alive have always been covered by the system. The European systems were started in the 1950s. The analysis in this chapter proceeded as if the system has always existed. Furthermore many systems have become more or less generous. Therefore actual development always differs from the structure inherent in a mature system
38. One can see that questions of justice have to be separated from that of a fair system. In case of pensions there is a problem of justice between generations. When the system was started, the generation which retired in the late 1950s and early 1960s had experienced two wars and a long economic depression. They gained at the expense of later generations, although later generations enjoyed a much higher standard of living.
39. This again, as in the case of expected utility theory, is a case in which ordinal utilities do not suffice.
40. Up to the late eighteenth century it was an important function of hospitals to keep people off the streets who could not care for themselves. It was a general welfare institution for the poor. The French name for municipal hospitals is *hôtel-Dieu*.
41. Austria in 1993, Germany in 1994, France in 1997, Luxembourg in 1998, Japan in 2000. The Netherlands introduced a long-term care insurance in 1968. The information were kindly provided by H. Rothgang, Centre for Social Policy, Bremen.

REFERENCES

Auerbach, Alan J. and Laurence J. Kotlikoff (1987), *Dynamic Fiscal Policy*, Cambridge (Mass): Harvard University Press.

Badelt, Christoph and August Österle (1998), *Grundzüge der Sozialpolitik*, Wien: Manz.

Barro, Robert J.(1974), 'Are Government Bonds Net Wealth', *Journal of Political Economy*, 82, pp. 1095–117.

Blake, David (1997), 'Pension Policy in the United Kingdom', in: Valdés-Prieto, S. (ed.), *The Economics of Pensions*, Cambridge: Cambridge University Press, pp. 277–317.

Blanchard, Oliver and Stanley Fischer (1989), *Lectures on Macroeconomics*, Cambridge (Mass): MIT Press.

Blanchet, Didier and Louis-Paul Pelé (1999), 'Social Security and Retirement in France', in: J. Gruber and D. Wise (eds), *Social Security and Retirement around the World*, Chicago: Chicago University Press, pp. 101–33.

Blundel, Richard and Paul Johnson (1999), 'Social Security and Retirement in the United Kingdom', in: J. Gruber and D. Wise (eds), *Social Security and Retirement around the World*, Chicago: Chicago University Press, pp. 403–35.

Breyer, Friedrich (1989), 'On the Intergenerational Pareto Efficiency of Pay-As-You-Go Financed Pension Systems', *Journal of Institutional and Theoretical Economics*, 145, pp. 643–58.

Breyer, Friedrich and Manfred Straub (1993), 'Welfare Effects of Unfunded Pension Systems when Labor Supply is Endogenous', *Journal of Public Economics*, 50, pp. 77–91.

Brown, Jeffrey R., Olivia S. Mitchell and James M. Poterba (2000), *Mortality Risk, Inflation Risk, and Annuity Products*, Cambridge (Mass.), NBER Working Paper 7812.

Brunner, Johann K. (1996), 'Transition from a Pay-As-You-Go to a Fully Funded Pension System: The Case of Differing Individuals and Intragenerational Fairness', *Journal of Public Economics*, 60, pp. 131–46.

Bundesamt für Sozialversicherung (1995), *Bericht des Eidgenössischen Departementes des Inneren zur heutigen Ausgestaltung und Weiterentwicklung der schweizerischen 3-Säulen-Konzeption der Alters-, Hinterlassenen- und Invalidenvorsorge*, Bern

Burckhauser, Richard V. and Jennifer L. Warlick (1981), 'Disentangling the Annuity from the Redistributive Aspects of Social Security in the United States', *Review of Income and Wealth*, 27, pp. 401–21.

Bütler, Monika and Georg Kirchsteiger (1999), *Aging Anxiety: Much Ado about Nothing?*, Tilburg, Center of Economic Research, Discussion Paper.

Crawford, Vincent P. and David M. Lilien (1981), 'Social Security and Retirement Decision', *Quarterly Journal of Economics*, 96, pp. 505–29.

Cubeddu, Luis (1998), *The Intragenerational Redistributive Effects of Unfunded Pension Programmes*, Washington D.C., IMF Working Paper.

Diamond, Peter A. and Jonathan Gruber (1999), 'Social Security and Retirement in the United States', in: J. Gruber and D. Wise (eds), *Social Security and Retirement around the World*, Chicago: Chicago University Press, pp. 437–73.

Disney, Richard, Carl Emmerson and Matthew Wakefield (2001), 'Pension Reform and Saving in Britain', *Oxford Review of Economic Policy*, 17(1), pp. 70–91.

Doyle, Suzanne, Olivia J. Mitchell and John Pigott (2001), *Annuity Values in Defined Retirement Systems: The Case of Singapore and Australia*, Cambridge (Mass.), NBER Working Paper 8091.

Edwards, Sebastian (1996), *The Chilean Pension Reform: A Pioneering Programme*, Cambridge (Mass.), NBER Working Paper 5811.

European Commission (1996), *Ageing and Pension Expenditure Prospects in the Western World*, Reports and Studies, No.3.

Finkelstein, Amy and Kames Poterba (2000), *Adverse Selection in Insurance Markets: Policy Holders Evidence from the U.K. Annuity Market*, Cambridge (Mass.), NBER Working Paper W8045.

Fox, Louise (1997), 'Pension Reform in Post-Communist Transition Economies', in: J. Nelson, Ch. Tilly and L.Walker (eds), *Transforming Post-Communist Political Economies*, Washington D.C.: National Academy Press, pp. 370–84.

Fox, Louise and Edward Palmer (2001), 'New Approaches to Multipillar Pension Systems: What in the World is Going On', in: R. Holzman and J. Stiglitz (eds) *New Ideas about Old Age Security*, Washington D.C.: The World Bank, pp. 90–132.

Fuchs, Victor R. (2001), *The Financial Problem of the Elderly: A Holistic Approach*, Cambridge (Mass.), NBER Working Paper 8236.

Gruber, Jonathan and David Wise (eds) (1999), *Social Security and Retirement around the World*, Chicago: Chicago University Press.

Holzmann, Robert (1988a), 'Ageing and Social Security Costs', *European Journal of Population Economics*, 3, pp. 411–37.

Holzmann, Robert (1988b), 'Zu ökonomischen Effekten der österreichischen Pensionsversicherung: Einkommensersatzraten', in R.Holzmann (ed.), *Ökonomische Analyse der Sozialversicherung*, Vienna: Manz, pp. 153–205.

Homburg, Stefan (1988), *Theorie der Alterssicherung*, Berlin, Heidelberg, New York: Springer.
Hubbard, Glenn R., Jonathan Skinner and Stephen P. Zeldes (1995), 'Precautionary Saving and Social Insurance' *Journal of Political Economy*, 103, pp. 360–99.
Jacobzone, S., E. Cambois, E. Chaplain and J.M. Robine (1998), *The Health of Older Persons in OECD Countries: Is It Improving Fast Enough to Compensate for Population Ageing*, Paris, OECD Labour Market and Social Policy Occasional Papers.
Iglesias, Augusto and Robert J. Palacios (2001), 'Managing Public Pension Reserves: Evidence from International Experience', in: R. Holzman and J. Stiglitz (eds), *New Ideas about Old Age Security*. Washington D.C.: The World Bank, pp. 213–53.
Jones, Michael (1996), *The Australian Welfare State*, 4th edition, St Leonards: Allen and Unwin.
Kapteyn, Arie and Klaas de Vos (1999), 'Social Security and Retirement in the Netherlands', in: J. Gruber and D. Wise (eds), *Social Security and Retirement around the World*, Chicago: Chicago University Press, pp. 269–302.
Kohl, Richard and Paul O'Brian (1998), *The Macroeconomics of Ageing, Pensions and Savings: A Survey*, Paris: OECD Ageing Working Papers 11.
Kotlikoff, Laurence J. and Avia Spivak (1981), 'The Family as an Incomplete Annuities Market', *Journal of Political Economy*, 89, pp. 372–91.
Lampert, Heinz (1998), *Lehrbuch der Sozialpolitik*, 5th edition, Berlin, Heidelberg, New York: Springer.
Liebman, Jeffrey B. (2001), *Redistribution in the Current U.S. Social Security System*, Cambridge (Mass.), NBER Working Paper 8625.
Lißner, Lothar and Josef Wöss (1999), *Umbau statt Abbau. Sozialstaaten im Vergleich: Deutschland, Österreich, Schweden*, Frankfurt/Main: Bund Verlag.
Miles, David (1999), 'Modelling the Impact of Demographic Change upon the Economy', *Economic Journal*, 109, pp. 1–36.
Miles, David and Allan Timmermann (1999), 'Risk sharing and transition costs in the reform of pension systems in Europe', *Economic Policy* 29, pp. 253–87.
Murphy, Kevin M. and Finis Welch (1998), 'Perspectives on the Social Security Crisis and Proposed Solutions', *American Economic Review*, Papers and Proceedings, 88, pp. 142–50.
Nelissen, Jan (1987), 'The Redistributive Impact of the General Old Age Pensions on Lifetime Income in the Netherlands', *European Economic Review*, 31, pp. 1419–41.
Obinger, Herbert (1998), 'Soziale Sicherung in der Schweiz', in: E. Tálos (ed.) *Soziale Sicherung im Wandel. Österreich und seine Nachbarstaaten im Vergleich*, Vienna: Böhlau, pp. 31–102.
OECD (1996), *Ageing in OECD Countries*, Paris.
Rein, Martin and Eskil Wadensjö (eds) (1997), *Enterprise and the Welfare State*, Cheltenham, UK and Lyme, US: Edward Elgar.
Rosner, Peter, Thomas Url and Andreas Wörgötter (1997), 'The Austrian Pension System', in: M. Rein and E. Wadensjö, (eds) (1997), *Enterprise and the Welfare State*, Cheltenham, UK and Lyme, US: Edward Elgar, pp. 33–64.
Rust, John and Christopher Phelan (1999), 'How Social Security and Medicare Affect Retirement Behavior in a World of Incomplete Markets', *Econometrica*, 65, pp. 781–831.
Samuelson, Paul (1958), 'An Exact Consumption-Loan Model of Interest with or without the Social Contrivance of Money', *Journal of Political Economy*, 66, pp. 467–82.

Schulenburg, J. Matthias Graf von der (1990), 'Demographischer Wandel, intergenerationale Gerechtigkeit und Stabilität des Generationenvertrages', in: B. Gahlen, H. Hesse and H.J. Ramser (eds), *Theorie und Politik der Sozialversicherung*, Tübingen: J.C.B.Mohr (Paul Siebeck), pp. 269–300.

Skocpol, Theda (1992), *Protecting Soldiers and Mothers. The Political Origins of Social Policy in the United States*, Cambridge (Mass.): Harvard University Press.

Stock, James H. and David A. Wise (1990), 'Pensions, the Option Value of Work and Retirement', *Econometrica*, 58, pp. 1151–80.

Venti, Steven F. and David A. Wise (1998), 'The Cause of Wealth Dispersion at Retirement: Choice or Chance', *American Economic Review*, Papers and Proceedings, 88, pp. 185–91.

6. Social Policy and the Labour Market

There is hardly a field of social politics more embattled than public regulation of the labour market. This is due to the fact that regulations of labour markets are at the core of ideological debates about market economies. Some consider any interference into the freedom to contract and any support of people not working as an infringement of rights or an unjustified burden on those working. Any state protection for employees is seen as root of the evil it pretends to cure.

On the other hand political groups which were – and to some extent still are – hostile to the idea of a market economy are important actors in labour policy: trade unions and political parties with socialist or social-democratic ideas. According to some of these ideas the employed stand against the employers, insofar as the latter can increase their profits by decreasing labour costs either through wage cutting or by making working conditions worse for the workers. The most elaborate of these theories are based on Marxist concepts of the economy.[1] Some socialist parties were for quite some time explicitly committed to a Marxist *Weltanschauung*.[2]

This is not the place to discuss these ideas. It suffices to say that they are different from the theoretical outlook of this book. Mainstream economics does not look at labour markets as a theatre of war between the working class and the capitalist class. Neither does it ask whether the infringement of the right to accept any contract, as is typical for most labour law stipulations, is really as bad as is sometimes suggested.

But the claim that the labour market is a market like any other market, and it is only the trade unions or state interference which hinder its proper functioning is surely a very strong statement. People cannot switch between different jobs as easily as they can do between different brands of soft drinks; they cannot hedge their wealth by investing in different assets if nearly all their wealth consists in their human capital. If someone loses her job, she might have to take any job if there were no unemployment insurance, because current consumption may depend on current income. To overcome poverty by working very hard may hinder a person to care much about health risks at a job. When a firm closes one of its sites in a small town this can have devastating effects for the economy and the social structure of a region. It cannot be denied that there are many social problems in connection with the labour market and labour relations. The basic reason is that the labour market is not a spot market, but characterised by long enduring contractual relations. The classical market model therefore can be misleading. That justifies a special chapter in the book.

In this chapter we will look into four aspects of the labour market: 1. unemployment; 2. unemployment insurance; 3. active labour market policy; 4. regulations of labour contracts. In the following chapters we will return to special aspects of the labour market. In Chapter 7, family policy, we look at labour market problems in relation to parental leave and other parental benefits. In Chapter 8, on poverty, we look at the problems of people whose integration in the labour market is tenuous.

6.1 UNEMPLOYMENT

6.1.1 Unemployment as an Issue for Social Policy

Unemployment was an important topic for economics for more than 70 years and it still is on the agenda. This is due to the traumatic experience with unemployment in the 1930s, having contributed to the rise of Nazism in Germany. Since then economists analyse what can be done to reduce unemployment. The theoretical setting is that of macroeconomics, namely whether fluctuations of aggregate demand are responsible for fluctuations of employment. The political question is whether the state can by means of fiscal and monetary policy contribute to dampening the fluctuations of aggregate demand and thus dampen the fluctuations of employment. Economists who consider aggregate demand failures to be the main cause of unemployment see unemployment as lack of jobs: in a downswing jobs are destroyed, in a boom new jobs are created.

Other economists disregard this idea and consider unemployment primarily as a problem of the functioning of the labour market. If only workers and employers were left alone to make contracts without any interference by unions, minimum wage regulations, unemployment benefits and other forms of state interference, while fluctuations of aggregate demand would affect wages and employment there would be no involuntary unemployment. If employment declines in case of declining aggregate demand, this is due to individuals leaving the labour market voluntarily because of wages becoming too low.

Be that as it may, that is not the way we look at unemployment in this book. The question of whether aggregate demand failures are a likely cause of unemployment and what the state can do about it is not pursued here. That question belongs to the field of macroeconomics. We look at situations without such aggregate demand problems. We also disregard, at least in this part of the chapter, the question of whether labour market regulation contributes to unemployment. We look at a situation with properly functioning markets.

There is a further distinction between the traditional economic concern for unemployment and the social policy aspect. In a macroeconomic context the loss of welfare due to unemployment is reduced welfare due to output lost. It is asked by how much GDP could be increased if there were no unemployment. In the social policy context we see the problem of unemployment primarily as that of the unemployed. If the rate of unemployment could be brought down from 8 per cent to 4 per cent, the increase in GDP may be in the order of 2 per cent to 3 per cent, as the marginal product of labour will decline. This is not very much. But for the unemployed that may have been a drastic change for the better, because it has become much easier to find a job.[3]

Is there no unemployment if only demand is sufficiently high? No, all modern economies must have some unemployment. Indeed, we have to look at the flows in the labour market, namely how people move into jobs and out of jobs. Each week people retire and young people enter the labour market. Each week firms close down some lines of their business, some go out of business completely; other firms open up new lines of business and new firms start. Each week some people decide to change employment and firms decide to replace some of their employees with other ones. All that takes time. At each instant of time, there are open jobs and unemployed people, even in situations without aggregate demand failures and with properly working labour markets. An equilibrium in the labour market cannot be characterised as a situation without any unemployment and without any vacant jobs. It has to be conceptualised as a state in which the number of new hires equals the number of ended labour contracts. (See Appendix 6.1 for a sketch of a standard model.)

To give an idea of the size of the flows in the labour market see Figure 6.1. The labour force in Austria comprises some 3.5 million people. The rate of unemployment was about 4 per cent in 2001. In that year there were about 750 000 spells of unemployment. About 20 per cent of the labour force experienced at least one spell of unemployment in a favourable macroeconomic environment![4] In the USA, with about 100 million people in employment, more than one million become unemployed each month and the same amount of people change from being unemployed to being employed. In Germany (West) with about 2.7 million unemployed throughout the year 1999, more than 5 million became unemployed in that year.

Is unemployment in such a situation a social problem at all? If the duration of the search for a new job were the same for all unemployed, that would hardly be considered a social problem: people would know that they would find a job. The loss of income due to unemployment would in this case hardly be experienced as a big problem. To be out of work for a few months once in a few years amounts to a loss of a few per cent of lifetime income. Unfortunately the situation is not like that. The duration of a spell of unemployment is not the same for all individuals. Some are never unemployed, some have more than one spell of unemployment in a year. The duration of some spells is a few days only, some spells last for years.

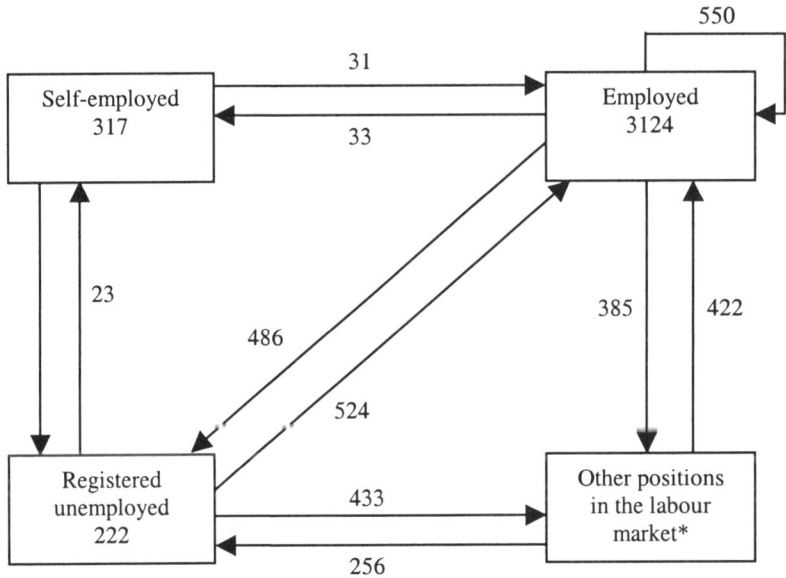

Notes: * out of labour force parental, leave, military service.
Though Austria is known for stable, long-lasting employment contracts with high protection of incumbents, there are large flows between the states employment – registered unemployment – out of the labour force. Total labour force: 3.5 million.

Source: Kubin and Rosner (2001).

Figure 6.1 Flows in the Austrian labour market for the year 2000 (in thousands)

To analyse these questions it is useful to conceptualise unemployment as a contingent event. First, some jobs last for a long time, some only for a short time. Though there are jobs with a known duration before the job starts, namely temporary jobs and seasonal jobs, in most cases it is not known when a job will end. The end of a job depends on many circumstances some of which cannot be influenced by the worker – change of technology, of tastes, of regulations, of owners of the firm. All these changes are accidental for the worker. The chance that a job ends can be captured by a probability distribution, namely the probability that a job is terminated within a given period. This distribution can be characterised by specific parameters (for example, the mean duration of a job).

Second, once an individual becomes unemployed, finding a job is a contingent event as well. Again the chance of finding a job can be conceptualised by a probability distribution. Even if all people were alike, having the same qualifications and the same characteristics which influence employment decisions, we should not expect that the length of unemployment experienced are the same for all. Some have more luck, others less. Moreover people are not alike: some have more qualifications than others. It may also be more difficult for women to find a job than for men. Members of ethnic minorities sometimes find it more difficult to find work. The probability of losing a job and the probability to find a job is not the same for everybody.[5]

Unemployment is a social problem – at least for some of those who get unemployed. That is the case without an aggregate employment problem. Even more so, when unemployment is an economic problem as well – whether due to an aggregate demand failure or due to other reasons for the non-clearing of the labour market.

6.1.2 The Measurement of Employment Problems

In this part of the chapter we want to look at different ways of describing labour market problems. There is no single measure to quantify labour market problems unambiguously.

6.1.2.1 The rate of unemployment
The most widely used statistical indicator to describe labour market problems is the rate of unemployment u. It is defined as:

$$\frac{\text{unemployed}}{\text{labour force}}$$

Neither the number of the unemployed nor the size of the labour force can be measured unambiguously.

An individual is considered (involuntarily) unemployed if she does not have a job and is prepared to take a job at the prevailing wage and at the prevailing working conditions. She is rationed in the labour market. It is important to take the wage and the working conditions into account. You are not an unemployed dishwasher if you are ready to take such a job for €100 per hour and do not find an employer. The equilibrium wage for dishwashing is probably less than 10 per cent of that value.

Unemployment is a clear theoretical concept, but it cannot be translated easily into a measurable concept. Many countries give several rates of unemployment. They differ in the number of people counted as unemployed and in the number of people being in the labour force. The EU and the OECD have managed to provide unified unemployment statistics which allows good comparisons between the rates of different countries.

Table 6.1   Unemployment rates

	1991	1995	2000
Austria		3.9	3.7
Czech Republic		4.1	8.9
Finland	6.7	15.3	9.8
France	9.5	11.7	9.5
Germany	4.2	8.2	8.1
Hungary		10.4	6.5
Ireland	14.8	12.3	4.2
Italy	8.6	11.6	10.5
Japan	2.1	3.2	4.7
Netherlands	5.8	6.9	2.8
New Zealand	10.3	6.3	6.0
Portugal	4.0	7.3	4.2
Spain	16.4	22.9	14.1
Sweden	3.1	8.8	5.9
Switzerland	2.0	3.5	3.0
United Kingdom	8.9	8.7	5.5
United States	6.8	5.6	4.0

Source: OECD (2001), p. 208, last value for Switzerland for 1999.

(i) The distinction between having a job and not having a job is not clear-cut. Many people registered as unemployed do work a bit – now and then a few hours, sometimes a full day. But they do not have a regular job. Some people with part-time regular jobs prefer to work full time. They are also rationed in the labour market if they cannot find a full-time job. However they are not counted as unemployed in the unemployment statistics of the EU and the OECD (see Table 6.1), though some of the national statistics do count them. Accepting only those who do not work at all as being unemployed leads to an underestimation of labour market problems, as there are many more who are rationed. On the other hand, including all people not working full time, but looking for a full-time job overstates the social problems because they have some income.

(ii) How can one tell whether an individual without a job is prepared to take a job at the prevailing wage? Some people who register as unemployed are not prepared to take the job at the prevailing wage – perhaps they already have a contract starting in a few weeks or are on the way out of the labour market. They register because they get unemployment benefits, health insurance or some other benefits. This leads to an overestimation of unemployment when counting these people as unemployed. On the other hand there are individuals who fit the economic criterion of unemployment but are not registered as unemployed – *hidden unemployment*. They do not register because they cannot get benefits. Nor do they expect to find a job through the unemployment agency.

In order to avoid these mistakes it is common to provide data from surveys for estimating the number of the unemployed. In the survey it is asked whether an individual without a job has looked for a job – has written applications for jobs, had interviews. The figures in the EU and the OECD tables are based on such data. The national statistics often rely on the numbers provided by the unemployment register.[6] Including hidden unemployed in the data affects not only the number of unemployed but the size of the labour force as well. They move in the same direction.

(iii) Even if we find all the people looking for a job and deduct all registered unemployed not looking for a job, the figures may still be misleading. The distinction between participating in the labour market and not participating is not as clear-cut as assumed in the definition of being unemployed. Individuals move in and out of the labour market, to some extent depending of the state of the labour market. The reason for that is that if it is easy to find jobs, people participate; if there are not many jobs, they drop out of the labour market (*discouraged workers*). That has become a relevant phenomenon. An increase of employment by 1000 people is not tantamount to a decrease in the number of unemployed by 1000, but usually results only in a smaller decline in measured unemployment. Labour force participation is pro-cyclical (Elmeskov and Pichelmann, 1993). This is easy to understand: consider the unemployed as people queuing up for jobs. If the queue is long, people hesitate to queue up. If more counters are opened to serve the queue, more people will come forward. In the context of the labour market: if unemployment is high, people may retire earlier, may stay in the education system a bit longer, or may stay at home. Therefore the phenomenon of discouraged workers is to be found primarily among people around retirement age, the young and women.[7]

6.1.2.2 The rate of employment

The last paragraph suggests that employment rates may also be considered as a factor in describing the state of the labour market. Employment rates are the share of employed and self-employed people of the population in working age. Usually individuals between the age of 15 and 65 are considered as of working age. Of course, it is not legitimate to see all people not working as somehow 'unemployed'. Many of them do not want to work. Young people prefer to remain in the educational system. Some people with small children, mostly mothers, prefer to stay at home for some time. Others stop working before the reach the age of 65. (We have seen in the chapter on pensions that in many countries there are incentives to retire early.) Still, low employment rates may point to the existence of labour market problems.

Table 6.2   International comparison of employment rates for 2000 (%)

	Total	Women	Men
Austria	67.9	59.7	76.2
Czech Republic	65.2	56.9	73.6
Finland	67.0	64.5	69.4
France	61.1	54.3	68.1
Germany	66.3	57.7	74.8
Hungary	56.4	49.7	63.3
Ireland	64.5	53.3	75.6
Italy	53.4	39.3	67.6
Japan	68.9	56.7	81.0
Netherlands	72.9	63.4	82.1
New Zealand	70.0	63.5	78.0
Portugal	68.1	60.4	76.2
Spain	56.1	41.1	71.4
Sweden	74.2	72.3	76.1
Switzerland	79.6	71.6	87.3
United Kingdom	72.4	65.5	79.1
United States	74.1	67.9	80.6

Source: OECD (2001), p. 209ff.

The lowest employment rates are to be found in southern Europe. Employment rates in the Scandinavian countries, the USA and other English speaking countries are the highest. Everywhere men's employment rates are higher than those for women. The spread of employment rates for women across states are bigger than for men. In Spain and in Italy less than 50 per cent of women are employed (see Table 6.2). However it is useful to look at details and to list employment and unemployment rates for different groups separately, not only according to gender but also according to age and education (Table 6.3).

The story does not stop here though, a high employment rate does not necessarily imply a high volume of labour. We also have to look at labour time. In the Netherlands unemployment was reduced and employment increased in the 1990s, but the volume of labour hardly increased. Most of the new jobs were part-time jobs. It may be socially better if more people are employed and working shorter hours (and earn less in comparison with a full working week) than if there are many unemployed.

Table 6.3   Unemployment rates (u) and employment/population ratios (e) according to sex, age and education

	Germany		Italy		Sweden		USA	
	u	e	u	e	u	e	u	e
by age								
15–24 m	8.1	52.5	28.4	30.2	12.3	46.7	9.7	62.0
25–54 m	6.7	89.4	6.4	84.6	5.2	85.8	2.9	89.0
55–64 m	12.6	48.2	4.6	40.3	6.9	67.8	2.4	48.7
15–24 f	7.2	44.2	35.3	22.0	11.4	45.4	8.9	57.6
25–54 f	8.0	70.8	12.5	50.7	4.6	81.7	3.3	74.3
55–64 f	15.0	29.0	4.9	15.2	5.3	62.5	2.5	50.5
by education.								
less than upp. sec. m	17.7	62.3	7.8	69.3	8.5	71.9	7.0	69.1
upp. sec. m	8.4	76.7	5.7	80.8	6.7	81.6	3.9	83.4
tertiary m	4.4	86.2	4.9	87.3	4.7	85.7	2.1	89.5
less than upp. sec. f	14.1	40.6	16.6	27.2	9.7	60.0	8.8	46.0
upp. sec. f	9.4	63.0	11.1	58.8	6.3	77.5	3.6	60.7
tertiary f	5.8	77.7	9.3	73.7	3.1	85.4	2.1	79.7

Note: u: unemployment; e: employment; m: male; f: female; upp. sec.: upper secondary education.

Source: OECD (2000), p. 212ff.; data according to age for 2000, according to education for 1999.

6.1.2.3 The distribution of unemployment

Whether unemployment is a relevant social problem does not only depend on the rate of unemployment but also on the distribution of unemployment: if all individuals were unemployed equally, a rate of 5 per cent would imply that within one year everybody is without a job for two to three weeks. In that case hardly anybody would be bothered. The problem is that during one year many people are not unemployed at all, some are unemployed for few weeks, but some are unemployed for the whole period under consideration.

To capture problems of unequal distribution of unemployment it is necessary to ask:

- how many spells of unemployment occur – the incidence;
- the length of unemployment spells – the duration;
- how many people experience unemployment.

If unemployment – measured in person-years – is constant, there is a simple relation between the average duration of unemployment, the probability of becoming unemployed and the unemployment rate:

$$u = U/L = (U/E) \cdot (E/L)$$

U: average number of unemployed spells during a year (unemployment-years); E: entry into unemployment (equals the exit from unemployment if unemployment is constant); L: labour force. The two expressions in the formula can be given an interpretation:

U/E: average duration of unemployment
E/L: rate of entry into unemployment (incidence)

The unemployment rate equals the average duration of unemployment times the probability of becoming unemployed.

The number of people experiencing unemployment P during a period is higher than its stock at any moment during this period if the average duration of unemployment is lower than a year. That is – fortunately – the case. But some individuals may have more than one spell of unemployment within a year. Taking account of multiple spells of unemployment:

$$u = \mu \cdot RI \cdot NS$$

$RI = P/L$: number of people experiencing unemployment as rate of the labour force. This is the risk of becoming unemployed.

NS = E/P: number of unemployment spells per person. This is a measure of the stability of re-employment.

μ = U/E: average duration of unemployment spells.

The importance of the decomposition of the rate of unemployment is due to the variation of the value of these parameters for different groups. For young people RI is usually high, but μ is small. They have a comparatively high risk of becoming unemployed, but most spells of unemployment are of short duration. For them it is comparatively easy to find a job. It is the other way round for older workers: the probability of becoming unemployed is small, but so is the chance of finding a job.

Table 6.4 Rates of inflow into and outflow from unemployment (1993)

	Inflows (per cent of employed)			Outflows (per cent of unemployed)		
	15–24	25–54	55+	15–24	25–54	55+
Germany	0.76	0.79	0.16	13.9	9.0	4.4
Italy	0.82	0.33	0.04	9.6	9.3	9.8
Sweden	2.58	1.10	0.41	18.1	9.8	4.5
Spain	1.07	0.52	0.12	2.8	1.2	1.2
USA	4.85	1.55	0.81	50.8	32.0	26.4

Note: The numbers for the rates of inflows are much lower than those of the rate of outflows. The denominator is in the first case the number of the employed, in the second case of the unemployed. The latter of course is much lower than the former.

Source: OECD (1995), p. 27.

Table 6.4 documents big variations across nations in the rates of inflow and outflow of unemployment. Amongst the economies compared in Table 6.4, the employed in the USA had the highest probability of becoming unemployed. Leaving unemployment was comparatively easy as well. The extreme at the other end of the spectrum is Spain.[8] If a person had a job, it was very likely that she could keep it, but if she became unemployed there were few opportunities find a job.

For many questions, particularly in the context of social policy, it is not sufficient to have knowledge of the average duration μ. It is important to have information about the distribution of unemployment. That cannot be gathered from macro-data as in the above given formula, only by using micro-data – data relating to individual spells of unemployment. We want to know how long people expect to stay unemployed – not only at the beginning of an unemployment spell, but also at points during the spell. Furthermore we want to know whether the probability of leaving unemployment changes during a spell, and if so in which way.

In order to determine what affects the probability of leaving unemployment one has to use a theoretical model describing this exit. From such a model one can calculate the probabilities of leaving unemployment and compare these probabilities with the actual data. In studies of exit rates it customary to use some specific statistics (Kiefer, 1988). If $G(t)$ is the distribution function of the length of unemployment spells

$$G(t) = \Pr(T < t),$$

then

$$S(t) = 1 - G(t) = \Pr(T \geq t)$$

is called the *survivor function*. It shows how many of those who became unemployed at a certain date (or in a certain period) are still unemployed at t. The *hazard rate* $\lambda(t)$ as a function of time is the density of the probability distribution over the survivor function – a conditional probability:

$$\lambda(t) = g(t)/S(t)$$

with

$$g(t) = dG(t)/dt.$$

The hazard rate can be interpreted as the probability that a spell of unemployment lasting until t will end between t and $t + \partial t$. Empirically, one has to count how many of those still unemployed at t find a job in the next period.[9]

An important question is whether the hazard-rate function is constant (see Figure 6.2). In that case the probability of leaving unemployment in the next period is independent of the length of prior unemployment. Most estimations show that the hazard rate decreases with the length of unemployment: the longer a spell of unemployment has already lasted, the less likely it is to leave unemployment within a given period of time.

This decrease of the hazard rate can be due to two effects. It can be caused by a dequalification due to unemployment: the longer an individual is unemployed, the more qualification is lost. *Unemployment causes dequalification.* The other possibility is that people entering unemployment at a certain date are not homogeneous. Some are more qualified, some are less qualified. The more qualified find a job within a shorter period than the less qualified. The longer an individual is unemployed the less likely she is to find a job in the next period, because the qualification an employer expects her to have is lower. *The unemployed are sorted by the passing of time.* The decrease of the probability of finding a job is not caused by unemployment, but is due to different qualifications at the beginning of the unemployment spell. Nowadays the statistical tests to discriminate between the two hypotheses for the decreasing hazard rate tend to see the falling hazard rates primarily caused by a sorting process.[10] (For an overview of the relevant statistical and theoretical problems see Layard et al., 1991, pp. 263–5.)

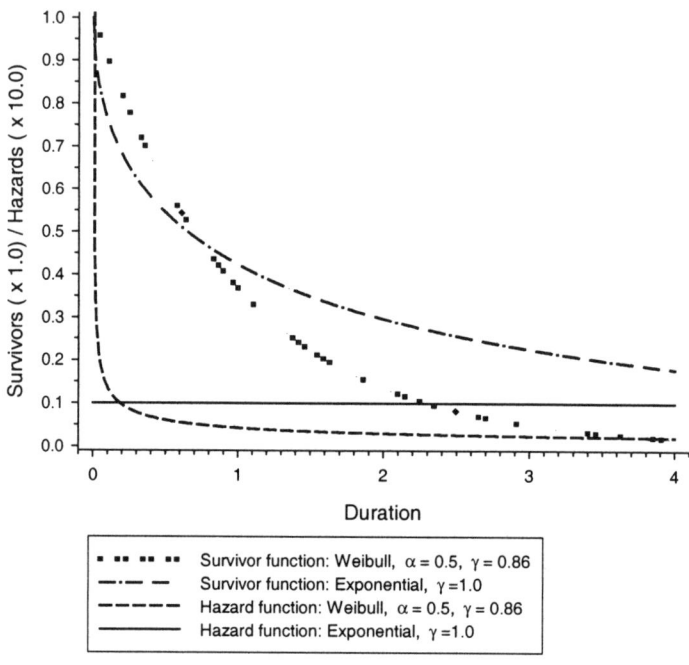

Notes: Exponential function: $F(t) = 1 - \exp(-\gamma t)$; $S(t) = \exp(-\gamma t)$; $\lambda(t) = \gamma$.
Weibull function: $F(t) = 1 - \exp(-\gamma t^\alpha)$; $S(t) = \exp(-\gamma t^\alpha)$; $\lambda(t) = \gamma \alpha t^\alpha$.
Note that the hazard is constant in the case of the exponential function but decreases in the case of the Weibull function.

Figure 6.2 Survivor and hazard functions for two distributions

The distinction between the two cases is important for policy questions. In the first case, namely decrease of human capital due to unemployment, it is very important to push the unemployed into employment. In the latter case, however this would not make much sense. It is more important to find those with less skills immediately after they become unemployed and to help them to get the necessary training.

The differences in the length of unemployment spells result in an unequal burden of unemployment. Though the greater part of those becoming unemployed within a year find a job within a short period, the greater part of unemployment within a year is concentrated among a much smaller number of people.

Table 6.5   Unequal burden of unemployment in Austria (1996)

Number of affected people: 708 753.

Decile	Average of the total duration in days	Annual average stock	Percentage of the total duration	Percentage of total duration (cumulative)
1.	8.8	1.708	0.7	0.7
2.	27.8	5.388	2.3	3.0
3.	46.9	9.086	3.9	6.9
4.	65.7	12.731	5.4	12.3
5.	85.3	16.520	7.0	19.3
6.	104.7	20.280	8.6	28.0
7.	129.9	25.146	10.7	38.6
8.	166.5	32.244	13.7	52.4
9.	233.5	45.226	19.2	71.6
10.	344.7	66.752	28.4	100.0
TOTAL	121.4	235.081	100.0	

Notes: How to read this table: out of 235 081 years of unemployment 1708 years (second row) were spent in unemployment by the 10 per cent with the shortest spells of unemployment. That was 0.7 per cent of total unemployment (third row). Their average duration of unemployment was 8.8 days (first row). The fourth row is the Lorenz curve of unemployment.

Source: Bundesministerium für Arbeit und Soziales (1998), vol. 2, p. 40.

6.1.3   Consequences of Unemployment

Unemployment can be a traumatic experience. Not only the loss of income matters, but most people see their work to be an important aspect of life. People often define their role in society through their job, even in cases where the job does not earn a high income or carry high social prestige. Becoming unemployed can result in losing self-esteem, particularly when the unemployed are considered by a wider public as being lazy or incompetent (Warr, 1987).

In the case of mass unemployment the unemployed will not experience their situation as an individual fate, rather the whole social fabric can be destroyed. This was documented in a pioneering study in the 1930s in a small Austrian town (Jahoda, et al., 1933, English translation, 1970; for a more recent study, see Winefield et al., 1993).

Here, we concentrate on the economic effects of unemployment in the narrow sense of the word: 1. loss of income and smoothing of consumption; 2. further spells of unemployment; 3. reduced wages in new jobs.[11]

6.1.3.1 Loss of income and consumption

The effect of unemployment which first comes to mind is the loss of income. How does that affect people? As income is the means to finance consumption, the relation between unemployment and consumption provides a basis for evaluating the effects of unemployment. It can be considered as a rough measure of the welfare loss for the unemployed.

It is clear that consumption is a function of income – $C = f(Y)$ – the higher the income, the higher is the consumption. This is standard economic theory. To understand the relation between unemployment and consumption it is necessary to be more specific. First, which income is the relevant argument in the consumption function? Second, are all types of consumption expenditures equally affected by unemployment?

In the simple introductory textbook version of the consumption function current consumption is a function of current income. This assumption is made for didactic purposes,[12] but it is not a realistic assumption. There are many causes which make the relation between current income and current consumption less strict. Many experience a rising wage profile, particularly those with higher qualifications. When young they expect to have a high income in the future. Their consumption may be more in line with future expected income than with current low income. The self-employed have fluctuating incomes. Some people withdraw purposely from the labour market for a certain period of time, for example, when caring for small children. It would hardly serve them best to have consumption fluctuating in the same way as income.[13]

The theoretical underpinning for the relation between consumption and income in a long-term context assumes that the utility function has to have the usual shape, namely declining marginal utility. Shifting wealth from periods of high income to periods of low income increases total utility. A change of income does not lead to changes of the same size in consumption. We should not expect the unemployed to decrease consumption as much as income decreases and we should not expect the re-employed to increase consumption in the same rate as income has increased.

How much reduction in consumption should we expect? Let us assume that there is full insurance against unemployment. In that case there would be no reduction in consumption due to individual experiences of unemployment.

Only changes of aggregate output influence consumption. When total output of consumption goods decline – that is, during the downswing of the business cycle or because of a collapse of the economy – consumption changes for all, whether unemployed or remaining employed, because higher unemployment goes together with the decline of production.

There are some types of unemployment against which full insurance is possible: *temporary lay-offs*. These are spells of unemployment with a return to the same employer, of the type that can be found frequently in seasonal jobs. As we will see below, the unemployment insurance systems create incentives for the occurrence of temporary lay-offs. Individuals who are temporarily laid off are unlikely to change their consumption much. After all, why should a construction worker, used to being unemployed during winter, let consumption go down during the period of unemployment? In summer he knows that he will be unemployed during winter – and will therefore take care; in winter he expects to be re-employed and does not have to worry.

That is different for other unemployed individuals. It is accepted that unemployment does affect consumption, implying lower utility during the period of unemployment (Dynarski and Gruber, 1997; Gruber, 1997; Bentolila and Ichino, 2001). For example, Bentolila and Ichino note that in Germany the unemployed reduce their total consumption per year by an average of something between 1.5 and 3 per cent (depending on the method of estimation) each additional month of unemployment. There is no full insurance for unemployment.

A slightly different interpretation of the relation between unemployment and consumption uses the assumption of the *Life-Cycle Hypothesis*: the argument in the consumption function is lifetime income. When deciding on consumption in period t, an individual takes account of expected income over her whole life. Current income is relevant only insofar as it provides the basis for estimating the expected income over the whole life. In that case an unexpected change in income affects total consumption insofar as the change influences expected life-time income. A wage increase due to an unexpected step upwards in the career ladder affects consumption habits more than a wage increase of the same size which was expected at the beginning of the career.

According to the Life-Cycle Hypothesis unemployment affects consumption via its effect on expected future income. It is not the loss of current income which makes the unemployed consume less, but the revised lower income over the whole life which has this consequence. If somebody becomes unexpectedly unemployed she may expect further spells of unemployment and a decline in her future wage. That this can be an important issue will be seen below.

Be that as it may, not all types of consumption expenditure are equally affected. One has to distinguish between durables and non-durables. During a period of income loss we should expect the reduction of expenditure for consumption to fall primarily on durables. That has been corroborated in the study by Dynarski and Gruber (1997): a period of unemployment made people spend, in the average, 7.6 per cent less on food and 34.6 per cent less on durables.

There is a further point in that expenditure for non-durables is to some extent a necessity and cannot be postponed. An individual can decide to go on holiday next year instead of this year or to postpone replacing the old car with a new one, because she is unemployed this year. The consumption of food or of a medical treatment cannot be shifted into another period.

BOX 6.1 UNEMPLOYMENT INSURANCE THROUGH THE FAMILY

In a study of differences in consumption by the unemployed between Italy and Spain on the one hand and the USA, Germany and the UK on the other, Bentolila and Ichino (2001) point to an interesting fact: although Spain and Italy provide lower unemployment benefits than Germany, Britain and the USA, in the two former countries the unemployed reduce consumption far less than the unemployed in the latter countries. The difference cannot be made up by savings, as the liquid resources of the unemployed are smaller in Spain and Italy than in the northern countries. Moreover, the possibility of getting a loan through the banking system is much smaller in the southern states. How come that the unemployed in Spain and Italy do not have to curtail their consumption as much as the unemployed in the north?

The authors argue, and support their argument with survey data, that this is due to the extended family networks – family ties beyond the household – which are still functioning in the countries of Southern Europe. These extended family ties provide transfers, help in finding a job in the underground economy, and they can give loans, as they have less problems with moral hazard. An unemployed individual cannot tell his cousins that there was no job available if they were offering him one, nor can he say that he has no means to pay back a loan if he has.

How do the unemployed make up for the income loss if the resulting curtailment of consumption is much smaller? There are three ways: (a) public transfers – the unemployment benefits system and social assistance; (b) self-insurance – savings; (c) private transfers – transfers within the family and the *added worker effect*.

It is clear that unemployment insurance, if any, is important for not having consumption strongly reduced in case of unemployment (Gruber, 1997). But the savings of the unemployed are important as well. Dynarski and Gruber (1997) note that between 25 and 40 per cent of consumption by the unemployed is financed by running down accumulated savings.

A further way to finance consumption is to rely on private transfers, mostly by the family. An important aspect is the possibility that another member of the same household increases his/her labour supply, either by entering the labour market or by extending hours worked – the *added worker effect*: if an individual becomes unemployed, the spouse starts to work or switches from part-time work into full-time work – so the story goes. This would be a rational response of a household to unemployment in the sense that the household has one common utility function underlying the decisions to earn income and to do the necessary tasks at home.[14] However the data do not confirm that prediction (Dynarski and Gruber, 1997). In the UK there is even a tendency for unemployment to become concentrated in households. Though unemployment was lower during the 1990s than in the decade before, more households were without workers in the latter decade (Gregg and Wadsworth, 2000). The concentration of employment and unemployment between households was also observed in other states (Förster and Pellizzari, 2000). Being unemployed goes together with an increased probability that the spouse is unemployed as well! Whether this is caused by incentives offered by the unemployment assistance system, by regional imbalances or any other cause is not clear.[15]

6.1.3.2 Recurrent unemployment

A spell of unemployment can have adverse effects on the behaviour of the unemployed and on the way a future employers looks at them. Both may in turn affect their chances of getting a new job, and if a new job is found, of keeping it. The unemployed can lose qualifications while unemployed. This does not mean that they forget their former qualifications, nor that technical progress is so quick that being unemployed for a year makes the former qualifications obsolete. That is not even the case with modern information technologies.

But there are other aspects of qualifications: the unemployed tend to develop different habits concerning the use of time, the regularity of living. Work habits can deteriorate (Jahoda et al., 1933). After a prolonged period of unemployment an individual may be less employable, not because he is not up to new technologies, but because his work habits have changed.

Employers may look differently at unemployed individuals applying for a job than at new entrants to the labour market or at individuals who switch from one job to another without an intermittent period of unemployment. They may think the arguments given in the last paragraph to be true. Or they may believe that an individual became unemployed because she was considered to be less productive than other workers by her last employer. In that case unemployment is like an invisible scar the applicant for a job cannot hide. An unemployed person has a smaller chance of a getting a lasting job than other applicants and therefore is more likely to take a job with a short duration, often a job with a fixed duration (Böheim and Taylor, 2000).

Moreover, firms tend to have last-in-first-out rules for dismissals if any. That is a protection for incumbents in a firm in order to fend off potential wage-cutting from outsiders.[16] It is often supported by trade unions. This contributes to making unemployment a recurrent experience.

BOX 6.2 DOES UNEMPLOYMENT CAUSE FUTURE UNEMPLOYMENT?

It is well documented that an individual unemployed at t has a higher probability of being unemployed at $t + 1$ than an individual working at t. But this does not imply that unemployment *causes* further unemployment through the mechanisms mentioned above. It can also be the case that an individual unemployed at t has characteristics which point to a higher probability of being unemployment at any period. When estimating the effects of unemployment on future unemployment it is necessary to control for such characteristics.

In a study of youth unemployment in the UK (Narendranathan and Elias, 1993) the authors used a sample from employment data of men between 1974 and 1980 of a cohort born during one week in 1958.* The raw data exhibited a much higher probability of unemployment for those who had had a period of unemployment before. When taking account of (a) the local unemployment rate, (b) marital status, (c) fathering a child, (d) father's social class, and (e) whether one had an above or below average score in maths and reading achievements when 11 years old, nearly all differences vanished in employment probabilities between those who had experienced unemployment before and the rest.

In a more recent study (Arulampalam et al., 2000) it was shown that the young were not negatively affected by unemployment concerning future unemployment, however for workers older than 25 there was a big effect.

> First we find that, for young men, only about 20 % of observed persistence in the unemployment probability is accounted for by state dependence.** However, for more mature men, roughly 38 % of observed persistence in the unemployment probability is accounted for by state dependence. (Arulampalam et al., 2000, p. 43)

The authors conclude that the employers expect the young to experience more spells of unemployment. It therefore does not signal lower productivity. That is different for older unemployed workers.

Notes:
*In many labour market studies only data of men are used. The reason is that men are usually active in the labour market, whereas women can stay at home without counting as being unemployed.
** A variable is said to be state dependent if its value at t depends on its value at $t-1$. The outcomes of a sequence of dices thrown is not state dependent. The value of a index of stocks, like the Dow-Jones Index is state dependent: jumps from one day to the other are limited in size. There is necessarily a correlation between the values of the index at two ensuing dates.

6.1.3.3 Reduced wages in a new job

If all jobs were alike, an individual would lose through unemployment only the foregone earnings. As soon as she finds another job her former situation would be fully restored. But jobs are different. Therefore wages can be different in new jobs. If a worker quits, the wage may go up, because it was the worker who took the initiative. If workers are discharged, one could not expect the wage in a new job to be higher than in the job which preceded the spell of unemployment. After all, it was the employer who took the initiative for the separation. We distinguish three reasons for discharging of employees:

- Temporary lay-off: the worker returns after some time to the same employer. Usually employees start with the same wage after the spell of unemployment as before that spell. In that case there is not much of a problem for the unemployed besides that of losing income for a short time.
- An employer dismisses an employee and fills the job with another employee. That is usually due to the employee no longer being considered sufficiently productive for the job. If she has a lower wage in a new job, it cannot be said that unemployment has caused the decline of the wage. It is the other way round: she became unemployed because

the wage was considered too high in relation to her personal productivity.
- The employee is discharged because the job is closed down. This is called *displacement*. It has nothing to do with the personal productivity of the worker. Any reduction of wages after a period of unemployment can be seen to be caused thereby. There is ample literature which shows that displaced workers experience reduced wages for a very long period after being displaced (for the USA see Hamermesh, 1989 and Fallick 1996; for the UK see Arulampalam, 2000). There are different reasons for that: first many employees have age-related wage profiles – the longer they stay in a firm the higher their wage. This wage increase is only partly due to increasing productivity. In a new job that wage will not cover that aspect. Furthermore employees lose firm-specific human capital. That means they have special skills and knowledge which can only can be used in the firm where this knowledge was acquired.[17]

BOX 6.3 THE MEASUREMENT OF THE WAGE LOSS

When measuring the loss of wages one needs a contra-factual wage with which the actual wage can be compared. Taking simply the wage before and after the period of unemployment can be misleading as the wages of those who were not displaced may have changed as well. If, for example, the wage in the new job is 5 per cent above the former wage, we still speak of a wage loss of 10 per cent if the wage of similar workers had increased meanwhile by 15 per cent.

A way to overcome this difficulty is to compare the difference between post-unemployment wages and pre-unemployment wages with the development of wages of a similar group of employees who did not experience unemployment during that period – *difference in difference* method.

In a study about long-term effects of unemployment Ruhm (1991) used data from 3813 employees, of whom 800 experienced displacement during the period 1971–1975. He had data reaching back three years before that period and four years after it had ended. It was asked whether displaced workers experienced more unemployment in the four years following displacement and how wages developed. Ruhm showed that, though the displaced workers experienced more unemployment in the period immediately following displacement, the difference in unemployment had nearly vanished after four years. The wage effect remained strong – about 14 per cent – even after four years.

> Displaced workers were also more than twice as likely to experience wage reductions exceeding 25 per cent between t − 2 [t: the year of displacement P.R.] and t + 2 (28.6 per cent vs. 14.1 per cent) and lost more than 10 per cent of previous wages 1.6 times as often (40.1 per cent vs. 25 per cent). Although displaced individuals averaged only 1.5 per cent earnings reductions over the four years, they missed out entirely on the 8.4 per cent real wage gain obtained by the control group over the same period. (Ruhm, 1991, p. 321)

There is a further point in that using the wage at the time of displacement for comparison can be misleading, because employees often experienced a reduction of their wage before the closure of the plant. Wage reductions are sometimes accepted as a way to avoid the closure of a plant. In a study of earning losses by Jacobson et al. (1993) the authors construed a contra-factual wage development taking account of wage losses prior to displacement. They used data from Pennsylvania where during the period of investigation big changes in employment occurred as many industrial sites, particularly in steel and related industries, were closed down. They showed that displaced workers experienced some wage reduction up to three years before displacement, a strong wage reduction immediately after displacement and some recovery in the following years.

> ...we find that high tenure, prime-age workers endure substantial and persistent earnings losses during or following mass lay-offs. Even six years after their separations, their quarterly earnings remain $1 600 below their expected levels. This loss represents 25 per cent of their predisplacement earnings. (Jacobson et al., 1993, p. 696)

There are other reasons for a wage loss after unemployment. Often plants which were closed down were unionised whereas the new jobs are in firms without unions (Fallick, 1996). This may be of relevance in countries where unionised firms pay higher wages than firms without unions (for example, in the USA).

6.2 HELPING THE UNEMPLOYED I: INCOME SUPPORT

What to do in face of unemployment depends on the political aim. Reducing unemployment is by definition a policy to help the unemployed. That is not always viable as there is a relation between unemployment and inflation – the Phillips curve: the lower unemployment is, the higher is inflation. That sets a limit on attempts to reduce unemployment by fiscal and monetary policy. Moreover it was argued above that there is always some unemployment due to structural changes in the economy.

There are other ways to help the unemployed, namely to better their social and economic situation. There are two ways to do it:

- Income support while unemployment lasts.
- Helping the unemployed to find a job.

As mentioned, even if lack of jobs at the aggregate level is an issue, it is unlikely that helping the unemployed to find a job is necessarily unreasonable. With the exception of situations such as the mass unemployment of the 1930s or after the closing down of many industrials sites in the former German Democratic Republic, there are always some jobs available as people retire or withdraw for other reasons from the labour markets and new firms start. On the other hand, even if the availability of jobs on the aggregate level is not a big issue, one cannot expect that jobs are everywhere and immediately available. People look for specific jobs at specific locations. An individual who has lost her job may have difficulties finding a suitable job in the same area within a short time, even in urban centres; even more so in sparsely populated areas or in a small town dominated by one company for employment. Therefore income support is always an important means for helping the unemployed.

6.2.1 Institutions and Rules

Giving a transfer to the unemployed is usually called 'unemployment benefit'. But one has to be careful with that expression. In most theoretical models unemployment benefits are treated as an income of an unemployed person. It is given unconditionally – that is, without regard to former contributions, without regard to search activities, without means-testing and without time limit. Hardly any unemployment insurance actually works that way (Atkinson and Micklewright, 1991).

One has to distinguish between unemployment insurance (UI), unemployment assistance (UA) and a guaranteed income. In an unemployment insurance system the benefits depend on former income, are usually given for a limited period and are not means-tested. In most UI systems one had to work for a specified period before becoming eligible for a transfer.

In an unemployment assistance system the benefits are means-tested, are given for much longer – sometimes even for unlimited periods – and are not necessarily related to former income. There is a further distinction between UI and UA: while receiving UI the individual is in most systems allowed to reject a job considered unsuitable without losing eligibility. Individuals on UA rarely enjoy this right.

In a guaranteed income scheme benefits given in case of unemployment are integrated with other welfare payments to fend off poverty. There is no relation to former income and no former contributions are required. Many countries have a mixed system – an unemployment insurance system for a certain period to be followed by unemployment assistance payments. But there are many unemployed who do not receive any unemployment benefit, in some economies more than 50 per cent.

Table 6.6 Unemployment benefit replacement ratios by duration and family circumstances* (1991)

	First year			Second and third year			Fourth and fifth year		
	(a)	(b)	(c)	(a)	(b)	(c)	(a)	(b)	(c)
Austria	42	45	25	40	43	0	40	43	0
Canada	58	58	58	13	25	0	13	25	0
France	58	58	58	37	37	30	28	28	0
Germany	37	41	37	33	36	0	33	36	0
Italy	7	8	7	0	0	0	0	0	0
Japan	25	25	25	0	0	0	0	0	0
Netherl.	70	70	70	56	56	56	34	48	0
Sweden	80	80	80	6	6	6	0	0	0
Switzerl.	63	72	63	0	0	0	0	0	0
UK	19	31	19	17	27	0	17	27	0
USA	24	26	21	5	10	0	5	10	0

Notes: * (a) single; (b) with dependent spouse; (c) with spouse in work.
Benefit entitlement before tax as a percentage of previous earnings before tax. Data shown are averages over replacement rates at two earnings levels (average earnings and two-thirds of average earnings).

Source: OECD (1994), part II, p. 175.

The unemployment insurance system is in many states a separate institution which collects contributions and pays the benefits. Unemployment assistance is in some states organisationally integrated with the UI system, in other states (for example, in the United Kingdom) it is part of the general social administration. In some countries the UI system is run by the unions or by funds closely associated with the unions (Sweden, Denmark, the Netherlands).[18] The unemployment insurance in the USA has another speciality: contributions are experience rated – the contributions that firms have to pay depend on past discharges.

The value of the benefits can be measured by the *replacement ratio* – the ratio of the benefit to former income – and the duration of the benefits. Table 6.6 gives an overview of replacement ratios for different countries for gross income. One extreme is Sweden: nearly full income is given for one year, but almost nothing afterwards. The Austrian system is not generous in the beginning, but can go on indefinitely where there is no other income in the household. The net replacement ratios can be up to 20 per cent higher, depending on the treatment of unemployment benefits in the tax system. In order to assess the structure of unemployment benefits for the long-term unemployed one has to take into account their relation to other welfare systems, particularly to social assistance.

6.2.2 Economic Effects of Unemployment Benefits

The problem of allocative effects is primarily the question of whether unemployment benefits increase unemployment. It is at the heart of many heated discussions among the wider public as well as in economic research. There is a systematic difference between the former and the latter discussions: economists discuss what happens if benefits are increased or decreased by a few per cent or, if in some situations in which currently benefits are given, there would be no benefits after a reform. This is not only the scientifically sensible approach, but also a politically sensible one. One can change social programmes only marginally – at least in a democracy. Among the wider public it is often discussed what will happen if an existing system of unemployment benefits is abolished completely. People ask what would the unemployed do if there were no benefits at all. In such a comparison unemployment benefits surely make a big difference and it is likely that many unemployed people would be prepared to accept jobs which they reject if they get a transfer.

However the idea that the unemployed should be prepared to accept any job misses an important point: it is one of the functions of the unemployment benefit system to prevent the unemployed from accepting any job offered whatsoever. They should be able to search for an adequate job, as that increases the probability that they will find a job which fits their qualification. If a qualified person is forced to accept a job demanding less qualifications, there is waste of human capital. That is the reason why many unemployment laws concede that for a specified period an unemployed individual has the right to refuse an offered job without losing eligibility for unemployment benefits, namely when the job requires less qualifications and offers wages far lower than in the former job. These stipulations are considered to contribute to the efficiency of the labour market.

Even if abolishing UI totally is not considered an option, economists are split over the question of whether unemployment benefits increase unemployment. Some are convinced that they are one of the main causes of high unemployment – particularly in the European context of the last 20 years. Others deny that there is a close relationship between unemployment benefits and the labour market outcome. As mentioned in the introduction, the empirical evidence using aggregate data is inconclusive (Atkinson, 1999). This is not surprising, because even if unemployment benefits contribute to unemployment they surely are not the sole cause for unemployment. Controlling for all other causes which may contribute to unemployment is not possible without a general and all encompassing theory of employment and unemployment. Furthermore to test such a model one needs more data than are available on an aggregate level for a few countries only and merely for a few decades.

To analyse how unemployment benefits affect unemployment one has to consider in which way they influence demand and supply of labour. The supply is affected through the following paths:

- Unemployment benefits increase the value of not-working. That reduces labour supply of those who are already eligible for unemployment benefits.
- Unemployment benefits increase the value of taking a job, because an individual can receive unemployment benefits as soon as she becomes eligible. That increases labour supply.

The demand for labour is not affected directly by unemployment benefits. In equilibrium less labour is employed at a higher wage if the former effect on supply is bigger than the latter.

Unemployment benefits influence the amount of labour employed in a further way: in models in which the wage is the result of bargaining between employers and employees or between employers and unemployed looking for a job, unemployment insurance affects the outcome of the wage bargain – it increases the wage *ceteris paribus*. The reason is, that the fall-back position of the employees is higher. Due to the increase of the wage, less labour is employed.

Taking into account that unemployment benefits have to be financed, labour demand is affected as well. If benefits are financed by a pay-roll tax levied on the employers, the wedge between the wage the employees receive and the wage the employer has to pay is increased. This shifts labour demand to the left – decreasing labour demand.[19]

Moreover, when estimating the effects of an unemployment benefit system the details of the institutional structure of the benefit system has to be considered, namely how benefits are related to former income, how long an unemployed remains eligible and so on. One has also to take social assistance into account.[20] In most cases these transfers are low, hardly more than 40 per cent of median income. Only for those with very few qualifications is it an interesting option not to work and to live on a transfer typical for UI or UA. For people with higher qualifications it implies a life in poverty which can be avoided by working. Figure 6.3 makes this precise.

Consider the case of UA which is given unconditionally for a long period. It is like a welfare payment, taken away if the individual works. Any effect on labour supply depends on the wage rate. In Figure 6.3 two cases are drawn. In the left panel the wage per hour is 0.5, in the right panel wage per hour is 2. Income increases with the number of hours worked. A UA transfer of 3 per day, hardly influences the labour supply of high-wage workers. Anyone with a high wage who has her optimum at a labour supply well above 1.2 hours is better off working than remaining unemployed. For individuals with an optimum slightly above 1.2 hours of work, it is also better not to work, namely if the indifference curve cuts the 3-units budget line. Still, most people with high qualifications work. For those with a low wage things are different. Not to work is better for all whose optimum amount of labour supply does not exceed 6 hours. For groups with access to transfers much closer to median income – for example, families with children, particularly lone mothers – it may be a relevant option to live on such transfers.[21]

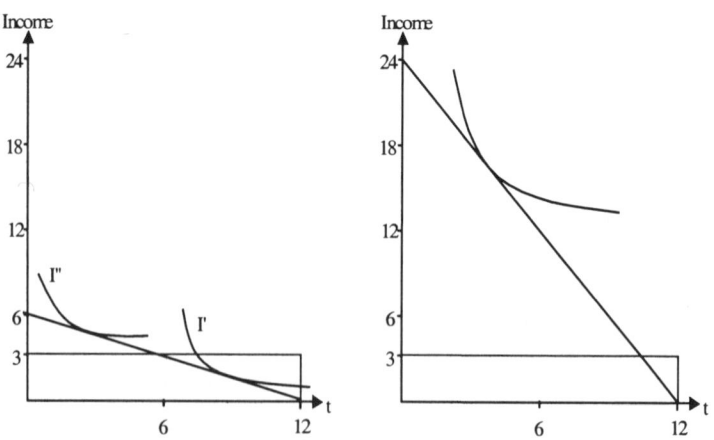

Figure 6.3 How UA affects labour supply in the case of low wages (left) and high wages (right)

A more promising approach to the analysis of the relation between unemployment benefits and unemployment is to ask how benefits influence the taking up of jobs, whether the unemployed tend to be less eager to take a job if benefits are higher. The theoretical framework is that of a search process. The basic idea is that the unemployed receive job offers as a stochastic process.[22] An unemployed individual can influence the rate of arrival by varying her search effort. If a job is offered she has to decide whether to accept it. The acceptance depends on the wage at the job and its expected duration, the expectations of future arrivals of jobs offers, as well as their wage, and the costs of being unemployed until a new offer arrives. If a job is rejected the unemployed cannot return to that offer later (no re-call). It can be shown that the optimal strategy for the unemployed is to set a wage – the reservation wage – and to accept the first offer with a wage not smaller than the reservation wage and to reject all offers below that wage (Mortensen, 1986). Unemployment benefits affect the reservation wage in two ways. First, the costs of unemployment until a new offer arrives is reduced. Second, the value of a job is higher if eligibility depends on having worked. If the former effect is stronger, then search duration is increased.[23]

For the empirical analysis one needs data on leaving unemployment for individuals who entered unemployment during a specific period. Thus it is possible to calculate for all t the survival rates for having remained unemployed up to t and the hazard rates for leaving unemployment at t. To evaluate the effects of the specific rules of an unemployment insurance system it is necessary to have data for people affected by these rules and data for other ones not affected by these rules (a so-called *control group*). The difference in the hazard rates are considered to arise due to the specific rules.

When taking the data of different individuals at the same time it is necessary to control for the sorting of individuals in the two groups, because the two groups compared may be different in some aspects.[24] If samples from different periods are used, it is necessary to control for different re-employment probabilities due to different aggregate effects – for example, whether there was a boom in the first period and a depression in the second.

The overwhelming evidence is that higher unemployment benefits tend to make unemployment spells longer, however the size of that effect is contentious. Usually this relation is expressed as an elasticity, namely the relative change of the duration over the relative change of the replacement ratio. The estimates vary between 0.3 and 1.0 for the USA and the United Kingdom during the 1980s (Atkinson and Micklewright, 1991, p. 1712). They may be different now and different in other countries.

So far only the effects on the individual unemployed have been discussed. In order to estimate the effects on aggregate unemployment it is necessary to consider further effects. In the short run the number of jobs available is limited. If an unemployed person takes a job, that reduces the number of open jobs. Thus the probability of finding a job goes down for all other unemployed people. This is an external effect. Therefore, making the unemployed looking more actively for a job by cutting benefits does not decrease aggregate unemployment accordingly.

BOX 6.4 HOW DOES (OR DID) THE REPLACEMENT RATE IN GERMANY INFLUENCE THE DURATION OF UNEMPLOYMENT?

Germany (before unification) changed the replacement rate of unemployment insurance in 1984 for those without dependent children by 5 percentage points. In the following year the period during which unemployment insurance could be received was extended for older workers. In the subsequent years that extension of benefits was extended to groups of slightly younger unemployed people. How did these changes influence the duration of spells of unemployment?

In a study by Jennifer Hunt (1995) the author could make use of the fact that the changes in the law did not affect all people equally. In the first instance those with dependent children were exempted, in the other changes younger employees fared differently from older employees. That is what economist call a *natural experiment*.

Hunt calculated the difference in the hazard rates between affected and non-affected individuals. To do so she took account of different hazard rates for leaving unemployment: some individuals move from unemployment to employment, others from unemployment to out of the labour force. The result of her estimation was that the cut in the size of the benefits had no discernible effects, but the extension of the duration of the benefits had a measurable impact on the duration of unemployment spells for those favourably affected by the change in the law. The duration increased in comparison to those whose benefits were not extended. For those between the age of 42 and 49 the hazard to leave unemployment for employment and for out-of-labour-force status was influenced, for those older only the probability of a switch from unemployment to out-of-labour-force was affected.

In the long run the number of jobs is not limited, as new jobs can be generated. The amount of new jobs depends, among other things, on the supply of a suitable employees. If the unemployed are more eager to take a job due to lower unemployment benefits, the employers create more new jobs. (See Appendix 6.1.)

Summing up: a sizeable reduction of unemployment rates by reducing the replacement rate can rarely be achieved, at least not unless benefits are to be cut drastically. Such a radical general curtailment of benefits would increase the caseload of other social assistance programmes.

In the late 1990s the discussion changed direction. Instead of a general reduction of benefits a different instrument became prominent for policy planning: sanctioning individuals who are suspected of not complying with the rules of the UI or the UA system, namely to accept jobs which are by the standards of the administration suitable. As mentioned above, most UI systems accept for a specified period a refusal to accept a job offer without withdrawing benefits if the job is below former qualifications. When on UA the protection of former qualification is usually less strong, although certain cases for non-acceptance of an offer are excused: travel-to-work-time, regional mobility, conscientious and religious objections, and so on (OECD, 2000). There are many ambiguities in the regulations, implying leeway for the administration and the possibility for moral hazard on behalf of the unemployed. Take the following cases:

- Should a vegetarian be allowed to refuse a job at a meat factory?
- Does a lone mother have to accept a job 25 miles from her home?
- Does a young single individual have to move to another city 200 miles away from home? What about a person whose spouse has a job?
- Should unemployment benefits be withdrawn if a Muslim wants to cover her head, something the employer does not accept because of some neutrality principles?[25]

How does the threat to end benefits affect unemployment duration? A way to analyse that is to integrate the reaction to the threat into the search model. This can be done in the following way: if an unemployed person rejects an offer considered suitable, there is a positive probability of being detected and losing benefit. The expected benefit of not accepting a job is reduced (Abbring et al., 2000). The evidence so far found supports the idea that sanctions make the unemployed move faster into employment.[26]

6.2.2.1 A special effect of unemployment insurance: subsidising temporary lay-offs

The unemployment benefit system does not only create incentives for people working, but also for firms, particularly concerning (i) seasonal production and (ii) the responses of firms to changes in demand for their output.

If production is concentrated in certain periods of the year, an unemployment benefit system allows laying people off during other periods. A typical example is the construction industry. In some countries many construction workers are unemployed during winter because it is too cold to work outside. A worker who decides to take a job in this industry expects recurrent spells of unemployment. In the absence of transfers the income during the months he works must suffice to keep him in that industry instead of moving to a job with all year round employment. *Ceteris paribus* the wage rate per time unit must be higher in seasonal jobs. If the seasonal unemployed receive a transfer while being unemployed they reduce their reservation wage. Unemployment benefits tend to lower the wages that employers have to pay without reducing income.

One finds such types of unemployment not only in clearly seasonal jobs, like agriculture, construction and tourism, but also in other industries with seasonal demand or with times of slack demand. Instead of building up inventories it becomes more profitable for the firms to lay people off and rehire them after a short period – temporary lay-offs. In the USA about 70 per cent of unemployment spells ended with a return to their former employer (recalls) (Borjas, 1996, p. 454). In Canada about half of all separations ended with a return to the same employer within two years (Robertson, 1988). Austria has two industries with strong seasonal components: construction and tourism.[27] The unemployment benefit system provides a subsidy for these industries and encourages their behaviour. That's why the USA introduced experience rating: firms who discharge workers have to pay higher contributions.

As the spells of temporary lay-offs are on average shorter than other spells of unemployment, the percentage of total unemployment (person-years) experienced by employees laid off temporarily is smaller than their share in the number of spells.

6.3 HELPING THE UNEMPLOYED II: ACTIVE LABOUR MARKET POLICY

6.3.1 Basic Ideas

The unemployed not only need means to live while they are unemployed, they may also need help to get a job. It is of course always easier for an unemployed person to find a job if there are many jobs available and if unemployment generally is low. A successful macroeconomic policy resulting in high employment is advantageous for the unemployed. However helping the unemployed to find a job does not imply that a new job has to be created. According to the flow approach, there are always some jobs available. Active labour market policy (ALMP) is primarily aimed at making the unemployed move more quickly into existing jobs.

The amount spent on active labour market policy is considerably less than the sum of all unemployment benefits. Only Sweden spends much on ALMP programmes. The stickiness of high unemployment in western Europe led to a reappraisal of the traditional means of dealing with unemployment: demand management to increase the number of jobs available and unemployment benefits to help the unemployed. Demand management is seen as contradicting price stability and/or has fallen prey to new theories of the working of the economy – namely the new macroeconomics, which had integrated rational expectations and problems of credibility in the models. Furthermore as mentioned already, the movement of unemployment and employment is not as close as assumed in most macroeconomic models.

Table 6.7   Incidence of long-term unemployment

	6 months and over	12 months and over
Austria	43.8	28.4
Belgium	71.8	56.3
Denmark	38.1	20.0
France	61.9	42.5
Germany	67.6	51.5
Italy	75.3	60.8
Netherlands	46.5	32.7
Spain	64.8	47.6
United Kingdom	43.2	28.0
United States	11.4	6.0

Note: A very high share of unemployment is concentrated among the long-term unemployed, though most spells of unemployment are of small duration. Only in the USA a small fraction of unemployment is long-term unemployed.

Source: OECD (2001), p. 228. Data for 2000.

Giving unemployment benefits without any further activity is not a good policy in the context of long-term unemployment: benefits are not sufficiently high to safeguard a standard of living above poverty lines. Increasing the benefits is rejected as the fear prevails that unemployment will thereby be increased. Help in finding a job is important, particularly for the long-term unemployed (Table 6.7).

We can distinguish between the following methods:

- Counselling and monitoring the unemployed when searching for a job.
- Training.
- Subsidising the unemployed for accepting a job.
- Subsidising the employer to accept an unemployed individual as an employee.

The distinction between the different methods is not always clear-cut. Does a course for training the unemployed to write CVs properly count as counselling or is it a kind of training? If a long-term unemployed individual is allowed to keep part of her unemployment benefits when beginning to work, is this a subsidy to her to accept the job, or a subsidy to the employer to accept the applicant? In some instances the unemployed have to accept counselling or have to enter a training programme in order to continue receiving benefits. Some active labour market policy measures can therefore be seen in the context of punitive strategies (for example, Dolton and O'Neill, 1996; Lalive, et al., 2000).

In order to plan a policy and to evaluate it afterwards one has to be clear what is its aim:

- Increasing overall welfare.
- Reducing unemployment.
- Increasing the hazard rate of leaving unemployment.
- Increasing the stability of jobs and/or wages of the re-employed.
- Increasing employment and/or wages of people having special problems – handicapped people, lone parents, individuals with a criminal record, addicts, and so on.

The most ambitious objective is increasing total welfare. It is necessary to weigh all the benefits of a policy against all its costs. The welfare loss due to the necessary taxation has to be taken into account as well as the disutility of the extra amount of work done. The pure distributional aspects can be left out. The reduced income of the taxed is cancelled by the increased welfare of the recipients of the subsidies. Only the excess burden of the extra taxes are a welfare loss.

Such an approach may be a bit overambitious. Most countries do not spend more than 1 per cent of GDP on such measures, spread over various programmes. To calculate what a difference is made on total welfare if about one-tenth of 1 per cent of GDP is spent differently, is a good exercise for the training of economists but can hardly be used for deciding about policies.

Reducing unemployment is probably the most often posed aim of ALMP, because any reduction in the rate of unemployment can be used as an easily understandable measuring rod in election campaigns, but as the basic idea of ALMP programmes is to make unemployed take existing jobs, how can total employment increase?

It can make the unemployed move more quickly into existing jobs. The matching process becomes more efficient, which increases employment and reduces unemployment. There is another mechanism discussed in literature (Layard et al., 1991) which is that the unemployed work as a check on wage increases. If unemployment goes down wages increase more quickly and labour demand is reduced. However there is good empirical evidence that the long-term unemployed do not affect wage increases. They are considered less of a threat for incumbent workers than people who have recently become unemployed. Therefore if for a given size of the rate of unemployment the share of the long-term unemployed is higher, the wage dampening effect is smaller. Increasing the hazard rate of the long-term unemployed works like an increase in the effective labour supply, as more individuals are considered apt for employment by the employers. That depresses wages and can thus increase employment.

The small size of all ALMP programmes together makes it unlikely that they will have a big impact on the overall unemployment rate, particularly when taking into account that more people will come forward to apply for a job if the registered unemployed move more quickly into jobs. Even less should be expected if ALMP programmes are used to boost employment in heavily depressed areas – as the *Neue Bundesländer* in Germany or the *Mezzogiorno* in Italy. If a region has not participated fully in the overall economic development of a state, ALMP programmes alone have little effect – though it might be socially and politically better to keep the unemployed in one way or another in contact with working life instead of leaving them on the streets.[28]

There is more chance of a success if the purpose of a programme is more modest: increasing hazard rates for leaving unemployment to employment, ensuring that the unemployed find lasting jobs with good wages or increasing the employability of groups with special problems are examples of such objectives for ALMP programmes.

6.3.2 Special Programmes

Various programmes to bring people into jobs have been suggested and some have been tried. They differ insofar as they emphasise particular problems faced by the unemployed in finding a job. Some aim at intensifying the search process by making the unemployed more active and more efficient in applying. Others aim to reduce the wage costs for a prospective employer by giving subsidies. Finally many programmes consist in training to increase the skills of the unemployed or make them otherwise more employable.

The programmes differ also insofar as some apply to a wide group of the unemployed on general terms – all long-term unemployed, all unemployed people with low qualifications – or whether a programme is for small groups only, requiring special admittance. Programmes to reduce wage costs tend to be available for wider groups, whereas qualification programmes hardly allow for general acceptance. The administrative capacity of employment agencies is usually not such as to organise useful and suitable trainings for a large numbers. The primary clientele for ALMP programmes are the long-term unemployed, as most new entrants to unemployment quickly return to employment.

If individuals to whom the programmes apply move quickly into employment, what happens to other people – those in employment and those of the unemployed not covered by the programme? Could it be that any success of ALMP is at the cost of these two groups, creating a higher probability of being laid off for those in employment and a lower probability of finding a job for those who are not covered by the programme? This is called the *displacement effect*.

If the number of jobs is fixed that must happen, but as mentioned, that is unlikely. There are always unfilled job openings, as there are always unemployed people. Reducing the duration of unemployment spells can be a way to reduce the spells of unfilled job openings. Furthermore more jobs are opened if the probability of finding a suitable employee increases. In the case of wage subsidies, the decrease of wage costs increases employment along the labour demand curve. Moreover wage setting may change if effective labour supply increases. A displacement effect cannot be ruled out, but it is unlikely that it will be one-to-one. (For an integrated approach to all these aspects see Appendix 6.1.) In the following paragraphs some examples are discussed.

(i) *Employment premiums* (Davidson and Woodbury, 1993; Meyer, 1995; Meyer, 1996). It was mentioned above that a threat to withdraw benefits can hasten the acceptance of a job. What about the other way round – giving a bonus to those who manage to find a job within a specified period of time? That was done in experiments in Illinois. A cash bonus of $500 was given if a job was found within eleven weeks and was kept for at least four months. Individuals who considered the UI benefit system a subsidy for a short period of leisure experienced an income effect, that could increase duration of unemployment as long as it remained below eleven weeks. For those with spells slightly above eleven weeks there was also a substitution effect making unemployment shorter. In a search theoretic context the eleven weeks rule made search more attractive before eleven weeks were over and had no influence afterwards.

The result was that unemployment duration decreased considerably, such that the UI system experienced net savings despite of giving the bonus (Meyer, 1995). Davidson and Woodbury got similar results. They found a negative effect for those who were not eligible for UI insurance and therefore were not offered a premium. There was a small displacement effect.

Meyer mentions the possibility that in the long run the positive effects can be much smaller. The experiment was carried out for about four months only. That was too short a period for the employed to react to the incentives the bonus provided: quitting a job and finding another one within a short time.

Moreover it is a programme specially designed for individuals in short-term jobs as the re-employment duration of merely four months hardly qualifies for a regular job.

(ii) *Training and counselling programmes.* In one way or the other many long-term unemployed lack skills and employability. There may be different reasons for that:

- Insufficient training when young, for example, school drop-outs.
- Technological changes can render qualifications obsolete or may demand the acquisition of new ones – not to be able to use a computer has become a hindrance in finding a clerical job. Some older clerical staff became unemployed because they lacked such skills.
- Long-term unemployed and frequently unemployed often find it difficult to adapt to working life. Some of them have other problems as well – problems with alcohol or drugs, individuals with a criminal record, with various mental problems.
- People who stayed for a long time out of the labour force – primarily women after years of childcare – also have problems with qualifications.
- Migrants sometimes face special problems, particularly when their language proficiency is not sufficient.

Training programmes can be of some use if appropriately tailored. That is not only a question of the amount of resources a society is prepared to spend but also of good administration. It is not easy to recognise the specific deficiencies of a long-term unemployed individual and to develop a special training to overcome it.

When evaluating the programmes one has to be realistic concerning what can be expected. A person who lost a long tenured job due to the introduction of a new technology can be expected to find another long-lasting job when properly retrained. For a individual with psychic problems or a criminal record it may already be a success if she manages to live most of the time off social assistance.

The overwhelming evidence suggests that the results of training programmes are modest (LaLonde, 1995; Heckman et al., 1999). That is not very surprising: if a programme spends €2000 for someone's training, a permanent increase of her wage of €200 per year would represent a rate of return of 10 per cent – that is a high rate.

Two things can definitely not be achieved by ALMP training: first, a general increase of skills and learning habits. If the school system does not work properly, if employers do not train their personnel, one cannot expect labour market policy to make good these deficiencies. Second, in regions with high unemployment, training can be used to keep the unemployed off the streets, but one should not expect all things to be fine when the training ends.

BOX 6.5   FORCED PARTICIPATION FOR THE LONG-TERM UNEMPLOYED

All through the last decades Switzerland had a very low rate of unemployment. When it increased in the late 1980s policy reacted by extending benefits and making the system more generous. As unemployment did not decrease the policy was changed in the mid-1990s. Since 1997 the unemployed are only entitled to seven months of unconditional unemployment benefits. For a further period of 17 months the unemployed can receive benefits under the condition that they participate in ALMP training and counselling programmes. Hand in hand with the enactment of that law went an extension of the administrative capacities of the employment service.

According to a study (Lalive et al., 2000) that resulted in higher hazard rates before the seven-months period had ended. People obviously avoided being put into these programmes. The hazard rates for those staying unemployed for more than seven months were reduced. According to the authors that reduction was caused by reduced search while participating in ALMP programmes.

(iii) *Subsidising employment.* In economic terms, if the expected productivity of an individual is below her wage, she will not find a job. What about subsidising the unemployed or the prospective employer such that wage costs are reduced? Two variants are discussed in the literature (a) targeted wage subsidies for the long term unemployed; (b) a lowering of wage cost without reducing wages for low-skill employees. There is a third variant (c), namely subsidies to employers to open new jobs, the most traditional way.

(a) *Employment vouchers* (Snower, 1994, 1997). The idea of training is to increase productivity and thus employability. Dennis Snower, an economist working for many years on labour market problems, made the following proposal: instead of supporting people while they are not working and thus increasing their problems in finding a job, one should subsidise them for a limited period when working – *employment vouchers*.

This should work according to the following scheme: after a spell of unemployment has reached a threshold, the unemployed individual gets a voucher for employment. The value of the voucher increases as the duration of unemployment increases further. When finding a job, the voucher is given to the employer, who in turn gets a subsidy. The subsidy decreases over time and ends after a specified period.

If low productivity is the consequence of long-term unemployment and the cause for not being accepted for a job, bringing people into employment should reduce their productivity gap. Therefore the wage subsidy is highest when employment starts and is slowly withdrawn. It is the higher the longer the spell of unemployment was before re-employment.

Snower suggests that employers know better what skills their employees need than the administration of the employment agency when planning training programmes. It is therefore better to have people in temporarily subsidised jobs than in subsidised leisure time.

In the last years some states have introduced subsidy programmes. There is an important difference between Snower's idea and most implemented programmes: subsidies are usually paid for a specific period of time and are then withdrawn completely, sometimes with the obligation to keep a formerly subsidised employee for a few more months. Such a scheme gives different incentives than Snower's original idea. The latter does not create kinks in the cost line of the employer, whereas the former does so.

The gradual withdrawal in Snower's scheme conforms to the idea that productivity increases gradually. When the subsidy ends, productivity should be on par with that of other employees with the same formal qualification. Giving a fixed amount of subsidy for a specific period which is then withdrawn totally gives incentives to hire people with very low productivity – that is warranted. However there is also an incentive to keep them even if productivity does not increase as long as the subsidy lasts (and not to care for any training). It is likely that these people will be discharged after the period of subsidy has ended.

(b) *Reducing wage costs of employees with low qualification.* From the mid-1980s to the end of the 1990s, unemployment went down in the USA, whereas in many European states it remained very high – 'Eurosclerosis' against the 'US-job-machine'. The different developments were linked to specific features of labour markets in the USA and in Europe. In the USA wage differences between the skills drastically increased. Real wages of low-skilled workers declined for many years in spite of a strong growth of the economy. Wage differences remained much narrower in Europe (with the exception of the UK). As unemployment among low-skill employees is higher than among other employees, some suggested subsidising low-skill employment. The idea was that if the net wages of low-skill workers cannot be reduced due to political or social reasons, a subsidy can reduce the wage costs to employers without reducing the welfare of low-skill workers.[29]

The Earned Income Tax Credit (EITC) in the USA as well as its British counterpart the Family Credit is a way of doing that (see below, Chapter 8.6). In states with high social security contributions the end should be achieved by reducing social security contributions for low-wage employees.

When evaluating this idea one has to consider two questions. First, who will reap the benefits from reduced social security contributions and who has to pay for it? Second, how big is the effect?

The first question can be posed slightly differently: who guarantees that a reduction of social security contributions reduces total wage costs? Is the result lower gross wages or higher net wages? It is generally assumed that workers pay in the long run for all benefits they get when they are financed by a pay-roll tax (see below 6.4.2). In that case net wages will increase after a reduction of social security contributions, leaving the wage the employer has to pay unchanged. However it might be the case that at the lower end of the wage distribution that does not hold.

The second questions relates to the problem of the elasticity of labour demand with respect to wage costs at the lower end of the wage distribution. There have been some attempts to evaluate the effect of such a subsidy, but there are no general accepted results. Kramarz and Phillipon (2000) using French administrative data suggest that the elasticity of demand is high. Others are more sceptical.[30]

(c) *Subsidising employers for investment* This is an old and traditional way for subsidising employment. The idea is that if investment is increased, there will be more jobs. To state it clearly: economists do not like such a policy – it is hardly discussed in the literature. A general subsidy of jobs distorts the price system and creates a welfare loss according to the ideas laid down in Chapter 3 above.

But it is not a simple misconception that investment subsidies are often legitimised by saying that they reduce unemployment. Though the total number of jobs is unlikely to be increased by such a policy, the location of jobs can be changed by subsidies. They are usually undertaken in order to attract jobs into a region. Whether that can be a reasonable policy is a difficult question. It has to be linked to policies concerning regions: if a region experiences high unemployment should jobs be brought to the people, or people to the jobs (migration)? The problem is that the unemployed may face many obstacles for regional mobility.[31] If all regions are prepared to subsidise investment, there is a danger that all may end up worse. In the end there are not more jobs but higher taxes. This is a prisoner's dilemma situation. That's why the EU made rules to restrict such subsidies.

6.3.3 How to Evaluate ALMP Programmes?

If one applies a programme to a group of unemployed people, one wants to know what effect it has. For example, if a programme's purpose was to make jobs steadier, we want to know in which way the programme influences the duration of employment in new jobs. Simply to look at the duration of the jobs after the programme will not do, because for any result we do not know what was the programme's contribution. For example, assume that the majority of people who took part in a programme ended in long-lasting jobs. That success may have been down to the programme. But the following may also have happened:

- People with higher inclinations for steady jobs may have applied to take part in the programme.
- The administrators of the programme may have accepted individuals with higher probabilities of success for participation in the programme.
- Those who left the programme prematurely were individuals whose prospects of success were dim.
- Due to an upswing of the economy more good jobs were available.
- The programme was started in a region where long-lasting jobs are more prevalent than in the rest of the economy.

The difficulty for the analysis is that for the same instance of time one cannot observe the same individual participating in a programme and not participating in it.

To overcome that problem it is necessary to estimate how the participants in a programme would have fared if they would not have taken part. One has to make a comparison with non-participants who are very similar. There are two ways to do that (i) using social experiments; (ii) extracting information about the influence of the characteristics of the participants on the outcome of the programme from existing data (non-experimental methods).

The basic idea of the experimental method is to take a random sample to whom the programme applies (treatment group) and a control group the members of which cannot take part. If individuals are randomly assigned to one of the two groups, the difference in outcome – for example, different wages at post-unemployment jobs – can be attributed to the programme. In the USA the administration undertook some experiments which are well documented in the literature (Meyer, 1995). In Europe there were only a few experiments (Björklund and Regnér, 1996).

BOX 6.6 A PURE EXPERIMENT: COUNSELLING AND MONITORING THE UNEMPLOYED IN THE NETHERLANDS

A rare case of a blind experiment was the Dutch Counselling and Monitoring programme (Gorter and Kalb, 1996). The treatment group was given more intensive counselling and monitoring than the control group. The staff spent more time with those from the treatment group and helped them more intensively to find a job. The unemployed were randomly appointed to the treatment and the control groups. They were not informed about the experiment. Using a job search model, the authors estimated differences in the hazard rates.

They distinguished between two aspects, namely change in the number of applications and change in the success of an application. They also distinguished between those who had a permanent job before the spell of unemployment, and those who were on a temporary job. The reason for this was that the latter group was helped to find a permanent job, which can contribute to staying unemployed for longer as it reduces the propensity to accept another temporary job.

The result was that the hazard rate for those who had a permanent job before unemployment was negatively affected (shorter spells of unemployment), though not really significant. The hazard of those with a temporary job before unemployment was positively affected by more intensive counselling, implying that they were less likely to look for another temporary job in comparison with the control group. Interestingly the acceptance rate did not change, the number of applications changed.

Unfortunately (for the analyst!) an ideal situation for experiments rarely exists. You cannot force individuals into programmes and you cannot deny rights merely because you want to test whether a training serves a useful purpose. Some voluntary collaboration is always necessary – from people in the treatment group and in the control group. That makes it likely that the individuals in the treatment group are different from those in the control group. If individuals self-select into the two groups, the results are biased.

For example, the employment agency asks a randomly chosen group of unemployed individuals to participate in a special training programme. If they agree, they are randomly allotted to the treatment group or the control group. The treatment group gets the training, the control group does not get it. The results can be affected by the following reaction of the unemployed: those who do not expect a favourable effect from the training will refuse to take part in the experiment. The unemployed who accept taking part are expecting something positive from the training. That biases the results upwards. This problem cannot be overcome by making participation obligatory. To force somebody to accept training she does not want does not make sense. Moreover those who accepted but were put into the control group may have looked for another training. Thereby results are affected, because the difference between the treatment group and the control group is reduced. The way to handle such problems is to look at the incentives to participate, to analyse the participation probabilities and how that influences the outcome.[32]

The second method, the non-experimental one, is more common. First, it is cheaper to handle data than to make an experiment. Second, there may be no control group available. With non-experimental methods it is necessary to control for special characteristics which may be differently distributed amongst the group of people affected by the programme compared with the employed, and for any incentives of the programme to self-select.

For example, consider a programme for making the long-term unemployed find lasting jobs. It is known from labour market research that different groups of people have different probabilities of being in such a job – married men are more likely to be in long-tenured job than single men of the same age and the same educational level. If among the long-term unemployed there are more single men than in the rest of the working population, one has to take that into account. Similar effects arise due to different education, gender, age and other characteristics.[33]

6.4 THE REGULATION OF LABOUR CONTRACTS

6.4.1 Why are Labour Markets so Intensively Regulated?

Not many markets are as heavily regulated as labour markets. That is true for all countries. Special labour codes fix many aspects of labour contracts, in most cases they confer rights to the employees and limit the freedom of the employers to command. These regulations concern the way the payment of wages has to be made,[34] the length of the working day or the working week, the minimum amount of holidays, the ways to terminate a contract, safety measures against accidents. But also minor aspects of a labour contract may be regulated by law – whether the employer has to provide special clothing, whether the time for change of clothing is part of the labour time, at which hours of the day the employer can order the employees to work, and so on. Non-discrimination and equal-opportunity laws are everywhere on the statutes, as well as regulations concerning political rights of the employed – to be represented by unions, to have shop stewards or other representatives. These rights are of course contentious. Are they really necessary or are they an unjustified privilege for some groups of workers? Do they increase the welfare of the employed, and if so at whose costs?

To begin to answer these questions it is necessary to appreciate a special feature of all labour contracts: they are long lasting and can therefore not be fully specified. When you go to the counter of a self-service restaurant and order something to eat, it is clear what the person behind the counter has to do. There is not much to be decided, probably only the amount of smiling and the way to say 'hello' and 'good bye'. In a working contract there are many things left open which are decided by order of the employer: when to work, where to work, what to do in a specific situation and many other things. It is an important feature of all labour contracts that the employee accepts the discretionary power of the employer. The labour laws and related laws set limits to that discretionary power.

What would happen if these rights did not exist? Some fear (others perhaps hope) that labour relations would be similar to the way they were during the nineteenth century. Then, so goes the saga, working conditions were set unilaterally by the employers and were very bad for the workers. But it is unlikely that we would observe a return to that structure even if there were no laws. In the absence of labour codes many regulations would still be part of the contract between an employer and the employed, often on an industry wide basis. For example, more than half of British and US employees have the right of a severance payment in case of being made redundant, though there is no legal obligation to grant it (Booth, 1997). Labour contracts would become more complicated as they would have to contain clauses on all the subjects which are now regulated in labour codes and related laws.

It cannot be claimed that individual or firm specific contracts would bring about precisely the same stipulations as existing law, though it is unlikely that without state regulations of labour contracts one would observe a return to nineteenth century relations. Indeed, if contracts without laws would result in the same structures, it would not be necessary for labour laws to deny the employed the right to accept less stringent conditions nor would it make sense for the employers to resist labour legislation.

It is not easy to understand the problems of labour relations in the theoretical model of a spot market. In such markets net benefits across different suppliers are equal. If one supplier of a service provides better quality for the same price, she would attract all demand. All differences in expected returns and risks of assets must be mirrored in different values of these assets. That is the content of all arbitrage conditions in financial markets. However this model assumes that transaction costs are very small. That is a reasonable assumption for most financial markets, and for many markets for goods and services. It is a very bad assumption for labour markets, unless workers are hired for the day only.

In most jobs employee productivity is much higher if they stay for a long period in the same job or the same firm. One can hire a worker for manual cherry picking and supplant him with another one the next day without productivity decreasing. But one cannot do that if cherry picking is done with special machinery, not to speak of the work of an accountant, of a teacher, of a nurse and all the other jobs for which firm specific knowledge is necessary. It is more profitable for the firms and also more rewarding for the employees to stick together in long-term jobs.

BOX 6.7 WHAT BELONGS TO PAID LABOUR TIME?

Florida Employees of Walt Disney World should be paid for time spent getting dressed as Mikey Mouse or Goofy, a federal mediator has ruled, opening the back door for thousands.

Arbitrator J. Chumley's decision stems from a complaint filed last year with the National Labor Relations Board by the Service Trades Council, which represents six unions at Disney World. The complaint alleged that in the fall of 1999, Disney unfairly stopped paying workers for time spent changing into or out of a costume or uniform and for the time spent wearing a uniform before reaching a work site.

About 3000 Disney employees at Epcot, the Magic Kingdom and Fort Wilderness Lodge were affected. (*International Herald Tribune*, 4 April 2001)

This has an important consequence: there is a pure distributional conflict between the employer and the employees. Employers can to some extent increase profits by reducing the wage and making working conditions harsher without making the workers quit the job. Workers can to some extent increase their utility by demanding higher wages, by shifting labour conditions in their favour and by reducing effort without endangering their jobs. Both may be effective for a short period only, but for workers with a limited period to continue working or for a firm which for one reason or the other wants to cut its costs, that may be sufficient in order to do it.[35] It is therefore incorrect to use the model of the spot-market as a reference when evaluating labour legislation.

To leave everything to private contracts is probably a disadvantage for employees, as they seldom have the skill to bargain for good contracts and lack the means to pay for professional help. It is easier for employers to take care of their interest by manipulating the conditions in 'small print' clauses. Unions and other representatives of employees can make a big difference in overcoming this deficiency of employees.

Be that as it may, we have to distinguish between two aspects of labour codes. Stipulation of laws may create costs for the employers, without influencing the working of the labour market – for example, safety regulations, maximum-hours-of-work regulations. Other rules affect the functioning of the labour market – namely laws structuring the ending of a labour contract: advanced notice of discharging an employee, requiring special legal procedures to end a labour contract, payments to the discharged employee, payments to a third party.

6.4.2 Who is Paying for It?

Are employees better off with such laws? If everything can be reduced to a pure distributional conflict between employees and the employer – whatever one side gains the other side loses without further effects – such laws increase the welfare of the employees and the employers lose accordingly. That can be the case in the short run only.

In the long run things are different. We have to assume that employers take account of the costs of such laws when deciding about investment. Employees, on the other hand, take them into consideration when thinking about their reservation wage: labour demand is shifted to the left and labour supply to the right by such laws. It is unlikely that the two shifts will cancel out completely.[36]

There is an effect on total employment. *Ceteris paribus* employment is lower and the money wage is also lower due to the existence of labour laws unless the shift of the labour supply curve to the right has a greater impact than the shift of the demand curve to the left.

Increasing non-wage labour costs is partly at the cost of people remaining unemployed. The amount of the reduction of employment depends on the difference between the shift of the labour demand function and the labour supply function. Only looking at the increased costs for the employers overstates the employment effect, as it does not take into account the reduction of the reservation wages of employees.

However one has to be careful when drawing political conclusions. Figure 6.4 compares the situation with labour laws with a situation without them under the condition that the labour laws do no influence productivity. As labour laws increase the duration of contracts, they affect productivity of workers. Productivity cannot be considered as given exogenously. Therefore the shift of the labour demand curve can be smaller, namely if productivity is affected positively.

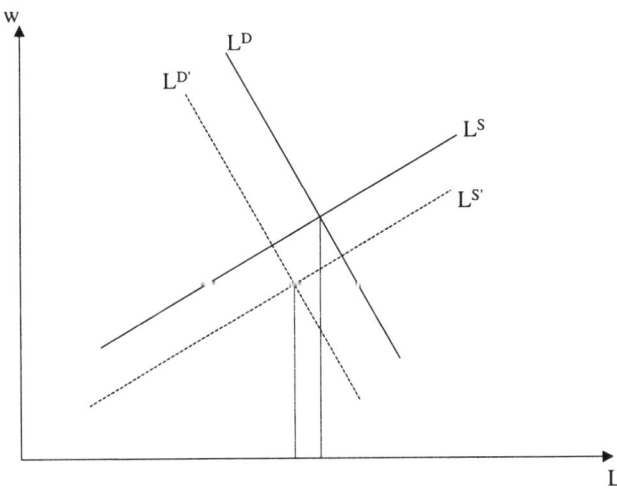

Note: Increasing non-wage labour costs shifts the labour demand curve to left. If the employees value the benefits positively, the labour supply curve is shifted to the right. The net-effect depends on the relative size of the two shifts. This diagram does not take into account any effects on productivity.

Figure 6.4 The comparative static effects of fringe benefits

Another way to look at this problem is to ask how would the wages of employees be affected if these laws did not exist, but everything else remained unaffected, that is leaving out the dynamic aspects of the labour laws. The overwhelming evidence is that wages would be lower. The employees pay for these benefits themselves.[37]

That is not surprising: the total wage costs of those in employment must be matched by their productivity. If wage costs go up due to an increase in benefits, one of three things (or a combination of them) must happen in the long run: (i) productivity increases; (ii) wages go down; (iii) less labour is employed as the demand curve shifts to the left. If you compare wage developments and development of non-wage labour costs, holding productivity for those in employment constant, the two must cancel out. In the long run the difference between a change in non-wage labour costs and changes in productivity must be seen in wage development.

BOX 6.8 WHO PAYS FOR WORKERS' COMPENSATION?

One of the earliest social policy measures was the introduction of an insurance scheme for compensation for job-related accidents. In Germany it was the beginning of modern social legislation under Bismarck in the late nineteenth century, in the USA the states began to introduce such legislation in 1910, the first state being New York. Before that workers had to rely on claims for liability for negligence to get compensation. That was a cumbersome undertaking with high costs for both sides.

> Pushing a suit through the court system often led to delays of two to four years between the date of the accident and a final court decision. In addition, there was a great deal of uncertainty about the results in the decision. As a result, the vast majority of workers sold their 'rights of action' in out of court settlements ...
>
> Evidence ... reveals that families of married fatal accidents victims bore the preponderance of the financial burden of industrial accidents. The studies reveal ... that the percentage receiving no compensation at all ranged from 22.2 per cent of Minnesota families in 1909–1910 to 60.9 per cent among men killed in Illinois before 1911 ... The mean ratio of compensation for fatalities ranged from a low of 38.3 per cent of annual earnings in Pennsylvania to 119.5 per cent in Minnesota. On average, however, the available evidence suggests that about 43 per cent of the families of fatal industrial accident victims would have received no compensation at all. (Fishback and Kantor 1995, p. 717)

The laws regulated compensation for job-related accidents and thus increased costs for the employers. How did these laws affect wages? The benefit of these laws was about 1 to 2.5 per cent of annual earnings (Fishback and Kantor, 1995, Table II). The authors

> took a sample of hourly wage rates for coal mining industries between 1911 and 1922, a sample from the lumber industry between 1910 and 1923 and a third sample of wages from the building industry between 1907 and 1913. They analysed data for three industries which are prone to industrial accidents, covering a period during which the reform of the laws were put on the statutes. In each year there was variation in the legal framework as the states did not introduce these laws in the same year. The authors controlled for divers factors influencing wages – product prices, unionisation and so on. Concerning the laws of compensation they write:
>
> In coal mining the presence of workers' compensation law was associated with a statistically significant 2.16 per cent decline in hourly earnings when evaluated at the mean hourly earnings. Similarly, the lumber industry wage offsets was 1.60 per cent and statistically significant. In the building trades, however, the decline was smaller at 0.33 per cent, and not statistically different from zero. (Fishback and Kantor, 1995, p. 728)
>
> Workers' compensation is an insurance the workers pay by themselves. Otherwise profits were reduced and capital were withdrawn from that industry.

Why, then, were employers always so much against all types of benefits? Were all the industrial disputes, often fought with bitterness, in vain? That may be partly due to the difference between the short run and the long run: in the short run workers can better their situation without jobs being lost. But I also suspect that this question is beyond the understanding of economics. Be that as it may, there is no country in the world where employees got these benefits without political fights. And there was also no country in the world where employers could not make good by increasing productivity.

6.4.3 Early Notification, Severance Payments and All That

It was mentioned above that some rights of employees limit the right of the employers to end a contract with an employee. To some extent employees are protected against being made redundant. Also dismissals for cause are made difficult by demanding to observe strict procedural norms. They make employers hesitant to dismiss workers whom they consider unproductive. That comprises severance payments, early notification rules and other legal procedures for dismissing employees. For example, in the USA firms have to pay higher contributions to the unemployment insurance if they dismiss workers. In Austria firms have to pay higher contributions to the pension system if they dismiss workers older than fifty.

Many economists consider such laws an important cause for the higher rate of unemployment in western Europe compared with the USA, because they are less strict in the USA than in most European states. Unemployment did not abate in western Europe after its increase in the early 1980s. In the USA it did so. One of the suspects was the statutory protection of existing labour contracts (Abraham and Houseman, 1993; Buechtemann, 1993). The protection of the employed contributed to what was termed *Eurosclerosis*.

Is this a reasonable conjecture? In what way do such laws affect employment and unemployment?[38] As usual, it all depends. Employment protection surely will have an effect if redundancy payments are very big or if it is completely forbidden to discharge employees. In that case employers are only prepared to hire employees if they are pretty sure that the job will last until the employee retires. Hardly any contract would survive that criterion. Of course, all people employed at the moment such a law is introduced can keep their job even if the productivity of their job declines due to an aggregate shock or a structural shock. For the unemployed it is extremely difficult to find a job.

To understand the functioning of such rules, consider the following case (Booth, 1997): an employer offers a job which is profitable with probability one for one period. With a probability smaller than one the job is profitable in the second period. If the worker can be discharged without costs, the employer will do so at the beginning of the second period when the job ceases to be profitable. If there are costs of discharging the worker, she will be kept as long as the loss for the firm is smaller than the costs of discharging. That provides a protection for the employed. However, when deciding how many jobs to offer in the first period, the employer takes the possibility of a loss in the second period into account. Fewer jobs will be offered. But in the second period more workers are employed in case of a slump compared with a situation without such costs (*labour hoarding*). There are fewer jobs, but they are steadier.

BOX 6.9　A TWO-LEVEL PROTECTION OF LABOUR CONTRACTS

Some countries with strong protection of existing labour contracts opened, to certain groups, the possibility of labour contracts with less protection. Particularly contracts with fixed duration were allowed. The contract expires automatically with no extra costs for the employer. A renewal leads under specific conditions to an indefinite labour contract subject to the strict rules of the labour law concerning the rights to terminate a contract. Such reforms were undertaken in order to give way to a more liberal labour market regime without reducing the benefits of those with jobs. What are the effects?

Blanchard and Landier (2001) studied such a reform in France. The institutional facts are that in France the employer can only discharge an employee with a contract of indefinite duration (CDI) due to personal reasons – the burden of proof is on the side of the employer – or for economic reasons. In that case complicated legal proceedings take place and the firm has to pay a severance payment. The government has expanded the former very limited possibilities for giving contracts with limited duration (CDD) for the young and for the long-term unemployed. Amongst the results:

> The proportion of [young P.R.] unemployed in a given 5-year cohort has remained roughly constant, from 15 per cent in 1983 to 16 per cent in 1999, and down to 12 per cent in 2000.
> Most relevant for our purposes, the proportion of CDIs has sharply dropped while the proportion of CDDs has sharply increased. In 1983, 60 per cent of a cohort (equivalently 95 per cent of those employed) were employed under CDIs; in 2000, the proportion was down to 21 per cent (54 per cent of those employed). And during the same period, the proportion of those employed under CDDs went from 3 per cent (5 per cent of employment) to 17 per cent (46 per cent of employment). (Blanchard and Landier, 2001, p. 28)

This reform – the authors call it partial reform – led to a higher rate of job turnover for the young compared to a situation without that reform. It was further shown that this reform was welfare decreasing.

Whether aggregate unemployment is higher or lower with such laws cannot be answered *a priori*. That depends on parameters of the specific model – that is on many features of the real world. There is a consensus among many economists working in that field that the contribution of such rules to unemployment, if any, is modest (Recently: Hunt, 2000; for contradictory evidence based on employment data see Lazear, 1990).

Such rules affect the working of the labour market and labour relations in other ways. Because they make it more difficult to terminate a labour contract, they give special incentives to invest in an existing contract. It pays for the employer to invest in the human capital of the employees. Actually severance payments are often provided by employers voluntarily to protect their expenditure for the training of their employees.

The existence of costs of ending a labour contract provides also an incentive to reduce working hours when demand decreases instead of relying on making workers redundant (Abraham and Houseman, 1993).

APPENDIX 6.1

An Integrated Model of Unemployment, Vacancies and Job Matching
(Mortensen and Pissarides, 1999)

The approach to an understanding of labour markets used in this chapter is to look at the flows of individuals between employment and unemployment. Corresponding to that flow must be a flow of jobs being open or filled with a worker. Indeed, if there were no vacancies, an unemployed individual could only find a job if a new one was created. The coexistence of vacancies and people looking for a job can be rationalised by assuming that finding a job or finding an employee are activities which take time. The unemployed and the vacancies are matched, that is, if an unemployed person and an employer meet and if the expected product y exceeds the sum of the reservation wage w^* and a minimum profit for the employer, they form a match after having decided about the wage. This minimal product is denoted y^*.

This process can be captured by a *matching function*. It is like a production function. The inputs are the vacancies v and the unemployed u. The output of this 'production' are the new matches. If the numbers of total working population and of the total jobs respectively are normalised to one, u is the rate of unemployment and v the rate of open jobs. The matching function can be written in the following way:

$$X = m(u,v)$$

X is the number of new matches.

The function increases in both arguments: the higher the rate of unemployment, the easier it is to find an unemployed individual taking an unfilled job; the higher the number of vacancies, the easier it is for an unemployed to find a job. One can assume that $m(0,v) = m(u,0) = 0$, that is, it needs open jobs and unemployed in order to get new matches. One can further assume that the matching function is homogeneous of degree one, that is, the function exhibits the property of constant returns to scale: doubling the number of unemployed and vacancies doubles the number of new matches per unit of time. In that case the function can be written slightly differently:

$$X = u \cdot m(1, v/u)$$

The term v/u, the ratio of vacancies to unemployment (θ), is an expression for the tightness of the labour market. The expression $m(1,v/u)$, or $m(\theta)$, is the hazard rate of unemployment, namely the probability of finding a job. The average duration of unemployment is $1/m(\theta)$, the average duration of a vacancy is $1/\theta \cdot m(\theta)$.

Assuming that the labour force is constant (with $1 - u$ in employment), the development of unemployment is characterised by the flows of new matches and of separations of employees from active jobs. A worker is separated from the job if its productivity falls below the value y^*. That happens when there is a shock making the job unproductive. In that case the worker becomes unemployed and starts anew with job search. In the simplest version all other causes for new matches are disregarded (people leaving and entering the labour force, employees looking for a job while being employed, employees being dismissed without closing down the job). The probability of a separation is π.

If unemployment does not change the number of new matches must equal the number of separations:

$$u \cdot m(\theta) = \pi \cdot (1 - u)$$

or, solved for the rate of unemployment:

$$u = \pi / (\pi + m(\theta))$$

This expression is known as the *Beveridge curve*, that is a relation between the rate of unemployment and vacancies under the condition that unemployment is constant, given the parameters of the matching function, the probability of finding a job and the probability of losing a job. That is a description of a macroeconomic relation between unemployment and vacancies characterised by the equality of flows into and out of employment.

In order to develop a model of labour market equilibrium it is necessary to look at the actors in the market – namely (i) individuals searching for employment and (ii) firms offering jobs. We have to ask what makes an unemployed individual accept a job, and employers accept an applicant for a vacancy. Furthermore we have to ask how many jobs are offered in equilibrium. (The size of labour force is exogenously fixed.)

These activities are conceptualised in an intertemporal context: an unemployed person accepts an offer by an employer if it is better for him than staying unemployed for one more period and looking for another job. An employer accepts a worker if expected profits by employing that applicant are higher than leaving the job open for one more period and waiting for another individual to apply for the job. Both actions are modelled with the same type of equation – the so called *Bellmann* equations. The idea is as follows: an asset promises a payment ρ per period. The debtor can at her discretion at the end of each period return the principal and stop paying ρ. In that case the owner of the capital has to look for another debtor and is in the same situation as one period before. That creates costs. When deciding whether to buy such an asset one has to subtract from the rate ρ a term taking account of the possibility that the principal is redeemed. This idea is being applied to the value of having a job, of remaining unemployed, of taking an employee and of having a vacancy.

Consider the unemployed: if a job is offered and she accepts it at the wage w, the asset value of that job, U^e, were w/r if the job would last forever (r is the rate of interest). However as the job may end after one period, namely if it becomes unproductive (probability: π), the wage w is secure for one period only. With probability π the employee becomes again unemployed and has to start searching a job. To take account of that when determining the asset value of taking a job, one has to deduct from the wage the difference in value between having a job and having to search anew – the value of being unemployed U^u.

$$rU^e = w - \pi \cdot (U^e - U^u)$$

The value of being unemployed can be determined in a similar way. If a person remains unemployed for one more period, having utility w^0, and can then look for another job, the probability of finding one is $m(\theta)$. Therefore, U^u, is the utility w^0 plus the expected value of a job found after one period of unemployment.

$$rU^u = w^0 + m(\theta) \cdot (U^e - U^u)$$

The utility w^0 depends on unemployment benefits, on utility of leisure, on the possibility of working in the shadow economy, and so on.

The decision of the employer is similarly structured. Assume for the moment that the number of jobs is fixed, and that some of the jobs are open – vacancies. To have a vacancy creates costs c per unit of time. The value of vacancy, V^v, is the expected profit if the job is filled after one period (probability: $\theta \cdot m(\theta)$) minus the costs of keeping the vacancy.

$$rV^v = -c + \theta \cdot m(\theta) \cdot (V^f - V^v)$$

If there is a worker in a job, the product is y and the profit is $y - w$. That profit is safe for one period only, as with probability π the job gets unproductive. The value of a filled job, V^f, is the profit of one period minus the expected difference between a filled job and a vacancy due to the possibility that the job becomes unproductive.

$$rV^f = y - w - \pi \cdot (V^f - V^v)$$

How many jobs will there be in equilibrium? The term V^v is a pure rent. Assuming competition employers invest until all pure rents have vanished: $V^v = 0$; the number of jobs is such that the costs of keeping a vacancy equals the value of filled job times the probability of a match ($c = \theta \cdot m(\theta) \cdot V^f$).

Up to now the determination of the wage w is open. Note that the wage is set in a bargain between the employed and the applicant. The usual condition for the wage, namely that it equals the marginal product cannot be used. Instead, if a worker and a firm meet, a match is formed if there is a positive surplus, that is, if y is higher than y^*. This surplus is split between the firm and the employee. That can be rationalised by Nash-bargaining, taking into account the outside opportunities, that is w^0 for the employee and the value of a vacancy for the employer, that is zero.

The equilibrium of this model are values for w, u, θ, V^f, U^e and U^u. This model can be used for the analysis of labour market policies: how the equilibrium values change if unemployment benefits are increased or decreased, if redundancy payments are introduced, if the long-term unemployed are helped to find a job, if matching is subsidised and so on.

NOTES

1. For a modern concise presentation of Marxist ideas in the framework of economic theory, see Roemer (1988), Foley (1986).
2. There was always some tension between social policy on the one hand and adherence to strict Marxism on the other. Marxist parties and groups tended to disregard social policy for its lack of revolutionary spirit. The debate about so-called revisionism began shortly after Marx's death and went on as long as socialist ideas were of political importance.
3. To see the difference between the general welfare loss of unemployment and the social policy aspect, increased leisure time due to unemployment must be counted positively in conventional welfare analysis. However the unemployed who have the extra leisure time have often a different feeling towards the increased leisure.
4. The size of the 'natural rate of unemployment' or 'non-accelerating inflation rate of unemployment' (according to the macroeconomic concepts) are closely related to the size of the flows in the labour market.
5. Usually one works with the same type of probability distribution for everybody, but the parameters may be different for members of different groups.
6. In some countries the self-employed are not counted in the labour force in the national statistics (for example, Germany, Austria). That makes the rate of unemployment higher.
7. On the other hand, if an individual loses his/her job, the spouse may start to look for one – the *added-worker* effect. That concerns also women, people near retirement and the young.
8. This has changed meanwhile.

9. The term 'hazard rate' originates from calculations of life expectancy, an accident or an illness, all are negative events. This is, of course, not the case with unemployment. Higher hazard means higher probability of finding a job.
10. The problem is that qualification – the stock of human capital – cannot be easily measured. Usually one takes years of schooling and perhaps prior work experiences into account. But it is clear that employers look not only at these characteristics when deciding whether to employ an applicant or not.
11. Unemployment affects the effort of employed people in their jobs. That is captured in *efficiency wage* models, which argue that the threat of unemployment makes employees work more assiduously (Akerlof and Yellen, 1986). Employers set the wage above the market clearing level to maximise profits. This causes a positive rate of unemployment in equilibrium.
12. It can be used to show strong aggregate effects of an increase of autonomous expenditure.
13. For the analysis of maximising utility over a long period, the technique of dynamic optimisation is used for calculating an optimal consumption path – that is, the amount of consumption at each instant of time.
14. It is not possible to draw the conclusion that both spouses are taking the decision together or that both are served equally.
15. Stephens (2001) found a positive added worker effect for spouses of displaced workers.
16. Such rules can contribute to aggregate unemployment (Lindbeck and Snower, 1988).
17. It was shown that employees who switch the firm but stay in the same industry experience only small wage reductions in case of displacement. If they move to another industry the loss of income is much bigger (Carrington, 1993; Neal 1995). It seems that human capital is to some extent industry specific.
18. In most states unemployment insurance was organised by unions and other workers' self-help organisations in the beginning.
19. For the analysis of distributional effects it is reasonable to assume that the pay-roll tax is shifted backwards to the employed. For the allocative effects that question is immaterial. Instead of the demand curve shifting to the left, the supply curve of labour would be shifted to the left. The equilibrium is the same.
20. For the unemployment register it can make a big difference whether individuals not working are supported by transfers related to the unemployment system or through other means of social assistance. When receiving payments through the latter, one is not necessarily registered as unemployed. In the former case non-participation may be disguised as unemployment. In the USA the former system of helping lone mothers – Aid for Families with Dependent Children – was given to non-working mothers. The recipients were not counted as unemployed. Some of them may have been looking for a job. In other systems, for example in Austria and in Germany, lone mothers are to some extent to be found in the unemployment registers even if they do not look for a job.
21. A study using data from a register of recipients of social assistance in the German town of Bremen calculated exit probabilities from that register (Gangl, 1998). The size of social assistance transfers bear no relation to former income. Even low labour incomes can be supplemented up to the limit. Though the recipients can be forced to take part in labour market programmes, this transfer comes pretty close to an unemployment benefit system as modelled in most theoretical papers on unemployment. For a single individual that transfer is about 40 per cent of mean German income. For a family with children the percentage is much higher. According to the study there was no difference in the probability of taking up a job for different implicit replacement rates.
22. Usually one assumes a Poisson process with a constant arrival rate λ.
23. The advantage of using the idea of a search process is that it is possible to rationalise the existence of different wages for very similar individuals. As the acceptance of a job depends on the expectations people have, that can result in different wages even where everybody has the same expectations about future arrivals: an offer pretty close to a good offer may be accepted because waiting for a further period does not pay.
24. In experiments individuals are randomly assigned to the two groups. However that is hardly possible in the unemployment benefit context.
25. Currently an issue in Germany and in France.

26. A policy relying on sanctions is perhaps politically easier to implement as it can use the widespread sentiment against people who are sometimes called 'welfare scroungers'.
27. 'The average male construction worker when being laid off in winter and having experienced a previous employment duration of more than 3 months faces a 50–60 per cent chance of being recalled by his former employer. If, additionally, this construction worker had already experienced a previous spell of temporary layoff unemployment, the estimated recall probability increases to 0.8–0.9.' (Pichelmann and Riedel, 1991).
28. ALMP programmes in depressed areas can hinder people from moving into other regions. Whether this is beneficial is an altogether different question.
29. Financing health by a pay-roll tax or other taxes as in most European states can be seen as a subsidy for low-wage workers. To see this, take the situation of a firm in the USA providing health insurance. The premium is independent of the employee's income and therefore a higher percentage of the income of low-wage employees than for employees with high wages.
30. It is often overlooked that there is a closely related issue, namely what are the effects of minimum wages. It is clear that if raising minimum wages does not have much influence on unemployment, reducing social security contributions will not have much influence either. Be that as it may, there is no unanimity concerning the effect of minimum wages (Card and Krueger, 1995).
31. An example: The industrial decline of northern England led to a decline in prices for houses. An unemployed person wanting to move to southern England where unemployment was much lower faced the problem that with the proceeds from a house sold in northern England it was impossible to buy a similar house in the south.
32. The classic method for evaluating the efficiency of a new drug, namely to give the members of the control group a placebo is not a viable option. It would necessitate giving the members of the control group a useless training without telling them.
33. For a not too technical introduction into the problems of statistical evaluation of experimental and non-experimental methods see Heckman and Smith (1996). An overview of the technical aspects is to be found in Heckman et al., (1999). For his work on these and similar questions James Heckman was awarded the Nobel price for economics in 2000. A comparison of experimental and non-experimental methods on a non technical level can be found in Heckman and Smith (1995).
34. Up to the beginning of the twentieth century some firms did not pay their workers in money – that is, they forced them to buy most things in specially designed shops. Often these shops either belonged to the firm or to a relative or a good friend of the owners of the firm. It took many industrial disputes to end this practice.
35. Note that most wages are set in bargains between the firm and the employed, or between unions as representatives of the employed and representatives of the employers. The unemployed – those looking for a contract – are not involved in bargaining about wages and working conditions. That is different from almost all other markets where prices are fixed by those wanting to make a contract.
36. In that case contracts without the laws would precisely mirror the laws.
37. It is also possible that the costs are shifted to the consumers. If the consumption habits of employers and employed are the same and if the labour law affects all employees uniformly that would not make a difference. If the law protects only a part of the employees, the shift of costs to the consumers is a serious issue. For example, if in an economy the expenditure for bread comprises a sizeable share of the budget of the poor, protecting the working conditions of the workers in mills and bakeries is at the expense of the poor. If the wages are on a subsistence level, the improvement of the working conditions for workers producing bread is at the expense of profits. That is similar to the problems discussed in the corn-law debate in England between the Napoleonic wars and 1847. See Ricardo (1817, ch. 22) and any book about the corn laws.
38. It is sometimes claimed that, if a payment is a pure transfer between the employer and the employed, it has not much influence. There is no social cost when ending a labour contract. The employer and the future employee take account of that payment when making the contract. Only in case that the law stipulates social costs which are not a pure transfer between the employer and the employee – costs of legal procedures, payment to third parties

– is there an effect at all. This is only correct if all wage bargains were between individuals looking for a job and firms looking for an employee. In that case the two sides could take account of the redundancy payment in the bargain. However most wage bargaining is between an incumbent employee and her firm. In that case redundancy payments influence the wage bargain and thereby employment and unemployment (Cahuc and Zylberberg, 1999).

REFERENCES

Abbring, Jaap H., Gerard J. van den Berg and Jan C. van Ours (2000), 'The Effect of Unemployment Insurance Sanctions on the Transition Rate from Unemployment to Employment', Amsterdam: Tinbergen Institute, mimeo.

Abraham, Katharine G. and Susan N. Houseman (1993), *Job Security in America. Lessons from Germany*, Washington D.C.: The Brookings Institution.

Akerlof, George A. and Janet L. Yellen (eds) (1986), *Efficiency Wage Models and the Labor Market*, Cambridge: Cambridge University Press.

Arulampalam, Wiji (2000), *Is Unemployment Really Scarring? Effects of Unemployment Experiences on Wages*, Bonn, IZA Discussion Paper, 189.

Arulampalam, Wiji, Alison L. Booth and Mark P. Taylor (2000), 'Unemployment Persistence', *Oxford Economic Papers*, 52, pp. 24–50.

Atkinson, Anthony B. (1999), *The Economic Consequences of Rolling Back the Welfare State*, Cambridge (Mass.): MIT Press.

Atkinson, Anthony B. and John Micklewright (1991), 'Unemployment Compensation and Labor Market Transitions', *Journal of Economic Literature*, 29, pp. 1679–727.

Bentolila, Samuel and Andrea Ichino (2001), *Unemployment and consumption: Are jobs losses less painful near the Mediterranean?*, Munich, CESIfO Working Paper.

Björklund, Anders and Håkan Regnér (1996), 'Experimental Evaluation of European Labour Market Policy', in: G. Schmid, J. O'Reilly and K. Schömann (eds), *International Handbook of Labour Market Policy and Evaluation*, Cheltenham and Brookfield: Edward Elgar, pp. 89–113.

Blanchard, Oliver and Augustin Landier (2001), *The Perverse Effects of Partial Labor Market Reform: Fixed Duration Contracts in France*, Cambridge (Mass.), NBER Working Paper 8219.

Böheim, René and Mark P. Taylor, (2000), *The Search for Success: Do the Unemployed find Stable Employment*, University of Essex, Discussion Paper.

Booth, Alison L. (1997), 'An analysis of firing costs and their implications for unemployment policy', in: D. Snower, and G. de la Dehesa (eds), *Unemployment Policy. Government Options for the Labour Market*, Centre for Economic Policy Research, Cambridge: Cambridge University Press, pp. 359–91.

Borjas, George J. (1996), *Labor Economics*, New York: McGraw Hill.

Buechtemann, Christopher F. (ed.) (1993), *Employment Security and Labor Market Behavior*, Ithaca, NY: ILR Press.

Bundesministerium für Arbeit und Soziales (1998), *Sozialbericht*, Wien.

Cahuc, Pierre and André Zylberberg (1999), *Job Protection, Minimum Wage and Unemployment*, Bonn, IZA, Discussion Paper 95.

Card, David and Alan B. Krueger (1995), *Myth and Measurement. The New Economics of the Minimum Wage*, Princeton: Princeton University Press.

Carrington, William J. (1993), 'Wage Losses for Displaced Workers – Is It Really the Firm that Matters?', *Journal of Human Resources*, 28, pp. 435–62.

Davidson, C. and S. Woodbury (1993), 'The Displacement Effect of Reemployment Bonus Programmes', *Journal of Labor Economics*, 11, pp. 575–605.

Dolton, P and D. O'Neill (1996), 'Unemployment Duration and the Restart Effect: Some Experimental Evidence', *Economic Journal*, 106, pp. 387–400.

Dynarksi, Susan and Jonathan Gruber (1997), 'Can Families Smooth Variable Earnings', *Brooking Papers on Economic Activity*, No. 1, pp. 229–303.

Elmeskov, Jorgen and Karl Pichelmann (1993), 'Interpreting Unemployment: The Role of Labour-Force Participation', *OECD Economic Studies*. No. 21, pp. 140–60.

Fallick, Bruce C. (1996), 'A Review of Recent Empirical Literature on Displaced Workers', *Industrial and Labor Relations Review*, 50, pp. 5–16.

Feather, Norman T. (1990), *The Psychological Impact of Unemployment*, Berlin, Heidelberg, New York: Springer.

Fishback, Price V. and Shawn Everett Kantor (1995), 'Did Workers Pay for the Passage of Workers' Compensation', *Quarterly Journal of Economics*, 112, pp. 713–42.

Foley, Duncan K. (1986), *Understanding Capital – Marx's Economic Theory*, Cambridge (Mass.): Harvard University Press.

Förster, Michael F. and Michelle Pellizzari (2000), *Trends and Driving Factors in Income Distribution and Poverty in the OECD Area*, Paris, OECD, Labour Market and Social Policy Occasional Paper, 42.

Gangl, Markus (1998), 'Sozialhilfebezug und Arbeitsmarktverhalten. Eine Längsschnittanalyse der Übergänge aus der Sozialhilfe in den Arbeitsmarkt', *Zeitschrift für Soziologie*, 27, pp. 212–32.

Gorter, C. and Kalb G.R.J. (1996), 'Estimating the Effect of Counselling and Monitoring the Unemployed Using a Job Search Model', *Journal of Human Resources*, 31, pp. 590–610.

Gregg, Paul and Jonathan Wadsworth (2000), *Two Sides to Every Story: Measuring Worklessness and Polarisation at Household Level*, Centre for Economic Performance Working Paper 1099.

Gruber, Jonathan (1997), 'The Consumption Smoothing Benefits of Unemployment Insurance', *American Economic Review*, 87, pp. 193–205.

Hamermesh, Daniel (1989), 'What Do We Know about Worker Displacement in the United States?' *Industrial Relations*, 28, pp. 51–9.

Heckman, James J. and Jeffrey A. Smith (1995), 'Assessing the Case for Social Experiments', *Journal of Economic Perspectives*, 9(2), pp. 85–110.

Heckman, James J. and Jeffrey A. Smith (1996), 'Experimental and Non-experimental Evaluation', in: G. Schmid, J. O'Reilly and K. Schömann (eds), *International Handbook of Labour Market Policy and Evaluation*, Cheltenham and Brookfield: Edward Elgar, pp. 37–88.

Heckman, James J., Robert L. LaLonde and Jeffrey A. Smith (1999), 'The Economics and Econometrics of Active Labor Market Programmes', in: O. Ashenfelter and R. Layard (eds), *Handbook of Labor Economics*, Amsterdam: North Holland, vol. 3, pp. 1865–2017.

Hunt, Jennifer (1995), 'The Effect of Unemployment Compensation on Unemployment Duration in Germany', *Journal of Labor Economics*, 13, pp. 88–120.

Hunt, Jennifer (2000), 'Firing Costs, Employment Fluctuations and Average Employment', *Economica*, 67, pp. 177–202.

Jacobson, Louis L., Robert J. LaLonde and Daniel G Sullivan (1993), 'Earnings Losses of Displaced Workers', *American Economic Review*, 83, pp. 685–709.

Jahoda, Maria, Paul F. Lazarsfeld and Hans Zeisel (1933), *Die Arbeitslosen von Marienthal*, English Translation: *Marienthal, the Sociography of an Unemployed Community*, Chicago: Adine Atheston (1970).
Johnson, G.E. and Layard, P.R.G. (1986), 'The Natural Rate of Unemployment: Explanation and Policy', in: O. Ashenfelter and R. Layard (eds), *Handbook of Labor Economics*, Amsterdam: North Holland, vol. 2, pp. 921–1000.
Kiefer, Nicholas N. (1988), 'Economic Duration Data and Hazard Functions', *Journal of Economic Literature*, 26, pp. 646–79.
Kramarz, Francis and Thomas Phillipon (2000), *The Impact of Differential Payroll Tax Subsidies on Minimum Wage Employment*, Bonn, IZA Discussion Paper 219.
Kubin, Ingrid and Peter Rosner (2001), 'Arbeitsmarktpolitik: Theoretische Grundlagen und österreichische Institutionen', in: R. Neck, E. Nowotny and G. Winckler (eds), *Grundzüge der Wirtschaftspolitik Österreichs*, Wien: Manz, pp. 88–126.
Lalive Rafael, Jan C. van Ours and Josef Zweimüller (2000), *The Impact of Active Labor Market Programmes and Benefit Entitlement Rules on the Duration of Unemployment*, Center of Economic Research Discussion Paper.
LaLonde Robert L. (1995), 'The Promise of Public Sector-Sponsored Training Programmes' *Journal of Economic Perspectives*, 9(2), pp. 149–68.
Layard, Richard, Stephen Nickell and Richard Jackman (1991), *Unemployment*, Oxford: Oxford University Press.
Lazear Edward P. (1990), 'Job Security Provision and Employment', *Quarterly Journal of Economics*, 105, pp. 699–726.
Lindbeck, Assar and Dennis Snower (1988), *The Insider-Outsider Theory*. Cambridge: Cambridge University Press.
Meyer, Bruce D. (1995), 'Lessons from U.S. Unemployment Insurance Experiments', *Journal of Economic Literature*, 33, pp. 91–131.
Meyer, Bruce D. (1996), 'What Have We Learned from the Illinois Reemployment Bonus Experiment?', *Journal of Labor Economics*, 14, pp.100–125.
Mortensen, Dale T. (1986), 'Job Search and Labor Market Analysis', in: O. Ashenfelter and R. Layard (eds), *Handbook of Labor Economics* Amsterdam: North Holland, vol. 2, pp. 849–920.
Mortensen, Dale T. and Christopher A. Pissarides (1999), 'New Developments in Models of Search in the Labor Market', in: O.Ashenfelter and R. Layard (eds), *Handbook of Labor Economics*, Amsterdam: North Holland, vol. 3, pp. 2568–627.
Narendranathan, Wiji and Peter Elias (1993), 'Influence of Past History on Incidence of Youth Unemployment', *Oxford Bulletin of Economics and Statistics*, 55, pp. 161–85.
Neal, Derek (1995), 'Industry-Specific Human Capital: Evidence from Displaced Workers', *Journal of Labor Economics*, 13, pp. 653–73.
OECD (1994), *The OECD Job Study*, Paris: OECD.
OECD (1995), *Employment Outlook*, Paris: OECD.
OECD (2000), *Employment Outlook*, Paris: OECD.
OECD (2001), *Employment Outlook*, Paris: OECD.
Pichelmann, Karl and Riedel, Monika (1991), *New Jobs or Recalls?*, Vienna, Institute for Advanced Studies, Research Memorandum 289.
Ricardo, David (1817), 'Principles of Political Economy and Taxation', in: P. Sraffa and M. Dobb (eds), *The Works and Correspondence of David Ricardo*, Vol. 1, Cambridge: Cambridge University Press, 1970.
Robertson, Matthew (1988), 'Temporary Layoffs and Unemployment in Canada', *Industrial Relations*, 26, pp. 82–90.

Roemer, John E. (1988), *Free to lose*, Cambridge (Mass.): Harvard University Press.
Ruhm, Christopher J. (1991), 'Are Workers Permanently Scarred by Job Displacements?', *American Economic Review*, 81, pp. 319–24.
Snower, Dennis (1994), 'Converting unemployment benefits into employment subsidies', *American Economic Review*, Papers and Proceedings, 84, pp. 65–70.
Snower, Dennis (1997), 'The simple economics of benefit transfers', in: D. Snower and G. de la Dehesa (eds), *Unemployment Policy. Government Options for the Labour Market*, Cambridge: Cambridge University Press, pp. 163–205.
Stephens, Melvin Jr. (2001), *Worker Displacement and the Added Worker Effect*, Cambridge (Mass.). NBER, Working Paper 8260.
Warr, Peter (1987), *Work, Unemployment and Mental Health*, Oxford: Claredon Press.
Winefield, Anthony H., Marika Tiggemann, Helen Winefield and Robert D. Goldney (1993), *Growing Up With Unemployment*, London: Routledge.

7. Families, Children and Gender

The support of families carries a heavy ideological burden, as does the policy concerning unemployment. However, unlike the case of unemployment, the ideology of family support relates not only to economics in the narrow sense of the word, but also to other aspects of social life. Often the ethical component of family life is emphasised. Some believe that an ethically good life without being married is only possible for people staying alone. Others point to the conservative element of life in families, because they see it as an institution which supports and strengthens the existing division of labour between men and women, the dominance of the husband-father-breadwinner over the rest of the family. Adherents of both political positions tend to demand that politics support their favoured life-style and that social policy should be a means for this end.

A different line of argument in favour of special family policy emphasises the usefulness of the family. They see the institution of the family as a basic element of the fabric of a society. If it is endangered, the stability of society is also in danger. The institution of the family is particularly important for children, because they have better chances to develop good characteristics if living in stable families.

Be that as it may, the notion of 'family' does not always mean the same. Traditionally it meant what is now sometimes called 'a nuclear family', namely two parents with children – it is used in this way in the context of the argument that children do better if living in a stable family. This notion of family was prominent at times when marriages rarely ended by divorce, and the birth of a child out of wedlock was considered immoral. Then, most single-parent households were a result of the death of one of the parents.

Whether one likes it or not, social realities have changed tremendously. Many marriages now end up in divorce. Having a child without being married only carries among particular groups a stigma.[1] In the context of social policy 'family' means in most instances any constellation of at least one parent with at least one dependent child.[2] Support of families is tantamount to the support of parents for bringing up children, independently of the legal form of the arrangement. This does not comprise all functions of the family, but it is the function which is emphasised in most discussions about family support. Other functions less prominent in the public discourse are support of the spouse (or partner) or support of the old. Problems of gender policy have become an issue for family policy as well.

In the first part of this chapter reasons for family support are discussed, in the second the instruments for child support are analysed. In the third the problems of maternity benefits are looked at and in the fourth part we consider the special problems of single-parent families.

7.1   WHY SHOULD FAMILIES BE SUPPORTED?

In the public discourse on family policy, different arguments for the support of families – that is, the upbringing of children – are emphasised. They are related to different normative positions. The strength of these positions vary in different cultures. For example, mothers with children below three are expected to stay with their children in Germany and in Austria. That is not the case to the same extent in France, where keeping children in a crèche is more common. Also social problems connected with special forms of family can be different. In the USA and the UK single mothers are a group at high risk of long-term poverty. Out-of-wedlock births are seen in connection with teenage pregnancies and unfinished high-school education. That is hardly a problem in most European states. Be that as it may, in order to evaluate policies it is necessary to be clear about their objectives, as the usefulness of the instruments of family support depends on the objective of the support.

7.1.1   Demographic Aims

For a long time a large population was considered to be good – the strength of a country was thought to depend on the size of its population. Policy should support the upbringing of children for the benefit of the nation or the state – a pro-natalistic policy. Today there are not many who attach a positive value to the 'strength' of a state without reference to the welfare of its inhabitants. Furthermore this policy was actively pursued by regimes which today are seen as extremely repulsive: Nazi Germany and Romania under Nicolai Ceaucescu are examples.[3]

An argument in favour of a pro-natalistic policy which is more in line with traditional economic thinking originates in the problems of the pension system (Chapter 5 above, particularly 5.6). The welfare of the old depends on the size of the young population. That concerns the pension system and the health system. Children provide external benefits if in future their contributions will support a PAYG pension system or health care system.[4]

However it is not clear whether or to what extent fertility can be influenced by public policy. Countries with high financial support for children do not tend to have higher fertility. Some people claim that a good public system for care of small children is more important for raising fertility, because women face difficulties in the labour market when they have to care for children. To what extent this is true is open. It is clear that the decline in fertility and the increased participation of women in the labour market, as well as the increased human capital of women are closely interrelated. If fertility can be raised by increasing transfers or by other public means, the elasticity of fertility with respect to public support seems to be low.

7.1.2 The Right to Establish a Family and Free Choice of the Number of Children

The right to establish a family was strictly limited in many cultures in the past. Today this is considered a human right. Article 16 of the Human Rights convention states:

1. Men and women of full age, without any limitation due to race, nationality or religion, have the right to marry and to found a family. They are entitled to equal rights as to marriage, during marriage and at its dissolution.
2. Marriage shall be entered into only with the free and full consent of the intending spouses.
3. The family is the natural and fundamental group unit of society and is entitled to protection by society and the state.

These are rights which, some believe, oblige the state to support families.

Moreover, a family should be free to have as many children as it likes. This has direct consequences: whereas a poor family hardly qualifies for public support when renting a big house or buying an expensive car, having many children is seen as legitimate reason for support. Note that in most religious denominations a strict observance of the tradition demands that people abstain from any non-technical means of birth control.

7.1.3 Rights of Children

Not only has the right to establish a family undergone tremendous changes in history, this is also true for the position of children. They used to provide cheap labour and a guarantee for old age support. Since child labour is prohibited nearly everywhere (though still existent in many poor economies) and old age support is organised in a cooperative way, children have lost their former position. Today children are seen as persons in their own right with claims even against their parents. Most states accept some responsibilities in safeguarding these rights and helping parents to care for their children. If parents are not able to provide sufficient resources or are otherwise unable to care for children the state may accept further responsibilities towards children. This idea is put on the statutes of the UN *Convention on the Rights of the Child.* Article 27 states:

1. States Parties recognize the right of every child to a standard of living adequate for the child's physical, mental, spiritual, moral and social development.
2. The parent(s) or others responsible for the child have the primary responsibility to secure, within their abilities and financial capacities, the conditions of living necessary for the child's development.
3. States Parties, in accordance with national conditions and within their means, shall take appropriate measures to assist parents and others responsible for the child to implement this right and shall in case of need provide material assistance and support programmes, particularly with regard to nutrition, clothing and housing.
4. States Parties shall take all appropriate measures to secure the recovery of maintenance for the child from the parents or other persons having financial responsibility for the child, both within the State Party and from abroad. In particular, where the person having financial responsibility for the child lives in a State different from that of the child, States Parties shall promote the accession to international agreements or the conclusion of such agreements, as well as the making of other appropriate arrangements.

This article probably mirrors a widely accepted normative position. It implies not only that the state should support families when raising children, but also that sometimes states should support children, because parents are not willing or able to do so. For example, if an individual refuses to work, her ensuing poverty is not as much of an issue as is the poverty of her children. They are not supposed to work. If they are poor, it is not their responsibility. Poverty among children raises different obligations for the state than poverty among adults.

7.1.4 Horizontal Redistribution: Support of Families with Many Children

Some consider it a question of equity that families with an above average number of children should be supported even if they have high income. This is argued by relating equity to the horizontal distribution within an income group: individuals within an income group are treated equally if the *per capita* income of individuals from families of unequal size remains within a reasonable close interval. This argument was used by the Austrian constitutional court, when ruling that the Austrian tax code does not give sufficient support for families. It was also used by the German constitutional court when deciding that families with children should not have to pay the same contribution for the insurance of old age care as families without children.[5]

A second line of argument can be that children from families with higher income are entitled to higher welfare, because parents have to share their income with their children. That argument draws on the right of children for adequate support by their parents. A further argument for horizontal redistribution makes use of the external benefits of raising children (Sinn, 1997). Families with an above average number of children create benefits for the rest, particularly for those without any children: everybody benefits from the labour of the next generation. Families with children are therefore entitled to some support for raising children regardless of their income.

7.1.5 Within Lifetime Redistribution: Support of Periods with Small Children

Even households with average or above-average lifetime income and merely an average number of children may face financial problems when children are small. Most households have small children during periods of low income. The wages of the young are often lower than wages of older employees. Moreover many households have a smaller supply of labour when caring for small children than at later periods of life. In some countries one adult member of the household is expected to stay at home when children are very young, or one member works only part time. Furthermore the period of small children frequently falls together with the period of establishing the household – buying a house, and so on. Households with high lifetime income often start to work late because of higher education. They cannot save much before having children. Finally buying child care in the market is very costly. In these cases redistribution of income during the life-cycle, namely towards earlier periods in life can be a sensible policy.

7.1.6 Support of Higher Education

A special political aim is to support the acquisition of human capital in order to increase people's future income. That can be argued on equity grounds, namely to decrease inequality of opportunities. Another argument can be derived from growth theory: increasing human capital is welfare enhancing.

Today all states have free education up to secondary level. The quality of public schools can be an important issue: if public schools are not of high quality, middle-class families might turn towards private schools. As they are often expensive, families may experience financial problems.

The costs households have to bear for post-secondary education of their children varies between states. In most states on continental Europe university education is either free, or fees are low. In the states of northern Europe, the UK, as well as Australia and New Zealand and the USA universities charge substantial fees, but states provide loans for students, which in some cases do not have to be repaid before earnings reach a threshold. In the Scandinavian countries these loans must be seen in the context of another normative position: it is no longer the responsibility of parents to finance their children beyond the age of eighteen.

7.1.7 Support of Special Family Structures

In many states particular ways of organising family life – namely raising children – gets special support. There are special provisions for helping single-parent families, mostly women with children. Various arguments are put forward for that. One being problems of poverty, but there is also a gender specific purpose: today many people think that a woman should have the opportunity to raise a child without being financially dependent on a man. Others want one adult – usually the mother – to stay at home when children are small. It is argued that this is better for children.

7.1.8 Gender Specific Policies

All families have to arrange the distribution of work for different tasks in the household and for getting income. It is clear that the distribution of tasks between spouses is strongly influenced by culture and tradition – namely that men are primarily responsible for earning income and women for tasks in the household and for raising children. However that no longer conforms to social realities and has been challenged by many political groups, primarily by feminist movements.

The changing social realities are: (i) higher professional qualification of women; (ii) lower fertility which allows more time for activities out of home; (iii) technical progress for household tasks; apart from caring for children, organising a household is no longer very time consuming. Such social changes and the changing consciousness of women are closely interrelated. There is no way to single out a basic cause from all the other aspects. Whether fertility was reduced because of more education, or reduced fertility allowed for a higher labour supply, which in turn made the acquisition of skills valuable cannot be decided. Be that as it may, all policies towards the family affect the relative position of genders. This raises special concern: many demand that family policy should support a more equal position of women, at least it should not strengthen the traditional roles of men and women.

7.2 INSTRUMENTS OF FAMILY SUPPORT

We can distinguish between the following instruments for the support of families:

- Giving financial support through the tax-transfer system.
- Accepting children without contributions in the health system.
- Accepting contribution-free years in the pension system.
- Survivor's pensions.
- Providing goods and services.
- Mandating and subsidising maternity benefits and parental leave.

Different countries put different emphasis on the various possibilities. There is no way to calculate the costs of all these activities. However one must not forget: there is no rich uncle. We can therefore ask: to what extent is it possible to subsidise families? Who is paying for it?

Note that about 70 per cent of women have at least one child.[6] The majority of households without dependent children are households before they have to care for children or after that period. Redistributing income to households with dependent children is primarily a redistribution towards households which presently have dependent children from those which currently do not (and of course from those which never have children). Where the number of children per household does not vary very much, and if the support of families is linear in the number of children, the financial support of households with children is primarily a redistribution over the life-cycle. A household receives a transfer during the period it is eligible for it – and pays for it at other times.

7.2.1 An Example: How Much Redistribution is in the Austrian System of Maternity Leave and Family Allowances?

Maternity leave and child allowances are financed by a special fund, the *Familienlastenausgleichsfond* (FLAF). This fund is financed largely from a earmarked pay-roll tax of 4.5 per cent. It is a special wage tax. The rest originates from general taxes. As wages and employment increased nearly every year and the number of births went down, from about 110 000 in 1970 to less than 80 000 per year in the late 1990s, there was a surplus in many years. The political system reacted by extending benefits. Cuts were rarely proposed. The following calculations rest on the law valid during the year 2000. Meanwhile some benefits have been extended.

After having given birth a woman can stay at home with full pay for 8 weeks (actually she is not allowed to work). The period of withdrawal from work could be extended for a further 22 months. This right could be used by the father and the mother. If only one parent took advantage of this opportunity the transfer ended when the child was 18 months old. If both parents made use of this programme, they could get the benefit up to the end of the second year. The payment was fixed and was given only to employed or formerly employed individuals. The size of the payment was about €400 per month, in the case of a single-parent household or a low-income household an extra payment of €190 per month was given.

For each child the family got a transfer depending on the age of the child – between €105 for the first and second child and €130 for the third and any further child per month below the age of ten, from €125 to €150 until the age of 19, and from €140 to €170 for children studying until the age of 26. A supplement of €30 was paid for the third and any further child except in the case of a very high income.

On top on this, there was a tax credit for each child of €50 per month. In order to make the payment independent from household income the tax credit was paid out if the tax bill was smaller than the credit (negative income tax).

A study calculated the net transfers to families according to the number of children and an assumed income stream over the whole life (Kothmayr and Rosner, 2000). In this study high income means an income typical for a person with university qualification. It starts at the age of 25, is not high in the beginning, but increases until retirement to at least the top quartile of the income distribution. A person with middle income starts to work at the age of 18, has a low income in the beginning and experiences only a moderate wage increase with age. Low income people start to work earlier and have an income which hardly rises until retirement. It was assumed that households with children have 1.5 wage earners. This is due to the fact that women earn less than men and reduce labour supply for at least a few years.

The payments into the system were a 4.5 per cent payroll tax. The transfer were the child benefits and the *Karenzgeld*. Two cases were calculated, support of children until the age of 18 and until the age of 25. The rate of discount was 2.5 per cent. As one can see in Table 7.1 households with only one child were net payers. In the case of two children not studying, high and middle-income families neither got a benefit nor did they lose through the system. Those with three children were net winners, particularly if their children studied. Note that for low-income households the net transfer is not only absolutely higher but makes an ever greater impact on the income of the household. Altogether for 4.5 per cent of all wage incomes there was not much redistribution achieved, as the share of families with more than two children is not more than 15 per cent.

There was also not much redistribution over the lifecycle, as benefits increased with age. Many families get benefits for more than 20 years and pay into the system for about 40 years. There cannot be much of an effect. One benefit which shifted income towards young households, namely a payment in connection with birth, was drastically cut in the late 1990s.

Table 7.1 Benefits and contributions over whole life in the Austrian child support system ($€$)

	Contributions		Income	
		High (93599)	Middle (80229)	Low (36279)
	Benefits	Benefits in % of contributions		
1 child till 18	34532	36.9	43.0	95.2
2 children till 18	69402	74.2	86.6	191.5
3 children till 18	104733	111.9	130.5	219.8
with supplement	109271			301.2
1 child till 25	42031	44.9	52.4	115.9
2 children till 25	85277	91.1	106.3	235.1
3 children till 25	126404	135.1	157.6	280.7
with supplement	132057			364.0

Source: Kothmayr and Rosner (2000), values were changed from schilling to euro.

For one aim of family policy this system is very efficient: reducing poverty. Low-income households and households without income would be extremely poor without the benefits. Actually there are few poor families with children who would not be poor without children.

7.2.2 Ways to Support Families

Financial transfers are given as special clauses in the tax system or as special payments. There is no systematic difference between the two, because transfers are nothing but negative taxes. Taxes and transfers can be discussed together.[7]

One has to distinguish between (i) tax deductions and (ii) tax credits. Tax deductions reduce the income used as basis for calculating the tax. Tax credits reduce the tax burden of a given income. If the marginal tax rate increases with increasing income, tax deductions of a given size are more valuable to the recipients of high income. Tax credits are the same for everybody, independent of income if the tax burden can be smaller than zero (Negative Income Tax).[8]

The redistributive effects of transfers can only be evaluated if the financing of the transfers is considered as well. For horizontal redistribution – favouring families according to the numbers of children within a given income class – tax deductions are a suitable instrument if the tax rates are adjusted such that in each income group the net transfers across the group are zero. If policy is more oriented towards vertical redistribution, tax credits (and cash benefits) are a more suitable instrument. Of course, the extra amount of taxes must not be financed by a regressive system.

Some countries set income thresholds for receiving some child benefits, as they consider fighting poverty in connection with children the main objective for family subsidies: these include the United States of America and the United Kingdom. Germany gives the households an option: they can choose between tax credits and tax deductions. Most low-income households opt for the tax credit, most high-income households for the deduction. Therefore nearly every family with dependent children is favoured proportionally to income – which in effect results in very little redistribution: the tax rates have to be higher. Similar systems can be found in other states as well: the USA has special system for the support of low-income families – the Earned Income Tax Credit (see Chapter 8.6). But they have also benefits which are more valuable for high-income families: benefits for child-care and for savings for the education of children (Ellwood and Liebmann, 2000). A precise evaluation of the child benefit system depends on the principles of the tax system. All tax systems are progressive and have increasing marginal tax rates. But the actual tax burden depends on many exemptions and how these exemptions interact.

The contribution-free health insurance or acceptance in a national health systems, as customary in most states – the exceptions are Switzerland and the USA – is, of course, a subsidy for families. This subsidy increases with the number of children. It is a special favour for single-earner families, as the non-working spouse is covered by the health system without any contribution. The same applies to survivors' pensions in regard to pensions for orphans. Widows' (widowers') pensions are also a subsidy for families: if there were no survivors' pension, the pension for all could be higher leaving contribution rates the same. (Or contribution rates could be lower without lowering pensions.)

States not only provide financial help for families with children but also services. The most important of them are publicly provided or publicly supported schools and facilities for child care. Public schooling up to secondary level is free nearly everywhere. Child-care for pre-school children is usually not free, though in some states contributions depend on income.

The primary reason for providing public schooling is that states have goals concerning education. First of all, everybody must get some schooling up to a certain level – schooling is obligatory. Second, states want to safeguard a certain quality of schooling. To some extent the content of what is taught in schools is also an important issue for the state. Altogether the purpose of public schooling is not primarily a social policy goal. The economic argument against providing goods and in favour of giving money cannot be invoked in the case of public schooling.[9]

The case for publicly provided or publicly supported child-care for smaller children however is weaker. Though it is widely accepted that some attendance at a kindergarten is good for children, in the sense of good for furthering their education, there is less unanimity concerning small children, particularly below the age of three. There are big variations between different states concerning the provision of kindergartens and crèches. This has much to do with ideas of how a family should organise its life: whether labour market participation of women with small children is considered as something normal, or rather as a sad necessity for those who cannot afford to stay at home.

In the Scandinavian countries and in France the provision of kindergartens and public child-care is much wider than in Germany or in Austria. If it were not, women could not take part in the labour market as much as they do. Private suppliers are politically accepted everywhere. In the UK and in the USA publicly provided child-care is less common. In the USA there are subsidies for low-income families for using day-care (Berger and Black, 1992).

Whether public assistance for child-care is something good, cannot be decided without determining, what is 'good'. If a high rate of participation of women in the labour market is considered good, cheap public child-care is important. If, on the other hand, that is seen as something of minor importance, public child-care need not be an important agenda. It goes without saying that this question is connected to the one of how different tasks in the household are allocated between genders.[10]

7.2.3 What are the Effects?

As shown above actual redistribution through different ways of supporting families with children need not be very big, even if these benefits amount to a sizeable part of GDP. Families with many children are subsidised by other households in nearly all systems. That is possible, because only a small fraction of families have many children.[11]

Low-income families are, in most states, also subsidised by public schooling and by free access to health services for children. If the latter is not provided and if the quality of public schooling is low, the redistribution in favour of low-income groups is much weaker. Moreover if high-income families enjoy tax deductions for children and have the opportunity of tax-deductible expenditures in connection with children (for higher education, for child-care) support for low-income families is further weakened.[12]

Important and much discussed are the effects on labour supply. Of course, there is an income effect and a substitution effect. Giving support to families implies increasing their income. Assuming that leisure is a non-inferior good that reduces labour supply. Men will be affected primarily concerning their hours of work, for women it may also affect participation. The substitution effect depends on the way child support works – whether it is means-tested or not, whether child-care is free or not; if not free, whether the contribution depends on income or is per-head; in which ways child benefits interact with other benefits and tax exemptions.

In general, any means-tested benefits increase effective marginal tax rates – that is the sum of the tax rate and the rate of withdrawal of the benefit – which affects the labour supply of low-income families, again particularly that of women. Tax exemptions and tax deductions for children can lower marginal tax rates. In that case there is a substitution effect in favour of more labour supplied.[13]

7.3 MATERNITY BENEFITS AND PARENTAL LEAVE

7.3.1 The Rights

Becoming a parent is an important event in the life of any adult, especially for the mother. As that has become a rare event during life – most mothers have fewer than three children – it is an interruption of 'ordinary' life, namely of working and having leisure time. To help with the 'big event' of a child, nearly all states provide some rights for women in connection with pregnancy and birth. There are rights to take leave without losing a job, in many states combined with a transfer. These rights have in may places also been extended to fathers.

Maternity leave means that the employed mother can stop working, or even has to stop working, a few weeks before and a few weeks after giving birth. In most states this right is accompanied by a transfer with a high replacement rate. The number of weeks vary. In 1992 the EU issued a Directive for the Protection of Pregnant Women which has 14 weeks minimum for maternity benefits (Fagan and Rubery, 1996) and for a transfer not smaller than in case of illness. Some states allow the employee to take off more weeks. This right is given to employed women, though there are some attempts to extend it to self-employed working women. Since 1993, women in the USA have the right to twelve weeks' unpaid leave following birth if working for an employer with more than 50 employees. Only about 45 per cent of women enjoy this right (Waldfogel, 1998b). If a firm pays any sickness benefits, they must continue to be paid during leave due to birth.[14]

These laws have to be seen in the context of the interrelation of health policy and labour protection. Though pregnancy and giving birth is not an illness, the pregnant woman and the mother immediately after birth is considered not to be fit for work.[15]

Parental leave is the right of the mother and the father to stay with the child while keeping a job, and can also be supported by a transfer. (For an overview see OECD, 1996.) The extent varies between 3 and 36 months. In the Scandinavian countries the transfer is bound to former income with a high replacement rate (up to 75 per cent for 12 months in Sweden and in Norway, in Denmark it is the same as full unemployment payment which depends on former income); Canada, Italy and Spain have wage dependent transfers with a much lower replacement rate. France, Germany and Austria give a fixed amount of money. The German transfer is partly means-tested (Laisney et al., 1999). The United Kingdom has a very short period for parental leave. The USA has none. In most countries these payments are reserved for the employed. The exceptions are the UK, Sweden, Denmark, Finland and recently Austria. France does not grant this right for staying with the first child.

The pick-up rates vary between states. The highest ones are to be found in the Scandinavian countries. That is not surprising given the high replacement rates. In Germany and in Austria the pick-up rates are high as well. That can be related to the small supply of public child-care facilities for children below three. Both states give benefits for a very long period: two years in Germany and, beginning with 2002, up to three years in Austria. Staying home with a small child is widely accepted in these two countries, though currently a political issue.

The right to parental leave is granted to fathers and mothers nearly everywhere, however, with the exception of Sweden, the percentage of men taking any leave is far below 10 per cent. Even in Sweden the percentage of weeks taken for parental leave by men is also only about 7 per cent.

7.3.2 The Effects

To understand how these rights influence the economic and social situation of people, it is necessary to distinguish two aspects: one, the right not to work without losing the job and, second, the transfer itself. The right to take leave is important as otherwise individuals who do not want to work for that period have to give up their job.

If labour markets were pure spot markets, the right to keep the job and to take leave would not be of interest for anybody. But as discussed in the chapter on labour markets that is not the case. Labour contracts are enduring, because that increases productivity. The right to take leave makes labour contracts steadier. That in turn makes it profitable for the firm to invest in young employees who are expected to give up working for some time because of child-care. On the other hand, employers hesitate to provide on-the-job-training for employees who are expected to take very long leaves. Which of the two effects dominates is an empirical question.

The transfers themselves strongly influence the labour supply around child birth. There are different effects to distinguish: if benefits are given only in case of prior employment, they increase women's supply of labour before having a child – the effective wage increases. For the analysis of effects on labour supply after giving birth one has to compare utility when working and not receiving the transfer and utility when not working and receiving a transfer.

The outcome of this comparison and the effect on labour supply after birth depends on many aspects. We expect that individuals enjoying high replacement rates are more likely to take leave. High replacement rates can be due to statutory high replacement rates, as in the case of the Scandinavian countries. Or they are due to low wages if the benefit has a fixed size, as in France, Germany and Austria. In the first case, taking leave will be more evenly spread among all employees than in the latter case. Also of importance for the comparison are the availability and costs of child-care facilities. If they do not exist or if they are very expensive, one person – mostly the mother – will take leave or quit working altogether.

These rights influence the position of women in the labour market and are important concerning the aim of increasing equality between genders. Without the right to take leave, training on the job would be more concentrated among employed men and employed women after childbearing age. On the other hand, if lengthy periods of leave are only taken by women, they are more likely to get jobs with little opportunities for promotion than men (Waldfogel, 1998a; 1998b).

BOX 7.1 MATERNITY LEAVE AND THE GENDER PAY GAP

It is a well-known fact that women earn less than men with similar qualifications. That is often called discrimination. That is difficult to understand for economists, as they assume that employers want to make profits. If women were prepared to work for lower wages than men with the same qualification, employers actually would prefer to employ women. That should drive up the wage of women.

This is not to deny that discrimination exists, but it shows that it is necessary to clarify how it works – what makes women's wages lower than those of men without increasing the demand for their labour. It is necessary to ask what affects the wage gap between men and women.

Jane Waldfogel (1998a, 1998b) relates the wage gap to the fact that mothers are differently affected when having children than fathers. Two facts: first, it is well established that the wages of men with families are *ceteris paribus* higher than the wages of men living without a family. That may be due to married men's higher feeling of responsibility making them work better. But it may also be the case that attributes increasing a man's probability of having a family also increases his productivity.

Second, the wage gap between single men and single women has markedly decreased in recent years. In some countries there is not much of a wage gap left between these two groups. However there remains a big difference in the wage gap between mothers and non-mothers with otherwise similar characteristics. Waldfogel reports that for a 30-year-old woman the difference is about 20 percentage points. Whereas non-mothers earn about 90 per cent of what men earn, mothers earn only about 70 per cent (1998b).

That difference can be the result of unobservable differences in qualifications as well: whereas years of schooling and training can easily be observed, there may be other differences in qualification which cannot be observed directly, but are not equally distributed between mothers and non-mothers. By comparing the wage gap at the age of 21 and at the age of 30 for the same women Waldfogel controlled for unobserved heterogeneity (*difference-in-difference* method). The assumption is that any unobserved differences in qualification must have had the same effect on wages when the women were 21 as at the age of 30. But the difference in the wage gaps between mothers and non-mothers was not affected, implying that it was not unobserved heterogeneity which produced the differences in the wage gap. Children do make a difference for wages.

The author further asked what difference does the right of maternity leave make. As she was only working with US and with British data, she could only evaluate the effects of protected jobs, not of long-term parental leave. The US data she used were from before 1993, when the right to maternity leave became mandatory. However many women had the right before that date. Waldfogel compared the development of women's wages with and without the right to leave. She not only controlled for characteristics of the women employed but also for characteristics of the employer –

> whether workers were represented by a union and the size of the employer. These characteristics as well may have influenced the development of wages independently of the right to maternity leave. She shows an effect of about 6 per cent in wages remaining after controlling for size and union coverage of the employer.

7.4 LONE MOTHERS, OCCASIONALLY LONE FATHERS[16]

Single-parent households, mostly headed by women, are an issue for social policy in many states. There are two reasons for this. First, these households are more likely than others to experience poverty. Second, being a lone mother is often seen an anomaly. Whereas the first reason can be given a precise meaning (see Chapter 8), that is not the case for the second reason if it implies something other than that the majority of mothers live in households with two adults. Indeed, there are many normative positions at stake, which to some extent call for different, sometimes contradictory policies.

Some consider the two-parent family a norm to be positively valued. Responsible people should avoid having children grow up in a single-parent household. This position can lead to a policy of non-support of lone mothers, as otherwise there are incentives for women to have children without living together with a man. Others emphasise the possibility of sharing the burden of care between spouses, and thus see lone mothers having a problem as they lack the help of a second adult. People sharing this value might favour support for lone mothers. A policy of support is particularly meaningful if one stresses the right of women to raise children without the support of men. A support for lone mothers is also sensible if one considers it important that a mother with small children quits working.

Differences also arise when considering who should be helped by a policy programme, namely whether the focus should be on the mother or on the children. In the first case, policy must aim at helping the mother to support herself and the children by working like anybody else. That is the approach taken in the Scandinavian countries (Lewis, 1997). If the focus is on the children, namely their poverty, if any, welfare payments are a reasonable means to achieve that objective. That does not help if labour market participation of women is seen an important agenda. However children's poverty is seen by all as an issue for social policy. Even those who are not in favour of lone mothers are usually in favour of helping children.[17]

In some countries there is a further point: many lone mothers have their first child below the age of 18, frequently they leave school or any other education early. That raises the danger of lifelong poverty due to too little qualification and of transmission of poverty from one generation to the next.

The share of lone-mother households has increased in the last decades, though it is much lower than the share of families with non-married mothers and mothers married to a man not the biological father of her children. Some women cohabit with the child's father, divorced women may start a new partnership leading to marriage. Therefore neither the number of out-of-wedlock births, nor of divorces are a reasonable indicator of the number of lone-mother households. Everywhere the share of lone-parent families is below 20 per cent, of which 80 per cent are lone mothers. In southern Europe the share of lone-parent households is much lower, the highest shares are to be found in northern Europe.

Lone mothers are not a homogenous group, all having the same problem. What they have in common is that whatever kind of problem there is, being a lone mother aggravates it: if a woman has low skills, having to care alone for a child makes it more difficult to earn a living above poverty level; if women have problems in integrating responsibilities for families into their professional life, that is an even greater problem if there is no help from a partner.

There are different types of programmes to help lone mothers:

(a) Helping mothers to get support from absentee fathers.[18]
(b) Help to fully participate in the labour market.
(c) Benefits in case of poverty, specially tailored for single mothers.

(a) *Alimony*. In all countries absentee parents have to contribute to financing the upbringing of children – alimony. That is an obligation according to civil law. Conflicts must be resolved by the courts as any other conflict over debts. Superficially, further activities by the state seem to be unnecessary. However non-paying of alimony can result in poverty of the child's household, particularly because they are mostly woman-headed households. In that case the state has to support the household if such poverty is seen as a problem (Pelikan, 1990).

Most countries have established programmes to help mothers to enforce their rights against the absentee fathers. In some states claims against absentee fathers have priority against claims of other creditors. Another way to help enforcing claims is to make alimony not dependent on actual income, but on income the absentee father can earn if he works regularly. The father should not be excused for not paying (or paying little) due to not working (working few hours or working in the underground economy). Often the instrument of wage assignments is used. Help for the legal proceedings can be of importance, particularly if a mother with little education wants to enforce her right.

Some states have a system of paying advances from public funds. In France these advances are means-tested. In Austria advances are paid only where a mother has a valid claim against the father. The state acts as debt collector. A burden for the public budget arises only insofar as some fathers manage to avoid paying though the mothers have a valid claim. The Scandinavian countries have the most generous systems of paying advances. There the advances are part of overall social policy to provide a minimum for all. They were also the first to introduce these advances. In Sweden the state guarantees a basic payment to all lone mothers. It is paid even in case the mother is not successful in demanding alimony. If the claim against the absentee father is below that minimum, the state makes good for the difference. The German regulations are somehow between the Austrian concept of debt-collecting and the Scandinavian social payments approach.

In the USA and in Great Britain helping mothers to enforce their rights are seen as a way to reduce the burden of social assistance payments for lone mothers. That is due to the importance of categorical social assistance benefits for lone mothers in these two countries. The assistance is paid, because the father does not pay. It can be reduced if only he would pay. The administration encourages mothers to make claims for alimony. Note that a woman has no reason to ask for alimony if she does not expect to get more from the father than the payment by social assistance. Going for alimony can even make her situation worse, namely if the absentee father is providing in one way or the other some help.

(b) and (c) *Participation in the labour market and poverty alleviation.* Though many women with children consider participation in the labour market as important for their welfare, lone mothers are even more dependent on opportunities to work. Alimony and child benefits hardly allow a life above poverty level. In many states lone mothers have higher participation rates in the labour market than married mothers (an exception is the UK, see Ermisch and Wright, 1991; Lewis, 1997), furthermore lone mothers more often work full time than married mothers. As discussed in Chapter 1.3, for lone mothers the income gained by working full time is often of higher importance than for married mothers, as there is no second adult to receive an income. The increase of labour market participation with increasing qualifications is more pronounced for single mothers than for married mothers (Staat and Wagenhals, 1996).

A particular problem is that lone-mother households have a higher probability of being poor than other households. As child poverty is considered a special plight, states tend to be more liberal in granting benefits for lone mothers than for other households. Some countries have categorical benefits for lone parents, others are more liberal in granting social assistance (see below, Chapter 8.7) or allow lone mothers to stay longer in unemployment benefit systems. This clearly works as a disincentive for participating in the labour market for women, as laid out in Chapter 6.2 (for the evidence in the UK: Ermisch and Wright, 1991).

NOTES

1. *Share of extra-marital births for selected countries*

Country	1960	1999
Austria	13.5	30.5
Denmark	7.8	44.9
Ireland	1.6	30.9
Italy	2.4	9.2
Netherlands	1.4	22.7
Sweden	11.3	55.3
Switzerland	3.8	10.0

    Source: Council of Europe (2000).

2. In other contexts the meaning of family may be different. The German constitution, the *Grundgesetz*, mentions as an objective of the German state the support of the institution of the marital status (Art 6(1) *Grundgesetz*). Married couples have some tax benefits even where they have no dependent child.
3. One can also find arguments in favour of a pro-natalistic policy in situations in which a majority nation in a state for one reason or the other finds itself threatened by the (often only imagined) higher fertility of a national minority.
4. New developments in growth economics show that density of population can be favourable for economic growth. The argument is that infrastructure in sparsely populated areas is very costly. However currently there are still many states who consider high demographic growth a problem.
5. Currently (autumn 2001) it is open whether that idea will be extended to the financing of the German pension system.
6. In the past, when fertility was much higher, the share of women who did not have a child was higher as well. That was due to medical reasons and because of social custom. Unmarried women were not supposed to have children.
7. If benefits are given outside the tax system, total tax burden is higher, as many people have to pay taxes and receive benefits. See the beginning of Chapter 1.
8. A progressive income tax need not have increasing marginal tax rates. A tax system with the formula $T = B + t \cdot Y$ with $B < 0$, $t > 0$ is a progressive tax, as the average tax rate increases with rising income.
9. The recent debate as to whether the state should give vouchers for schools to give parents more choice is also not primarily a social policy issue. The question is rather whether the state should enjoy a (near) monopoly for supplying schools for low- and middle-income families.
10. In Germany as well as in Austria, most schools work half-days, which is a problem for women working full time. That is contentious in both states now. Groups who consider the equality of women as an important issue want to increase the supply of public child-care, others who put less emphasis on that aim, are reluctant in that respect. The communist countries had a very broad supply of child-care facilities, as they were interested in women working full time. After the planned economies had collapsed it was reported that many people saw again the positive aspect of women staying at home. Labour market

participation of women declined. Whether that conformed to the wishes of the women or whether it was a way to reduce unemployment amongst men, has to be left open. In the former GDR it was clear that women wanted to continue working.
11. In the USA, among women 40–44, 19 per cent had no child, 16.4 per cent one child, 35 per cent two children, 19.1 per cent three children, and slightly more than 10 per cent had more than three children (data for the year 2000, source: US Census Bureau).
12. To make a calculation of these effects can be difficult. It is usually not so difficult to get data for transfers when they are paid. But to calculate the effects of tax deductions, namely by how much the overall tax rates could be reduced if special tax benefits were withdrawn goes beyond book-keeping.
13. Moreover one has to consider whether the unit of taxation is the household or the individual. If the household is the tax unit, all incomes of all members are added together for calculating the tax. To avoid having a very progressive tax system, the income is in that case to some extent split between the spouses. In Germany the tax burden of a family is twice the tax on half the income. In the USA there are many instances in which a married couple pays higher taxes than if taxed as individuals independently from each other – the so called *marriage penalty*. In any case, household taxation discourages labour force participation of women. The higher the income difference between the spouses, the bigger the effect.
14. Providing a payment when on leave creates problems if there is no central fund for financing the benefit. An individual employer can face big costs, though in the average wage costs increase only slightly by giving that transfer.
15. There are also laws forbidding pregnant women to carry out tasks which can be a danger for her or the unborn child.
16. As problems of lone parents are mostly problems of lone mothers, I did not attempt in this part to formulate everything in a gender-neutral way.
17. Groups which reject the right to terminate a pregnancy (right-to-life) are often in favour of supporting lone mothers, because they consider it a way to reduce the demand for abortions.
18. Claims against an absentee parent are also of relevance for families with two adults, if one of the biological parents is not living with the children.

REFERENCES

Berger Mark, C. and Dan A. Black (1992), 'Child Care Subsidies, Quality of Care, and the Labor Supply of Low-Income, Single Mothers', *Review of Economics and Statistics*, 74, pp. 635–42.

Council of Europe (2000), *Recent Demographic Developments in Europe*, Luxembourg.

Ellwood, David L. and Jeffrey B. Liebmann (2000), *The Middle Class Penalty: Child Benefits in the U.S. Tax Code*, Cambridge (Mass.), NBER Working Paper 8031.

Ermisch, John F. and Robert E. Wright (1991), 'Welfare Benefits and Lone Parents' Employment in Great Britain', *Journal of Human Resources*, 26, pp. 424–56.

Fagan, Colette and Jill Rubery (1996), 'Transition between Family Formation and Paid Employment', in: G Schmid, J. O'Reilly and K. Schönmann (eds), *International Handbook of Labour Market Policy Evaluation*, Cheltenham and Brookfield: Edward Elgar, pp. 348–78.

Gupta, Datta Nabanita and Nina Smith (2001), *Children and Career Interruptions: The Family Gap in Denmark*, Bonn, IZA Discussion Paper No. 263.

Kothmayr, Regina and Peter Rosner (2000), 'Wie effizient ist die österreichische Familienpolitik', *Wirtschaft und Gesellschaft*, 26, pp. 99–118.

Laisney, François, Michael Lechner, Matthias Staat and Gerhard Wagenhals (1999), 'Work and Welfare of Single Mothers in Germany', *Economie Publique*, 3, pp. 111–44.

Lewis, Jane (ed.) (1997), *Lone Mothers in European Welfare Regimes. Shifting Policy Logics*, London and Philadelphia: Jessica Kingsley.

Pelikan, Christa (1990), *Strafrechtliche und Zivilrechtliche Unterhaltssicherung*, Vienna: Institut für Rechts- und Kriminalsoziologie.

OECD (1996), *Employment Outlook*, Paris: OECD.

Ruhm, Christopher (1998), 'The Economic Consequences of Parental Leave Mandates: Lessons from Europe', *Quarterly Journal of Economics*, 113, pp. 285–315.

Sinn, Hans-Werner (1997), *The Value of Children and Immigrants in a Pay-as-you-go Pension System. A Proposal for a Partial Transition to a Funded System*, Cambridge (Mass.), NBER Working Paper 6229.

Staat, Matthias and Gerhard Wagenhals (1996), 'Lone Mothers: A Review', *Journal of Population Economics*, 9, pp. 131–140.

Waldfogel, Jane (1998a), 'Understanding the 'Family Gap' in Pay for Women with Children', *Journal of Economic Perspectives*, 12, pp. 137–56.

Waldfogel, Jane (1998b), 'The Family Gap for Young Women in the United States and Britain: Can Maternity Leave Make a Difference', *Journal of Labor Economics*, 16, pp. 505–42.

8. Poverty

It is often unclear what is meant by poverty. It is a vague concept which we have to make precise in order to use it for the analysis of social policy. It is a bit like pornography: though it is difficult to define poverty, one can recognise it when one sees it. However to say that somebody is poor is a value judgement.

In bygone times the poor were the working people; people had to work only if they were poor. A gentleman was not expected to work. Poverty was not seen being a social evil – after all who would work for the gentleman if nobody were poor? Working hard was not supposed to be a relief from poverty. The labourers should remain poor. This went together with the fear that a person stops working as soon as she is not poor any more (Furniss, 1920).

Later the view changed: it became accepted that working should be a way out of poverty. The poor were seen as being unable to earn an income sufficiently high to lift them out of poverty. Either they did not work enough or their wages were too low. The change in outlook began in the last decades of the eighteenth century. It was connected with the normative idea that working was an activity to earn a living sufficiently high to alleviate poverty, and with the economic idea that labourers with income above subsistence do not reduce labour supply. This was closely connected with two other new normative ideas. First, working was not any longer considered dishonourable. Second, poverty was considered a social plague. And that is the position which holds today: poverty is considered a problem – primarily for those who are poor, but also for society at large.

We have to distinguish between two aspects: poverty as a problem of income distribution and poverty due to poverty of the overall economy, mostly due to low productivity and/or a small capital stock. The reason for this distinction is that in the latter case poverty can be abolished only through economic growth, whereas in the former case redistribution can be an important reduction factor.

The fact that in many countries today there is much less poverty than a hundred years ago is of course due to economic growth. But there were many instances of economic growth which were accompanied, at least for some time, by growing poverty. Obviously the link between economic growth and reduction of poverty is not straightforward. Be that as it may, as this is a book about social policy we are only concerned with poverty insofar as it can be mitigated by redistribution.

In the first part of the chapter, we try to define the concept of poverty such that it can be used for research and for making decisions about policies. The second part discusses the way in which the fact that people live together in households affects the concept of poverty. Duration of poverty is discussed in the third part, and in the fourth part we clarify what is to be understood by the expression 'there is more poverty in A than in B'. The fifth part looks at the extent of poverty in rich economies and discusses the importance of personal versus social factors. The last two parts are concerned with policies to help the poor: the sixth part deals with wage supplements and the final part with social assistance.

8.1 DEFINING POVERTY – CONCEPTUAL ISSUES

8.1.1 Which Metric to Use

The first question to address is which metric to use when deciding whether an individual is poor. Economics uses utility as a metric of the quality of life. But this would not be practical for defining poverty, as the utility an individual experiences is a subjective concept. It needs strong assumptions to give an objective account of the utility an individual experiences. It is better to stick to narrower concepts of a metric, namely command over resources.

There are limits to using this metric. First, people may prefer to have very little command over resources for other reasons – they may enjoy leisure or they may prefer less resources if access to them is possible only through some other disadvantages, for example, some kind of bondage.[1] Second, individuals may have special needs which can only be satisfied if they have more resources available than would alleviate their poverty – a wheelchair, special medical treatments, and so on. Be that as it may, even if poverty cannot be measured directly by lack of resources, one can consider lack of resources as an indicator of poverty.

There is a further aspect: in each society there are goods provided freely or at subsidised prices. They can make a big difference. For example, in most rich economies nearly everybody has access to medical services and to reasonable schools for children. In a society in which these important goods are not provided freely, a person needs a much higher income to avoid poverty (Smeeding et al., 1993). Other important public goods may include a public transportation system, good access to recreational areas and public safety.[2]

There are three different ways to define lack of resources: (i) lack of goods; (ii) low expenditures; (iii) low income. Lack of goods is closely connected to a low standard of living. After all, our welfare depends on the goods which are available for our consumption. Usually a set of goods is taken which are considered as basic consumption goods. If an individual lacks one or more of them she is considered poor.

There is a big drawback to this metric in that it is difficult to distinguish whether a person lacks command over specific goods because she cannot afford them or whether she does not value them highly. Not having a car, or a TV set, or a special evening dress for going out would in many instances raise the suspicion of poverty. But amongst professors living in big cities one can find some without any of these three goods, though they are not poor.

This metric can be used when the goods under consideration are really very basic – enough calories, access to minimal health services, access to clean water, a basic shelter for having privacy, basic education for children. There are not many people who voluntarily refrain from consuming these goods. However to classify an individual living in a rich economy as non-poor because she has all these goods would be very modest. In a poor economy such a list of very elementary goods can be sensible for defining poverty.

It is a further disadvantage of that metric that one needs data over goods households can use. Not many administrative data are available. It is necessary for the social scientist to collect them.

Using the amount of expenditures for goods as an indicator of poverty avoids the pitfalls of people's preferences. Furthermore it is a scalar expression. That has the advantage that it is always possible to say whether an amount is above, below or equals to a threshold. The disadvantage is that expenditures may not be a reliable metric for welfare, because people may have access to goods without spending for them – public provision of goods, stored-up goods, particularly durables, and goods from their own production.

Low income as an indicator for poverty has the advantage that administrative agencies provide more data on income than data relating to either command over goods or expenditures. Second, using the metric of income makes the comparison with non-poor individuals much easier. For example, to say that an individual has half the income necessary for being non-poor, is an easily understandable assertion. To make a similar statement in the metric of command over goods is more difficult.

Using income also has important drawbacks. The relation between income and welfare is less direct than between expenditure and welfare. We have seen in Chapter 6.1.3.1 that expenditure for consumption is much less volatile than income. Most people save or take recourse to loans for smoothing expenditure. Expenditure in turn is more volatile than command over goods, as expenditures for durables can be shifted over time without major effects on command over goods.

Whether one uses income, expenditure or consumption of goods as standards of poverty makes a difference for determining who is considered poor. There are people who are poor when taking income as defining criterion, but who are not poor according to expenditure and vice versa. Nor is the relation between income and having specific goods very close.

Table 8.1 The relative movement of households between deciles as ranked by expenditure and by income

	1	2	3	4	5	6	7	8	9	10
1	30.8	20.5	15.0	9.1	6.0	5.4	4.1	2.9	4.0	2.1
2	29.4	25.7	17.5	11.6	6.6	3.1	2.6	1.4	1.6	0.6
3	20.5	20.0	21.1	12.5	9.8	6.8	3.6	2.6	1.7	1.3
4	8.3	12.8	15.4	19.0	15.3	8.8	6.4	6.8	4.4	2.7
5	4.1	7.8	12.0	14.8	15.4	15.7	10.8	9.0	6.3	4.1
6	2.6	4.7	7.7	10.6	15.3	16.4	15.4	11.3	9.6	6.6
7	2.0	2.7	5.6	10.4	11.7	15.1	16.5	15.1	11.4	9.4
8	1.3	3.0	3.0	5.4	9.0	13.8	15.3	17.5	19.5	12.1
9	0.9	1.4	1.4	4.1	6.7	9.8	16.5	19.4	20.0	19.7
10	0.1	1.3	1.3	2.4	4.4	4.8	8.7	14.0	21.5	41.5

Notes: Rows: expenditure; columns: income.
There were 233 households poor according to income but not poor according to expenditure. On the other hand 550 expenditure-poor households were not poor according to income. The poverty level used was that of the supplementary benefit level. The data were taken from the British expenditure survey.

Source: McGregor and Borooah (1992).

In Table 8.1 households are ranked in deciles according to expenditure (rows) and according to income (columns). Though the diagonal is always the largest number, there is quite some movement. Some households with very low incomes have high expenditures and vice versa.

Table 8.2 provides data about the relation between the possession of goods, the rank of income (RCDR) and the rank of expenditure (REXP). In the second and third decile, according to income, there are more people without cars, without videos and without freezers than in the lowest decile. This is not the case for ranking according to expenditures.

Table 8.2 Household characteristics by decile

Decile	Council house		No car		No video		No freezer	
	RCDR	REXP	RCDR	REXP	RCDR	REXP	RCDR	REXP
1	55.9	62.2	65.5	84.9	80.9	93.7	69.7	81.0
2	62.6	50.5	78.4	70.2	89.3	86.3	76.6	71.6
3	51.6	45.9	67.6	58.9	86.7	79.2	70.6	63.0
4	35.7	35.2	47.2	41.2	76.4	76.3	61.8	63.9
5	25.8	29.2	33.4	34.4	69.2	68.0	58.9	58.3
6	24.2	20.8	25.4	26.1	66.6	65.6	58.5	60.2
7	19.1	21.4	19.4	20.1	60.6	61.9	61.2	57.9
8	15.7	17.5	17.4	17.4	57.5	59.0	56.8	59.6
9	9.7	12.8	12.4	11.6	59.5	53.5	58.3	57.8
10	4.1	8.8	5.0	7.1	52.2	55.3	60.2	59.2

Note: RCDR: Ranking according to income; REXP: ranking according to expenditure.

Source: McGregor and Borooah (1992).

8.1.2 Absolute Standards or Relative Ones?

Should we say that a person is poor if her command over resources, her income or her expenditure falls below a threshold in absolute values or is it the differential between individuals which is decisive? Taking an absolute standard conforms to the idea that poverty implies the absence of essential consumption goods. Using relative standards throws light on the position of the poor in the overall distribution of income or of goods.

Using the metric of command over resources for an absolute standard of poverty comes close to the idea of basic needs. An individual is considered to be poor if she cannot satisfy certain needs for which these goods are essential. It is clear that such a standard of poverty requires a clear identification of such basic needs – for example, nutritional standards. In older economic literature a distinction between basic needs and higher needs, or between needs and wants was often made. This can be sensible for analysing poverty in very poor societies, but not being hungry or not having running water are not sufficient criteria for absence of poverty in a rich society.[3]

If poverty is defined and described by the lack of certain goods, that does not necessarily mean that these goods are essential to experience utility. Lack of goods is not a direct expression of poverty, although it is considered as an indicator of poverty. Individuals who lack a range of commonplace goods are suspected to be too poor to have bought them.

In a study of poverty in Austria the following list was used: possession of (i) a stove; (ii) a TV set, (iii) a telephone; (iv) availability of a washing machine; (v) housing without need of repair; (vi) at least one person reads daily a newspaper; (vii) at least one person had some holidays last year (Lutz et al., 1993). It is clear that a household may lack some of these goods due to preferences. In this study a household was considered to be poor where at least four of the seven items were missing. A report about deprivation in the UK used a list of more than 20 items, namely different household appliances, heating, a regular warm meal, but also the ability to buy presents, to have an evening out once a while, to receive friends (Callan et al., 1993). The way to establish such lists is to look for goods which are common in most households. This provides the information about 'normal' consumption bundles, against which poverty in the sense of lack of consumption goods can be estimated. The study for Great Britain compared the availability of the goods on their list in income-poor households with that of other households.

If poverty is measured in the metric of income or expenditure, as well as an idea about necessary consumption bundles for specifying an absolute standard, one needs data on prices. It can be difficult to get these data, as prices for the poor are not the same as for the rest of the society. Keeping quality constant, prices are often higher for the poor. The reason is that in order to buy at low prices, people have to be mobile and have to buy larger quantities of the same good. Poor households are often restricted in their mobility and are constrained in their liquidity – they neither have reserves, nor can they borrow against future income.

An example of an absolute concept of poverty is the basis for its definition in the USA: poverty is defined by a relation between income and expenditure for food. An individual in a household of three and more is considered poor if her income is lower than three times the expenditure for the necessary food for that household (Dalaker and Proctor, 2000). The idea behind this definition of poverty is that a household's share of expenditure for its food declines with income and, given income, increases with the size of the household (*Engel curves* – after the German statistician Engel, see below, 8.2).

The metric of goods is not suitable for relative thresholds. It is better to use a percentage of median income or expenditure as the relevant threshold (40, 50 or 60 per cent). The median is preferred to the mean income because of the long right tail of the income distribution. When defining poverty it is sensible to leave the very rich out of the picture. That is achieved by taking the median. The advantage of using a relative measure is that one does not have to bother much about appropriate levels of consumption or income. We define somebody as poor, when she has less than 40, 50 or 60 per cent of the median, whatever the median may be.

However relative standards also have some disadvantages. When a country gets richer or poorer without changing the income distribution, poverty does not change according to relative criterion. If everyone in a country became poorer, but the income distribution did not change, it would be questionable to argue that poverty has not increased. It may even happen that by using a relative standard, poverty may decrease where many people become poorer. Compare the following two income distributions and take 60 per cent of the median as poverty threshold:

$$2, 3, 4, 5, 6, 10.$$
$$1, 1, 1, 1, 1, 12.$$

Whereas in the first case there is one poor person, in the latter case poverty has vanished! Everybody except the one very rich person has lost. It is counter-intuitive to say that poverty has decreased.

In general, relative poverty thresholds are very sensitive to the development of mean income. If that income declines in relation to the top income, poverty can decrease. This can happen even in cases where people in the lowest income range lose as well. It may have occurred in some of the transformation countries where a big share of the population lost, partly through redistribution, partly through the decline of aggregate output. In some of the transformation economies those in the middle of the income distribution lost a great deal. They came nearer to those at the bottom, therefore poverty was reduced when using a relative poverty threshold. That may be the reason why according to some studies the transformation did not increase poverty (Torrey et al., 1997), while according to others it did (Kornai, 1997). Whereas the former study used relative poverty thresholds, the latter one took different concepts of poverty into consideration.

Besides its pragmatic advantage there are other reasons for using a relative concept of poverty, for example, inequality itself can be a disadvantage. If people below a minimum are not considered as socially equal, this can lead to social exclusion. Assume that there are good and bad schools. The former are private and charge fees to cover costs, the others are public without fees. Assume further that the probability of getting a good job is much higher for former pupils of the private schools – they are the better schools. Rich families send their children to the good private schools, families with low income send their children to the public schools. A relative disadvantage, which need not be big, generates a social stratification.

A special case are *positional goods*. These are goods which cannot be reproduced and are therefore allocated to those who have the highest willingness to pay for them – usually the rich. The classic example of positional goods are 'old masters'. Their prices depend on the willingness of the richest individuals to pay for them. All others are excluded from their possession as they cannot be produced. The income distribution determines the allocation. Of course, an individual should not be considered poor, if she cannot buy a Rembrandt or a Van Gogh. However there are cases of positional goods which are of more social concern. For example, if recreational areas can be bought off by wealthy people, others may be excluded from an essential good. Zoning codes can be of importance for the distribution of utility across a population. A small city of wealthy people can restrict the construction of new houses and thus keep prices up. People with low incomes may be forced to remain in neighbourhoods with low environmental qualities.

BOX 8.1 INFANT MORTALITY AND THE SHARE OF THE RICH

A study (Waldmann, 1992) established a relation between income distribution and infant mortality. Keeping the absolute income of the bottom 20 per cent constant, infant mortality is higher in countries with a higher share of income going to the top 5 per cent. The following equation was estimated:

$$\log(\text{infant mortality}) = \beta_0 + \beta_1 \log(\text{poor income}) + \beta_2 \log(\text{middle income}) + \gamma \text{ rich share}$$

poor: bottom 20 per cent;
middle: between 20 per cent and 95 per cent.

It turned out that γ is positive.

> The estimates ... imply with 95 per cent confidence that a rise in the real income of the rich by 1 per cent of national income (holding the income of the poorer strata constant) is associated with a rise in the infant mortality rate of between 0.72 and 4.24 per cent of its original level. (Waldmann, 1992, p. 1287)

The author controlled for measurement errors, statistical outlayers and other problems which may have influenced the result. But γ remained positive. He also checked whether he could point to a plausible reason for that result, for example, urban–rural differences, access to health services and others. He could not find a coherent theory fitting the data. There was no 'story' which could tell in a sensible way how income distribution affects infant mortality.

An important aspect of loss of welfare due to having less than others can arise in the case of medical need. Assume that a country spends at most 10 per cent of GDP for medical purposes. (In most poor countries it is much less.) In poor countries with an unequal distribution of income that implies that if the wealthy manage to have good medical treatment, not much remains for the poor. Note that this can be the outcome of an allocation of health services in line with the market. The rich buy all resources available for health services.

8.1.3 An Integrated Approach: Functionings and Capabilities

Obviously neither an absolute standard of poverty nor a relative one is satisfying. How much income a person needs not to be poor depends on the society in which she lives. That relates not only to the problem that goods may be more expensive in one society than in another one, but that you need different goods in different societies for doing the same thing. For example, in a society where most people live with their families in the same village all through their life, people can communicate with their extended family and with friends by walking from one house to the other. Neither a telephone, nor a car is necessary for an important aspect of welfare – namely to be able to communicate with friends and family. Compare that with a society with high regional mobility: without a telephone and without access to means of transportation it is very difficult to communicate regularly with friends and family. For the same basic function one needs different resources in different societies. Furthermore people vary in their ability to use goods. A bicycle can be used for transportation by somebody physically able to ride it. For a severely handicapped individual the same bicycle does not serve any purpose.

According to Sen (1983, 1985), to understand poverty – and other aspects of the standard of living – one has to break up the close connection between goods and utility. This is done in a few steps. First, we do not assign utility to goods directly, but it is their characteristics (c) which are considered useful – it is one of the characteristics of a bicycle to be useful for transport over shorter distances.[4] The characteristics are a function of the good.

$$c = c(x)$$

The characteristics are objectively given properties of the goods.

Second, by using goods, that is, making use of their characteristics, an individual can achieve something – she can move with a bike within a small region. The achievements (b) depend on the individual, but they can, at least to some degree, inter-subjectively be determined. They are a function of the characteristics of a good.

$$b = f(c(x))$$

with f(.) being a function of the utilisation. Though these achievements are due to people's activities, they are not fully subjective as they do not depend on preferences.

Third, the subjective aspect is the valuation of the achievement by the individual.

$$u = h(f(c(x)))$$

Utility is a function of a person's achievements – of what she does with the goods.

Take food: its characteristics are its nutritional value, whether it serves dietary criteria, whether it has ethical properties, whether it is tasty, and so on. The achievements are to be well nourished, to enjoy good food, to live in accordance with ethical principles. It is the individual who values these achievements. Some people value food primarily because of its nutritional value, others consider ethical aspects also important – for example, food produced with a small amount of energy, or food which conforms to the principles of a creed.

Instead of the traditional economic question of how much utility does a person experience, one should, according to Sen, frame the analysis of welfare by asking which capabilities does a person enjoy to achieve something. He considers this question to be decisive for defining poverty. The achievements are in the space of the b's not in the u's. Poverty should be defined absolutely in the space of achievements (the b's). It should be agreed upon what an individual should be able to do in absolute terms to not be poor – what functions he or she can achieve. In the space of goods this is defined relatively, namely by the goods necessary to achieve the accepted function in a particular society.

It may be sensible, for example, to consider the possibility of communicating regularly with friends and family to be essential. That is not to say that an individual who does not have such contacts is poor, because a particular individual may not value contacts highly and may even prefer not to have them. However if somebody lacks the opportunity of communicating with friends and family because she lacks the required resources, she is considered poor. Which goods an individual needs for such communication depends on the social and technological structures of a society – whether friends and family live nearby or whether it is necessary to travel. It also depends on personal circumstances – a handicapped individual needs special goods for that function. Other basic functions are being adequately nourished, raising children, having some privacy, going out without being ashamed,[5] having the ability to live in accordance with one's ethical principles.

Up to now Sen's concept has hardly been used in practical research. It is part of a larger research programme to supplant the concept of utility in welfare analysis. However in many ways it comes close to widely held ideas of poverty, namely that people who cannot function in a way which is typical for a society should be counted as poor. That approach is also more in line with actual policies regarding poverty than a strict adherence to a fixed threshold. For example, if in a society the aggregate number of calories is a problem, breastfeeding mothers and people with physically demanding jobs are given priority at the allocation of food. Poor handicapped people may be helped with a wheelchair, without regard to any threshold in monetary terms.[6] People in need of care are helped if they are too poor to buy the necessary services in the markets. A poverty threshold in monetary terms would not be considered sensible if it were to include expenses for care even where there is no need for it. Sen's idea is an attempt to define what many consider as common sense, namely to take into account special needs and not to bother whether people manage to have utility.

8.1.4 Earnings Capacity

Up to now we have only looked at the outcome – how much income, expenditure or goods an individual actually has. Some people may be poor because they are unable to earn sufficient income, whereas others are poor because they do not work enough – either they are unemployed or they prefer leisure to more income. As the policy in the two cases should be different, it can be useful to define poverty according to *earnings capacity* (Garfinkel and Haveman, 1977). This is defined as the ability of an individual or a household to generate an income stream, if it were to use its physical and human capital at capacity.

The earning capacity of an individual was defined as earnings for 50 weeks of full-time work. For a household the gross earnings capacity (GEC) is the sum of the earning capacities of all adults of a household. Weeks of unemployment or sickness must be deducted (WSU). Y is non-earned income.

$$GEC = \sum EC[(50 - WSU)/50] + Y \text{ (summation over all adults)}$$

A household with children has obligations which reduce the time available for earning income. Therefore the authors defined a net earnings capacity (NEC) by deducting a certain amount of money for each child.

$$NEC = GEC - (\$1520 \text{ per child aged 5 or younger} + \$ 376 \text{ per child aged 6–14})$$

Earnings equations for individuals with specific characteristics were estimated in order to calculate the values for earnings capacity.[7]

The change of perspective by using earning capacity instead of actual income changes the composition of the poor (Table 8.3). If actual income is used, less than 31 per cent of the poor population in the USA are Afro-American. But if NEC is used, more than 38 per cent of the poor population are Afro-American. Especially striking is the change of composition of the poor if one looks at family size. Using actual income, most poor households are small and most poor individuals live in small households. But when using GEC or NEC, people in bigger households make up the bulk of the poor population. That implies that individuals in small households are more likely to be poor because they cannot make use of their human capital. Poor individuals living in big households are often poor even if they work full capacity. (For a more recent application of the concept of earnings capacity, see Haveman and Buron, 1993.)

Table 8.3 *Percentage distribution of earnings capacity and current income-poor individuals and current income-poor households, by selected socio-economic characteristics, total population (USA)*

Characteristics	NEC Individuals	GEC Individuals	Current income Individuals	Current income Households
Race of head				
White	59.96	60.90	67.70	76.37
Black and other	40.04	39.10	31.15	23.89
Sex of head				
Male	49.88	40.57	45.60	45.95
Female	50.12	59.43	54.40	54.05
Family size				
1	6.25	13.99	19.29	48.67
2	6.26	11.40	14.64	18.47
3–4	22.94	23.30	22.06	16.04
5+	64.75	50.78	44.01	16.82
Years of schooling				
0–8	46.71	51.23	48.94	49.53
9–12	47.76	42.37	41.65	38.19
13–16	5.23	5.46	8.36	10.81
17+	0.31	0.44	1.06	1.47

Source: Garfinkel and Haveman (1977).

8.2 INDIVIDUALS AND HOUSEHOLDS

Up to now no distinction has been made between individuals and households. But one has to take account of the fact that individuals living together in one household share to some extent income and goods. That affects poverty. A non-working spouse without any income need not be poor. Children usually have no income but only some of them are poor. Taking that into consideration raises normative and conceptual problems when defining and measuring poverty.

It is a normative issue whether individuals living together – under one roof – are considered as one household. To what extent does a household comprise more than two generations? Do people who are neither related by marriage or common ancestors constitute a common household if they reside together? (That is currently a hotly debated issue as it also concerns households of people of the same sex.) What about dependent children not living with their parents? All that can affect whether individuals are counted as being poor.

The most important conceptual problem is that of equivalence scales: how much extra resources must a household be given in order that the addition of one more member should not change the prevailing economic situation. A second problem relates to the *equal sharing* assumption – that is, do individuals in a household have equal access to its resources.

8.2.1 Equivalence Scales

It is clear that a larger household needs more resources to avoid poverty than a smaller household. But the need for resources does not increase proportionally with the number of individuals living together in a household. This is due to economies of scale in the consumption of some goods. For example, most families can do with one bathroom and one kitchen. These are household-specific public goods.

There are different ways to account for the extra costs for a household due to having more members: (i) objective standards and (ii) using the concepts of analysis of demand.

Objective standards relate to the needs of children – food, clothing, schooling. Costs are estimated directly – for example, how much does a child cost until it can support itself. These estimates are made by experts. As mentioned already, in the USA the poverty lines for different structures of families use calculations for food expenditures. This conforms to the idea on which the US poverty line is based, namely a relation between income and food expenditure.

Using data from expenditure is problematic when using this method for applied research: children are not born with an endowment of goods. Their parents either have to reduce the rate of saving or substitute from other consumption goods if there is one more child. Therefore it is not possible to infer anything about supplementary costs for children from actual expenditure.

In order to draw conclusions from actual expenditure of households for children it is better to make use of the concepts of economic theory (Deaton and Muellbauer, 1986). Ideally one has to start with the following utility function for parents:

$$u = u(q, a)$$

q are consumption goods, and a is the demographic characteristic of the household. One can then calculate cost functions or expenditure functions for a given level of utility u^* (p is the vector of prices).[8]

$$c = c(u^*, p, a)$$

The difference in costs due to one more person present while keeping utility constant is:

$$\Delta c = c(u^r, p^r, a + 1) - c(u^r, p^r, a)$$

with u^r a fixed utility level and p^r given prices. That is an expression for the difference in costs due to one more child, holding utility of the incumbent family members and prices constant. Writing it down as relative costs:

$$E = \frac{c(u^r, p^r, a + 1)}{c(u^r, p^r, a)}$$

There is a problem in that children are a source of utility as well – their number is a choice variable, not a parameter. In this context that is not a normative statement, but we observe people having children although they create costs. To take account of that, one has to use the function $\theta(u^*,a)$ instead of u^*. The cost-function is therefore:

$$c[\theta(u^*,a), p, a]$$

Though the demand functions are independent of θ, they cannot be identified, because the parameter a appears twice. It would be necessary to calculate interdependent demand functions for children and goods.

To overcome this problem the following path is pursued: it is asked how much extra does a household need to be compensated for one more member.

The criterion of compensation is taken from observed expenditure patterns for households with given income for different household size. That is, one assumes that the incumbent members of the household are equally well off if the expenditure patterns remain the same with one more child.[9]

Two methods are used:

(a) Engel method;
(b) Rothbarth method.

The Engel method uses the assumption that the standard of living of adults can be represented by the share of food expenditure. As mentioned, this assumption is based on the following observations: holding the size of the household constant, a higher income implies a lower food share. Holding income constant, a bigger family implies a higher food share. These two propositions are empirically well documented. The Engel approach has the following criterion for compensation: the members of a household are compensated for one more member, if the incumbent members spend the same share of income on food in the presence of the new member as without her.

The Rothbarth method does not pursue the question of basic goods, but looks for so called 'adult goods'. These are goods the consumption of which is curtailed when a household experiences higher costs due to a new member in the household. To make reasonable inferences from household data, one has to use goods with high income elasticity of demand. Rothbarth considered expenses for alcohol and cigarettes to be such goods. When he made his study in England in the late 1930s, cigarettes and drinks were such goods. That may have changed meanwhile. Be that as it may, his compensation criterion is the following: how much additional income is necessary to allow for the former consumption of 'adult goods'?

How do the two compensation methods compare? This is shown in Figure 8.1. On the horizontal axis is food q_1, on the vertical axis the 'adult good' q_2. The expansion curves H and O show combinations for the acquisition of the two goods with different incomes. The curve O gives the expansion path for the reference household, the curve H for the bigger household. At R the bigger household spends as much on non-food goods as the smaller household at S, the original position. This is the Rothbarth compensation. At E the bigger household spends the same percentage on food as the smaller household in the original position – the Engel compensation. Engel compensation is higher than Rothbarth compensation. What are the actual differences between these two compensation methods? Deaton and Muellbauer calculated both equivalence scales using data from Sri Lanka (10 000 observations) and Indonesia (6500 observations) (Table 8.4).

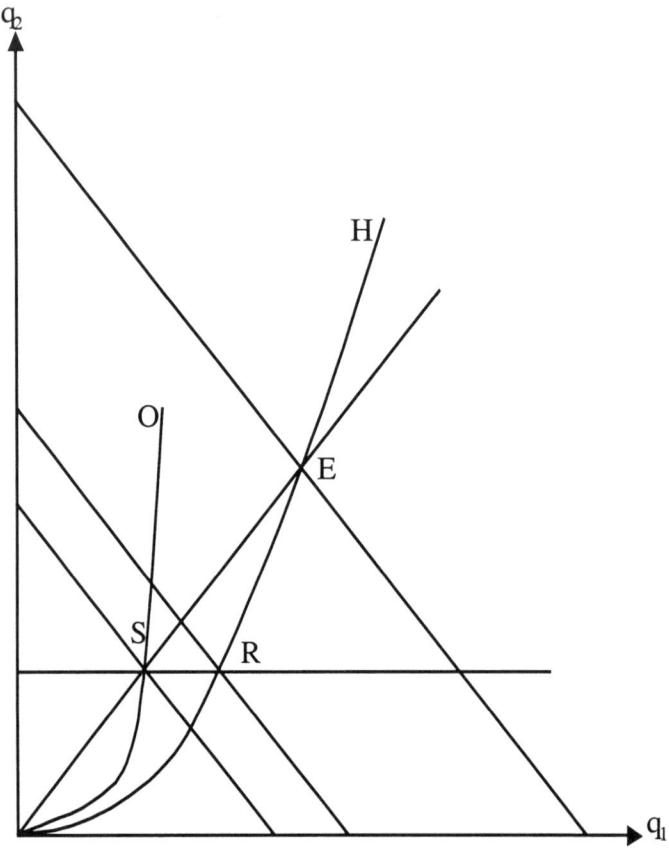

Figure 8.1 The compensation criterion according to Engel and Rothbarth

Table 8.4 Estimated equivalence scales (couples only = 1)

	Engel equivalence scales		Rothbarth equivalence scale	
	one child	two children	one child	two children
Sri Lanka	1.41	1.77	1.12	1.21
Indonesia*	1.45	1.86	1.10	1.16
Indonesia**	1.58	2.22	1.12	1.22

Note: * refers to children up to 5 years, ** refers to children older than 5.

Source: Deaton and Muellbauer (1986).

The equivalence scales as shown in Table 8.5 are common in international comparisons. Note that the Leyden scale (see Appendix 8.1) which is based on subjective evaluations is radically different from other scales: more individuals in a household do not much increase the necessary expenditure. A reason can be that households with children do not pursue the same expenditure patterns as households without children.

There are limits for the use of equivalence scales based on these methods: (i) the value of an equivalence scale can depend on the income people have (Conniffe, 1992); and (ii) the equivalence scales are calculated from annual data, although having children does not last forever. It may be part of a normal life plan to consume certain goods during periods without children (Nelson, 1992; Pashardes, 1991).

Table 8.5 Scales used in international context

OECD scale	First adult person	= 1.0
	Each further adult person	= 0.7
	A child	= 0.5
EU compromise scale	First adult person	= 1.0
	Each further adult person	= 0.5
	A child	= 0.3
Leyden scale	First person	= 1.000
	Second person	= 0.235
	Third person	= 0.160
	Fourth person	= 0.136
	Fifth person	= 0.099

Source: Lutz et al. (1993).

Does it make any difference which equivalence scale is used? As Tables 8.6(a) and 8.6(b) from an Austrian study show, there is quite some difference. Not only is the number of poor people affected by the choice of the equivalence scale, also the composition of the poor population changes when using different scales. There are poor households and poor people when using one scale, who are not poor when using another scale. Not surprisingly, when using the Leyden scale the correspondence is very low. This is due to the low weight which is given to further members of the household. Though one gets the highest number of poor households when using the Leyden scale, one gets the lowest number of poor individuals. The choice of an equivalence scale can have a big impact on the measured poverty of subgroups.

Table 8.6 Overlapping of poor when using different equivalence scales

(a) Number of poor households in 1000s

Poor households according to	ÖSTAT standard	Not poor according to			Total poor households
		OECD	Leyden	EU compromise	
ÖSTAT standard*	–	30	145	71	518
OECD	14	–	133	57	503
Leyden	192	196	–	139	566
EU compromise	55	57	75	–	503

(b) Number of poor individuals in 1000s

Poor individuals according to	ÖSTAT-standard	Not poor according to			Total poor individuals
		OECD	Leyden	EU compromise	
ÖSTAT standard	–	114	740	344	1541
OECD	64	–	695	292	1491
Leyden	212	217	–	157	1014
EU-compromise	62	60	403	–	1260

Note: * ÖSTAT Standard refers to the equivalence scales used by the Austrian statistical office. A second adult was given 0.8. Children were weighted between 0.33 and 0.8 depending on age.

Source: Lutz et al. (1993).

8.2.2 Inequality within Households

The relation between poverty on a household level and poverty for individuals is complicated by the fact that one cannot infer that all members of the household are poor if the per capita income of a household falls below the poverty threshold. Nor can we conclude that nobody in a household is poor if the per capita income is above that threshold. We have to take into account that the use of resources of an household may be unequally distributed within the household (Haddad and Kanbur, 1990; Jenkins, 1991).

This would not be much of a problem for measuring poverty if the intra-household distribution were randomly distributed. There is ample evidence that this is not the case: in many instances women have less access to the wealth of a household than men. In some societies women have less access to food or to health services than men (Sen, 1984). We will see below that neglecting intra-household inequality can affect measured poverty in either direction – that is, it can both increase and decrease the amount of poverty showing in statistics.

8.3 DURATION OF POVERTY

Many people are without income for short periods. For example, when quitting a job without cause most unemployment systems do not pay any benefit for a specified period. It would be wrong to consider all such spells without income as cases of poverty. If somebody loses his income for a few weeks only, it should not cause a big headache for social policy. For the analysis of poverty it is necessary to look at the duration of low income or periods without income. Whatever standard for defining poverty is used, the social effects depend to a large extent on for how long an individual or a household falls below this threshold.[10]

There are the same questions to be tackled as in the case of unemployment – are very low incomes concentrated among a small segment of the population or do many individuals experience very low incomes for merely short spells? It is clear that in the former case poverty creates a more important problem for social policy than in the latter one.

The methods used to pursue these questions are similar to those used for analysing spells of unemployment and need not be repeated here – study of poverty periods, probability of leaving poverty, and so on. However there is one difference: unemployment spells are mostly characterised by expressing them in weeks or days. Long-term unemployment begins when an individual is unemployed for more than half a year. The relevant duration of poverty spells is much longer, often extending to years and even decades (see Table 8.7).

As in the case of unemployment, poverty within a year is concentrated among a small part of the population, though a high percentage of the poor leave poverty within a short period (Bane and Ellwood, 1986). More recent studies from other countries confirm these findings (Stevens, 1994; for Austria, Stelzer-Orthofer, 1997; for Germany, Buhr, 1995).

The difference in length of poverty spells may be a cause for the difference between poverty according to income, to expenditure and to access to goods. People living in a household with a short spell of income-poverty may still enjoy a high standard of living if goods are available from earlier periods.

There is a different perspective when pursuing the question of duration of poverty from research on unemployment. Entry to and exit from unemployment are mostly analysed in a stochastic framework. Losing a job and finding one is not treated as influenced by the behaviour of the unemployed other than through her optimising choice when looking for a job. One does not ask why a specific individual became unemployed and why she found a new job. Such an approach is inappropriate in research on poverty. One wants to know why a particular person became poor and why she ceased to be poor. Entry to and exit from poverty are seen as events in which individuals (except

296   *The Economics of Social Policy*

poor children) are actively involved. After all, only very few people left poverty after having won the lottery.

Table 8.7   Distribution of length of poverty spells in the USA

Spell length to date (years)	Exit probability	People beginning a spell — Completed spell distribution	People poor at a given time**	
			Completed spell distribution	Uncompleted spell distribution
1	0.445	44.5	10.6	23.9
2	0.285	15.8	7.6	13.3
3	0.246	9.8	7.0	9.5
4	0.208	6.2	5.9	7.1
5	0.197	4.7	5.6	5.7
6	0.145	2.8	4.0	4.5
7	0.128	2.1	3.5	3.9
8	0.074	1.0	2.0	3.4
9	0.083	1.1	2.3	3.1
over 9	0.100*	12.0	51.5	25.6
Average	4.2	12.3	25.6	6.2

Note: * Value assumed   ** Distributions derived assuming no growth steady state.

Source: Bane and Ellwood (1986).

Due to the different outlook in poverty research compared with analysing unemployment, a different concept of duration is sometimes used. When analysing duration of unemployment one looks at the duration of individual spells, often reinforced by checking for multiple spells. In research on poverty it is also asked for how long an individual experienced poverty out of a given period, independent of the number of spells. Second, it is asked how long did a period of poverty last, meaning by that the time from the beginning of the first period of poverty to the end of the last.[11]

8.4   MEASURING POVERTY

In 8.1 we discussed how to fix a threshold of poverty, now we are going to measure it. The purpose of this exercise is that we want to give a precise meaning to sentences like: 'In country A there is more poverty than in country B' or 'Poverty has decreased in the last years'. It is also important to measure poverty if it is to be reduced efficiently, as otherwise it is not possible to say how much a specific policy contributed to its reduction. As in the case of defining poverty, there are different ways to do it. Each method has advantages and disadvantages which will be discussed in the following sections (Ravallion, 1992).

8.4.1 Head-Count

The most frequently used measure is simply to count the number of the poor – head-count. As a ratio it is the share of the poor in a population:

$$H = P/N$$

P: number of poor individuals; N: size of the reference population.

The head-count measure is very popular because the data necessary to calculate it are often available without detailed research. Moreover it is easy to understand. But it has important drawbacks. Consider the following distribution of 10 units of income among four individuals:

$$1, 2, 3, 4$$

Assuming a poverty threshold of 2.1, there are two poor individuals. If wealth gets redistributed to:

$$0.1, 0.5, 3.5, 5.9$$

poverty has not increased. If it is changed to:

$$0.1, 2.2, 3, 4.7$$

poverty has actually decreased! That is counter-intuitive.

Simply counting poor households or poor individuals means being insensitive to the depth of their poverty. In order to take account of it, it is sensible to look for a poverty measure which has the following properties:

Monotony Axiom: if the wealth of an individual below the poverty line is reduced, poverty must increase.

and

Transfer Axiom: if the wealth of an individual below the poverty line is redistributed towards another one with higher wealth, poverty must increase.

Any reasonable poverty measure should comply with these two axioms. For doing that individuals with different severity of poverty should be given different weight in the poverty measure. In the head-count measure all the poor have the same weight, independently of the severity of their poverty.

8.4.2 The Poverty Gap

The poverty gap (PG) is a weighted sum of the poor. A poor person's weight in that measure is her relative distance from the poverty line. If z is the poverty line, and y_i is the income of individual i, her weight in the poverty measure is $(z - y_i)/z$.

$$PG = (1/N) \cdot \sum (z - y_i)/z$$
$$= (1/N) \cdot \sum (1 - y_i/z)$$

The summation is taken over all poor individuals or poor households. The poverty gap equals the share of the poor times the average normalised distance of the wealth of the poor to the poverty line.

$$PG = \Gamma H \quad \text{with} \quad \Gamma = 1 - \mu/z$$

with μ the mean income of the poor. The size of Γ alone is not a good indicator of poverty: if an individual is moved from slightly below the threshold to a point above it, the average income of the remaining poor is lower. We observe an increase of Γ. But poverty surely has decreased. Therefore one has to multiply Γ by the share of the poor.

There is a further interpretation of the poverty gap: it is the minimal wealth necessary to eliminate poverty, namely taken as share of income necessary to keep the total population at the poverty line (if perfect targeting were possible).

The poverty gap fulfils the transfer axiom and the monotony axiom. It also has a drawback: inequality within the poor is not taken seriously. Consider the following two distributions:

$$1,2,3,4$$
$$2,2,2,4$$

If the poverty line is 3.1, the head-count measure H is in both cases 3, the poverty gap PG is also the same in both cases, namely 0.2661. But is it sensible to say that poverty is the same in both situations?

If one wants to take inequality within the group of poor households into consideration, that can be done with the *monotony-sensitivity axiom*:

Individuals are ordered according to their wealth, 1 is the poorest, n is the richest person. If ΔP_i is the increase in poverty as a consequence of a reduction of the wealth of the i-th person, then $\Delta P_i > \Delta P_j$ for $j > i$.

8.4.3 The Generalised Poverty Gap

The monotony-sensitivity axiom requires that a person's weight in the poverty measure should increase more than proportionally with the distance of her income from the poverty line. This can be achieved by a generalisation of the poverty gap:

$$P_a = 1/N \cdot \sum (1 - y_i/z)^a$$

If $a > 1$, the weight of poorer individuals in the measure is higher in a non-linear way; if $a \to \infty$, only the poorest individual has a positive weight. For $a = 0$ this is the head-count; if $a = 1$ one gets the poverty gap. The P_a measure satisfies all three axioms for $a > 1$. In the literature one finds the expression *Foster-Green-Thornbeck* (FGT) index. There is one drawback when using this index: it does not have a nice interpretation if $a > 1$. In that case it is not illustrative.[12]

Table 8.8 Ranking of poverty according to different poverty measures

Household type	H	PG	P(a=1.5)	P(a=2)	P(a=2.5)
Single pensioners	0.361 (1)	0.098 (7)	0.044 (2)	0.053 (2)	0.064 (2)
Pensioner couples	0.163 (2)	0.093 (8)	0.018 (3)	0.022 (4)	0.025 (4)
Single non-pensioners	0.060 (4)	0.204 (5)	0.017 (4)	0.023 (3)	0.028 (3)
Non-pensioner couples	0.018 (8)	0.270 (3)	0.006 (7)	0.006 (7)	0.007 (7)
Couples (1–2 children)	0.022 (6)	0.297 (1)	0.008 (6)	0.009 (6)	0.010 (6)
Couples (3+ children)	0.028 (5)	0.280 (2)	0.010 (5)	0.012 (5)	0.013 (5)
Lone parents	0.134 (3)	0.253 (4)	0.047 (1)	0.060 (1)	0.072 (1)
Others	0.019 (7)	0.143 (6)	0.003 (8)	0.003 (8)	0.004 (8)

Source: Clark et al. (1981).

Is it important which measure is used? Yes, if changes in income distribution do not affect all the poor in the same way. Table 8.8 is from a study on poverty indices with data taken from the UK. Note that single pensioners have the highest incidence of poverty according to head-count, and pensioner couples the second highest, but they are the least poor group according to the poverty gap, and are amongst the better-off groups for any P_a measure $a > 1$. Obviously, most of the poor pensioners are not very poor, whereas poor couples with one and two children are very poor. Lone parents fare worst if one takes P_a as poverty measure for all $a > 1$.

8.4.4 Three Special Problems of Poverty Measurement

8.4.4.1 Inequality within households

If one transforms the value of a poverty measure for households into that of individuals, one has to consider that wealth may be unequally distributed within families. As already mentioned, this is primarily a gender specific problem, as women tend to have less access to the resources of a household than men. This can result in a smaller value for H for individuals than for households: if a couple are just below the poverty level, one of them may be above that threshold, namely when he is better off at her cost. The poverty gap increases if a couple is ε away from the poverty line, and she gives 2ε to him (or he takes it), he is ε above the poverty line, whereas she is 3ε below.

To see the relevance: Haddad and Kanbur (1990) calculated different poverty measures while taking intra-family inequality into consideration. The material came from a southern province in the Philippines (2900 individuals in 450 households). It concerned calorie intake. C_i: calorie intake of person i, R_i: calorie requirement of person i, Φ_{ij}: calorie adequacy of person i in household j (C_i/R_i). There is a natural poverty threshold, namely

$$\Phi_i = 1$$

There are M people in N households. The size of the household i is n_i ($i = 1,2...N$). Summing over all n_is gives M.

Consider the two statistics:

$$\Phi = (1/M) \sum\sum \Phi_{ij}$$
$$\Phi 1 = (1/N) \sum \Phi 1_j$$

with

$$\Phi 1_j = (1/n_j) \sum \Phi_{ij}$$

Φ is the average of the calorie adequacy taken over all individuals separately; $\Phi 1$ averages over individuals when everybody of household j has the average calorie adequacy of that household ($\Phi 1_j$). The difference between poverty measured for the distribution of Φ and $\Phi 1$ shows the difference between poverty of individuals, when summing over individual calorie adequacy (Φ) and when assigning to everybody the average calorie adequacy of the person's household ($\Phi 1$) (see Table 8.9).

Table 8.9 Poverty according to different poverty measures for households and individuals

	$P_0(\Phi)$	$P_1(\Phi)$	$P_2(\Phi)$	$P_0(\Phi 1)$	$P_1(\Phi 1)$	$P_2(\Phi 1)$
All	0.70243	0.18640	0.06759	0.76875	0.15201	0.04093
Owner	0.68345	0.17584	0.06342	0.74964	0.14021	0.03716
Tenant	0.68865	0.17792	0.06445	0.76253	0.14202	0.03822
Labourer	0.74310	0.20589	0.07605	0.83276	0.17269	0.04884
Male	0.72372	0.19017	0.06863	0.77089	0.15058	0.04016
Female	0.67980	0.18240	0.06648	0.76648	0.15353	0.04175
Adult	0.48615	0.10074	0.03259	0.75231	0.14757	0.03957
Non-adult	0.85494	0.24681	0.09226	0.78034	0.15515	0.04189

Source: Haddad and Kanbur (1990).

Using the head-count ratio P_0, poverty is lower when taking individuals separately than when calculated with household averages. That implies that some are escaping poverty by consuming an above household average share of calories. When using P_1, the poverty gap, as measure, poverty is higher with individuals taken separately then when calculated with household averages. The same is true if poorer individuals are given an even greater weight, as in P_2. Looking at households there are more poor individuals than when taking data for calorie intake of individuals separately. However poverty in the sense of shortfall of calorie intake is underestimated by taking data for households.

8.4.4.2 The relation between the poverty line and poverty measurement

The purpose of measuring poverty is, as mentioned, to say whether poverty in situation 1 is higher or lower than in situation 2. But that depends, amongst other things, on the chosen level of the poverty line. Take the following two distributions of income for the bottom half of 10 individuals. Median income is 5 (incomes above the threshold do not influence the poverty measures).

$$A: 1.0, 1.0, 3.1, 3.1, 5$$
$$B: 2.1, 2.1, 2.1, 3.6, 5$$

The poverty lines are: a) 2; b) 2.5; c) 3; d) 3.5

Poverty according to head-count measure:

A: a) 0.2 b) 0.2 c) 0.2 d) 0.4
B: a) 0   b) 0.3 c) 0.3 d) 0.3

Poverty according to poverty gap:

A: a) 0.1 b) 0.120 c) 0.133 d) 0.165
B: a) 0   b) 0.048 c) 0.090 d) 0.120

When taking 2 as the poverty line (40 per cent of the median) distribution A has more poverty than B for both measures, with 2.5 as the poverty line (50 per cent of the median) A has less poverty for the head-count but more poverty when taking the poverty gap. This is also true for the poverty line at 3 (60 per cent of the median). If the poverty line is 3.5 (70 per cent of the median), the head-count shows again more poverty for A, but less poverty where the poverty gap is used.

There is a condition under which the ranking of poverty for a set of distributions of welfare within a population (wealth, income, calorie intake, and so on) is independent from the chosen value of the poverty line (Kakwani, 1989; Lambert, 1989, p. 54ff). To state this condition, we need the concept of the *Lorenz curve* (see above, Chapter 3, Appendix 3.2). It shows the cumulative share of the population against the cumulative share of income (or any other welfare indicator).

As was stated in Chapter 3, Lorenz curves cannot be ranked unambiguously, because they can cross (this is the case for the Lorenz curves of the two distributions A and B). If Lorenz curves do not cross up to the highest poverty line and the underlying distributions have the same mean, then the curve closer to the axis (the more unequal distribution) has higher poverty for all poverty lines and all poverty measures P_a.

That condition seldom applies, because different income distributions rarely have the same mean. But the idea of using Lorenz curves can be extended to the case of unequal means: if two Lorenz curves do not cross up to the highest poverty line and the mean of the Lorenz curve closer to the diagonal (the more equal distribution) is higher than the mean of the dominated Lorenz curve, then there is less poverty for all poverty lines and all poverty measures P_a.

8.4.4.3 Does less poverty imply more social welfare?

Does a lower value of a poverty measure necessarily indicate more welfare? Is a situation with less poverty necessarily better than another one with more poverty? This is not to deny that poverty is bad, but consider the following two situations:

A: 1, 4, 4, 4
B: 1, 1, 4, 4, 4

If the poverty threshold is above 1 and below 4, there is more poverty in B for all poverty measures P_a, because there are two poor individuals. But having one more individual cannot be worse.

The case as described by a change from A to B is a realistic one. Assume that there are two groups, one with a high incidence of poverty and the other with a low incidence.

share of population:	50	50	
poverty rates:	10	18	average: 14

Assume that the population with higher incidence of poverty grows faster than the other one. The shares of the two groups shift in the following way:

shares of population:	25	75	
poverty rates:	10	16	average: 14.5

There is overall more poverty in the second situation (according to head-count), but nobody is worse off. The welfare of individuals in the first group did not change; the chance of being poor remained the same. The situation in the second group improved, at least according to the head-count measure, because the probability of being poor decreased.

That is a realistic setting: the overall number of poor people has increased in the last decades. The share of the poor has increased as well, because poor regions have higher demographic growth than rich societies. However it is not justified to say that the situation has deteriorated merely because there are more poor people. In some respect the very poor are better off today: their life expectancy is much higher than it was 30 years ago.

Fighting poverty can even be the cause of increased poverty. That does not imply that fighting poverty fails, rather that it is effective: if mortality rates among the poor decrease in consequence of implementing a social programme, there will be more of them. Decreasing mortality can be the consequence of a programme generally fighting poverty, or of an increase in health expenditure for poor people. All measures aimed at reducing infant mortality have this effect. If fewer children of the poor are stillborn, the consequence is more poor people.[13] If the incomes of the households remain the same, the per-capita income goes down and poverty increases even more for other measures. However it is sensible to consider the reduction of mortality as an increase of welfare.

The increase of overall poverty in the world is to some extent the consequence of a decline of mortality (see Table 8.10). Infant mortality decreased in nearly all countries and life expectancy increased. The poor were more strongly affected than others, as they were disproportionally afflicted by short life expectancy and high infant mortality. Be that as it may, stating that the increase of poverty is partly due to positively valued developments should not lead to a benign attitude towards poverty.

Table 8.10 Increase of life expectancy at birth for countries with high incidence of poverty

	Before 1970		About 1990	
	m	f	m	f
Angola		33	44	48
Brazil		60	63	70
Cameroon	35	38	54	57
Ethiopia		41	46	49
India	42	41	57	58
Zaire		43	59	54

Source: *United Nations Demographic Yearbook* (1972 and 1995).

8.5 THE POOR: HOW MANY, HOW POOR AND WHAT MAKES THEM POOR

After the methodological preliminaries about defining and measuring poverty some information about poverty demonstrates the application of the concepts. Of course, the bulk of the poor live in poor countries. They are often extremely poor. According to the criteria of the United Nations and of the World Bank an individual is extremely poor if she has less than $1 a day. When using this standard there are no poor people in the industrialised countries – he or she would have starved to death already. This does not imply that there is no poverty in rich countries, but one needs a much higher income merely to avoid starving to death.

8.5.1 The Empirics of Poverty

8.5.1.1 Absolute poverty: the United States of America
The USA not only has the highest incidence of poverty among rich economies, it also has the best official documentation of its poverty. This is due to the importance of fighting poverty as an objective of official social policy and of the great weight it has in the public discussion of social policy. There is an official poverty line which is updated yearly. Official estimates of the extent of poverty in the USA are provided. The data are easily accessible on the internet: www.census.gov/hhes/www/povty99.html.

As mentioned above, poverty is defined in the following way: a household is poor if its share of expenditure on food is at least a third of its income. This definition goes back to research on poverty sponsored by the Social Security Administration in the years 1963–1964 (Orshansky, 1965). To apply this definition, the costs of a basket of 'least costly nutritionally adequate food plans' are calculated and annually updated. Thus it is not necessary to use an equivalence scale based on different information (see Table 8.11)

Table 8.11 *Poverty thresholds in 1999 by size of family and number of related children under 18*

Size of family unit	Related children under 18 years				
	None	One	Two	Three	Four
One person unrelated					
Under 65 years	8,667				
65 years and over	7,990				
Two people					
Householder under 65 years	11,156	11,483			
Householder 65 years and over	10,070	11,440			
Three people	13,032	13,410	13,423		
Four people	17,184	17,465	16,895	16,954	
Five people	20,723	21,024	20,380	19,882	19,578

Source: Dalaker and Proctor (2000).

According to this definition nearly 12 per cent of the US population were poor in 1999. This was the smallest number for about 20 years. Poverty rates are different for different groups (see Table 8.12). Amongst children poverty is more widespread, Blacks have the highest incidence, non-Hispanic whites the lowest. Female headed households a have higher incidence of poverty than married-couple families. There are big regional variations in poverty rates between states. In New Mexico the poverty rate reaches more than 20 per cent, in Utah and Maryland it is below 8 per cent. However one has to take into account that a unique poverty threshold for a country as big as the USA is very problematic. As the average (or the median) income varies between different states, the price level for basic goods may vary as well. A dollar in a poor state can be of higher value than a dollar in a rich state. An individual at the poverty level is in that case better off in a poor state than in a rich state.

Table 8.12 Poverty rates in the USA according to demographic characteristics

All people	11.8
Under 18	16.9
18 to 64	10.0
65 and over	9.7
White non-Hispanic	7.7
Asian and Pacific Islander	10.7
Hispanic	22.8
Black	23.6
All families	10.2
Married-couple families	5.8
Female householder families	30.4

Source: Dalaker and Proctor (2000).

The average poverty gap per family was $6687, the average poverty gap per person in poor households was $1908. For unrelated people the average poverty gap was $4206. The total poverty gap was approximately $80 billion. That was less than 1 per cent of GDP. Although it does not take much to eliminate poverty completely, a substantial share of the population experience it.

8.5.1.2 Relative poverty: the Luxembourg Income Study

An ambitious programme to make data on income distribution and on poverty comparable across different countries is carried out by the Luxembourg Income Study (LIS) (Smeeding et al., 1990). It was started in the 1980s and is still going on. It is based on the use of microdata which are made comparable across nations. In such a setting an absolute poverty level cannot be used as poverty in countries with different average incomes are compared. Therefore a relative poverty threshold is used.[14] In the first studies 50 per cent of median income was taken (Smeeding et al., 1990). In more recent publications poverty rates for 40, 50 and 60 per cent of median income are presented. Thus more insight into the distribution of income in low-income households is gained. To take account of the size of households the square root of the number of people in a household was used for calculating equivalent income (Table 8.13).

The data confirm the general impression (or prejudice) that a higher percentage of the population is poor in the USA than anywhere else. The lowest poverty rates are to be found in the Scandinavian countries. Single-parent families are everywhere at a higher risk of becoming poor.

Table 8.13 *Percentage of people who are poor at different poverty thresholds*

		Total population			Children			Elderly		
Poverty line (% of median)		40	50	60	40	50	60	40	50	60
Belgium	1992	1.9	5.2	10.7	1.6	4.6	9.3	4.2	12.1	24.6
Canada	1997	7.3	11.9	18.4	9.6	15.7	23.1	1.4	5.3	17.3
Czech. Rep.	1992	0.7	2.3	6.5	1.0	2.2	5.4	0.3	5.0	18.3
Finland	1995	2.2	5.2	10.6	1.7	4.3	8.3	1.2	5.3	18.2
France	1994	3.4	8.0	14.1	2.9	7.9	14.3	3.4	9.8	18.5
Germany	1994	4.2	7.5	13.1	6.0	10.6	16.2	4.0	7.0	15.3
Hungary	1994	6.0	10.1	15.0	7.0	11.4	15.6	3.9	8.8	18.6
Ireland	1987	4.4	11.1	20.0	4.7	13.8	25.1	4.7	8.2	25.2
Italy	1995	9.4	14.2	21.1	14.6	20.2	28.8	4.5	12.2	20.3
Netherlands	1994	4.9	8.1	13.7	4.9	8.1	12.9	3.3	6.4	21.4
Norway	1995	3.1	6.9	13.1	2.2	3.9	9.6	0.7	14.5	29.4
Sweden	1995	4.7	6.6	10.0	1.3	2.6	5.5	0.8	2.7	7.8
Switzerland	1992	6.7	9.3	14.7	7.1	10.0	16.4	4.7	8.4	19.0
UK	1995	6.1	13.4	22.1	8.4	19.8	30.1	4.0	13.7	29.1
USA	1997	10.8	16.9	23.9	14.8	22.3	31.0	12.0	20.7	29.9

Source: http://lisweb.ceps lu/publications/incomeproject/povertytable.html.

Some countries with low poverty rates at the 40 per cent level have pretty high poverty rates at the 60 per cent level (Ireland, UK). That suggests that there are many households with income around the 50 per cent threshold, but only a small number of very poor households.

Table 8.13 can be used for comparing the two approaches. The official US poverty threshold was about 42 per cent of US median household income (Smeeding et al., 2000). Therefore the official poverty rates in the USA are rather in line with the 40 per cent threshold of Table 8.12 than with the 50 per cent thresholds.

There are also calculations of poverty gaps (Table 8.14). Interestingly many of those who are poor in countries with low poverty expressed by head-count (Sweden and Norway) are very poor by these calculations. This can be due to being very efficient at fighting moderate poverty (old age poverty due to low pensions, low-wage poverty). However the 'hard cases' – people dropping out of the labour market, people being on the fringes of organised society – cannot be reached by the existing means of social administration.

Table 8.14 Poverty gap: equivalent income deficit as percentage of poverty line

Country	Total	Elderly families	Single-parent families	Two-parent families	Other families
Sweden	40.0	45.2	33.4	28.2	43.2
UK	16.0	10.9	17.7	10.8	24.3
Israel	16.3	13.4	13.7	20.4	13.3
USA	39.9	29.1	43.0	33.3	50.6
Norway	40.8	48.3	27.7	29.2	47.6
Canada	33.9	18.8	37.0	30.5	41.8
West Germany	30.6	28.5	31.4	23.2	48.4

Source: Smeeding et al. (1990).

8.5.1.3 Duration of poverty

Measuring the duration of poverty needs much more data. Calculations are usually based on panel data and income surveys which follow the income of families over long periods. Again the USA provides the best data (for example, Naifeh, 1998 for the period 1993–1994). Though 30 per cent of the population were poor for at least two months during 1993–1994, only 5 per cent were poor all through the two years. Nearly half of all poverty spells lasted between two and four months, and more than 75 per cent lasted for up to one year. The structure of the duration of poverty spells for Blacks and Hispanics were similar, though the entry and exit rates of the former were markedly below that of the latter. Whites not only had the lowest poverty rates but also the highest exit rates from poverty. Children and older people had lower exit rates.

In a study comparing poverty in different OECD countries (OECD, 2001) data on average duration and distribution of length of poverty spells were provided (Table 8.15). For most countries surveyed the former does not exceed 1.9 years, only the USA has an average duration of 2 years. Looking at entry and exit rates countries with high poverty rates have low or not particularly high entry rates but low exit rates. That raises the suspicion that there is an underclass whose way of living is markedly distinct from that of mainstream middle-class society.

8.5.2 Personal or Social Factors?

As mentioned at the beginning of this chapter, poverty is not considered to be a normal state in modern societies. People should be able to earn enough not to be poor. That is a basic normative value. Therefore poor individuals must be seen as not earning enough by working. Why do some people not earn enough?

There are structural factors and personal factors that ensure that among people living in the same society, having the same opportunities, experiencing more or less the same aggregate shocks, the occurrence of poverty can be very different. Sometimes it is simply chance that makes one individual poor and another not. Some are lucky and never become unemployed. Others get a job demanding considerable firm-specific skill, but due to a shift in consumer preferences or changed rules for international trade the job is suddenly closed down and the firm-specific skills cannot be used at another job. For some individuals, rebellious behaviour while young turns into hard working to show parents that they can make it. Others leave school too early, maybe they end up with a criminal record or an addiction. Some are affected by long-lasting illness or by some other impairment of working ability. Most people are able to overcome a separation from the spouse, but for a few it can be the start for a long-lasting social decline.

Table 8.15 Gross rates of entry and exit of poverty (1993–1995)

Country	Annual poverty rate	Yearly rate of entry[a]	Yearly rate of exit[b]
Belgium	9.8	4.7	48.2
Canada	10.9	4.8	36.4
Denmark	4.7	3.1	60.4
France	9.6	4.6	46.9
Germany	12.1	5.1	41.1
Ireland	8.2	5.0	54.6
Italy	13.5	5.3	40.6
Netherlands	7.8	4.2	55.7
Spain	12.0	5.9	49.6
United Kingdom	12.1	6.0	58.8
United States[c]	16.0	4.5	29.5

Notes: [a] Number of people entering poverty between t and t + 1 as share of the population not in poverty in t, averaged over the period.
[b] Number of poor in t who exit poverty in t + 1 as share of the population in poverty in t, averaged over the period.
[c] Data refer to 1987–1989.

Source: OECD (2001), p. 50.

Under structural factors is to be understood that *ceteris paribus* the probability of becoming poor is not the same for everybody but varies systematically with social characteristics. Poverty is concentrated in specific groups of the population, defined by economic and social characteristics:

ethnic and racial minorities, people with low qualifications, people living in distant regions or in inner-city ghettos, and so on. These structures are closely related to the probabilities of low income. They reflect systematic inequalities in society.

Is there a theoretical relation between the poverty of some and the wealth of others? Some think that inequality necessarily begets poverty. The wealth of the rich rests on others' poverty, (as Marx has argued that at length in his famous idea of the immiseration of the working class). Others think that some countries remained poor because they were exploited by other countries through different kinds of dependency (colonialism, imperialism). Today the integration of markets into worldwide markets ('globalisation') is by many considered responsible for making people poor.

There are too many theoretical problems at stake to satisfactorily discuss them here in a few paragraphs. For the purpose of this book it suffices to state that in rich economies there is no social group the members of which are necessarily poor. The structural factors do not 'cause' poverty, in the way that individuals to whom these factors apply are necessarily poor.[15] According to economic theory having low skills implies earning a low wage. But this does not imply that individuals with low skills must be poor. Being an Afro-American in an inner-city ghetto, or a young French individual of Arab or African origin in the *banlieu* of a city, or a lone mother is no reason for being poor. There is no theoretical connection between belonging to one of these groups and being poor, although it is true that individuals from these groups have a higher probability of being poor. All one can say is that among these groups there are relatively more individuals without appropriate skills and/or without the opportunity to use their skills for gainful employment. There is always a personal factor.[16]

People earning low wages are at high risk of becoming poor. There are three reasons for that. First, they experience unemployment more often than others. Second, low-wage households cannot build up reserves for interruptions of working life. It does not need much to make people with low wages experience poverty – a medium length spell of unemployment, an accident, a short-term mental disturbance. Third, low wages are usually the consequence of low skills. That again may contribute to having difficulties overcoming adverse events.

But not all the poor earned low wages before becoming poor. Many people experience periods of poverty. These spells are usually linked to specific events, which some individuals are less apt to overcome than others (Leisering and Leibfried, 1999). These events can be:

- A fall of income due to unemployment, health problems or the death of an earning member of the household.

- The household grows.
- Needs rise for whatever reason.
- A new household is started (divorce, children become independent).
- A child is born into poverty.

In more traditional societies it is often the extended family which provides assistance. In modern societies family assistance is usually reduced to the support between spouses and individuals in direct lineages. It is expected that public support systems provide help in case of adverse circumstances. How much poverty there is in a society depends also on the efficacy of social programmes.

The states of western Europe differ in the extent of their overall social protection. The Scandinavian countries, the Netherlands, Belgium, Austria and Germany have very comprehensive systems of social protection, which reduce poverty. Spain, Portugal and Italy provide less public support, but there is more support through families than in northern countries. The United States clearly fares much worse in that respect. In the former planned economies there was hardly any poverty, as avoiding it was a prime objective of social and economic policy.[17] There was also no unemployment. Nobody was dismissed merely for not really working. Only people with deviant behaviour were poor – and that often led to imprisonment.

A hint of the efficacy of social programmes is given in Table 8.16. The highest poverty gap and the highest share of pre-transfer poor are in Sweden and in West Germany! These states are very efficient at reducing poverty. The importance of the social policy provision becomes even clearer when one looks at poverty rates for groups: in Sweden more than 98 per cent of the elderly would be poor without public transfers. With transfers less than 1 per cent are poor.

This does not imply that without the welfare state everybody with pre-transfer income below the poverty threshold would be poor. When estimating what the situation would be without transfers one has to take into account that in that case people would pay much lower taxes and would take care of themselves. That is the other side of what was said above in Chapter 5: People who do not save because there is a public pension system have no income when old.

Summing up, the extent of poverty in a society depends on three factors:

- Poverty is smaller in countries with low unemployment and low employment in casual and irregular jobs.
- The lower the inequality of wages at the lower end of the income distribution the lower is overall poverty.

- The more assistance people get when affected by an adverse event, the lower poverty is.

Table 8.16 Pre- and post-transfer poverty rates and poverty gaps

Country		Percentage poverty gap*	Percentage of people who are poor
Sweden	Pre-transfer	80.7	41.0
	Post-transfer	40.0	5.0
	Percentage reduction	50.4	87.8
United Kingdom	Pre-transfer	72.6	27.9
	Post-transfer	16.0	8.8
	Percentage reduction	78.0	68.5
Israel	Pre-transfer	57.6	29.0
	Post-transfer	16.3	14.5
	Percentage reduction	71.7	50.0
United States	Pre-transfer	71.0	27.3
	Post-transfer	39.9	16.9
	Percentage reduction	43.8	38.1
Norway	Pre-transfer	79.7	24.1
	Post-transfer	40.8	4.8
	Percentage reduction	48.8	80.1
Canada	Pre-transfer	69.8	25.6
	Post-transfer	33.9	12.1
	Percentage reduction	51.4	52.7
West Germany	Pre-transfer	86.3	28.3
	Post-transfer	30.6	6.0
	Percentage reduction	68.2	78.8

Note: * Equivalent income deficit as percentage of poverty line.

Source: Smeeding et al. (1990).

8.6 ASSISTING THE POOR I: WAGE SUPPLEMENTS

What can be done? This question will be discussed in the last two sections of the chapter. But why not simply fill in the gap – giving all the poor the difference between their income and the poverty line? If that is done, the earned income of the poor goes down: if a poor person increases her income by working, this extra income is taxed away euro by euro by the reduction of the transfer. This amounts to a tax rate of 100 per cent. There are two ways to deal with that:

- Reducing the effective tax rate by creating special schedules for transfers – wage supplements.
- Combining transfers with attempts to make recipients of welfare work – social assistance and welfare-to-work programmes (8.7).

These are not mutually exclusive.

Wage supplements are of big importance in the USA – the Earned Income Tax Credit, EITC – and in the UK, Family Credit. The EITC applies primarily to families with dependent children. For each dollar a family earns, it gets 34 cents for one child and 40 cents for two children. The benefit rises until it reaches $2312 for one child ($3816 for two children). It stays at that level until income reaches $12 460.[18] As income increases further the benefit gets withdrawn at a rate of 15.98 per cent in the case of one child and 21.06 per cent for two children (Ellwood and Liebmann, 2001; Hotz and Scholz, 2001; see Figure 8.2). Payment of EITC transfers are provided for people with incomes above the poverty threshold. (In 1999 the poverty threshold for a family consisting of one adult and two children below 18 was $13 423.)

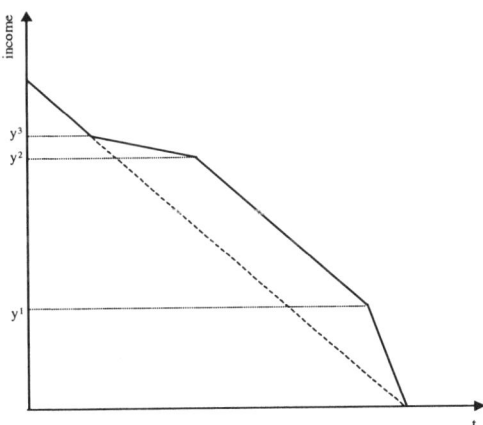

Note: The transfer for a working person increases until he reaches income y^1, it stays constant until y^2 and is then withdrawn. At income y^3 the transfer is zero.

Figure 8.2 The budget constraint of low-wage employees in the presence of the EITC in the USA

Family Credit in the UK is paid to all families below a threshold level working at least 16 hours a week. A fixed amount is given to all families with income up to £79 per week. The benefit is £48.80 for an adult and between

£12.35 and £25.40 for each child depending on age. For incomes higher than the threshold the benefit is reduced by 70 per cent of the difference between the actual income and the threshold. An extra £10.80 is given to those working at least 30 hours (www.west-dunbarton/gov.uk/couninfo/benefits/famcredt.html).

The basic ideas of such schemes is to 'make work pay', as the political slogan says. For very low incomes the benefit is increased with each hour worked, for some income brackets the size of the benefit is independent of income, for still higher incomes there is a tax on further income. The tax rate is much smaller than the 100 per cent tax rate, as in the case of the transfer being withdrawn completely at the poverty threshold. This transfer increases labour supply for the very poor; it may have opposite effects at higher wages (for the UK see Duncan and Giles, 1996; for the USA, Ellwood, 2000).

BOX 8.2 HOW TO PREDICT THE EFFECTS OF WAGE SUPPLEMENTS

What were the effects of the reform of the UK Family Credit on labour supply – namely the extra £10? For those who had been working less than 30 hours, there was an incentive created to work more hours. For those who had been working more than 30 hours before the reform an income effect was created which might have decreased labour supply. The extra £10 was an incentive to reduce working time for some women, as long as it remained at least 30 hours. Furthermore, some married women might have reduced their labour supply or may even have dropped out of the labour market completely, where the spouse could claim the extra £10.

To evaluate these effects empirically it is necessary to estimate labour supply functions of individuals in different situations – married people, lone parents, and so on. With the results of these estimations one can predict the response of the affected people to the change of the benefits. A study by Duncan and Giles (1996) reported that the overall labour supply response was negative.

> We predict some movements towards 30 hours of paid work for married women receiving Family Credit on the basis of their own employment, but there is a significantly larger cluster of women reducing their hours away from 30 hours level. Indeed, as many women as are predicted to increase their hours level are predicted to leave the labour market altogether. These seemingly contradictory results arise because the effect of the reform may result from a change in their own entitlement or that of their spouse. (Duncan and Giles, 1996, p. 152)

8.6.1 The Efficiency of Wage Subsidies

The ability of tax credits and other form of wage subsidies to eliminate poverty is limited, as it does not attempt to give those with very low earnings a transfer which would enable them to evade poverty completely. It mitigates poverty. It is a reasonable concept under two conditions: first, as its idea is to reduce the disincentive to work, low-skill jobs must be available. During the 1990s this condition was fulfilled in the USA and in the UK. Second, there must be other programmes for individuals unfit to work.

To evaluate the efficiency of such a programme one can make use of Figure 8.3. Consider the following simple case: The recipients of incomes are uniformly distributed in the interval (y_{min}, y_{max}). There is an income support scheme which applies to all incomes not greater than $y' > z$, the poverty threshold, according to the formula $b \cdot (y' - y)$, $b<1$; that is, a percentage b of the difference between the target income y' and the actual income is given. In figure 8.3 the working of such a transfer is drawn. (It rather resembles the UK FC than the EITC scheme.) The areas B and C are inefficiencies, because transfers are given to those not in need. B representing transfers to the poor in excess of what they need to reach the poverty line. The area C represent transfers to the non-poor.[19] The area D signifies inefficiency, because the poverty line is not reached. Even with the transfer some people's incomes remain below the poverty line.

There are two definitions of efficiency:

(i) vertical efficiency: share of transfers going to the poor
   (A/(A + B + C)).

(ii) horizontal efficiency: transfers going to the poor as share of poverty gap
   (A/(A + D)).

There is a problem in that the higher the horizontal efficiency the lower the vertical efficiency, unless the withdrawal rate is very high. Indeed, if the minimum income is set sufficiently high, vertical efficiency can reach one, namely all poverty is eliminated. But due to the withdrawal rate of less than 100 per cent there is vertical inefficiency as nearly all incomes with the transfer are well above the poverty line. On the other hand increasing vertical efficiency reduces horizontal efficiency.

The success of such a scheme depends also on the wage distribution at the lower end. To see that, assume that the wage distribution is as drawn in Figure 8.3 right. There are only a few people with very low incomes, the bulk of poor people are slightly below the poverty line. In that case a wage subsidy is not efficient unless it has a very high withdrawal rate. That is the situation in many European states: minimum wages are about half the average wage. The poverty line is half the median income. Most low-skill employees working full time are already at the poverty threshold unless they are single earners with many children. A wage supplement for low-skill employees brings many people far above the poverty threshold. Note that EITC payments reach households up to a level of about 200 per cent of the poverty threshold. In many European states that would imply paying wage supplements to employees at about median income. It would reach more households than if the wage distribution were more unequal. The costs of such a scheme would be high. Wage supplements are a reasonable policy when the wage distribution is very unequal at the lower end.[20]

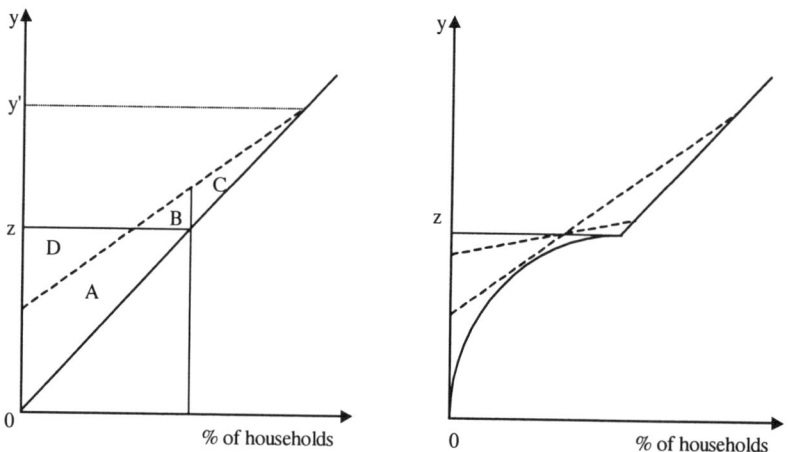

Figure 8.3 Measuring efficiency of an income support scheme

8.7   ASSISTING THE POOR II: SOCIAL ASSISTANCE

8.7.1 Institutions

The basic idea of wage supplements is to help low-income individuals without considering special needs, without caring whether poverty is totally eliminated or merely reduced. Furthermore, individuals not working cannot receive that transfer. Their big advantage is that they are easy to administer and recipients do not face extremely high tax rates. Social assistance works on another principle: it should take care of needs and it does not mind high marginal tax rates. To make it work it needs considerable administrative capacity. It is not only necessary to distinguish the poor from the non-poor, but also to distinguish between eligible poor and non-eligible poor. The problem of eligibility arises because social assistance should reduce or eliminate poverty, but it is not considered to be a basic income. It should not supplant labour income. Individuals living in non-poor households are in general not entitled to any benefit, even if they have no income.

The basic structures are the same everywhere, namely an individual in need, whether due to low income or due to special needs can turn to the social administration. Its job is to assess the need and to allocate resources. It should also empower the individual to escape poverty. That means counselling, training, helping to find a job, but also sometimes withdrawing benefits.

The institutional structures can be very different. (For detailed information, see Eardley et al., 1996; Lødemel and Trickey, 2001). They not only differ between states, there are also big variations within states, as poor relief is traditionally provided by regions and cities. The extent of central government interference varies. In the United Kingdom all laws concerning social assistance are centrally decided (that may change now due to devolution) and all administration works under the guidance of the Secretary of State for Social Security (Trickey and Walker, 2001). There is not much discretion for regions and cities, beside the usual differences which arise if different people apply the same law. In the USA, the federal programmes are implemented by state laws. The federal budget provides block grants, which can be supplemented by state budgets. Germany meanwhile has a unified code for social assistance, although there is discretion for regional decision making. In Austria the federal state has up to now ceded its prerogative to put a law on the statutes in favour of the provinces. In Sweden, there is a national law for social assistance, but the communes have more discretion to decide things than in Germany (Buhr, 1998).

The interaction with other social policy programmes differ between countries. Again the British case is unique in Europe, as there is no systematic separation between contributory programmes (for example, basic pension, unemployment benefits) and social assistance. Australia and New Zealand have hardly any social security system and most benefits are means-tested. Therefore social assistance is much broader than in most European states (Eardley et al., 1996) (Table 8.17). Also in the USA social assistance covers aspects which in most European states are handled by other social policy institutions – access to health services and family allowance. In states with more elaborate programmes of income maintenance – the Scandinavian countries and most states of continental Europe – social assistance should merely help individuals who are not adequately covered by other social policy programmes. Social assistance is merely the residual supplier of help.

The interplay with other social policy programmes is also of importance insofar as other programmes may have also poverty averting aspects. The pension systems in the Scandinavian countries, in Switzerland, France, Italy, the Netherlands and Austria grant almost all people with any right to a public pension a minimum around the poverty line. In the UK, the USA, and in Germany this is not the case. Therefore social assistance has a greater role to play for the elderly in these countries. In Ireland even unemployment benefits are paid by the social assistance system.

The same applies to family support. In states with generous, not means-tested, family benefits (Germany, Austria, France, Spain) the need for social assistance of families is *ceteris paribus* smaller than in states where family benefits are small or are means-tested (UK, USA). In the USA social assistance is primarily concerned with helping families with children.

Table 8.17 Share of beneficiaries and share of expenditure on social assistance

Country	Population share of beneficiaries	Total assistance expenditure as share of GDP	Total assistance expenditure as share of social protection
Australia	15.9	5.2	40.6
Austria	4.8	1.4	4.6
Canada	13.7	2.0	10.7
Denmark	–	1.2	4.4
France	2.1	1.8	6.8
Germany	6.2	1.8	7.6
Ireland	11.6	4.3	21.6
Italy	4.6	1.4	5.6
New Zealand	24.4	12.5	65.4
Sweden	6.2	1.0	3.1
Switzerland	2.4	0.8	n/a
UK	13.4	3.0	13.4

Note: In New Zealand nearly a quarter of the population gets transfers of social assistance programmes. In states with extended social security programmes the share is fare below 10 per cent. It is a residual programme.

Source: Eardley et al. (1996).

A further point is that much depends on the definition of a household. In Denmark, Finland, Norway and Sweden parents are not legally obliged to finance their children beyond the age of 18, even if they reside in the same household. Young people without income living with their non-poor parents may therefore be entitled to some benefits. In some countries living in one house is the decisive criterion for forming one household, even where more than two generations are involved. At the other end of the spectrum lies

Germany and Austria, where parents can be asked to reimburse the social administration for the assistance their children get, independently of living arrangements, and children can be asked to reimburse the assistance their parents receive.

Some systems of assistance are universal, in the sense that whoever has a need can turn to social assistance (Scandinavian countries, Germany, Austria, Netherlands, Belgium). Other have created categorical benefits – for lone parents, for the young, for special groups of long-term unemployed, and so on (USA, France, Spain, Italy, UK).

8.7.2 Evaluating Social Assistance

There is no country without social assistance. It is accepted everywhere that there is a need for it. Everywhere it is discussed whether the benefits are too generous or are not generous enough, though there are not many who want to abolish them completely. Providing help for the 'unlucky' is a principle of charity. Some want to replace it by a basic income.

To analyse the merits of assistance systems it is necessary to be precise as to what is to be understood under the phrase 'help the unlucky'. As mentioned above, social assistance has two objectives in helping the poor:

1. Reducing actual poverty.
2. Empowering for escaping poverty.

These two objectives will be discussed separately.

8.7.2.1 Reducing actual poverty

The ability of a social assistance system to reduce actual poverty depends on the following characteristics:

- The statutory provisions of how much to give.
- The statutory provision for eligibility – whom to give it to.
- The propensity to apply for a benefit – take-up rates.

The statutory rules for the size of the benefits are due to political fiat. Some states are more generous, others are less so. That is primarily a normative question. There is no economic theory why that is so. It has probably something to do with the perception of the poor: whether they are seen as morally guilty – not working hard enough, consuming too much – or as a problem of the society. It is very much a cultural phenomenon. Interestingly there is no relation between *per capita* income and generosity in the support of the poor (Table 8.18).

Table 8.18 Level of social assistance entitlements as percentage of median income

	Germany	Sweden	United Kingdom
Single 35	51	67	46
Single 68	56	67	58
Couple 68	67	65	57
Couple 35, one child 2	73	69	48
Couple 35, one child 7	56	70	48
Single parent 35, one child 2	90	71	54
Single parent 35, one child 7	56	73	54
Single parent, two children, 2,7	85	75	52

Note: For the calculation of the equivalent median income the modified OECD equivalence scales were used (0.5 for a second adult, and 0.3 for each child).

Source: Behrendt (2002).

The rules for eligibility are also determined by political fiat. They have much to do with the distinction between 'deserving poor' and 'non-deserving poor' – again a normative distinction. Usually individuals who are not expected to work are considered more deserving than others. That relates to age, health, disabilities and obligations to care for somebody, mostly for children. Men below the age of 60 without any obvious disability rank last in the list of people excused for not working.[21]

The third factor, namely the take-up rates are the result of individual decisions and are therefore apt to being modelled in the economist's way. Poor individuals apply if the utility of doing so is higher than the utility of not applying. This utility increases with:

- The size of the benefit to be received. This depends on the difference between the statutory benefits and an individual's income. People with income only slightly below the threshold are less likely to apply.
- The duration of the benefit. Individuals who expect to receive an income above the poverty line within a short period are less likely to apply.
- The absence of stigma. Any stigma attached to receiving benefits reduces the probability of an application (Moffitt, 1983).
- The friendliness of the administration. Administrative practices influence the decision to apply. They can encourage the poor to do so – or they can be a disincentive. (Providing information; help with filling out forms, the possibility for applicants to use their native language – ethnic minorities are over-represented among the poor.)

Actually only a part of the eligible poor apply for social assistance. In Germany less than 50 per cent do so (Riphahn, 2000). In the USA take-up rates for some important programmes are about 60 per cent (Blank and Ruggles, 1996). That does not imply that only less than 50 per cent or 60 per cent of the poverty gap is filled by social assistance. As expected, individuals who are very poor are more likely to apply than individuals whose income is only a bit below the threshold for eligibility. Furthermore individuals with short spells of poverty are less likely to apply for assistance. Table 8.19 confirms the above given predictions for the United Kingdom and Germany, namely the more severe the poverty the higher the probability that a household gets benefits. For Sweden that is not the case.[22]

Table 8.19 *Percentage of households receiving means-tested transfers at different levels of poverty*

		Germany 1994	Sweden 1994	United Kingdom 1995
No poverty	Y ≥ 60 per cent	7	24	7
Near poverty	50 per cent ≤ Y < 60 per cent	32	25	42
Moderate poverty	40 per cent ≤ Y < 50 per cent	42	47	66
Severe poverty	30 per cent ≤ Y < 40 per cent	47	52	73
Extreme poverty	Y < 30 per cent	65	51	86

Note: Y: income before means-tested benefit.

Source: Behrendt (2002).

Behrendt (2002) also calculated, how much poverty was reduced by the transfers received. The result was that in Germany poverty was reduced by 27 per cent (minus 2.8 percentage points), in Sweden by 32 per cent (minus 4.4 percentage points) and in the United Kingdom by 60 per cent (minus 14.4 percentage points). The high result for the UK is due to the general importance of means-tested benefits.[23]

Looking at the statutory level of social assistance and the eligibility rules, poverty is greatly reduced and in many states extreme poverty is largely eradicated.

8.7.2.2 Duration of assistance and policies to reduce dependence

Helping the poor would hardly be an issue if it were not for the duration of assistance. This is often called *welfare dependency*. It means that individuals on assistance are getting used receiving benefits and stop attempting to earn a living. They are caught in the *poverty trap*: when taking a job their initial income is not much higher than the assistance they receive. When working, they lose the benefits. Their marginal tax rate is therefore not far below 100 per cent. However by not working they forgo the possibility of getting a job with a higher wage.

Their has been a lot of research on the duration of dependency. The necessary data are *panel data* or data from administrative files. A panel is a collection of data for a sample of the population over a long period. The same households are interviewed at periodic intervals. In that way it is possible to trace the dynamics of particular household characteristics – income, poverty, employment and unemployment, consumption habits, changes of household size, and so on. Administrative assistance files allow the analysis of the dynamics of the population receiving assistance. The main difference between these two types of data is that administrative data only provide data for households which have applied for assistance. They are not representative of all poor households. Panels provide a representative sample from the whole population. The question of pick-up rates can only be handled by a panel.

Be that as it may, social assistance is not considered a basic income. All systems demand that individuals work if possible. However it is clear that individuals receiving assistance face special problems in finding employment.

BOX 8.3 THE BREMEN APPROACH TO ANALYSING SOCIAL ASSISTANCE

A special approach to the analysis of social assistance data was developed at the Centre of Social Policy Research at the university of Bremen (Leisering and Leibfried, 1999). Instead of using data of recipients of social assistance at specific dates, a continuous time profile of income support was used. For that purpose it was necessary to use administrative files, as panel data do not contain this information.

Although these data restrict the research to poverty of individuals who had applied for social assistance, thereby neglecting the poor who have not applied, they have two important advantages. First, the reasons why poverty spells began and why they ended are recorded in the files. Second, short-term interruptions of poverty spells are precisely recorded.* Thus it is possible to pursue the question of what were the reasons why people asked for assistance, why people stopped receiving assistance and what caused the interruptions to receipt of assistance if any. In that context the duration of poverty is considered to last from the beginning of the first spell to the end of the last spell.

In turned out that only a small fraction of recipients depend without interruption for a long period on assistance. Many are either short-term recipients or switch a few times between receiving assistance and being able to support themselves. A categorization into five types was developed.

1. The *bridgers*: transitory recipients.
2. The *marginalized*: long-term recipients.
3. The o*scillators*: people swinging between assistance and sufficient income.
4. The e*scapers*: long-term recipients who eventually escape assistance for a long time.
5. The e*xternalized*: people receiving assistance who have no contact with the labour market (for example, old people without any pension).

These different types have different characteristics concerning the amount of their autonomy as active individuals. Whereas the *bridgers* and the e*xternalised* hardly lose autonomy and the *escapers* regain it, the *marginalized* have lost their autonomy. The o*scillators* are in danger of losing it.

Note: * It is necessary to distinguish between real interruptions of receiving transfers and purely administrative interruptions.

All through the 1990s states pursued policies to bring people into work. The disincentive to work inherent in the assistance programmes, namely providing an income slightly below half the median income, was increasingly regarded as a problem. Social assistance programmes were supplemented by schemes designed to make people work: the slogan is *welfare-to-work* or *workfare*. Nearly all countries developed divers schemes under different titles to get the poor to work unless there were specific reasons for not working – age, small children, health (Lødemel and Trickey, 2001).

The approach was by training and subsidising jobs, similarly to ALMP programmes. Under the guidance of social assistance, special programmes were developed: subsidising jobs in non-profit organisations, providing jobs at communal levels for divers activities (cleaning parks, helping with repair jobs, and so on). Whether such jobs are productive or not, is not the issue. The point is that it should make people active. In Europe many programmes are specifically aimed at young people, as youth unemployment was considered a special problem. When refusing to participate, people may lose the right to assistance.[24]

> ### BOX 8.4 A EUROPEAN EXAMPLE OF ACTIVATION: DENMARK
>
> The first scheme of activation was the *Youth Allowance Scheme* (1990), in the beginning for individuals at age 18 and 19, then extended to all up to 24 and later extended to those above 25.
>
> The right to benefit was matched with an obligation to work. Activation took place after only two weeks on social assistance. The wage was a special low 'project wage'. (Rosdahl and Weise, 2001, p. 169)
>
> Since 1998 all people on social assistance must be activated unless sick, pregnant or with a small child if no public childcare is available. Individuals below 30 must participate after 13 weeks of getting social assistance, those above 30 only after 12 months.

The most ambitious programme to make welfare recipients participate in the labour market was started in the USA. Its purpose was to reduce the number of individuals whose income depended to a great extent on welfare payments. The reforms were successful insofar as this number declined drastically. Therefore other countries' policy planners became interested.

Besides the general social assistance programme for the poor, namely Food Stamps and the EITC support for people with low labour income, the most important programme was the federally legislated and federally funded 'Aid to Families with Dependent Children' (AFDC). It reached a comparatively high percentage of the population. It was started in the 1930s and was then considered primarily a help for widows. The AFDC transfers should supplant the male breadwinner. As married women with children were not supposed to work, widows with small children were considered to belong to the deserving poor. The disincentive to work was not seen a problem. The caseload remained small, somewhere between 1 and 2 per cent of the population.

In the mid-1960s things began to change. First, the number of households receiving AFDC transfers increased to about 5 per cent of the population. Second, the biggest group of AFDC recipients became never-married women with children, who often became recipients of welfare payments. Third, it was no longer seen as appropriate for women with children not to work.[25] The question of work incentives became important.

Starting in the mid-1980s, reforms were actively pursued, first on an experimental basis. In 1995 the whole system was changed at the federal level. The most important changes were, first, to limit the period of eligibility for transfers and, second, to fix the amount of federal funds handed over to the states. The first aspect should create incentives for the recipients to take a job, the second was aimed to encourage the states to implement reforms. The system is now known as 'Temporary Assistance for Needy Families' (TANF).

The states were given a great deal of freedom for detailed regulations. They differ in their strictness and liberality. By being more liberal a state cannot increase the funds it gets from the federal government. If a state decides to be more liberal, it has to use more of its own resources.

There is an upper limit of 60 months for which a household can be supported by using federal money. This rule does not apply to one spell of poverty, but to the period in receipt of TANF-support over a lifetime. Some states have legislated even shorter periods. Besides these rather punitive measures some incentives to take a job were introduced as well. First, people can remain for some time with Medicaid after having begun to work. Second, earning disregards were in many states extended. That means that for a specified period an individual taking a job can continue to receive a fraction of TANF- support. A dollar earned does not decrease the transfer by a dollar. Third, support for child-care was increased in many states. Fourth, funds for special training and counselling programmes were increased.

What are the effects of these changes? There are different aspects. First, how were the number of women receiving TANF-support affected? Second, how did labour market participation develop? Third, how were women leaving welfare affected?[26]

Within a period of three years the caseload has been halved. Labour force participation of single mothers with children increased between 1989 and 2000 by nearly 10 percentage points (Blank and Schmidt, 2000). It would be wrong to attribute the entire decrease of mothers receiving TANF benefits and the increase of labour force participation to the new social policy approach, as married mothers also increased labour supply, though at a lower rate. Indeed, labour market development in the USA was characterised by very strong demand in the 1990s. Even without a change of welfare legislation the number of people receiving support would have declined and labour market participation would have increased. In fact, the number of people receiving TANF benefits had already started to decline by 1994, two years before the reforms became effective. Nevertheless there is unanimity amongst studies that the new laws contributed to the decline of the numbers of families on welfare and the increase in labour market participation of single mothers with children.

There is a lot of research undertaken on how women fared who left welfare. It is clear that those who are pushed off welfare without having started to work are worse off after the reforms. It is too early to say how many will be affected this way as the first time the 60-month rule applied was at the end of the year 2000. Concerning women who started to work, it is unclear whether they are better off or not. The difficulty is in estimating how the same group would have fared had welfare laws not changed, in the same favourable macroeconomic circumstances and with the same changes of minimum wages. There are no data directly available to compare with. Cancian et al. (2000), using data from Wisconsin, report that money income did not increase for women leaving welfare in 1997, though earnings rose. Poverty remained high amongst those who had left welfare for work.[27] Schoeni and Blank (2000) conclude that family income increased and poverty was reduced, though the reforms before the switch to the TANF system had the greatest impact.

Be that as it may, it is far too early to say what will be the effects of increased labour market participation on long-term earnings. Furthermore, nobody knows what will happen if macroeconomic circumstances cease to be as favourable as they were in the 1990s.

APPENDIX 8.1

A Subjective Definition of Poverty
(Goedhart et al., 1977)

Could one ask people how much they need to break free of poverty? It is clear that different people would give different answers. The average of the answers cannot not be used for a threshold, because the answers may depend systematically on the actual situation of the person – that is, the threshold may be higher for individuals with higher income. There is an attempt to tackle this problem. As it was worked out at the University of Leyden (in the Netherlands) it is called the Leyden concept.

Assume a cardinal utility concept. The level of utility is not a definite number, but utility differences are expressed by a number. The way to find such a utility representation was to ask people how much income a household needs to feel excellent, to feel good, to have enough, to have just enough, to have barely enough, to have not enough, to be badly-off, and to be very badly-off. The interval [0,1] was divided into intervals of equal length and each of the statements was allocated to one of the points in the interval (1 = excellent, 0 = very badly-off). Each person responded according to his or her individual utility function.

If one assumes that for each individual the difference between the worded expressions of utility signifies the same utility difference, one can interpret data from a survey as information about different utility functions of individuals. Based on earlier work the authors argue that the utility function U(z) (z: income) can be fairly well approximated by a log-normal distribution with μ and σ as parameters.

$$U(z) = (1/\sigma\sqrt{2\pi})\int_0^z (1/t)\exp\{-1/2[\ln(t-\mu)/\sigma]^2\}dt$$

$$\equiv \Lambda(z;\mu,\sigma) \equiv N[\ln(z);\mu,\sigma]$$

The two parameters μ and σ cannot be interpreted as mean and variance of a probability distribution, as there is no uncertainty involved. They are individual welfare parameters, namely $\exp(\mu)$ was interpreted as the necessary income to be in the middle of the welfare scale. The higher μ, the more an individual needs for being at the middle of the utility scale (0.5). The parameter σ gives the slope of the utility function around its mean. It can be considered a measure of sensitivity of welfare to income at the mean. Figure 8.4 shows the distribution of perceived utility between zero and one depending on income for different values of μ (with the same $\sigma = 0.4$).

From a survey of 2500 households (1750 answers could be used) the authors calculated a regression for the parameter μ according to the following formula (fs: size of family, y: income of the household):[28]

$$\mu = \beta_0 + \beta_1 \ln(fs) + \beta_2 \ln(y) + \varepsilon$$

The estimated values of the parameters were:

$$\beta = 4.41; \beta_1 = 0.13; \beta_2 = 0.53.$$

The value of β_2 show that as actual income increases the household demands more to be at the middle of the welfare scale.

It was further asked how much the household needs as an absolute minimum. That question comprised two issues: first, how much satisfaction a household considered necessary for not being poor; second, how much income it needs for achieving that level of satisfaction. Households with higher actual income not only may demand higher income for achieving a specific position on the utility scale, they might require a higher grade on the utility scale as a minimum as well.

To test for that effect the relation between actual income and minimum required income was estimated. That gave different parameters from those estimated for the relation between μ and actual income.

$\beta_0^* = 3.60; \quad \beta_1^* = 0.12; \quad \beta_2^* = 0.60$

That is, the relation between the minimum income necessary for not being poor is different from the income necessary to be at the middle of the welfare scale. The income necessary to be at the middle of the welfare scale increases with growing income, while the minimum income for not being poor increases even faster.

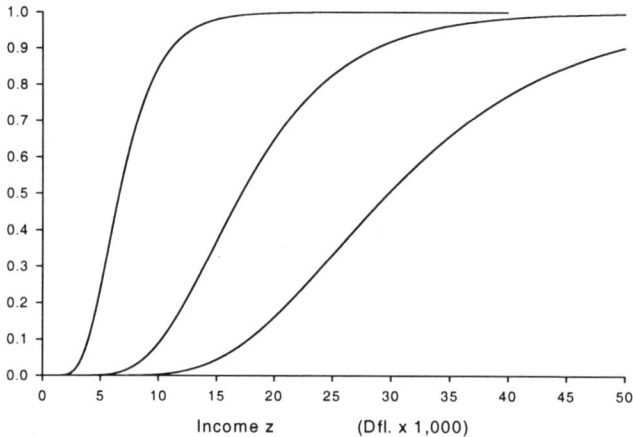

Figure 8.4 Utility as a function of income for a log-normal distribution

These two observations were used for construing a poverty threshold. To do so, the fact that poorer households need less income is interpreted in the following way: one can get accustomed to lower income – that is, if a person loses income she gets used to it and will finally have higher utility than she thought she would have with that income when she actually had a higher income. The converse applies when income is rising (see Figure 8.5).

Line I gives the minimum income as a function of actual income according to the estimation with the β^* values. For a household with income Y1 the minimum is M1. If the household experiences a decline of its income to M1, it will after some time assign to it a higher utility value because of the adaptation process. If the income is further reduced to the minimum income according to the new evaluation at M1 to M2, a further round of adaptation will occur. At y_{min}^* the process has come to an end. The value of y_{min}^* is considered a poverty line: those below have a minimum above their actual income if their income is increased; those above have a minimum below their actual income if their income is decreased.

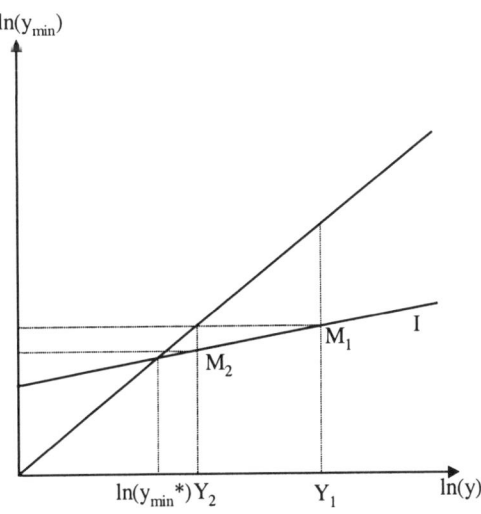

Figure 8.5 The construction of a poverty line

Table 8.20 Weighted means of income, official poverty thresholds, subjective income thresholds by family size for the Netherlands and the USA

USA $/year	Actual before tax income	Official poverty threshold	Subjective income threshold
1 person, <65 [a]	14.062	5.019	12.144
1 person, >=65 [a]	8.016	4.626	9.668
2 persons, <65 [a]	26.921	6.482	16.753
2 persons, >=65 [a]	17.102	5.837	15.641
3 persons	27.755	7.686	19.694
4 persons	30.815	9.860	22.374
Netherlands Dfl/year			
1 person, <65 [a]	22.922	12.890	17.173
1 person, >=65 [a]	21.048	13.173	22.498
2 persons, <65 [a]	37.952	18.788	22.025
2 persons, >=65 [a]	32.631	18.822	21.707
3 persons	33.487	19.731	23.753
4 persons	38.516	21.616	25.984

Note: [a] Age of reference person.

Source: de Vos and Garner (1991).

Table 8.20 gives the estimated poverty thresholds and compares them with administratively fixed thresholds. It is not surprising that the official thresholds are much lower. After all, administratively fixed thresholds influence some transfers. Keeping the threshold at a lower level reduces the burden on the budget. The relation between the two thresholds changes with the size of the household. This points to a different weighting scheme for children and further adults (see section 8.2 above). Children seem to be perceived as less of a burden by their parents than suggested by research based on the concept of compensation according to either the Engel method or the Rothbarth method. Interestingly the Dutch thresholds are more in line with each other than the American ones.

APPENDIX 8.2

Sen's Index of Poverty

In section 8.4. it was argued that simply counting the poor is not an appealing way to measure aggregate poverty – no information concerning the actual income of poor individuals is used. To calculate the aggregate poverty gap is a way to overcome this deficiency. However no information about inequality among the poor is used, as the weight of each poor person in the measure is simply the distance of income from the poverty line. The generalised poverty gap, the FGT index, avoids this flaw by making the weight rise non-linearly with the shortfall of income. As mentioned, this poverty measure has the disadvantage that it does not allow a suggestive interpretation.

Sen proposed a different measure of aggregate poverty (Sen, 1976) which takes into account inequality among the poor. The weight a poor person has in the measure is their rank order among the poor.[29]

$$P = H[\Gamma + (1 - \Gamma)G]$$

with H the head-count ratio, Γ, as in 8.4.2, the mean shortfall of income among the poor, and G the Gini-coefficient of income among them.

He showed that this index conforms to the monotony axiom, the transfer axiom and the monotony-sensitivity axiom. Furthermore if there is no inequality among the poor (G = 0), it is precisely the poverty gap (HΓ).

Though the absolute value of Sen's poverty index has no suggestive interpretation, differences between two poverty rates can be decomposed into a change of incidence of poverty (H), a change of intensity of poverty (Γ) and a change of inequality as expressed by the Gini coefficient (G) (Table 8.21).

This index has also a drawback in that it is not additively separable – that is, aggregate poverty of a population cannot be expressed as the weighted sum of poverty of its subgroups. This is due to the rerankings as analysed in Appendix 3.2. If two groups of a population are merged, it is likely that the rankings of some individuals change. A comparison of poverty rates is impossible in that case.

Table 8.21 Change of poverty according to Sen's poverty index and decomposition into components

	Percentage change in Sen poverty index	Incidence poverty rate	Intensity Income gap ratio	Inequality Gini (poor)
Austria 1983–1993	–10	–92	99	93
Canada 1985–1995	–17	66	20	14
Denmark 1983–1994	–31	91	4	5
Finland 1986–1995	–20	16	47	38
France 1984–1994	–32	14	52	34
Germany 1984–1994	63	76	14	9
Hungary 1991–1997	–35	36	30	34
Ireland 1987–1994	–48	–4	54	50
Italy 1984–1993	66	63	19	19
Japan 1984–1994	23	52	26	22
Mexico 1989–1994	2	142	5	–47
Netherlands 1984–1995	76	145	–30	–16
Sweden 1983–1995	25	35	44	21
Turkey 1987–1994	–3	54	46	0
USA 1985–1995	–5	135	–5	–30

Source: Förster and Pellizzari (2000).

APPENDIX 8.3

Economic Growth and Poverty – a Statistical Analysis

Can poverty vanish merely through as a result of economic growth? Namely when all incomes grow at the same rate? This, of course, is only possible when the poverty threshold in no way depends on the wealth of the economy.

A simple calculation: y, average income of a poor person; z, poverty threshold; g, rate of growth. How many years does it take until y equals at least z?

$$z = y(1 + g)^T$$

therefore

$$T = \ln(z/y)/\ln(1 + g)$$

If $g = 3$ and $y = z/2$, then $T = 20$. It will take 20 years until an average poor person has grown out of poverty. This doesn't seems bad, but it is a strong assumption that poverty levels which do not change with the wealth of an economy are reasonable welfare indicators. It is safe to assume that it will take much longer until the poor have escaped poverty through growth.

Nevertheless it is sensible to ask how much growth can contribute to the reduction of poverty. In order to do so empirically it is necessary to look at the changes of income distribution concomitant with economic growth. We want to know to what extent the change in poverty is a result of the changing income distribution and to what extent economic growth caused a decline of poverty. To pursue this question the change in poverty is analytically decomposed into a growth component, a redistribution component and a residual (Datt and Ravallion, 1992).

Let P_t be an index of poverty depending on the poverty line z, the mean income μ_t and the Lorenz curve L_t as a description of the income distribution.

$$P_t = P(z/\mu_t, L_t),$$

Poverty may change due to a change in any of these parameters. For the following analysis z is kept constant – an absolute standard of poverty which does not change as a result to economic growth. The growth component of the change of poverty is its change when mean income changes and the Lorenz curve remains constant at L_t.

$$G(t, t+n) \equiv P(z/\mu_{t+n}, L_t) - P(z/\mu_t, L_t)$$

The redistribution component is the change in poverty due to a change in the Lorenz curve, while holding μ_t constant.

$$D(t, t+n) \equiv P(z/\mu_t, L_{t+n}) - P(z/\mu_t, L_t),$$

If one wants to decompose a change in poverty between t and t + n into a change resulting from to higher mean income and changing income distribution, there is a difficulty, as the two components do not add up nicely. There is interaction between the two terms. To determine the total change of poverty it is necessary to add a residual.

$$P_{t+n} - P_t = G(t, t+n) + D(t, t+n) + R(t, t+n)$$

Poverty

This residual can be given an interpretation. A rearrangement of terms gives the following:

$$R(t, t+n) = G(t+n, t+n) - G(t+n, t)$$
$$= D(t+n, t+n) - D(t, t+n).$$

It is either the difference in the growth components with Lorenz curves at the beginning and the end of the period, or alternatively the difference of the redistribution components with the mean at the two ends of the period.

Data for India show that in India poverty was reduced due to strong growth and a slight redistribution in favour of the poor between 1977 and 1988. Holding the poverty threshold fixed, poverty was reduced. In Brazil poverty remained constant, though there was some growth of mean income. However that was countered by redistribution away from the poor (Tables 8.22 and 8.23).

Table 8.22 Poverty in India and Brazil since the late 1970s[a]

Poverty/inequality measure	1977–78	1981	1988
Rural India			
H	52.68	–	38.66
PG	16.03	–	9.40
P_2	6.67	–	3.25
Brazil			
H	–	26.46	26.47
PG	–	10.07	10.71
P_2	–	4.96	5.58

Table 8.23 Decomposition of the change of poverty

(a) Rural India (excluding consumer durables)

Period	Growth Component	Redistribution component	Residual	Total change in poverty
Head-count index (H)				
1977–78 to 88	–12.74	–0.46	–0.82	–14.02
Poverty gap index (PG)				
1977–78 to 88	–5.31	–1.26	–0.06	–6.63
P_2				
1977–78 to 88	–2.56	–0.99	0.13	–3.42

(b) Brazil

Period	Growth Component	Redistribution component	Residual	Total change in poverty
	Head-count index (H)			
1977–78 to 88	–4.49	4.46	0.04	0.01
	Poverty gap index (PG)			
1977–78 to 88	–2.34	3.19	–0.21	0.63
	P_2			
1977–78 to 88	–1.42	2.31	–0.27	0.62

Note: ^aPoverty measures in per cent; those for India are based on consumption excluding expenditure on durables. H: Head-count, PG: Poverty gap, P_2 : FGT Index with $\alpha = 2$.

Source: © with permission from Elsevier Science.

NOTES

1. It was customary to consider the consumption of meat as sign of not being poor. Meanwhile being a vegetarian is not uncommon among non-poor people.
2. In areas where poor people are concentrated public safety is often lower than in other areas. Though the crimes which are particularly disruptive of everyday life – small thefts, burglary, mugging – are more often committed by comparatively poor people, the majority of the victims are also poor – they live in the same area.
3. One should be aware that nutritional requirements are to some extent endogenous. People working hard need more calories.
4. This idea was introduced into economics by Lancaster (1966).
5. Sen mentions Adam Smith's example: a British labourer needs a cotton shirt to appear in public without being ashamed. A French labourer does not feel ashamed when having merely a linen shirt. In a rich society people need more in order not to feel as outsider.
6. It does not make sense to put a wheelchair in the basket of goods everybody must have for not being poor.
7. Wages were taken to be independent of time worked.
8. The cost function $c(u^*, p, a)$ determines the minimal costs of a bundle of goods to reach utility level u^*, when prices are the vector p, and the demographic characteristics are a.
9. To base this method in the standard utility framework, it is necessary to make special assumptions for the utility function, see Gronau (1988). For the handling of household-specific public goods, Nelson (1992).
10. There is another aspect to problems of time. The loss of welfare due to low income depends on the expected level of total income. For example, many students have low income and low consumption possibilities. If they had to stay on that level of consumption throughout their life, they would be poor. However low incomes and low command over resources are accepted by students for a short period.
11. There is a further reason to characterise the duration of poverty by measuring the time from the beginning of the first spell to the end of the last spell: when social assistance data are used as proxy for poverty, the statutes and administrative practices can influence the length of individual spells. Some systems accept repeated spells only if the assisted person manages to support himself from time to time. Other systems are prepared to give long term support without intermittent periods of self-support. A study by Kazepov and Voges (1998),

comparing social assistance in 13 European cities of 5 states, related the duration of the first spell of social assistance to its statutory construction and its administrative practices.
12. Poverty measures of GFT type have a further advantage: they are additive. That means that poverty of population can be expressed as the weighted sum of poverty of subgroups; for example, a country's poverty is the weighted sum of poverty in different regions, where the weights are the relative size of the regions. Other poverty measures depending also on values of distribution of income as well (for example, the Gini coefficient) do not have this property. See Appendix 8.2.
13. In the long run fertility will decrease if infant mortality goes down.
14. One of the advantages of using a relative poverty threshold as in the LIS is that one does not have to bother about purchasing power in different countries. Consider the following example of poverty rates in Germany, separately documented for the western parts and for those which formed the GDR.

The first column gives the head-count ratio of poverty at the 50 per cent of median income level, where the reference income is the income of the region. For the last three lines the common income distribution was used. For the second column the West German poverty level was used. This created extremely high poverty rates for East Germany. Poverty is declining according to that column, whereas according to column 1 it was increasing. In column 3 a common poverty threshold without correcting for different purchasing power parities was used. The poverty ratios for both parts of Germany are lower, however in West Germany poverty is increasing, whereas it was stable according to column 1. For column 4, again the threshold of the western parts were used, however a correction for different purchasing power was applied. Poverty rates for the eastern part are still smaller. Finally, in column 5 a common poverty threshold and corrections for purchasing power were used. Poverty is lower in both parts.

		Separately 1	Without correction for purchasing power		With correction for purchasing power	
			West 2	Together 3	West 4	Together 5
West	1990	10.3	10.3	5.5	10.3	7.3
	1991	9.9	9.9	6.5	9.9	7.5
	1992	10.1	10.1	7.4	10.1	7.9
East	1990	3.4	64.9	31.0	30.1	21.7
	1991	4.4	46.8	34.3	20.1	16.3
	1992	5.3	28.9	22.6	17.8	14.8
Together	1990	8.8	22.1	15.3	14.6	10.4
	1991	8.7	17.7	12.4	12.0	9.4
	1992	9.1	13.9	10.5	11.6	9.3

Source: Andreß (1999), p. 126.

If the same absolute level for a threshold were used all over the EU states, poverty rates would diverge much more strongly between different countries. Correcting for different purchasing power does not suffice to give a realistic picture of poverty, as absolute living standards are very different.
15. Marx had a theory as to why workers must become poor in a capitalist economy.
16. This does not imply that the individual is in one way or another accountable for his or her poverty. Once more, the difference between a positive statement – namely that there are personal characteristics which contributed to poverty – should not be mixed with a normative statement.
17. Many activities which carry a high risk of becoming poor were simply forbidden: migration, not working, and so on.
18. That income is achieved at about 2000 hours of work per year at the minimum wage. That is far above the normal working time in Europe or the USA.
19. Resources are squandered from the point of view of poverty reduction.

20. Another way to look at wage supplements is to consider them as wage subsidy or to make very low wages socially acceptable.
21. Whether lone mothers are seen as 'deserving' or 'not deserving' is a politically interesting problem. On the one hand, it is accepted that lone mothers do have special problems and therefore their children as well. On the other hand, having a child without being married is by some considered inappropriate. Nadine Lefaucher (1995) notes that the generosity of the French scheme of support for lone mothers was shaped by the decision to pacify anti-abortion groups.
22. That may be due to the fact that Sweden considers every individual above the age of 18 as a household on its own whether living on parent's income or not. That very much affects the student population.
23. The data cannot be compared with those of Table 8.16. There, poverty reduction was calculated for income before any transfers. Behrendt's study considered poverty for incomes including social security transfers.
24. There is a legal problem. These activities should not turn into real jobs as that would demand complying with minimum wage regulations, job protection, and so on. On the other hand, some consider that type of work as forced labour which contradicts human rights. Neither Germany nor Austria developed special workfare programmes (up to 2002) which may be due to their experiences with forced labour during the Nazi period.
25. That may be partly due to the general change of outlook concerning labour market participation of women and partly due to the fact that never-married mothers were by many seen as having inflicted their poverty on themselves. Furthermore many think that AFDC transfers contributed to the increase in the number of births out of wedlock births.
26. A further question was whether the number of children born out of wedlock decreased.
27. The state of Wisconsin became famous for the early implementation of welfare reforms.
28. For σ no systematic estimation was attempted. A value of 0.4 for σ was assumed.
29. In a welfarist interpretation this amounts to making the shortfall of utility of an individual dependent not on the shortfall of income from the poverty line but on the number of poor individuals with higher income.

REFERENCES

Andreß, Hans-Jürgen (1999), *Leben in Armut*, Opladen: Westdeutscher Verlag.

Bane, Mary Jo and David T. Ellwood (1986), 'Slipping Into and Out of Poverty: The Dynamics of Spells', *Journal of Human Resources*, 21, pp. 1–23.

Behrendt, Christina (2002), *At the Margins of the Welfare State: Social Assistance and the Alleviation of Poverty in Germany, Sweden and the United Kingdom*, Aldershot: Ashgate (forthcoming).

Blank, Rebecca M. and Patricia Ruggles (1996), 'When Do Women Use Aid to Families with Dependent Children and Food Stamps', *Journal of Human Resources*, 31, pp. 57–89.

Blank, Rebecca M. and Lucie Schmidt (2000), 'Work and Wages', mimeo, University of Michigan, mimeo.

Buhr, Petra (1995), *Dynamik von Armut*, Opladen: Westdeutscher Verlag.

Buhr, Petra (1998), *Armut im Wunderland? Wege in die und aus der Sozialhilfe in Schweden und Deutschland*, Universität Bremen, Sonderforschungsbereich 186, Arbeitspapier No.51.

Buhr, Pera, Stephan Leibfried, Monika Ludwig and Wolfgang Voges, *Passages through Welfare. The Bremen Approach to the Analysis of Claimants' Careers in 'Publicly Administered Poverty'*, Discussion Paper 3.

Callan, Tim, Brian Noland and Christopher T. Whelan (1993), 'Resources, Deprivation, and the Measurement of Poverty', *Journal of Social Policy*, 22, pp. 141–71.

Cancian, Maria, Robert Haveman, Daniel R. Meyer and Barbara Wolfe (2000), *Before and After TANF: The Economic Well-Being of Women Leaving Welfare*, Institute for Research on Poverty, Special Report 77.

Clark, Stephen, Richard Hemming and David Ulph (1981), 'On Indices for the Measurement of Poverty', *Economic Journal*, 91, pp. 515–25.

Conniffe, Denis (1992), 'The Non-Constancy of Equivalence Scales', *Review of Income and Wealth*, 38, pp. 429–44.

Dalaker, Joseph and Bernadette D. Proctor (2000), *Poverty in the United States*, www.censu.gov/prod/2000pvos.

Datt, Gaurav and Martin Ravallion (1992), 'Growth and Redistribution Components of Changes in Poverty Measures', *Journal of Development Economics*, 38, pp. 275–95.

Deaton, Angus S. and John Muellbauer (1986), 'On Measuring Child Cost: With Applications to Poor Countries', *Journal of Political Economy*, 94, pp. 720–44.

de Vos, Klaas and Thesia I. Garner (1991), 'An Evaluation of Subjective Poverty Definitions: Comparing Results from the U.S. and the Netherlands', *Review of Income and Wealth*, 37, pp. 267–85.

Duncan, Alan and Christopher Giles (1996), 'Labour Supply Incentives and Recent Credit Reforms', *Economic Journal*, 106, pp. 142–55.

Eardley, Tony, Jonathan Bradshaw, John Ditch, Ian Gough and Peter Whiteford (1996), *Social Assistance in OECD Countries*, London: HMSO.

Ellwood, David T. (2000), 'The Impact of Earned Income Tax Credit and Social Policy Reforms on Work, Marriage, and Living Arrangements', mimeo, John F. Kenndedy School of Government, Harvard University.

Ellwood, David T. and Jeffrey B. Liebmann (2001), *The Middle Class Parent Penalty: Child Benefits in the U.S. Tax Code*, Cambridge (Mass.), NBER Working Paper 8031.

Förster, Michael F. and Michele Pellizzari (2000), *Trends and Driving Factors in Income Distribution and Poverty in the OECD Area*, OECD, Labour Market and Social Policy-Occasional Paper No. 42.

Furniss, Edgar S (1920), *The Position of the Laborer in a System of Nationalism*, New York: August M. Kelley, 1985.

Garfinkel, Irwin and Robert Haveman (1977), 'Earnings Capacity, Economic Status, and Poverty', *Journal of Human Resources*, 12, pp. 49–69.

Goedhart, Theo, Victor Halberstadt, Arie Kapetyn and Bernhard van Praag (1977), 'The Poverty Line: Concept and Measurement', *Journal of Human Resources*, 12, pp. 503–19.

Gronau, Reuben (1988), 'Consumption Technology and the Intrafamily Distribution of Resources', *Journal of Political Economy*, 96, pp. 1183–205.

Haddad, Lawrence and Ravi Kanbur (1990), 'How Serious is the Neglect of Intra-Household Inequality?', *Economic Journal*, 100, pp. 866–81.

Haveman, Robert and Lawrence Buron (1993), 'Escaping Poverty through Work: The Problem of Low Earnings Capacity in the United States, 1973–88', *Review of Income and Wealth*, 39, pp. 141–57.

Hotz, Joseph V. and John Karl Scholz (2001), *The Earned Income Tax Credit*, Cambridge (Mass.), NBER Working Paper 8078.

Jenkins, Stephen P. (1991), 'Poverty Measurement and the Within-Household Distribution: Agenda for Action', *Journal of Social Policy*, 20, pp. 457–83.

Kakwani, Nanak (1989), 'On Measuring Undernutrition', *Oxford Economic Papers*, 41, pp. 528–51.
Kazepov, Yuri and Wolgang Voges (1998), 'Benefit Recipients: Characteristics and Temporal Patterns', in: Chiara Saraceno (coordinator) *Evaluation of Social Policies at the Local Urban Level: Income Support for the Abel Bodied*, ESOPO Contract No. ERB-SOE2-CT-95-3001.
Kornai, Janos (1997), 'Reform of the Welfare Sector in the Post-Communist Countries: A Normative Approach', in: J. Nelson Ch. Tilly and L. Walker (eds), *Transforming Post-Communist Political Economies*, Washington D.C.: National Academy Press, pp. 272–98.
Lambert, Peter (1989), *The Distribution and Redistribution of Income*, Oxford: Basil Blackwell.
Lancaster, Kevin J. (1966), 'A new approach to consumer theory', *Journal of Political Economy*, 74, pp. 132–57.
Lefaucher, Nadine (1995), 'French Policies towards Lone Parents: Social Categories and Social Politics', in K. McFate, R. Lawson and W.J. Wilson (eds), *Poverty, Inequality and the Future of Social Policy*, New York: Russell Sage Foundation, pp. 275–89.
Leisering, Lutz and Sephan Leibfried (1999), *Time and Poverty in Western Welfare States*, Cambridge: Cambridge University Press.
Lødemel Ivar and Heather Trickey (eds) (2001), *'An Offer You Can't Refuse'. Workfare in International Perspective*, Bristol: The Policy Press.
Lutz, Hedwig, Michael Wagner, Walter Wolf (1993), *Von Ausgrenzung bedroht*, Forschungsberichte aus Sozial- und Arbeitsmarktpolitik, Wien: Bundesministerium für Arbeit und Soziales.
McGregor, P.P.L. and V.K. Borooah (1992), 'Is Low Spending or Low Income a Better Indicator of Whether or Not a Household is Poor: Some Results From the 1985 Family Expenditure Survey', *Journal of Social Policy*, 21, pp. 53–69.
Moffitt, Robert (1983), 'An Economic Model of Welfare Stigma', *American Economic Review*, 73, pp. 1023–35.
Naifeh, Mary (1998), 'Trap Door? Revolving Door? Or Both?' US Census Bureau, *The Official Statistics*, 8 July.
Nelson, Julie A. (1992), 'Methods of Estimating Household Equivalence Scales: An Empirical Investigation', *Review of Income and Wealth*, 38, pp. 295–310.
OECD (2001), *OECD Employment Outlook*, Paris.
Orshansky, Mollie (1965), 'Counting the Poor: Another Look at the Poverty Profile', *Social Security Bulletin*, 28, pp. 3–29.
Pashardes, Panos (1991), 'Contemporaneous and Intertemporal Child Costs', *Journal of Public Economics*, 45, pp. 191–214.
Ravallion, Martin (1992), *Poverty Comparison*, Washington D.C.: The World Bank.
Riphahn, Regina T. (2000), *Rational Poverty or Poor Rationality. The Take-up of Social Assistance Benefits*, Bonn, IZA Discussion Paper No.124.
Rosdahl, Anders and Hanne Weise (2001), 'When all must be active – workfare in Denmark', in: I. Lødemel and H. Trickey (eds) (2001), *'An Offer You Can't Refuse' Workfare in International Perspective*, Bristol: The Policy Press, pp. 159–80.
Schoeni, Robert F. and Rebecca M. Blank (2000), 'What Has Welfare Reform Accomplished? Impacts on Welfare Participation, Employment, Income, Poverty and Family Structure', mimeo, University of Michigan.
Sen, Amartya (1976), 'Poverty: An Ordinal Approach to Measurement', *Econometrica*, 44, pp. 219–31.

Sen, Amartya (1983), 'Poor, Relatively Speaking', *Oxford Economic Papers*, 35, pp. 153–69.
Sen, Amartya (1984), 'Family and Food: Sex Bias in Poverty', in: A. Sen, *Resources, Values and Development*, Cambridge (Mass.): Harvard University Press, 1997, pp. 346–68.
Sen, Amartya (1985), *Commodities and Capabilities*, Amsterdam and New York: North Holland.
Smeeding Timothy M., Michael O'Higgins and Lee Rainwater (eds), *Poverty, Inequality and Income Distribution in Comparative Perspective*, New York: Harvester/Wheatsheaf.
Smeeding, Timothy M., Lee Rainwater, Martin Rein, Richard Hauser and Gaston Schaber (1990), 'Income Poverty in Seven Countries: Initial Estimates from the LIS Database', in T. Smeeding, M. O'Higgins and L. Rainwater (eds), *Poverty, Inequality and Income Distribution in Comparative Perspective*, New York: Harvester/Wheatsheaf, pp. 57–76.
Smeeding, Timothy M., Peter Saunders, John Coder, Stephen Jenkins, Johan Fritzell, Aldi J.M. Hagenaars, Richard Hauser and Michael Wolfson (1993), 'Poverty Inequality, and Family Living Standards Impacts across Seven Nations: The Effects of Noncash Subsidies for Health, Education and Housing', *Review of Income and Wealth*, 39, pp. 229–56.
Smeeding, Timothy M., Lee Rainwater and Gary Burtless (2000), *United States Poverty in a Cross-National Context*, Luxembourg Income Study, Working Paper 244.
Stelzer-Orthofer, Christa (1997), *Armut und Zeit*, Opladen: Leske+Buderich.
Stevens, Ann Huff (1994), 'The Dynamics of Poverty Spells', *American Economic Review*, Papers and Proceedings, 84, pp. 34–7.
Torrey, Barbara B. Timothy M. Smeeding and Debra Bailey (1997), 'Vulnerable Populations in Central Europe', in: J. Nelson Ch. Tilly and L. Walker (eds), *Transforming Post-Communist Political Economies*, Washington D.C.: National Academy Press, pp. 351–69.
Trickey, Heather and Robert Walker (2001), 'Steps to compulsion within British labour market policies', in: I. Lødemel and H. Trickey (eds), *'An Offer You Can't Refuse' Workfare in International Perspective*, Bristol: The Policy Press, pp. 181–213.
Waldmann, Robert J.(1992), 'Income Distribution and Infant Mortality', *Quarterly Journal of Economics*, pp. 1283–302.

Index

Abbring, J.H. 225
Abraham, K.G. 244, 246
absentee fathers, *see* alimony
accident insurance 43, 91, 242–3
active labour market policy 226–37
  basic ideas 226–9
    methods 227–8
    objectives 228–9
  evaluation of 235–7
  special programmes 229–35
    employment premiums 230–31
    subsidising employment 232–5
    training and counselling
      programmes 228, 231–2, 236
added worker effect 213, 249n.
addiction 66, 85, 228, 231, 309
Adema, W. 2, 3
admission rates to inpatient care
    institutions 119
'adult goods' 291–2
adverse selection 38–9
  in insurance market 45–6, 100, 114, 165
ageing
  and employment/unemployment
    rates 204, 215
  health policy and 85, 98, 100, 119, 124
  see also care services; pensions
Aid to Families with Dependent
    Children (AFDC) 324
AIDS/HIV 83, 101, 102, 103, 104, 108, 117, 120, 126–7n.
Akerlof, G. 40n., 250n.
Algemeene Wet Bijzondere Ziektekosten
  (AWBZ) 92
alimony 272–3
allocative effects of social policy 49, 51–5
  family policy 267, 269, 274

  health insurance 55, 111–20
  poverty alleviation programmes 55, 314
  unemployment benefits 220–25
Altman, D. 114
altruism 46, 47, 66
Anand, P. 108
Andreß, H.-J. 335n.
Anell, A. 89
Angola, life expectancy in 304
annuities 144, 147, 156–7, 162, 164–6
Aronson, J.R. 74–6
Arulampalam, W. 214–15
asset portfolios, choice of 162–4
asset value of a job 248
Association génerale des institutions
  de retaite des cadres (AGIRC)
  137–8
Associations pour le regime de retaite
  complementaire des salaries
  (ARRCO) 137–8
Assurance-maladie 87
asymmetric information 38–9, 42, 44, 100, 115
Atkinson, A.B. 4, 218, 221, 223
Auerbach, A.J. 185
Ausgleichszulage 139
Australia
  care services in 189
  pension system in 134
  pensions expenditure in 133
  return on annuities in 166
  social assistance programmes in 317, 318
Austria
  birth rate in 179, 262
  dependency ratios in 180
  emergency fund in 47
  employment rates in 203
  extra-marital births in 274n.

family policy in 257, 259, 262–4, 266, 268, 269, 273, 318
health services in 82, 87, 89–91, 106
  admission rates to inpatient care institutions 119
  care services 188, 189–90
  employment in 118
  expenditure on 79, 80
housing policy in 30
labour market flows in 198–9
life expectancy in 178
long-term unemployment in 227
pension system in 138–41, 156, 160, 167, 168, 174, 175, 182–3, 318
pensions expenditure in 133, 181
population aged 75 or over in 188
poverty in 281–2, 293–4, 331
  programmes to reduce 317, 318, 319
unemployment benefits in 219, 220, 226
unemployment distribution in 209
unemployment rates in 201

Badelt, C. 190
Baily, M.N. 89, 120, 125n.
Bane, M.J. 296
Barendregt, J.J. 84, 125n.
Barro, R.J. 156
basic needs 281
Baumol's disease 117, 188
Becker, I. 122
Behrendt, C. 320, 321
Behrens, C.S. 123, 124
Belgium
  long-term unemployment in 227
  pension system in 182
  pensions expenditure in 133
  poverty in 307
    programmes to reduce 319
Bellmann equations 248
benefit–cost ratio 60
Bentolila, S. 211, 212
bequests 150, 154, 155–6, 165, 169
Berger, M.C. 266
Berk, M.L. 80
Berndt, E.B. 117
Besley, T. 89
Beveridge, William 20n.
Beveridge curve 247

Beveridge plan 82
Bird, E.J. 57
birth control 258
birth rates 120, 124, 145, 179, 257–8, 261, 262
Bismarck, Otto von 17, 20n., 242
Björklund, A. 236
Black, D.A. 266
Blanchard, O. 154, 245
Blanchet, D. 136, 172
Blank, R.M. 15, 321, 325, 326
Blumenthal, D. 127n.
Blundell, R. 172
Böheim, R. 214
Booth, A.L. 238, 244
Borjas, G.J. 84, 226
Borooah, V.K. 280, 281
borrowing constraints 170
bounded transfers 62–5
  economic arguments in favour of 65–8
Brazil
  life expectancy in 304
  poverty in 333–4
Breyer, F. 154, 156, 190n.
Broome, J. 107
Brown, J.R. 165
Brunner, J.K. 156
Buechtemann, C.F. 244
Buhr, P. 295, 317
Bundesamt für Sozialversicherung 145
Bundesministerium für Arbeit und Soziales 209
Burckhauser, R.V. 191n.
Buron, L. 288
Busse, R. 91
Bussemaker, J. 20n.
Bütler, M. 180

Cahuc, P. 252n.
Callan, T. 282
calorie intake, poverty measured by 300–301
Cameroon, life expectancy in 304
Canada
  family policy in 268
  pensions expenditure in 133
  poverty in 307, 308, 331
    programmes to reduce 312, 318
  unemployment benefits in 219, 226
Cancian, M. 326

capital market imperfections 173
capital stock 150–51, 154, 155, 156, 178, 186
capitation fees 88, 92, 97, 113, 114, 120
car insurance 46
Card, D. 251n.
cardiovascular disease 87
Cardon, J.H. 46
care services 187–90
Carrasquillo, O. 94
Carrington, W.J. 250n.
Casperson, E. 8
Ceaucescu, Nicolai 257
Chiappori, P.-A. 46
child benefits 19n., 262, 263–5, 267
child care provision 257, 258, 265, 266, 267, 268, 269, 325
children
   health insurance for 96, 103, 106, 110, 118
   number of 6, 51, 57, 67, 73, 94, 122, 123, 179, 187, 258, 259–60, 265, 266
      extra costs for household due to increase in 289–94, 330
      poverty threshold varying with 305
   parental responsibility for 318–19
   poverty rates of 307
   rights of 258–9
Children's Health Insurance Programme (CHIP) 96
Chile, pension system in 147–8, 161, 162, 165
choice, rational, *see* choice theoretic approach; rational choice assumption
choice theoretic approach 81–4, 107
Clark, S. 299
Cochrane, J.H. 100
communication, resources necessary for 285, 286
compensated (Hicks') demand function 68–70
compensating variation 68–70
concentration curve 74–6
Conniffe, D. 293
consistency assumption 11
constrained optimisation 13–14
consumption
   durable and non-durable 212, 280
   reduction due to unemployment 210–13
consumption bundles 282
consumption tax 7–8, 13–14
contagious diseases 99, 102
Cooper, P.F. 94
co-ordination failures 46–7
corn laws 251n.
cost function, household 290
costs of health services, increases in 111–16
Council of Europe 274n.
Crawford, V.P. 191n.
crèches, *see* child care provision
Cubeddu, L. 186–7
Culyer, A.J. 109
Cunningham, P.J. 98
Currie, J. 118
Cutler, D.M. 80, 87, 94, 100, 114, 125 and n., 126nn.
Czech Republic
   employment rates in 203
   health expenditure in 79
   pensions expenditure in 133
   poverty in 307
   unemployment rates in 201

Dalaker, J. 282, 305, 306
Daniels, N. 110
Datt, G. 332
Davidson, C. 230–31
de Vos, K. 142, 329
Deaton, A.S. 127n., 290–92
deductibles 45, 103, 104, 113, 126n.
defined benefit systems 136, 138, 143, 144, 168
defined contribution systems 136, 137, 138, 143, 144, 168
demand management 197–8, 227
demographic aims of family policy 257–8
demographic changes
   and health services 119–20, 124
   and pension systems 152–4, 157–60, 178–84
Denmark
   care services in 189
   extra-marital births in 274n.
   family policy in 268
   long-term unemployment in 227

poverty in 331
dental care 84, 85, 110
dependency ratios 179–80
diabetes 89, 110, 111
Diagnosis Related Group Rates 113, 114, 127n.
Diamond, P.A. 94, 145
difference in difference method 216, 270
diminishing marginal utility 84, 85, 210
disability pensions 59–61, 133, 139, 142, 147, 164
discouraged workers 202–3
Disney, R. 143
displacement, wage reduction due to 216–17
displacement effect 230, 231
distributional effects of social policy, *see* redistribution
divorce 146, 256, 272, 309, 311
doctors
  general practitioners 88, 106
  number of 89, 90, 102
Dolan, P. 107
Dolton, P. 228
Doyle, S. 165, 166
Drèze, J. 31
Duncan, A. 314
Dworkin, R. 77n.
Dynarski, S. 211, 212, 213

Eardley, T. 317, 318
early notification rules 243
early retirement 139, 142, 143, 145, 147, 164, 166, 170–73, 174, 203
Earned Income Tax Credit (EITC) 234, 265, 313, 316, 324
earnings capacity 287–8
economic approach to social policy 9–14
economic growth, and poverty 277–8, 331–4
education
  access to 4, 8, 58, 66, 265–6, 278, 279, 283
  and earnings capacity 288
  and employment rates 204
  financing of 4, 8, 39, 58, 260–61
  and pensions 177–8, 186–7
  vouchers for 63, 126n., 274n.
Edwards, S. 147

effects of social policy 49–61
  allocative effects, *see* allocative effects of social policy
  distributive effects, *see* redistribution
efficiency 3–4
  in health services provision 107–8, 111–16
  of wage subsidies 315–16
efficiency wage models 250n.
Elias, P. 214
Ellis, R.P. 104, 126n.
Ellwood, D.T. 15, 265, 296, 313, 314
Elmeskov, J. 202
emergency funds 47
emergency treatment 94, 98
employment in health services 118–19
employment premiums 230–31
employment rates
  female 169, 203–4, 273, 325
  international comparisons of 169, 203–4
  as labour market measure 203–4
  male 169, 203–4
employment vouchers 233
endowments, changes in 30–31, 152–4
Engel curves 282
Engel method 291–2, 330
Equitable Life 164
equity 3–4
  in health services provision 104, 105, 108–11, 118
equivalence scales 289–94, 326–30
equivalent variation 77n.
Ermisch, J.F. 273, 274
Esping-Andersen, G. 16
Ethiopia, life expectancy in 304
EU compromise scale 293–4
European Central Bank 191n.
European Commission 182
Eurosclerosis 234, 244
evaluation of ALMP programmes 235–7
expected utility function, *see* Neumann–Morgenstern utility function
expenditures, low, as indicator of poverty 279–82
experience rating 226
experimental method 235–7
extra-marital births 256, 257, 272, 274n., 336n.

Fagan, C. 267
fair insurance 36–7, 42, 44–5, 54–5, 121, 157, 174
Fallick, B.C. 216, 217
Familienlastenausgleichsfond (FLAF) 262
families
 health insurance and 103, 123
 pensions and 175
 policies supporting, *see* family policy
 private transfers within 213
 structures of 212, 256, 261, 271
 unemployment insurance through 212
Family Credit 234, 313–14
family policy 5, Ch. 7
 ideology of 256–7
 instruments of family support 262–7
  allocative effects of 267
   Austrian system of maternity leave and family allowances 262–4
   distributive effects of 263–5, 266
   ways to support families 264–6
 and poverty alleviation 264, 265, 271–2, 273–4, 318
 reasons for 257–61
 see also lone mothers; maternity benefit; maternity leave; parental leave
farmers, pensions for 137, 138, 141, 160
Fattore, G. 89
Felder, S. 127n.
fertility rates, *see* birth rates
Finkelstein, A. 165
Finland
 employment rates in 203
 family policy in 268
 pension system in 171, 182
 poverty in 307, 331
  programmes to reduce 318
 unemployment rates in 201
firms, state regulation of 5
first welfare theorem 26–8
Fischer, S. 154
Fishback, P.V. 43, 242–3
fixed-term contracts 244, 245
Foley, D.K. 249n.
food
 characteristics and achievements associated with 286
 expenditure on 282, 289, 292–3, 305

food stamps 62, 324
Förster, M.F. 213, 331
Foster-Green-Thornbeck (FGT) index 299
Fox, L. 136, 148
France
 dependency ratios in 180
 employment rates in 169, 203
 family policy in 257, 266, 268, 269, 318
 health services in 87
  admission rates to inpatient care institutions 119
  care services 189
  employment in 118
  expenditure on 79, 80
 labour contract regulation in 245
 life expectancy in 178
 long-term unemployment in 227
 pension system in 136–8, 168, 182, 318
 pensions expenditure in 133
 population aged 75 or over in 188
 poverty in 307, 331
  programmes to reduce 318, 319
 social security wealth in 172
 unemployment benefits in 219
 unemployment rates in 201
Fuchs, V.R. 191n.
funded pension schemes 135–6, 141, 143, 145–9 *passim*
 asset portfolios selected by 162–4
 compared with PAYG systems 149–60, 183, 186–7
 basic ideas 149–54
 effect of shocks 157–60, 178
 risks in 163–4
Furniss, E.S. 277

Gangl, M. 250n.
Garber, A.M. 89, 120, 125n.
Garfinkel, I. 287–8
Garner, T.I. 329
gender pay gap 269–71
gender specific policies 261
general equilibrium, welfare properties of 22–31
general practitioners (GPs) 88, 106
generalised poverty gap 299–301, 330
Gerdtham, Ulf-G. 80, 125n.

Germany
  accident insurance in 242
  active labour market policy in 229
  birth rate in 179
  consumption reduction due to
    unemployment in 211, 212
  dependency ratios in 180
  employment rates in 169, 203, 204
  family policy in 257, 259–60, 265,
    266, 268, 269, 273, 318
  health services in 43, 82, 87, 91–2,
    122, 184
    admissions to inpatient care
      institutions 119
    care services 188, 189
    employment in 118
    expenditure on 79, 80, 116
  life expectancy in 178
  long-term unemployment in 227
  pension system in 141–2, 149, 160,
    168, 171, 182, 183–4, 318
  pensions expenditure in 133, 181
  population aged 75 or over in 188
  poverty in 307, 308, 331, 335n.
    programmes to reduce 311, 312,
    317–21 passim
  unemployment benefits in 219, 224
  unemployment rates in 201, 204,
    206
Giles, C. 314
Gini coefficient 71–6, 330, 331
Glennester, H. 88
Glied, S. 114
Goedhart, T. 326
Goodin, R.E. 16
goods
  characteristics and achievements
    associated with 285–7
  lack of, as indicator of poverty
    279–82
Gordon, M. 82
Gorter, C. 236
government bonds 165
government insurance 94, 95
Greece, life expectancy in 178
Gregg, P. 213
Gronau, R. 334
Grossman, M. 81
Gruber, J. 53, 94, 114, 118, 145, 211,
  212, 213

Haddad, L. 294, 300–301
Hadorn, D.C. 109, 111, 127n.
Hamermesh, D. 216
Harvard University 100, 114
Haveman, R. 287–8
hazard rate 207–8, 223, 224, 228, 229,
  232, 236, 247
head-count measure 297–303, 330, 331,
  333–4
health
  monetary value of 81, 86–7
  utility of 107
health insurance 5, 6, 14, 17, 18
  access to, see health policy
  adverse selection in market for 46,
    100, 114
  allocative effects of, see health policy
  competition between providers of 43,
    87, 91–3, 99, 103
  distributive effects of, see health
    policy
  employer-provided 94, 95, 102
  for high-risk individuals 98, 102,
    103–4, 123
  maternity benefits included in 53
  objectives of, see health policy
  organisational structures for, see
    health policy
  premium for 42, 89, 91–2, 93, 96,
    100, 103, 114
    subsidy for 87, 94, 97
  private 2, 88, 89, 92, 94, 95, 106
  see also disability pensions; sickness
    benefits
Health Maintenance Organisations
  (HMOs) 114
health policy Ch. 4
  allocative effects of 55, 111–20
    cost increases 116–20
    efficiency problems 111–16
  approaches to 81–6
  children and 257, 262, 265, 266
  distributive effects of 56–7, 76–7,
    121–5
    horizontal redistribution 123
    intergenerational 124–5, 184
    over life-cycle 123–4
    vertical redistribution 121–2
  health expenditure 79–80, 84, 85, 87,
    88–9, 93, 95, 116

objectives of 98–111
    health insurance contracts and 98–9
    market problems and 99–101
    social policy aims (normative aspects) and 101–11
  organisational structures for 87–98
    mandatory public insurance 87, 92, 93, 97, 101
    public support of access to health services 87, 94–8
    publicly organised 87, 88–9
    social insurance institutions 87
      with competition 91–3, 103
      without competition 98–91
  see also health insurance
'healthy', definition of 84–5
Heckman, J.J. 232, 251n.
Hendel, I. 46
Hicks' demand function 68–70
HIV/AIDS 83, 101, 102, 103, 104, 108, 117, 120, 126–7n.
Höchstbeitragsgrundlage 138
Holmlund, B. 53
Holzmann, R. 179, 183
Homburg, S. 157
homelessness 10, 12, 25, 26, 29–30
hospital beds, number of 89, 102
hospitals 90, 92, 93, 96, 97, 114, 187
  admission rates to 119
  length of stay in 120
Hotz, J.V. 313
household, definition of 289, 318–19
Houseman, S.N. 244, 246
housing policy 10, 12, 29–30, 55
  rent subsidies 64–5
Hubbard, G.R. 191n.
Human Rights Convention 258
Hungary
  employment rates in 203
  health expenditure in 79
  life expectancy in 178
  pensions expenditure in 133
  poverty in 307, 331
  unemployment rates in 201
Hunt, J. 224, 245
Hurley, J. 81, 107, 125n.

Ichino, A. 211, 212
Iglehart, J.K. 95–6
Iglesias, A. 136

immunisation 66
income, low, as indicator of poverty 279–85
income distribution, measures of 59, 70–77, 302; *see also* poverty
income effect 54, 62–3, 70, 230, 267
indefinite labour contracts 245
India
  life expectancy in 304
  poverty in 333–4
Indonesia, equivalence scales for 291, 292
inequality, measures of 59, 70–77, 302; *see also* poverty
infant mortality 284, 303
inflation, annuities affected by 164–5
information
  asymmetric 38–9, 42, 44, 100, 115
  lack of 48–9, 83, 101
intergenerational accounting (IA) 185–7
International Monetary Fund (IMF) 182
investment subsidies 234–5
Ireland
  employment rates in 203
  extra-marital births in 274n.
  health services in
    care services 189
    expenditure on 80
  life expectancy in 178
  pensions expenditure in 133
  poverty in 307, 331
    programmes to reduce 318
  unemployment benefits in 318
  unemployment rates in 201
Israel, poverty in 308
  programmes to reduce 312
Italy
  active labour market policy in 229
  birth rate in 179
  consumption reduction due to unemployment in 212
  dependency ratios in 180
  employment rates in 169, 203, 204
  extra-marital births in 274n.
  family policy in 268
  health services in 87, 89
    admission rates to inpatient care institutions 119
    care services 189
    employment in 118

Index

life expectancy in 178
long-term unemployment in 227
pension system in 168, 182, 318
pensions expenditure in 181
population aged 75 or over in 188
poverty in 307, 331
  programmes to reduce 318, 319
social expenditure in 2
unemployment benefits in 219
unemployment rates in 201, 204, 206

Jacobson, L.L. 217
Jacoby, H.G. 67
Jacobzone, S. 119, 189
Jahoda, M. 210, 213
Jamaican Nutrition and Milk Programme 67–8
Japan
  birth rate in 179
  dependency ratios in 180
  employment rates in 203
  health expenditure in 116
  pension system in 182
  pensions expenditure in 181
  population aged 75 or over in 188
  poverty in 331
  unemployment benefits in 219
  unemployment rates in 201
Jenkins, S.P. 73, 294
job matching 246–9
Johnson, P. 172
Johnson, R.F. 81
Jones, M. 190n.
Jönsson, B. 80, 125n.

Kahneman, D. 40n.
Kakwani, N.C. 73, 302
Kalb, G.R.J. 236
Kanbur, R. 294, 300–301
Kantor, S.E. 43, 242–3
Kapetyn, A. 142
Kazepov, Y. 334n.
Kiefer, N.N. 207
Kieke, G.H.O. 93
Kirchsteiger, G. 180
Kohl, R. 156
Kornai, J. 283
Kothmayr, R. 263–4
Kotlikoff, L.J. 157, 185
Kramarz, F. 234

Krankenkassen 87, 89–92, 106, 142
Krueger, A.B. 251n.
Kubik, J.D. 118
Kubin, I. 199
Kuttner, R. 95, 97, 102

Labelle, R. 113
labour contracts, regulation of 238–46
  burden of payment for 240–43
  reasons for 238–40
  termination of contracts 243–6
labour demand 54, 55, 221, 229, 240–42
labour hoarding 244
labour market
  characteristics of 196–7
  flows in 198–200, 206, 246–9
  measurement of problems in 200–209
  participation rates, *see* employment rates
  see also active labour market policy; labour contracts, regulation of; labour demand; labour supply; unemployment; unemployment benefits
labour supply
  family policy and 267, 269, 274
  in intergenerational accounting models 185, 186
  labour market regulation and 240–41
  pension systems and 156, 168–73
  unemployment benefits and 220–25
  wage supplements and 314
Laisney, F. 20n., 268
Lalive, R. 228, 232
LaLonde, R.L. 232
Lambert, P.J. 74–5, 302
Lampert, H. 141
Lancaster, K.J. 334n.
Landier, A. 245
Latvia, pension system in 148–9
Layard, R. 208, 229
Lazear, E.P. 245
Lefaucher, N. 336n.
LeGrand, J. 126n.
Leibfried, S. 310, 322
Leisering, L. 310, 322
Levison, A. 114
Lewis, J. 271, 273
Leyden scale 293–4, 326–30
Liebmann, J.B. 145, 177, 265, 313

Life-Cycle Hypothesis 211
life expectancy 89, 119–20, 121, 124, 143, 147–8, 161, 165, 167, 173–80 *passim*, 186, 303–4
life insurance 163–4
Lilien, D.M. 191n.
Lißner, L. 142, 143
loading 36, 37
Lødemel, I. 317, 323
lone mothers
 policies supporting 250n., 257, 261, 271–4
  alimony 272–3
  labour market participation and poverty alleviation 273–4, 324–6
 poverty rates of 305–6, 326
 share of households with 272
 unemployment among 10–11, 222, 250n.
 working patterns of 10–11, 273
Lorenz curves 71–6, 302, 332–3
Lubitz, J.D. 119
Lutz, H. 282, 293, 294
Luxembourg Income Study (LIS) 139, 306–8

managed care 94, 97, 114
mandatory public insurance 87, 92, 93, 97, 101
mandatory savings plans 147–8, 150, 161, 162
Mann, J.M. 98
Manning, W.G. 113
market failure
 and public health insurance 99–101
 types of 28–9
 uncertainty and 37–9
married couples
 pensions of 146, 176
 poverty rates of 305–6
Marx, K. 310
Marxism 196
matching function 246
maternity benefits 53, 262–3, 267
 effects of 268–9
maternity leave 50, 262–3, 267–8
 effects of 268–71
Matsaganis, M. 88
McClellan, M. 121
McGregor, P.P.L. 280, 281

mean income, poverty defined in relation to 139, 282, 283, 332–3
means testing 15
 for care provision 188, 190
 for family benefits 267, 268, 273, 318
 for pensions 134, 136, 139, 140, 144, 147, 175
 for social assistance 317, 321
 for unemployment benefits 218
median income, poverty defined in relation to 282–3, 301–2, 306–8, 315
Medicaid 87, 95–6, 109–11, 114, 118, 121, 325
medical research 120, 126–7n.
Medicare 3, 80, 87, 95, 97, 101, 121–2, 124, 125
meritoric goods 66
Metcalf, G. 8
Mexico, poverty in 331
Meyer, B.D. 230–31, 236
Micklewright, J. 218, 223
Miles, D. 144, 155
minimum wage 10, 12, 251n.
 pensions related to 142
Moffit, R. 320
Monheit, A.C. 80, 94
monopoly 28–9, 99
monotony axiom 297–8, 330
monotony–sensitivity axiom 298–9, 330
moral hazard 38, 39, 100, 225
Morgenstern, O. 31
mortality rates 87, 114, 119, 165, 177–8, 303–4
 infant 284, 303
Mortensen, D.T. 223, 246
Muellbauer, J. 290–92
Murphy, K.M. 125n., 145
Myles, G.D. 30
myopic behaviour 162

Naifeh, M. 308
Narendranathan, W. 214
National Bureau of Economic Research (USA) 172
National Health Service 14, 16, 82, 83, 87, 88–9, 114
Neal, D. 250n.
Nelissen, J. 175
Nelson, J.A. 293, 334n.

Netherlands
  active labour market policy in 236
  dependency ratios in 180
  employment rates in 169, 203, 204
  extra-marital births in 274n.
  health services in 43, 87, 92–3
    care services 189
    expenditure on 79, 80
  long-term unemployment in 227
  pension system in 142, 182, 318
    redistributive effects of 174, 175–6
  population aged 75 or over in 188
  poverty in 307, 329–30, 331
    programmes to reduce 319
  unemployment benefits in 3, 219
  unemployment rates in 201, 204
Neumann, J. von 31
Neumann–Morgenstern utility function 31–3
New Zealand
  employment rates in 203
  pension system in 134
  social assistance programmes in 317, 318
  unemployment rates in 201
Newhouse, J.P. 45, 100, 114
Nikkei-index 163
Nolan, B. 109
non-experimental method 235–6, 237
non funded pension schemes, see pay-as-you-go (PAYG) pension schemes
Nordhaus, W. 117
Norway
  family policy in 268
  health services in 87
    admission rates to inpatient care institutions 119
    care services 189
  employment in 118
  life expectancy in 178
  poverty in 307–8
    programmes to reduce 312, 318
  notional defined contribution systems 136
Nozick, R. 20n.
nursing homes 188, 190
Nyman, J.A. 112

O'Brian, P. 156
O'Flaherty, B. 20n.

O'Neill, D. 228
Obinger, H. 145
objectives of social policy 4, 5–8
Occupational Safety and Health Authority (OSHA) 91
OECD 79, 80, 118, 119, 133, 169, 180, 181, 182, 188, 201, 202, 203, 204, 206, 219, 225, 227, 268, 308, 309
OECD scale 293–4
Office of Strategic Planning 97
old-age pensions, see pensions
Oleske, D.M. 114
Oregon Department of Administrative Services (ODAS) 96
organisational structures of social policy 16–17
Orshansky, M. 305
ÖSTAT standard 294
Österle, A. 190
overlapping generation models 149–54
  changing assumptions of 155–7
  intergenerational accounting (IA) 185–7

Palacios, R.J. 136
Palmer, E. 136
panel data 322
parental leave 262–3, 268
Pareto-efficiency 26–31
  economic conditions for 28–9, 37–9
  of pension systems 151–4
  and redistribution 28, 29–31
part-time working 11, 201–2, 204, 213
partial equilibrium approach 52
Pashardes, P. 293
paternalism 66, 101
patient's charters 115
pay-as-you-go (PAYG) pension schemes 135–6
  compared with funded systems 149–60, 183, 186–7
    basic ideas 149–54
    changing assumptions 154–7
    effect of shocks 157–60, 178
  distributive effect of 174
  examples of 136–46 *passim*, 148, 149
  pro-natalistic policy to support 257
  risks in 166–8
payroll taxes 53, 54, 58, 61, 142, 221, 234, 262, 263

350 *Index*

Pederson, S. 17
Pelé, L.-P. 136, 172
Pelikan, C. 272
Pellizzari, M. 213, 331
pensions 5, 17, 18, Ch. 5
  allocative effects of 168–73
  disability pensions 59–61, 133, 139, 142, 147, 164
  distributive effects of 54–5, 59–61, 173–8
    intergenerational 183–4, 186–7
  funded and PAYG systems compared 149–60, 183, 186–7
    basic ideas 149–64
    changing assumptions 155–7
    effect of shocks 157–60, 178
  insurance premium for 42
  and poverty alleviation 6, 135, 161, 317–18
  pro-natalistic policy to support 257
  public expenditure on 133–4
    demographic shifts and 181
  purpose of 133
  reasons for public provision of 160–68
  survivors' pensions 133, 147, 175, 191n., 262, 265
  systems of 134–49
    basic pension related to minimum wage plus savings (Netherlands) 142
    combined system with minimum pension (Sweden) 142–3
    definitions 135–6
    flat rate pension plus mandated income insurance (UK) 143–4
    incomes related pension with redistribution towards low-income groups (USA) 145
    integrated two-tier system plus state supported third tier (Switzerland) 145–7
    mandatory savings plans plus means-tested basic pension (Chile) 147–8
    notional contribution scheme on PAYG basis plus a funded scheme (Latvia) 148–9
    pure PAYG with unclear redistribution (Austria) 138–41
    strict PAYG (Germany) 141–2
    two-tier PAYG with minimum pension (France) 136–8
Phelan, C. 173
Philippines, poverty measurement in 300–301
Phillipon, T. 234
Pichelmann, K. 202, 251n.
Pissarides, C.A. 246
planned economies 19n.
Poelert, J.D. 93
political science aspects 14–17
pooling equilibrium 45
population changes, *see* demographic changes
Portugal
  employment rates in 203
  social expenditure in 2
  unemployment rates in 201
positional goods 283–4
Poterba, J.M. 116
Poterba, K. 165
poverty Ch. 8
  attitudes to 277
  definition of (conceptual issues) 278–88
    absolute or relative standards? 281–5
    choice of metric 278–81
    earnings capacity 287–8
    integrated approach: function and capabilities 285–7
  duration of 295–6, 308, 309
  economic growth and 277–8, 331–4
  empirics of 304–8
    absolute poverty (in US) 304–6
    duration of poverty 308, 309
    relative poverty (Luxembourg Income Study) 139, 306–8
  of households 289–94
    definition of household 289
    equivalence scales and 289–94, 326–30
    inequality within households 294
    objective standards and 289–90
  measurement of 296–304
    generalised poverty gap 299–301, 330
    head-count 297–303, 330, 331, 333–4

poverty gap 298–9, 301, 302, 306, 307–8, 312, 315, 321, 330, 333–4
Sen's index of poverty 330–31
special problems of 300–304
  inequality within households 300–301
  relation between poverty line and poverty measurement 301–2
  relation between poverty measure and social welfare 302–4
personal and social factors causing 308–12
programmes to reduce, *see* poverty alleviation
poverty alleviation
  family policy and 264, 265, 271–2, 273–4, 318
  pensions and 6, 135, 161, 317–18
  programmes for
    allocative effects of 55, 314
    distributive effects of 311, 312, 315–16, 321
    social assistance 316–26
      Bremen approach to analysing 322–3
      duration of assistance and policies to reduce dependence 321–6
      eligibility criteria 319, 320, 324
      institutions 316–19
      reduction of actual poverty due to 319–21
      size of benefits 319–20
      take-up rates 319, 320–21
    wage supplements, *see* wage subsidies
  as social policy objective 5–6, 15, 319
poverty gap 298–9, 301, 302, 315, 321, 330
  empirical estimates of 306, 307–8, 312, 333–4
poverty threshold
  definitions of 278–88
  for extreme poverty 304
  independent of wealth of economy 331–2
  Leyden scale used to construct 328–30
  in Luxembourg Income Study 139, 306–8

relation between poverty measurement and 301–2
  in UK 313–14
  in US 282, 289, 304–5, 307, 313
poverty trap 322
precautionary saving 157
pregnancy, health care during 118
prescriptions 106
price increases in health services 117
principal–agent problem 113, 115–16
prisoner's dilemma 46–7, 235
private health insurance 2, 88, 89, 92, 94, 95, 106
private social expenditures 1–2
Proctor, B.D. 282, 305, 306
productivity increases
  employment vouchers and 233
  in health services 117
  labour laws and 241–2
  and pension systems 152–4, 157–60, 178, 180, 186
profit maximisation 23–5, 28, 33, 35
progressive tax-transfer systems 73
psychiatric treatment 90, 92
public debt 135
public goods 29, 278, 279
  household-specific 289
public health services 87, 88–9; *see also* National Health Service
public housing 30
public transport 4–5, 278
Puelz, R. 46

quality
  fixed 67–8
  increases in 117
Quality-Adjusted-Life-Years (QALYs) 107–10
QWB (quality of well being) 110–11

race
  and pensions 177–8, 186–7
  and poverty 288, 305–6, 308
Ramsey, John 155
Ramsey-model 155
Rand Study 113
rational choice assumption 9–12
  problems with 47–9, 65–6
rationing
  of food 31

of health services 84, 85, 105–7
of housing 229–30
Ravallion, M. 297, 332
Rawls, J. 20n.
Reagan, Ronald Wilson 15
Reber, S. 114
recreational areas 5, 278, 284
recurrent unemployment 213–15
redistribution
   data for measuring 59–61
   goods or money? 61–8
   or insurance? 56–7
   Pareto-efficiency and 28, 29–31
   payers and beneficiaries 8, 53, 57–8, 121
   as social policy objective 5–6, 22
   social programmes resulting in 43–4, 49–51 *passim*, 55–61, 103, 121–5, 173–8, 183–4, 186–7, 259–60, 262–6, 311, 312, 315–16, 321
      characterising change in inequality due to 59, 70–77
   standard for comparing 55–6
   types of 6–8
   unit for calculating 56
redundancy payments 50, 238, 243, 244, 245–6
Reeder, W.J. 64–5
regional policy 235
Regnér, H. 236
regressive tax-transfer systems 73
regulations, constraints imposed by 12–14, 49, 50
relative input prices 54
relative prices, changes in 53–4, 58, 62–3
renal disease 95, 102
rent subsidies 64–5
replacement ratios
   maternity benefits 267, 269
   parental leave payments 268
   pensions 138–46 *passim*, 161, 167, 177
   unemployment benefits 219, 220, 223, 224, 225
reproductive treatment 85
reservation wage 223, 226, 240, 241, 246

resources, lack of, as indicator of poverty 278–81
   absolute or relative? 281–5
retirement age 139, 140, 141, 142, 143, 144, 145, 147, 168, 170–73, 174;
   see also early retirement
retirement provisions, *see* pensions
Ricardo, D. 251n.
Ricardo-equivalence 156
Richardson, E. 87, 125n.
Richtsatz 139, 140
Riedel, M. 251n.
Riley, G.F. 119
Riphahn, R.T. 321
risks
   in funded systems 163–4
   preferences for 34–5, 44, 45–6, 115
   protection against 5–6, 22–3
   in public PAYG systems 166–8
   separation of 42–5, 91, 93, 100, 103–4
   uninsurable 102
   see also uncertainty
Robarth method 291–2, 330
Robertson, M. 226
Roemer, J.E. 249n.
Rosdahl, A. 324
Rosner, P. 138, 199, 263–4
Ross, T.W. 66
Rubery, J. 267
Ruggles, P. 321
Ruhm, C.J. 216–17
rule of rescue 84, 109, 110
Rust, J. 173

Sabin, J. 110
safety 91, 278
Salanié, B. 46
Samaritan's dilemma 47, 66, 101, 162, 163
Samuelson, P. 190n.
Sappington, D.E.M. 116
Schmidt, L. 325
Schoeni, R.F. 326
Scholz, J.K. 313
school vouchers 63, 126n., 274n.
Schulenburg, J.M. Graf von der 183, 184
Schulz, E. 92
Scott, F.A. 94
second welfare theorem 30–31, 93

self-employed persons
  flows in and out of self-employment 199
  inclusion in employment/unemployment statistics 203, 249n.
  incomes of 210
  maternity leave for 267
  pensions of 135, 137, 138, 141, 146, 147
Sen, A. 31, 285–7, 294, 330–31
separating equilibrium 45
severance payments 50, 238, 243, 244, 245–6
Sheiner, L. 125
Shiffrin, S.V. 40n.
Short, P. 126n.
sickness benefits 59–60, 88
Singapore, return on annuities in 166
single-earner households, redistribution in favour of 123, 175, 265
single mothers, *see* lone mothers
Sinn, H.-W. 260
Skinner, J. 121
Skocpol, T. 17, 160
Slutsky equations 68
Smeeding, T.M. 278, 306–8, 312
Smith, J.A. 251n.
smoking 52, 81–4 *passim*
Snow, A. 46
Snower, D. 233
social exclusion 283
social expenditure as share of GDP 1–3
social health policy, *see* health insurance; health policy
social marginal utility 112
social policy approach 81, 82, 84–6, 107
social security wealth 170–72
Spain
  birth rate in 179
  consumption reduction due to unemployment in 212
  employment rates in 203
  family policy in 268, 318
  health services in
    care services 189
    expenditure on 79, 80
  life expectancy in 178
  long-term unemployment in 227
  social assistance programmes in 319
  unemployment rates in 201, 206
Speenhamland system 57
Spence, M. 40n.
Spivak, A. 157
spot markets 239–40, 268
Sri Lanka, equivalence scales for 291, 292
Staat, M. 273
Ståhlberg, A.-C. 59–61
State Earnings Related Pension Scheme (SERPS) 144
Stelzer-Orthofer, C. 295
Stephens, M. Jr. 250n.
Stevens, A.H. 295
Stiglitz, J. 40n.
Stock, J.H. 191n.
Straub, M. 156
student loans 39, 261
substitution effect 54, 62–3, 66, 68, 230, 267
Supplemental Security Income (SSI) Programme 118
supplier-induced demand 113
survival rates 207, 208, 223
survivors' pensions 133, 147, 175, 191n., 262, 265
Svarvar, P. 89
Sweden
  birth rate in 179
  dependency ratios in 180
  employment rates in 169, 203, 204
  extra-marital births in 274n.
  family policy in 268, 273
  health services in 82, 87, 89
    admission rates to inpatient care institutions 119
    care services 189
    employment in 118
  life expectancy in 178
  pension system in 142–3, 149, 168, 171, 182
  pensions expenditure in 181
  population aged 75 or over in 188
  poverty in 307–8, 331
    programmes to reduce 311, 312, 317, 318, 320, 321
  redistributive effects of welfare state in 59–61
  social expenditure in 2
  unemployment benefits in 219, 220

unemployment rates in 201, 204, 206
Swedish Health Care Act 82
Switzerland
  active labour market policy in 232
  employment rates in 169, 203
  extra-marital births in 274n.
  health system in 43, 87, 93, 101, 103, 114, 121, 265
    expenditure on 79, 80, 93
  life expectancy in 178
  pension system in 145–7, 162, 174, 318
  poverty in 307
    programmes to reduce 318
  unemployment benefits in 219, 232
  unemployment rates in 201, 232

Talos, E. 16, 17
targeting benefits 67–8; *see also* means testing
tax-benefit incidence 8, 53, 57–8, 121
tax credits 263, 264–5, 267
tax deductions 264–5, 267
tax expenditures 1–2
taxation of benefits 2–3
Taylor, M.P. 214
technical progress 101, 117, 120, 187, 231, 261
Temporary Assistance for Needy Families (TANF) 325–6
temporary employees 94, 236
temporary lay-offs 211, 215, 225–6
Thatcher, Margaret 14
time inconsistency 48
Timmermann, A. 144
Tobin, J. 104
Topel, R.H. 125n.
Torrance, G.W. 107
Torrey, B.B. 283
trade unions 16, 17, 23, 160, 196, 214, 217, 219, 238, 240, 271
training and counselling programmes 228, 231–2, 236, 323–4, 325
transaction costs 239
transfer axiom 297–8, 330
transplants 110
transport, *see* public transport
Trickey, H. 317, 323
Tu, Ha T. 98
Turkey, poverty in 331

Tversky, A. 40n.

Ullman, F. 114
UN Convention on the Rights of the Child 259
uncertainty
  concerning time of death 150, 156–7
  elements of analysis of 31–9
  see also risks
unemployment
  consequences of 209–17
    loss of income and consumption 210–13
    recurrent unemployment 213–15
    reduced wages in new job 215–17
  dequalification caused by 207
  distribution of 205–9
  duration of 199–200, 205–9, 223, 224, 225, 227, 229, 230, 231, 233, 247, 295–6
  hidden 202
  income support during, *see* unemployment benefits
  insurance against risk of 37
  integrated model of unemployment, vacancies and job matching 246–9
  of lone mothers 10–11, 222, 250n.
  natural rate of 249n.
  Pareto-inefficiency of 26
  policies to reduce 217–18
    see also active labour market policy
  rate of, as labour market measure 200–203, 204
  rates of inflow and outflow to/from 206
  social policy aspect of 197–200
  temporary lay-offs 211, 215, 225–6
  voluntary 9–10
  wage level and 9–10, 54, 201, 215–17, 221–3, 226, 229
unemployment benefits 5
  allocative effects of 220–25
  conditional on participation in ALMP programmes 232
  and consumption 213
  duration of 218–20, 224
  guaranteed income schemes 218, 219
  institutions and rules for 218–20, 225, 318

Index   355

replacement ratios for 219, 220, 223, 224, 225
taxation of 3
temporary lay-offs subsidised by 211, 225–6
unemployment assistance (UA) system 218–19, 222, 225
unemployment insurance (UI) system 218–20, 225
Unfallversicherung 91
uninsurable risks 102
United Kingdom
  consumption reduction due to unemployment in 212
  dependency ratios in 180
  employment rates in 169, 203
  family policy in 257, 265, 266, 268, 273
  health services in 82, 83, 87, 88–9, 106, 114
    admission rates to inpatient care institutions 119
    care services 188, 189
    employment in 118
    expenditure on 79, 80, 88–9, 116
  inflation in 165
  long-term unemployment in 227
  pension system in 134, 143–4, 162, 174, 182, 318
  population aged 75 or over in 188
  poverty in 282, 307–8
    programmes to reduce 312, 313–14, 317–21 *passim*
  social security wealth in 172
  unemployment benefits in 3, 219, 223
  unemployment rates in 201
  wage subsidies in 234
  welfare state reforms in 14, 88
United Nations Demographic Yearbook 178, 179, 304
United States
  accident insurance in 242
  birth rate in 179
  consumption reduction due to unemployment in 212
  dependency ratios in 180
  employment rates in 169, 203, 204
  family policy in 53, 257, 265, 266, 267, 273

  health services in 3, 14, 46, 53, 80, 87, 88, 89, 94–8, 101, 102–3, 114, 118, 121–2, 124, 125, 265, 325
    admission rates to inpatient care institutions 119
    care services 189
    employment in 118
    expenditure on 79, 80, 95, 116
  inflation in 165
  labour market flows in 198
  life expectancy in 178
  long-term unemployment in 227
  pension system in 134, 145, 149, 156, 160, 171, 182, 318
    redistributive effect of 174, 177–8, 186–7
  pensions expenditure in 181
  population aged 75 or over in 188
  poverty in 282, 288, 289, 296, 304–8, 329–30, 331
    programmes to reduce 312, 313, 316, 317, 319, 321, 324–6
  rent subsidies in 64–5
  retirement age in 145, 173
  unemployment benefits in 219–20, 223, 226
  unemployment rates in 201, 204, 206
  wage subsidies in 234
United States General Accounting Office 94, 98, 102–3, 126n.
universities 260–61
US Census Bureau 95, 275n.
utility function 24
  aggregated for each period 47
  demographic characteristic of household entering 290
  expected, *see* Neumann–Morgenstern utility function
  for housing 64–5
  in intergenerational accounting models 185
  pensions and 150, 155, 168–9
  risk preferences and 34–5

vacancies 246–9
Value Added Tax (VAT) 8, 58
van de Ven, W.P.M.M. 93, 104, 126n.
van Doorslaer, E. 76–7, 104, 111
Venti, S.F. 161
Vienna, housing policy in 30

Viscusi, K. 81, 84
Voges, W. 334n.
voluntary contracts, enforcement of 25–6

Wadsworth, J. 213
wage assignments 272
wage subsidies 228, 229–30, 232–4, 312–16
  allocative effects of 314
  efficiency of 315–16
wage supplements, *see* wage subsidies
Wagenhals, G. 273
wages
  differentials in 234
    gender pay gap 269–71
  health risks and 84
  labour market regulation and 240–43
  payment of 238
  and poverty 310, 311, 315–16
  reductions in 217
  reservation wage 223, 226, 240, 241, 246
  taxes and benefits affecting 53
  and unemployment 9–10, 54, 201, 215–17, 221–3, 226, 229
Wagstaff, A. 104, 109
Wailoo, A. 108
waiting lists 89, 106
Waldfogel, J. 267, 269–71
Waldmann, R.J. 284
Walker, R. 317
Walzer, M. 104
Warlick, J.L. 191n.
Warr, P. 209
Weise, H. 324
Welch, F. 145
welfare dependency 321–2
welfare loss, quantitative evaluation of 68–70
Wet op de Toegang tot Ziektekostenverzekeringen (WTZ) 92

widows 324
willingness-to-pay 103, 105
Winefield, A.H. 210
Wise, D.A. 161, 191n.
women
  access to household wealth 294, 300
  earnings capacity of 288
  employment rates of 169, 203–4, 273, 325
  insurance premiums for 42, 103
  life expectancy of 178
  pensions of 167, 174, 175, 186–7
  redistribution in favour of 61
  retirement age for 139, 140, 142, 143, 147, 174
  rights of 12
  unemployment rates of 204
  wages of 269–71
  see also gender specific policies; lone mothers; maternity benefits; maternity leave; parental leave
Woodbury, S. 230–31
workfare programmes 323–4
working hours 204, 213, 240, 246, 313–14; *see also* part-time working
World Health Organisation 81, 84, 102
Wöss, J. 142, 143
Wright, R.E. 273, 274

Yellen, J.L. 250n.
young people, programmes aimed at 323–4
Youth Allowance Scheme (Denmark) 324

Zaire, life expectancy in 304
Zeckhauser, R.J. 80, 94, 100, 126nn.
Zieckenfondsbesluit (ZFW) 92–3
zoning 284
Zweifel, P. 113, 119
Zylberberg, A. 252n.